IN DEFENSE
OF
JUSTICE

IN DEFENSE OF JUSTICE

THE GREATEST DISSENTS OF RUTH BADER GINSBURG

Edited and Annotated for the Non-Lawyer

by

Sarah Wainwright

Mockingbird
Press

Publisher's Cataloging-In-Publication Data

Wainwright, Sarah, author;
In Defense of Justice: The Greatest Dissents of Ruth Bader Ginsburg: Edited and Annotated for the Non-Lawyer / Sarah Wainwright.

Paperback	ISBN-13: 978-1-946774-65-1	ISBN-10: 1-946774-65-0
Hardback	ISBN-13: 978-1-946774-66-8	ISBN-10: 1-946774-66-9
Ebook	ISBN-13: 978-1-946774-67-5	ISBN-10: 1-946774-67-7

Library of Congress Control Number: 2019948183

1. Law In General—Biography. 2. Biography & Autobiography—Lawyers & Judges. 3. Law—General. 4. Jurisprudence & General Issues. 5. Law & Society, Gender Issues. 6. Constitutional Law & Human Rights, 7. Collection, Series, Collected Works, I. Sarah Wainwright. II. Title. III. Title : The Greatest Dissents of Ruth Bader Ginsburg: Edited and Annotated for the Non-Lawyer.

K-170 / BIO020000 / LAW000000 / LA / LAQG / LNDC1 / AC1-999

Type Set in Century Schoolbook / **Franklin Gothic Demi**

Mockingbird Press, Augusta, GA

CONTENTS

Acknowledgements vi
Editor's Note vii
Preface ix

WOMEN'S RIGHTS
Introduction 3
Ledbetter 11
Hobby Lobby 33
Coleman 63
Carhart 85

MINORITY RIGHTS
Introduction 113
Gratz 121
Ricci 133
Adarand 171
Vance 181
Shelby County 205
Masterpiece Cake Shop 239

ACKNOWLEDGEMENTS

This book, like most, was a group effort and could not have been completed without the input and hard work of my collaborators. I want to thank John Saxon for making sure the opinion summaries in this book accurately reflected the case law and importance of these pivotal decisions.

I want to thank Nathan Inks for doing the tedious job of inspecting the citations and footnotes to ensure the grammarians and blue book champions would not cringe when reading them.

Special thanks to Joshua Davis and Jenny Frank, the artists of the group, who brought a bit of flare to the cover and transformed what was coming out to be a stuffy legal text into a colorful creation that looks great in the book case.

Finally, I want to thank Abigail, my project partner, for keeping me on track and giving meticulous feedback which vastly improved the finished product.

EDITOR'S NOTE

Our purpose in putting together a book of Justice Ginsburg's greatest dissents was to showcase the Justice herself: her style, method of writing and spirit. To the non-lawyer, reading a legal brief or opinion can be tasking; the text is riddled with inline citations that strain the attention, especially when the reader is not versed in the coded language of the law. While most practitioners develop the ability to move effortlessly through heavily cited text by the end of their One-L year, the uninitiated find it burdensome and distracting.

Legal citation serves a weighty purpose in the practice of law. It gives authority to the claims made by the writer and assures the reader the author has not simply made it up as they went along. Precedence in the law is paramount. A lawyer may be well respected for their brilliance, but it would be a rare occasion when a court accepted an argument without assurance it was supported by some past decision. The same holds for judicial opinions. A judge can use the weight of authority to press their position in an opinion; when done successfully, it is difficult for an opponent to simply ignore.

To balance the value of heavy citation with its distraction to our intended audience, we decided to remove all inline citations and place them in the footnotes. In doing so, however, we broke a cardinal rule of book formatting, which holds that heavy citing should always be placed in endnotes. Our decision was made to ensure the value of the citations were not lost to the readers. Those wanting to observe the Justice "show her work" could do so without laboriously turning to the back pages in search of an endnote. Additionally, legal citations themselves often contain valuable text in the form of parentheticals, which can explain why the precedent is relevant to the argument it supports or showcase text from the source as compelling as the argument it follows.

The decision to keep the citations in the footnotes does come at a slight cost. As you will see, the number of citations is large, and the footnotes can often overwhelm the page. Additionally, Justice Ginsburg's dissents contained their own original footnotes which we needed to distinguish from the converted inline citations. It must be mentioned that judicial opinion footnotes, especially from the Supreme Court, can carry significant weight and should be read as a part of the whole opinion. Such an example is the famous "Footnote Four" of *U.S.*

v. Carolene Products Co.[1], which outlined the parameters of appropriate judicial review. Footnote Four itself was a small aside in one of a number of New Deal cases, but it took on a life of its own under the Warren Court and, some say, can be credited as the precedent which allowed for the major liberalization of our constitutional doctrine. In order to save Justice Ginsburg's own footnotes from being lost among the other citations, we designated each with the prefix "FN" followed by the number given by the original opinion.

In the end, we hope our formatting strikes the right balance between ease of reading for the non-lawyer and an in-depth account of the dissents of this great justice.

---

[1] 304 U.S. 144 (1938).

PREFACE

Sometime in the mid to late 2010s, Ruth Bader Ginsburg—a diminutive, soft-spoken Jewish grandmother who, by that time, had served as a Supreme Court Justice for approximately two decades—became, however improbably, a modern-day superhero.

It is hard to pinpoint the commencement of Ginsburg's elevation from judge to hero for millions of idealistic Americans. Perhaps it was in 2015, with the publication of *Notorious RBG: The Life and Times of Ruth Bader Ginsburg*,[1] a New York Times bestseller that chronicled Ginsburg's life in the informal argot of its self-described "#millennial" authors.[2] Though surely the process began earlier than that, on June 25, 2013, with the first post[3] (celebrating Ginsburg's dissent lamenting the Supreme Court's gutting of the Voting Rights Act) on a blog devoted to celebrating all things Ginsburg—a blog which would later inspire the book's authors to write *Notorious RBG*.[4] Regardless, it is safe to say that by 2018, Ginsburg's status as a cultural icon was cemented. That year saw the release of two films about Ginsburg—*On the Basis of Sex*, a biopic chronicling her years as a women's rights lawyer, and *RBG*, a documentary about her life. Both collectively grossed over $50 million worldwide at the box office,[5] and the latter

---

[1] IRIN CARMON & SHANA KNIZHNIK, NOTORIOUS RBG: THE LIFE AND TIMES OF RUTH BADER GINSBURG (2015).

[2] *Id.* at viii.

[3] Notorious R.B.G., TUMBLR (June 25, 2013), https://notoriousrbg.tumblr.com /post/53878784482/throwing-out-preclearance-when-it-has-worked-and.

[4] The name of the blog, https://notoriousrbg.tumblr.com/, is a portmanteau of the name of the late rap artist "Notorious B.I.G." and Ginsburg's initials, "RBG." The blog, which was founded by one of the authors of *Notorious RBG*, *see* CARMON & KNIZHNIK, *supra* note 1 at viii, chronicles the obsession of many left-leaning millennials with Ginsburg, as expressed in a variety of mediums ranging from the traditional, such as images of quotations of Ginsburg's opinions supporting civil rights, to the modern, such as memes of Ginsburg, to the eccentric, such as in the form of pictures of Ginsburg's image as imprinted upon manicured fingernails. *See generally* Notorious R.B.G., *Archive*, TUMBLR, https://notoriousrbg.tumblr.com/archive.

[5] *RBG* grossed $14,383,034 worldwide. RBG *(2018)*, NUMBERS, https://www. the-numbers.com/movie/RBG-(Documentary)-(2018)#tab=summary (last visited July 25, 2019). *On the Basis of Sex* grossed $38,797,996 worldwide. On the Basis of Sex *(2018)*, NUMBERS, https://www.the-numbers.com/movie/On-the-Basis-of-Sex-(2018)#tab=summary (last visited July 25, 2019).

also received two Academy Award nominations.[6] Indeed, *RBG*'s tagline is "Hero. Icon. Dissenter."[7] Not long after the success of these films, in January 2019, clothing retailer Banana Republic re-released a necklace whose first iteration became Ginsburg's famous "dissent jabot," or the special collar that Ginsburg wears with her judicial robe on days when she issues a significant dissent.[8]

While Ginsburg has only worn her special "dissent jabot" since approximately 2012,[9] it is, primarily, the many eloquent and impassioned dissents which Ginsburg has authored since her elevation to the Supreme Court in 1993 that led to her role as the principal antagonist to the conservative-leaning majority which has dominated the Court for essentially the entirety of Ginsburg's tenure. Those impassioned dissents—usually on behalf of women and minorities whom Ginsburg views as having been given short shrift by the Court's majority—have led directly to her role as a cultural touchstone, a feminist icon, and hero to millions of Americans both young and old. In short, without Ginsburg's dissents, she might well be just another in a long line of Justices of the Court, distinguished but largely indistinguishable to most Americans outside the legal bar and academy. Because of her dissents, Ginsburg has come to embody the zeitgeist of the cultural moment.

This book features some of Ginsburg's best-known dissents and aims to situate those dissents within their proper context—both historically and in terms of how they reflect Ginsburg's life experience

---

[6] *RBG* received Oscar nominations for Best Documentary Feature and Best Original Song ("I'll Fight"). Kimberly Nordyke, *Oscars: 'Roma,' 'Favourite' Top Nominations With 10 Apiece*, HOLLYWOOD REP. (Jan. 22, 2019), https://www.hollywoodreporter.com/lists/oscar-nominations-2019-complete-list-nominees-1172407.

[7] *Hero. Icon. Dissenter.*, WARNERMEDIA (May 1, 2018), http://www.timewarner.com/blog/posts/20180501-hero-icon-dissenter.

[8] For a history of the provenance of the necklace and how it came into Ginsburg's possession, see Holly E. Thomas, *Proof That D.C. Style Is Evolving? Ruth Bader Ginsburg's New Jewels*, REFINERY29 (Nov. 12, 2012), https://www.refinery29.com/en-us/2012/11/39750/ruth-bader-ginsburg-necklace, and Chloe Foussianes, *Ruth Bader Ginsburg's "Dissent Collar" Is Being Reissued by Banana Republic*, TOWN & COUNTRY (Jan. 7, 2019), https://www.townandcountrymag.com/style/jewelry-and-watches/a25779929/ruth-bader-ginsburg-dissent-collar-banana-republic-reissue/. The story behind the re-issue of that necklace in early 2019 is recounted at Notorious R.B.G., TUMBLR (Jan. 7, 2019), https://notoriousrbg.tumblr.com/post/181805871929/were-so-excited-to-announce-that-banana-republic. The necklace itself can be found (and purchased) at *Notorious Necklace*, BANANA REPUBLIC, https://bananarepublic.gap.com (last visited Aug. 5, 2019).

[9] *See* Thomas, *supra* note 8.

and jurisprudential philosophy. It focuses on two principal areas where Ginsburg's dissents have proven most noteworthy or compelling: the protection of women's and minority rights. These two sections are prefaced by introductions which review different aspects of Ginsburg's life and professional experience to illuminate how Ginsburg came to be such a fierce defender of the rights of those who have traditionally had too few champions. Where relevant, the real-world impact or potential future influence of Ginsburg's dissents are also discussed.

But before diving into Ginsburg's dissents specifically, it is important to situate those dissents within a broader historical context. Why does the practice of dissenting, and of doing so in writing, exist? Do dissents matter? Do they ever have lasting impact? Why do judges write dissents? Why, even, do judges write at all? Does the written opinion, and especially the written dissent, impart special impact to the words of the court or judge issuing it? And what do these conclusions tell us about Ruth Bader Ginsburg's role and legacy—both as a justice and as the Court's most recent famous dissenter?

The Importance of the Written Decision

The writing of judicial opinions is rooted in both Roman and English law, though only beginning in approximately the eighteenth century did English judges issue anything remotely comparable to the formal modern written judicial opinion.[10] Yet contrary to popular

---

[10] By contrast, in the eighteenth century, many U.S. states had already "adopted the statutory requirement that judges write their opinions rather than merely state them orally," thereby enshrining the practice early in American law. Patricia M. Wald, *The Rhetoric of Results and the Results of Rhetoric: Judicial Writings*, 62 U. CHI. L. REV. 1371, 1371 n.1 (1995). For a more comprehensive discussion of this history, as well as comparisons between and among the judicial practices of various countries, see *id.* and sources cited therein; *see also* William J. Brennan, Jr., *In Defense of Dissents*, 37 HASTINGS L.J. 427, 432–34 (1986); Ruth Bader Ginsburg, *Remarks on Writing Separately*, 65 WASH. L. REV. 133, 134–138, 145–47 (1990); Kevin M. Stack, *The Practice of Dissent in the Supreme Court*, 105 Yale L.J. 2235, 2235 n.2 (1996); JOHN P. DAWSON, THE ORACLES OF THE LAW 406 (1968). For a comprehensive discussion of "existing standards governing courts' issuance of opinions," see Chad M. Oldfather, *Writing, Cognition, and the Nature of the Judicial Functions*, 96 GEO. L.J. 1283, 1288–97 (2008). For a general discussion of the variety of approaches to the issuance of formal opinions which have been adopted by various nations around the world, see generally Kurt H. Nadelmann, *The Judicial Dissent: Publication v. Secrecy*, 8 AM. J. COMP. L. 415, 415–18, 420–29 (1959).

belief, there is not and never has been any formal requirement in many American courts that judges issue written opinions. While some state constitutions have requirements that judges give reasons, write opinions, or both, "these requirements usually apply only to the state Supreme Court," although "a few also apply generally to all the courts of the state."[11] In federal courts, by contrast—including the Supreme Court—"[a] few statutory and doctrinal mechanisms exist to constrain federal judges' reason-giving, but they do not amount to a universal duty to give reasons. A court must enter *some* judgment in order to dispose of a case, but need not necessarily provide [a written] explanation of that judgment."[12]

If there are no formal requirements mandating a written opinion, then why do judges bother to write them? Scholars who have studied the history of courts and of the legal systems upon which the United States based its own have concluded that, in essence, the written opinion accomplishes two principal functions: it confers legitimacy upon the judicial process and helps hold both judges, individually, and the judiciary, generally, accountable to the citizenry for decisions rendered.[13]

---

[11] Mathilde Cohen, *When Judges Have Reasons Not to Give Reasons: A Comparative Law Approach*, 72 WASH. & LEE L. REV. 483, 526 n.252 (2015). Many state courts do not issue written opinions for a significant portion of their rulings, and even federal judges follow the same practice on occasion: "Our English forebears did and do announce decisions from the bench with no off-the-bench deliberative time. This is still common practice in many state courts that suffer the heaviest flood of cases, and our district court judges regularly make oral rulings in the middle of trials to keep things moving. Absence of rhetoric is principally an appellate court problem." Wald, *supra* note 10, at 1375.

[12] Cohen, *supra* note 11, at 526 (footnotes omitted).

[13] To these functions some scholars add a third which contemplates the participatory role of the citizenry in the civic life of society, though this role has been conceptualized in different ways. *See, e.g.*, Michael Serota, *Intelligible Justice*, 66 U. MIAMI L. REV. 649, 655 (2012) (one of three "primary functions" of judicial opinions, in addition to "legitimacy" and "constraint," is "to enable litigants to respond to a court's decree and to inform the public of its legal rights and responsibilities (rule of law)"); Cohen, *supra* note 11, at 505 ("reason-giving" in the form of written opinions "treats parties and the general public as rational moral agents who are entitled to evaluate and sometimes to participate in judicial decisions"). *See generally* Michael Wells, *French and American Judicial Opinions*, 19 YALE J. INT'L L. 81, 82, 85–92 (1994) ("An opinion is an instrument for achieving systemic goals: providing guidance to lawyers and lower courts, persuading readers of the rightness of the decision, constraining arbitrary action on the part of judges, and legitimating their efforts."). Meanwhile, left unsaid by most scholars, but recognized explicitly by at least one distinguished jurist, is the practical necessity of the written

Legitimacy is perhaps the most important of these functions: "while the elected branches of government are able to secure legitimacy *qua* consent at the ballot box, an unelected and life-tenured federal judicial branch cannot. These judges must instead rely upon the power of persuasion; that is, by providing reasoned justifications for their rulings, judges are able to secure the 'tacit approval and obedience of the governed.'"[14] The Supreme Court itself seems to agree with this approach, having noted that "the judiciary's legitimacy hinges upon the practice of producing 'legally principled decisions under circumstances in which their principled character is sufficiently plausible to be accepted by the Nation.'"[15] Notably, Justice Ginsburg also seems to appreciate the role of the opinion in conferring legitimacy: she has written that judges "do not alone shape legal doctrine but . . . they participate in a dialogue with other organs of government, and with the people as well."[16]

As for accountability, one distinguished American jurist has expounded the point succinctly: "[f]or a conscientious judge, the simple obligation to write an opinion persuasively explaining the outcome of a case is a profound constraint on judicial discretion."[17] In effect, written opinions ensure that judges are accountable, at minimum by reputation, for their decisions, and such accountability implicitly confers, at least in theory, circumspection and restraint upon the jurists' moral and legal reasoning.

---

opinion: "[I]s it possible to have reasonably consistent justice administered by hundreds of judges for millions of people without any permanent record as to why cases come out one way or the other? Surely not." Wald, *supra* note 10, at 1376. For a well-reasoned hypothetical discussion of what such a legal system might look like, and how functional (or not) it might be, see generally James Boyd White, *Judicial Opinion Writing—What's an Opinion For?*, 62 U. CHI. L. REV. 1363 (1995).

[14] Serota, *supra* note 13, at 649 (quoting Ray Forrester, *Supreme Court Opinions—Style and Substance: An Appeal for Reform*, 47 HASTINGS L.J. 167, 173 (1995)). *See also* Wald, *supra* note 10, at 1372 (noting that judges write reasoned opinions to reinforce their "oft-challenged and arguably shaky authority to tell others—including our duly elected political leaders—what to do").

[15] Serota, *supra* note 13, at 653 (quoting Planned Parenthood of Se. Pa. v. Casey, 505 U.S. 833, 865 (1992)).

[16] Ruth Bader Ginsburg, *Speaking in a Judicial Voice*, 67 N.Y.U. L. REV. 1185, 1198 (1992).

[17] Patricia M. Wald, *Some Thoughts on Judging as Gleaned from One Hundred Years of the Harvard Law Review and Other Great Books*, 100 HARV. L. REV. 887, 904 (1987).

The Evolution and Role of the Dissent

If legitimacy and accountability are bound up with the written opinion, which is itself—at least in the United States—the foundation of the judicial house, then the long history of spirited and vociferous dissent by Justices of the Supreme Court provide the mortar with which the walls of that house are cemented.

This statement is not an uncontroversial one; in the 200-plus years since the first dissent in 1806,[18] jurists have assailed the dissent, labeling it as "useless and undesirable"[19]; excoriating it as "subversive literature"[20]; faulting it for "cancel[ing] the impact of monolithic solidarity on which the authority of a bench of judges so largely depends"[21]; and lamenting that "[t]he only purpose which an elaborate

---

[18] As Justice William Brennan recounts, "in 1806, Justice [William] Paterson delivered the first true dissent from a judgment and opinion of the Court in *Simms v. Slacum.*" William J. Brennan, Jr., *In Defense of Dissents*, 37 HASTINGS L.J. 427, 434 (1986) (citing Simms v. Slacum, 7 U.S. (3 Cranch) 300, 309 (1806) (Paterson, J., dissenting)). Arguably, however, the first substantive "dissent," though one which went by another name (that of "special concurrence") came one year earlier, from the pen of Justice William Johnson, in *Huidekoper's Lessee v. Douglass*, 7 U.S. (3 Cranch) 1, 72 (1805). Prior to this date, the Court alternated between delivering opinions *seriatim*—a longstanding practice in English law whereby each judge of a tribunal announced his (for they were all men) individual opinion on each case—and the practice instituted by Chief Justice John Marshall whereby one "opinion of the Court" was announced by a single sitting Justice (who was, in almost every case, Chief Justice Marshall). There were occasional opinions prior to 1805 that differed from that of the majority of other Justices or from the "opinion of the Court," but those opinions were neither in form nor design formal dissents as presently conceived. The history and evolution of these practices, as well as a history of the genesis and role of dissenting opinions in Supreme Court jurisprudence generally, is discussed in detail in Karl M. Zobell, *Division of Opinion in the Supreme Court: A History of Judicial Disintegration*, 44 CORNELL L. REV. 2, 187–207 (1959). For more on William Johnson, in a piece that argues that he was the true author of the first dissent, see Scott Bomboy, *Remembering the Supreme Court's First Dissenter*, NAT'L CONST. CTR. (Dec. 27, 2018), https://constitutioncenter.org/blog/remembering-the-supreme-court s-first-dissenter.
[19] N. Sec. Co. v. United States, 193 U.S. 197, 400 (1904) (Holmes, J., dissenting).
[20] *See* Brennan, *supra* note 18, at 429 (quoting Justice Potter Stewart, his colleague and contemporary on the Court for more than twenty years); *see also* M. Todd Henderson, *From 'Seriatim' to Consensus and Back Again: A Theory of Dissent* 1 n.6 (University of Chicago Public Law & Legal Theory Working Paper No. 186, 2007); Meredith K. Lewis, *Justice William Johnson and the History of Supreme Court Dissent*, 83 GEO. L.J. 2069, 2089 (1995).
[21] LEARNED HAND, THE BILL OF RIGHTS 72 (Harvard University Press 1958).

dissent can accomplish, if any, is to weaken the effect of the opinion of the majority, and thus engender want of confidence in the conclusions of courts of last resort."[22] And yet the dissent has endured—and, in so doing, has functioned both to strengthen the Supreme Court as an institution and to cement the reputation of several of its justices as both iconoclasts and visionaries, making their indelible mark upon the history of the Court and of American jurisprudence.

To understand the dissent's importance to the Court, it is necessary to situate the dissent in both its proper jurisprudential and historical contexts. In an often-cited lecture delivered at a California law school, Justice William Brennan, who served on the Supreme Court from 1956 until 1990, set out to "examine some of the many different functions of dissents."[23] Paramount among these, said Brennan, is the role of the dissent as a "corrective."[24] In this role the dissent, "[i]n its most straightforward incarnation . . . demonstrates flaws the author perceives in the majority's legal analysis . . . in the hope that the Court will mend the error of its ways in a later case."[25] If the dissent has an "essence," it is this—the dissent functions as the formal notice which the losing, minority side provides to both the majority and to posterity that, in the minority's view, the majority has made a grave mistake. In this vein, Justice Brennan's sentiment was not original, for it borrowed from one of the most famous statements ever issued about the nature of the dissent. In the words of Charles Evans Hughes, the Eleventh Chief Justice of the United States: "A dissent in a court of last resort is an appeal to the brooding spirit of law, to the intelligence of a future day when a later decision may possibly correct

---

[22] Pollock v. Farmers Loan & Tr. Co., 157 U. S. 429, 608 (1895) (White, J., dissenting); see reprinted remarks by Henry Wollman, along with unsigned introduction, *Evils Of Dissenting Opinions*, 57 ALB. L.J. 74, 75 (1898), for an argument that "[n]othing of any benefit to the public can be gained by a dissenting opinion." By contrast, one scholar has written that "[i]f such a view is correct there should be no faith in the court for the history of that body since the days of [Chief Justice John] Marshall has been one of constant and, at times, vitriolic dissent." John T. Ganoe, *The Passing of the Old Dissent*, 21 OR. L. REV. 285, 285 (1942). As well, in the words of Justice Robert Jackson— widely considered one of the most eloquent writers even to sit on the Court, if not in fact the most: "Those who begin coercive elimination of dissent soon find themselves exterminating dissenters. Compulsory unification of opinion achieves only the unanimity of the graveyard." W. Va. State Bd. of Educ. v. Barnette, 319 U.S. 624, 641 (1943).

[23] Brennan, *supra* note 18, at 430.

[24] *Id.* For a more detailed discussion of the dissent as a "corrective device," see Meredith K. Lewis, *Justice William Johnson and the History of Supreme Court Dissent*, 83 GEO. L.J. 2069, 2083 (1995).

[25] Brennan, *supra* note 18, at 430.

the error into which the dissenting judge believes the court to have been betrayed."[26]

All other purposes to which a dissent might aspire flow directly from and through this one. Another purpose which naturally follows is, in the words of Justice Ginsburg herself, the dissent's ability "to lead the author of the majority opinion to refine and clarify her initial circulation"—in other words, to make improvements upon the majority opinion's first draft.[27] As Ginsburg herself would doubtless concede, this strategy is sometimes effective: channeling Justice Louis Brandeis, whose "counsel" Ginsburg has stated she tries to follow, she observed that "[a] few of [her] favorite" dissenting opinions "remain unpublished" because the majority made "ameliorating alterations" to the majority opinion.[28] This function of the dissent harkens back to

---

[26] CHARLES EVANS HUGHES, THE SUPREME COURT OF THE UNITED STATES 68 (1928). This quote is also discussed by Justice Ginsburg herself in her lecture entitled *The Role of Dissenting Opinions*, 95 MINN. L. REV. 1, 4 (2010). The same lecture is printed, in slightly different form, in RUTH BADER GINSBURG, The Role of Dissenting Opinions, Lecture at Tulane University Law School Summer Program (July 2013), *in* MY OWN WORDS: RUTH BADER GINSBURG 278–86 (2016). As well, Justice Brennan shared a similar sentiment later in his lecture on the dissent, observing that "[a] dissent challenges the reasoning of the majority, tests its authority and establishes a benchmark against which the majority's reasoning can continue to be evaluated, and perhaps, in time, superseded." Brennan, *supra* note 18, at 435.

[27] Ginsburg, *The Role of Dissenting Opinions, supra* note 26, at 3. Justice Ginsburg's colleague on the Court and close friend, Justice Antonin Scalia, went a step further, stating that dissents improved not only the Court's opinions, but also the Court's judges. "It forces them to think systematically and consistently about the law, because in every case their legal views are not submerged within an artificially unanimous opinion but are plainly disclosed to the world. Even if they do not personally write the majority or the dissent, their name will be subscribed to the one view or the other. They cannot, without risk of public embarrassment, meander back and forth—today providing the fifth vote for a disposition that rests upon one theory of law, and tomorrow providing the fifth vote for a disposition that presumes the opposite." Antonin Scalia, *The Dissenting Opinion*, 19 J. SUP. CT. HIST. 33, 42 (1994). Notably, Scalia's observation does not always hold true. As Justice Ginsburg herself demonstrated in a dissent featured in this collection, the reasoning supporting Justice Anthony Kennedy's opinion for the majority in *Planned Parenthood of Southeastern Pennsylvania v. Casey*, 505 U.S. 833, 851 (1992), which reaffirmed the constitutional right to an abortion, should logically have led the majority in *Gonzales v. Carhart*, 550 U.S. 124 (2007)—which had a majority opinion also written by Justice Kennedy—to the exact opposite conclusion from that which it reached. This matter is discussed in the chapter of this work addressing Ginsburg's dissent in *Carhart*.

[28] GINSBURG, The Role of Dissenting Opinions, *supra* note 26, at 281, 286. She continues, "And even when Brandeis gained no accommodations, he would

the role of the written opinion as providing both legitimacy and accountability: as Justice Brennan explained, the dissent "safeguards
the integrity of the judicial decision-making process by keeping the
majority accountable for the rationale and consequences of its decision. . . . [V]igorous debate improves the final product by forcing the
prevailing side to deal with the hardest questions urged by the losing
side."[29] By challenging the rationale and result of the majority opinion, dissents thus allow the superlative argument and reasoning to
rise to the top.[30]

   A related function of the dissent, insofar as it might fail sufficiently
to corral the majority opinion or to limit its scope, is as "a sort of
'damage control' mechanism," whereby the dissent is "used to
emphasize the limits of a majority decision that sweeps, so far as the
dissenters are concerned, unnecessarily broadly."[31] The dissenter
might distinguish the majority opinion from related cases; show how
it differs in type or scope from those cases; or draw out subtle
distinctions in the factual scenarios addressed in the case—all of

---

retract his dissent if he thought the Court's opinion was of limited application
and unlikely to cause real harm in future cases. He once explained: one must
husband resources; dissenting too often will weaken the force of a dissent
when it becomes important to write." *Id.* at 281. As noted *supra* in note 26, a
lecture entitled "The Role of Dissenting Opinions" appears as written by
Ginsburg at least twice in scholarly publications; both are cited in note 26.
There are some deviations in the content of the two texts, and the quotation
provided in the text accompanying this footnote is not identical between the
two sources. Where only one of these printings is quoted, the language quoted
does not necessarily appear in identical form, or even at all, in the other
printing.

[29] Brennan, *supra* note 18, at 430. He continued: "In this sense, this function
reflects the conviction that the best way to find the truth is to go looking for it
in the marketplace of ideas. It is as if the opinions of the Court—both for majority and dissent—were the product of a judicial town meeting." *Id.* Professor
Lewis expands upon this reasoning: "Just as competition in economic markets
generally results in better products than those produced by a monopolist with
a captive market, better judicial opinions will result when Justices know
their interpretations will be compared with those of any Justice who differs.
If no one can concur or dissent, however, the majority has a monopoly over
the opinion and thus does not have to concern itself with competing view-
points that may reveal defects in the Court's result or analysis." Lewis, *supra*
note 24, at 2084.

[30] Or, as Justice Brennan put it: "For simply by infusing different ideas and
methods of analysis into judicial decision-making, dissents prevent that process from becoming rigid or stale. And, each time the Court revisits an issue,
the justices are forced by a dissent to reconsider the fundamental questions
and to rethink the result." Brennan, *supra* note 18, at 436.

[31] *Id.* at 430.

which are, in Brennan's words, "designed to furnish litigants and lower courts with practical guidance—such as ways of distinguishing subsequent cases."[32] Brennan further counseled that a dissent may even "hint that the litigant might more fruitfully seek relief in a different forum—such as the state courts."[33]

All of these tools are employed by Justice Ginsburg in some of her best-known dissents, and all are on evidence in the cases and dissents which feature here. Consider two examples. First, in *Adarand Constructors, Inc. v. Peña*[34]—a case in which the majority effectively made it more difficult for affirmative action policies to withstand a legal challenge[35]—Ginsburg used her dissent to demonstrate how the majority's own reasoning, which implicitly set forth means to undermine laws helping minorities, could be parsed to demonstrate how, in the future, affirmative action policies could be designed to withstand judicial scrutiny.[36] Second, in *Coleman v. Court of Appeals of Maryland*[37]—where the majority opinion limited the types of claims which could be sustained under the Family and Medical Leave Act[38]—Ginsburg used a portion of her dissent to demonstrate mechanisms prospective litigants could use to obtain relief of the type which the majority had effectively barred by seeking redress via other legal or administrative means.[39]

Both the dissents in *Adarand* and *Coleman* are prototypical Ginsburg: eloquent, impassioned, and (usually) understated rhetoric directed with laser precision at the inconsistencies, inaccuracies, fallacies, and, especially, implicit moral failings found in the majority's reasoning. Perhaps not coincidentally, these are qualities frequently associated with what Justice Brennan described as the "most enduring dissents": those in which the dissenters speak as "Prophets with Honor," authoring "dissents that often reveal the perceived congruence between the Constitution and the 'evolving standards of decency that mark the progress of a maturing society,' and that seek to sow seeds for future harvest. These are the dissents that soar with passion and ring with rhetoric. These are the dissents that, at their best, straddle the worlds of literature and law."[40] The dissents in this lofty

---

[32] *Id.*

[33] *Id.*

[34] 515 U.S. 200 (1995).

[35] *See id.* at 227.

[36] *See id.* at 274–76 (Ginsburg, J., dissenting).

[37] 566 U.S. 30 (2012).

[38] *See id.* at 36–39.

[39] *See id.* at 64–65 (Ginsburg, J., dissenting).

[40] Brennan, *supra* note 18, at 430–31 (quoting Trop v. Dulles, 356 U.S. 86, 101 (1958)); *see also* Edward McGlynn Gaffney, Jr., *The Importance of Dissent*

echelon number few, and are those whose discernment leaps from the page into the consciousness of the modern reader because they contain the irreducible essence of substantiated moral truth—truth which was, for whatever reason, lost to the dissenter's erstwhile contemporaries.

Several famous dissents ring with such moral clarity. Perhaps the earliest is that of Justice Benjamin Curtis in the Court's notorious 1857 decision of *Dred Scott v. Sandford*.[41] There, the Court held, in a 7–2 decision, that African-Americans could never become United States citizens. In a dissent which Ginsburg herself has lauded as a "classic example" of an opinion which invokes Chief Justice Hughes' notion of a dissent "appealing to the intelligence of a future day," Curtis wrote that "[a]t the founding of our Nation . . . African Americans were 'citizens of at least five States, and so in every sense part of the people of the United States,' thus 'among those for whom and whose posterity the Constitution was ordained and established.'"[42] Curtis's words, which can be read as an entreaty cloaked as a statement of law, would not come to fruition for more than 100 years.

In the context of moral reckoning, probably the most famous dissent of all is the lone dissent by the first Justice John Marshall Harlan[43] from the majority opinion in *Plessy v. Ferguson*,[44] the infamous case which enshrined the doctrine of "separate but equal" as the law of the land. In the lauded dissent's most famous passage, Harlan wrote that "[t]here is no caste here. Our constitution is color-blind, and neither knows nor tolerates classes among citizens. In respect of civil rights, all citizens are equal before the law."[45] Harlan's

---

and the Imperative of Judicial Civility, 28 VAL. U. L. REV. 583, 590–91 (1994).

[41] 60 U.S. (19 How.) 393 (1857).

[42] Ginsburg, *The Role of Dissenting Opinions*, *supra* note 26, at 4–5 (quoting *Scott*, 60 U.S. (19 How.) at 582 (Curtis, J., dissenting)). More forcefully, Curtis also argued that when a strict interpretation of the Constitution, according to the fixed rules which govern the interpretation of laws, is abandoned, and the theoretical opinions of individuals are allowed to control its meaning, we have no longer a Constitution; we are under the government of individual men, who for the time being have power to declare what the Constitution is, according to their own views of what it ought to mean. *Scott*, 60 U.S. (19 How.) at 621 (Curtis, J., dissenting).

[43] This is not a typo. The "first" John Marshall Harlan was an Associate Justice of the Supreme Court from 1877 until his death in 1911. His grandson and namesake, the "second" John Marshall Harlan, also served as an Associate Justice, from 1955 until 1971.

[44] 163 U.S. 537 (1896).

[45] *Id.* at 559 (Harlan, J., dissenting). Ironically, at the time he wrote his famous *Plessy* dissent, Harlan "happened to be the only Southern member on the Court . . . . All others were either born in or appointed from the North."

perspective was decades ahead of its time; it foretold a future which would not arrive for more than half a century, when a unanimous Court declared, in *Brown v. Board of Education*,[46] that segregated schools are unconstitutional. Harlan's dissent led the editorial board of the *New York Times* to proclaim that the country had witnessed "an instance of which the voice crying in the wilderness finally becomes an expression of a people's will and in which justice overtakes and thrusts aside a timorous expediency."[47] It also caused Harlan, in the astute words of one scholar, "to be regarded as something of a judicial folk-hero,"[48] and led directly to his unofficial moniker: "The Great Dissenter."[49]

While Harlan has long been celebrated by enlightened jurists, Justice Oliver Wendell Holmes is perhaps the only Supreme Court Justice other than Ginsburg whose writings have attained substantial renown beyond the confines of the legal academy—due in large measure to the strength and eloquence of his prose. Holmes is another Justice to whom the label "The Great Dissenter" has been attached.[50] The

---

Henry J. Abraham, *John Marshall Harlan: A Justice Neglected*, 41 VA. L. REV. 871, 883–84 (1955); *see also* H. B. Brown, *The Dissenting Opinions of Mr. Justice Harlan*, 46 AM. L. REV. 321, 336 (1912).

[46] 347 U.S. 483 (1954).

[47] ZoBell, *supra* note 18, at 201 (quoting Editorial, N.Y. TIMES, May 23, 1954, at 10E).

[48] *Id.* at 199; *see also* Abraham, *supra* note 45, at 890–91 ("If further proof still be required of the contributions that [Harlan] made to American constitutional law, one need but point in review to several of his leading dissents that have since been vindicated by becoming accepted governmental practice, either as a result of Court reversals or legislative action. The roll is an impressive one."). Abraham then lists eight additional cases where Harlan's dissent ultimately became the law. *See id.* at 891.

[49] ZoBell, *supra* note 18, at 202. While Justice Harlan grew in renown in the decades after his tenure on the Court for both the probity of his dissents and for his moral and judicial foresight, he was best known in his time for the volume of his output, authoring 316 dissenting opinions across his career, in addition to 703 majority opinions and 100 concurrences. *Id.* at 199 (citing Abraham, *supra* note 45, at 872). But as early as 1917—only six years after Harlan's death—scholars were writing law review articles labeling him as "The Great Dissenter." *See, e.g.*, Thomas Jefferson Knight, *The Dissenting Opinions of Justice Harlan*, 51 AM. L. REV. 481, 484 (1917) (stating that Harlan "acquired by reason of the vigor and frequency of his dissenting opinions the appropriate title of 'The Great Dissenter.'").

[50] Justice Holmes, by contrast to Justice Harlan, "is so described not because of the frequency but because of the power of his dissents." Gaffney, *supra* note 40, at 590 n.7. This label given to Holmes is particularly ironic, considering that Holmes himself once called dissents "useless" and "undesirable." N. Sec. Co. v. United States, 193 U.S. 197, 400 (1904) (Holmes, J., dissenting).

moniker is especially befitting of a man who once wrote—in dissent—
that "if there is any principle of the Constitution that more impera-
tively calls for attachment than any other it is the principle of free
thought—not free thought for those who agree with us but freedom
for the thought that we hate."[51] So poignant and forceful is the
strength of Holmes' writing that "[i]t has been remarked that Holmes'
contribution to Anglo-American jurisprudence was the destruction of
the myth of judicial certainty."[52] After Holmes, "[d]issent became an
instrument by which Justices asserted a personal, or individual, responsibility which they viewed as of a higher order than the institutional responsibility owed by each to the Court, or by the Court to the
public."[53]

Justice Ginsburg is a natural heir to the legacy of Justices Harlan
and Holmes. As one of her biographers has observed, many of Ginsburg's dissents form the "seeds" of the "agonizingly long process" that
is "[c]hanging the culture on subjects such as affirmative action, defendants' rights, and employment discrimination."[54] Perhaps more
than those of any other recent Justice, Ginsburg's dissents shoot
flaming arrows across the bow of the "myth of judicial certainty."
Many of these dissents feature prominently here, including six which
feature an attribute of the dissent not unknown in Court history, but
reinvigorated and employed for devastating emphasis by Ginsburg:
the practice of proclaiming the dissent orally from the bench.[55]

As Ginsburg herself has explained, "[o]rdinarily, when Court decisions are announced from the bench, only the majority opinion is
summarized. . . . A dissent announced orally [from the bench], therefore, garners immediate attention. It signals that, in the dissenters'
view, the Court's opinion is not just wrong, but, to borrow Justice Stevens' words, 'profoundly misguided.'"[56] While several notable dissents

---

[51] United States v. Schwimmer, 279 U.S. 644, 654–55 (1929) (Holmes, J.,
dissenting).
[52] ZoBell, *supra* note 18, at 202 (citing Philip B. Kurland, *The Supreme Court
and the Attrition of State Power*, 10 STAN. L. REV. 274, 277 (1958)). As one
scholar has wryly observed: "If the authority of the Court is weakened by a
dissent, it is probably because it ought to be weakened." Brown, *supra* note
45, at 351.
[53] ZoBell, *supra* note 18, at 203.
[54] LINDA HIRSHMAN, SISTERS IN LAW: HOW SANDRA DAY O'CONNOR AND RUTH
BADER GINSBURG WENT TO THE SUPREME COURT AND CHANGED THE WORLD 210
(2015).
[55] The six cases in question are *Gonzalez v. Carhart, Ledbetter v. Goodyear
Tire & Rubber Co., Vance v. Ball State University, Shelby County v. Holder,
Fisher v. University of Texas at Austin*, and *Burwell v. Hobby Lobby Stores,
Inc. See* Ginsburg, The Role of Dissenting Opinions, *supra* note 26, at 287–316.
[56] *Id.* at 279. Ginsburg, whose tenure on the Court overlapped with Justice

have been read from the bench throughout Court history,[57] Ginsburg's frequent recent adoption of the practice—which has been said to function as "a scream for reconsideration"[58]—has contributed to her reputation as an iconoclast and a champion for civil rights.

Ginsburg's Fierce Advocacy for Civil Rights

Nowhere is Ginsburg more impassioned—or more rhetorically fierce—than when dissenting in cases where she believes the majority has either unduly restricted or failed to uphold the rights of the traditionally disenfranchised. The introduction to the section of this book on minority rights discusses a number of these dissents in considerable detail. It will suffice here to quote the words of one Ginsburg biographer, who writes that she is "disinclined by nature to try to patch together a centrist compromise" and has "repeatedly produced radically confrontational rhetoric directed at her retrograde male colleagues."[59] While this characterization is somewhat incendiary, its essence is not inaccurate; though Ginsburg's career has been marked at times by incrementalism, she has never settled for half measures, and she has never been afraid of confrontation.

In this regard, Ginsburg is the natural heir to Justice Harlan, who, over the course of his long career, became "determined to secure unto the . . . underprivileged the equal rights he was convinced the Constitution meant to impart to them."[60] In many ways, theirs is a kinship of both philosophy and circumstance. "Harlan's struggle on behalf of civil rights was a frustrating one on both the state and national level . . . . It was one long, heartbreaking series of dissents upon dissents, frequently alone among the justices."[61] While Ginsburg is frequently joined in dissent by some or all of the Court's other more liberal members, in all other respects the comparison rings true. As

---

Stevens for the better part of two decades, did not specify the source from which she obtained these words. In the alternate version of "The Role of Dissenting Opinions," Ginsburg did not cite Stevens, and instead stated that announcing dissents orally "signals that, in the dissenters' view, the Court's opinion is not just wrong, but grievously misguided." Ginsburg, *The Role of Dissenting Opinions*, supra note 26, at 2.

[57] For a discussion of some of these, see Andrew Lowy, *Reading a Dissent from the Supreme Court Bench*, NAT'L CONST. CTR. (July 18, 2014), https://constitutioncenter.org/blog/reading-a-dissent-from-the-supreme-court-bench/.

[58] *Id.*

[59] HIRSHMAN, *supra* note 54, at 292.

[60] Abraham, *supra* note 45, at 881.

[61] *Id.*

well, it has also been said of Harlan that it "is a pity that he did not live to see his philosophy triumph in some of the many other cases in which his dissents would ring out during his tenure."[62] While no talisman can foretell how the Court's jurisprudence will change in future decades, there can be no realistic doubt that even if a future Court topples existing precedent in favor of her minority perspective, Ginsburg—whose dissents from the conservative majority became even more vociferous and frequent as she entered her ninth decade of life—will, like Harlan, not survive to see it.

It is worth considering that such result was not necessarily predestined. The pique and passion of which Ginsburg's dissents are redolent mark a noticeable change from her early career, when Ginsburg earned a well-deserved reputation as an advocate for women's rights who, while skilled and conscientious, was also measured and strategic. Ginsburg advanced women's rights not through aggressive assaults, but tactically, in incremental phases that, in isolation, represented small victories, but, taken together, helped to bring about a sea change in the legal status and rights of women in the United States.[63]

One journalist who has long covered the Court observed that Ginsburg's early success as an advocate resulted from her conscious decision to be "the very opposite of a firebrand."[64] Later in her career, Ginsburg herself spoke frequently of her approach at that time, viewing herself "as a kind of teacher to get [the Justices] to think" about civil rights issues from a different perspective.[65] Ginsburg was a master tactician and promoter employing an approach long advocated by great writers: when trying to illustrate or emphasize a point, the best approach is show, don't tell.

Working with various women's and civil rights organizations, Ginsburg advanced cases featuring carefully chosen plaintiffs whose circumstances demonstrated the inherent absurdity of inequalities

---

[62] *Id.*

[63] This undoubtedly helps to explain why years later, during her confirmation hearings, Ginsburg stated that as a Supreme Court Justice, "[s]he should be ever mindful, as Judge and then Justice Benjamin Nathan Cardozo said: 'Justice is not to be taken by storm. She is to be wooed by slow advance.'" Neil A. Lewis, *The Supreme Court; Ginsburg Promises Judicial Restraint If She Joins Court*, N.Y. TIMES (July 21, 1993), https://www.nytimes.com/1993/07/21/us/the-supreme-court-ginsburg-promises-judicial-restraint-if-she-joins-court

[64] Dahlia Lithwack, *The Irony of Modern Feminism's Obsession with Ruth Bader Ginsburg*, ATLANTIC (Jan./Feb. 2019), https://www.theatlantic.com/magazine/archive/2019/01/ruth-bader-ginsburg-feminist-hero/576403/.

[65] Jessica Weisberg, *Supreme Court Justice Ruth Bader Ginsburg: I'm Not Going Anywhere*, ELLE (Sept. 23, 2014), https://www.elle.com/culture/career-politics/interviews/a14788/supreme-court-justice-ruth-bader-ginsburg/.

prevalent in then-existing law—such as one which functioned to assume military servicemen's wives were dependent on their husbands for support, but that servicewomen's husbands were not similarly dependent on their wives.[66] In this manner and in numerous cases, Ginsburg, hearkening back to her days as a law school professor, mustered logic and legal acumen to shepherd the Justices to the only natural result reason would tolerate.

Ginsburg as a Modern Feminist Icon

The indirect approach that was a hallmark of Ginsburg's early career would not forever endure. While Ginsburg was at the vanguard of the women's movement, so were many other activists whose names are now mere footnotes in history. It is Ginsburg's persistent, forceful, and eloquent advocacy for the rights of women (as well as for the rights of traditionally disenfranchised minorities) in her dissents that cemented her status as a modern feminist icon.

It is no accident that Ginsburg's prevalence in American popular culture—in the form of a proliferation of books, movies, magazine profiles, internet memes, an opera,[67] "Halloween costumes, a bobblehead doll, tattoos, t-shirts, coffee mugs, and a children's coloring book"[68]—is the result of endeavors spearheaded, in nearly every instance, by women. Setting aside critique and criticism within the legal academy of her judicial philosophy, while Ginsburg does have the occasional detractor—one notable piece is entitled "The Dark Side of the Cult of Ruth Bader Ginsburg"[69]—most publicity directed toward or about Ginsburg has taken the form of hagiography, elevating her almost to the level of a demi-god. She has been called "indomitable"[70]; a "feminist hero" [71]; "notorious"[72]; an "icon"[73]; "a legit

---

[66] The case was *Frontiero v. Richardson*, 411 U.S. 677 (1973). It is discussed extensively in HIRSHMAN, *supra* note 54, at 69–77.

[67] In 2015, Ginsburg and her long-time friend and colleague on the Court, Justice Antonin Scalia, whose friendship flourished in part due to their shared love of opera, were fictionalized in *Scalia/Ginsburg*, an opera by Derrick Wang. Susan B. Apel, *Opera Preview: "Scalia/Ginsburg" — Mining (and Minding) the Political Gap*, ARTS FUSE (Oct. 2, 2018), http://artsfuse.org/1742 30/opera-preview-ginsburg-scalia-mining-and-minding-the-political-gap/.

[68] *Ruth Bader Ginsburg*, WIKIPEDIA, https://en.wikipedia.org/wiki/Ruth_Bader _Ginsburg#In_popular_culture (last visited Aug. 5, 2019).

[69] Mari Uyehara, *The Dark Side of the Cult of Ruth Bader Ginsburg*, NATION (Jan. 30, 2019), https://www.thenation.com/article/notorious-rbg-scotus.

[70] Yasmin Omar, *Why Ruth Bader Ginsburg Is Our Feminist Hero*, HARPER'S BAZAAR (Jan. 4, 2019), https://www.harpersbazaar.com/uk/culture/entertainment/a25722034/why-ruth-bader-ginsburg-is-our-feminist-hero/.

pop-culture icon"[74]; and—all in one single article, a formidable triumph of encomium—a "feminist gladiator," "the most conservative radical in the women's movement," "the American ideal of power and authority for millions of women and girls," and "what we dream of for our toddler daughters."[75] One almost expects to learn that Judy Chicago is making room, four decades after its creation, for an additional place setting in her famous feminist art installation, *The Dinner Party*.

What do millions of women see in Ginsburg? She is, quite simply, the embodiment of nearly everything both inspirational and aspirational about the better angels of the American experiment. Born into a lower-middle class family of Jewish immigrants who "never achieved much material success,"[76] Ginsburg worked hard and earned admission to three separate Ivy League institutions—Cornell for her undergraduate education and both Harvard and Columbia for law school—and was the highest-ranked student in the class at all three of them. Yet despite her success, she faced immense personal adversity in the form of invidious gender discrimination, and struggled either to find or to retain jobs for years after graduation. Against all odds, she prospered professionally and became a leading activist in the burgeoning feminist movement, responsible alone or in collaboration with others for numerous substantive concrete victories on various fronts. She then parlayed this professional success into multiple life-tenured presidential appointments to the federal bench, ultimately becoming the second and longest-serving female Supreme Court Justice in United States history. At every step of the way she has used her abilities, talents, influence, and brilliance either to effectuate or to advocate forcefully for substantive, systemic, lasting changes to American law aimed at bolstering and expanding the civil rights of all Americans. And while doing all of this, she lived for decades in domestic tranquility, devoted and beloved wife to an equally devoted and beloved husband, mother to two healthy and successful children, and grandmother of four.[77]

---

[71] *Id.*

[72] CARMON & KNIZHNIK, *supra* note 1.

[73] *Hero. Icon. Dissenter.*, supra note 7.

[74] Patrick Ryan, *"RBG": How Ruth Bader Ginsburg Became a Legit Pop-Culture Icon*, USA TODAY (Nov. 9, 2018), https://www.usatoday.com/story/life/movies/2018/05/01/rbg-documentary-shows-how-ruth-bader-ginsburg-became-pop-icon/562930002/.

[75] Lithwack, *supra* note 64.

[76] HIRSHMAN, *supra* note 54, at 6.

[77] Gail Collins, *The Unsinkable R.B.G.: Ruth Bader Ginsburg Has No Interest in Retiring*, N.Y. TIMES (Feb. 20, 2015).

In short, Ginsburg has both lived the American Dream and worked as few have to ensure its continued viability. Starting from the bottom, Ginsburg reached the top of the mountain, then turned back and reached down, pulling up as many of her fellow citizens her miniscule frame could carry.

Why Study Ginsburg's Dissents?

Every accomplishment noted above would have been true had Ginsburg never written a single dissent during her tenure on the Court. But her dissents are where she has left her truly indelible mark—the place where Ginsburg stands athwart history, battling to hold back the tides that threaten the principles she spent her life's work fighting to uphold.

One constant since Ginsburg's early days as an advocate is the resolute precision of her legal arguments. That is uniformly true of her legal briefs, her petitions for certiorari to the Supreme Court, her oral arguments, and most assuredly in the opinions she has written on behalf of the Court. But the practice of her craft—her decades spent thinking, researching, writing, preparing, arguing, and advocating—has as its magnum opus her dissents, which advocate a United States that adheres more faithfully to the noble ideals enshrined in the country's founding documents. As Ginsburg herself has said, "the founders stated a commitment in the Declaration of Independence to equality and in the . . . Bill of Rights to individual liberty. Those commitments had growth potential."[78]

True, it is difficult to engage in any serious review of Ginsburg's dissents without hyperbole coming to mind. Time after time, Ginsburg's dissents function to skewer, dissect, and eviscerate the reasoning of her judicial foes with the force of their incontrovertible logic, empirical scrutiny, and air-tight legal arguments—not to mention their carefully deliberate construction[79] and implicit moral clarity. But while the dissents are paradigmatic examples of cogent and persuasive legal writing, their staying power is inextricably

---

[78] Ginsburg, *supra* note 16, at 1188.

[79] As Ginsburg has explained "[t]he most effective dissent, I am convinced, 'stand[s] on its own legal footing'; it spells out differences without jeopardizing collegiality or public respect for and confidence in the judiciary. I try to write my few separate opinions each year as I once did briefs for appellees— as affirmative statements of my reasons, drafted before receiving the court's opinion, and later adjusted, as needed, to meet the majority's presentation." *Id.* at 1196 (quoting Collins J. Seitz, *Collegiality and the Court of Appeals*, 75 JUDICATURE 26, 27 (1991)).

bound up with the ideals they advocate, both in the force of their argument in support of how best to uphold those ideals and as foundational expressions of the nobility and timelessness of such ideals.

Justice Brennan, in his lecture on the role of dissents, stated that they are "critical to an understanding of the [individual Supreme Court] justice. Just as we judge people by their enemies, as well as their friends, their dislikes as well as their likes, the principles they reject as well as the values they affirmatively maintain, so do we look at judges' dissents, as well as their decisions for the court, as we evaluate judicial careers."[80] To truly understand Ginsburg then—and in keeping with the history of the dissent both in jurisprudence and as a form of expression—we must analyze and seek to comprehend the reasons why she chose, each time she so chose, to face the majority head on and state unequivocally, "you are wrong."

Those reasons can be found in her dissents. Ginsburg has stated that she learned early in her academic career from one of her college literature professors, the famed Russian novelist Vladimir Nabokov, that "[w]ords could paint pictures."[81] The pictures she paints are of real human lives, diminished by prejudice, minimized by history, and limited by the destructive impact of Constitutional promises unfulfilled and noble ideals unattained. But if we wish to evaluate Ginsburg by her dissents, then we should see her not just as a painter of words, but through the lens of another former jurist frequently quoted by Ginsburg, Justice Benjamin Cardozo, who wrote that the "dissenter speaks to the future, and [their] voice is pitched to a key that will carry through the years"; against the majority, the dissenter "is the gladiator making a last stand against the lions."[82]

Ginsburg is a gladiator. As a woman, she is one of the first of her kind. To the fight, she brings nothing but a pen. When the lions roar, she roars back, and with equal aplomb. She is ferocious. She is unafraid.

---

[80] Brennan, *supra* note 18, at 428.

[81] Ruth Bader Ginsburg, *Ruth Bader Ginsburg's Advice for Living*, N.Y. TIMES (Oct. 1, 2016), https://www.nytimes.com/2016/10/02/opinion/sunday/ruth-bader-ginsburgs-advice-for-living.html.

[82] Benjamin N. Cardozo, *Law and Literature*, 14 YALE REV. 689 (1925), *reprinted in* J. M. Landis, *Law and Literature*, 48 YALE L.J. 489, 490–507 (1939). The quoted material appears at Yale L.J. pages 714–15.

WOMEN'S RIGHTS

LEDBETTER V. GOODYEAR TIRE & RUBBER COMPANY

BURWELL V. HOBBY LOBBY STORES, INC.

COLEMAN V. COURT OF APPEALS OF MARYLAND

GONZALES V. CARHART

WOMEN'S RIGHTS

"I ask no favor for my sex. All I ask of our brethren is that they take their feet off our necks."

The personal history of Ruth Bader Ginsburg is a story of a tenacious woman who steadfastly refused to accept the circumstances to which an unjust world relegated her. Time and again throughout her long and accomplished career, Ginsburg overcame discrimination resulting from her status as a woman in an overwhelmingly male profession. Ginsburg's personal experiences led her, as an advocate, to challenge numerous discriminatory laws that unfairly prejudiced women who simply wanted to be treated equally to men. As a Supreme Court Justice, those same experiences informed Ginsburg's perspective that the Constitution's broadly egalitarian language means nothing if it does not provide remedies for the discrimination and systematic inequality which women in the United States have faced for so long.

When Ginsburg was an undergraduate at Cornell University, it was generally understood that women went to college to find a man, not to learn. Ginsburg, of course, had other ideas. Yet, to avoid sticking out among her peers, she did most of her studying in bathrooms—an anecdote she recounts in good humor to this day.[1]

She did land a man, however, meeting Martin Ginsburg, her late husband of fifty years, at Cornell. But unlike many of her contemporaries, her success in love did not herald a retreat from work or intellectual pursuits. Ginsburg's mother had instilled in her daughter the importance of being independent: "Even if you meet Prince Charming," she told her daughter, "be able to fend for yourself."[2] Ginsburg heeded her mother's advice while pursuing her undergraduate education. And, along with a lifelong partner, she discovered and pursued a passion for the law that led her to become one of the most influential and respected women in American history.

Ginsburg traced her desire to become a lawyer to her work as a research assistant in Cornell's Department of Government, where she was asked to compile data on the "black lists" of individuals in the entertainment industry accused of having Communist ties or sympathies

---

[1] *Ruth Bader Ginsburg: Justice for All*, WHAT IT TAKES (Sept. 26, 2018), https://whatittakes.simplecast.fm/40ca4a6b, 7:28.

[2] *Id.* at 4:55.

during the McCarthy era.[3] As Ginsburg followed the Congressional investigations into alleged Communist activity, she realized she wanted to be like the people she read about in the hearing transcripts: someone who stood up for the accused, who reminded Congress about the First Amendment and its protection of the freedom of speech and the Fifth Amendment and its protection against self-incrimination, and who made the system better for all.[4] Accordingly, after giving birth to her first child Jane in 1956, Ginsburg joined her husband Marty as a student at Harvard Law School.

Ginsburg began her studies at Harvard six years after the first woman was admitted to its law school. Her class of 500 included just eight other women, and Ginsburg was the only one who was also a mother.[5] She has said that motherhood is to credit for the balanced approach she took toward the normally overwhelming responsibilities of the typical law student. In her own words, "[e]ach part of my life provided respite from the other and gave me a sense of proportion that classmates trained only in law studies lacked."[6] Having a young child gave Ginsburg the perspective to understand that there was ultimately something "more important" than the law.[7] Her days consisted of attending class and then hurrying home to care for her young daughter.

Then, as if the responsibilities of being a full-time student and mother were not enough, Marty was diagnosed with testicular cancer during his final year of law school. In addition to managing her own coursework and managing his care, Ginsburg went to Marty's classes, took notes for him, and transcribed his papers so that he would not fall behind during his recovery.[8]

Such a grueling schedule would be impossible for most people, which makes Ginsburg's early success all the more impressive. This trying period of her life is when she developed her now-famous nocturnal character—one of Ginsburg's former clerks has joked that a

---

[3] Jon Craig, *Ruth Bader Ginsburg Reminisces About Her Time on the Hill*, CORNELL CHRON. (Sept. 22, 2014), http://news.cornell.edu/stories/2014/09/ruth-bader-ginsburg-reminisces-about-her-time-hill.

[4] *Ruth Bader Ginsburg, supra* note 1, at 14:24.

[5] *Id.* at 10:34.

[6] Ruth Bader Ginsburg, *Ruth Bader Ginsburg's Advice for Living*, N.Y. TIMES (Oct. 1, 2016), https://www.nytimes.com/2016/10/02/opinion/sunday/ruthbader -ginsburgs-advice-for-living.html.

[7] Stephanie Francis Ward, *Family Ties*, ABA J. (Oct. 2010), http://www. aba-journal.com/magazine/article/family_ties1?icn=most_read.

[8] Ryan Park, *What Ruth Bader Ginsburg Taught Me About Being a Stay-at-Home Dad*, ATLANTIC (Jan. 8, 2015), https://www.theatlantic.com/business /archive/2015/01/what-ruth-bader-ginsburg-taught-me-about-being-a-stay-at-home-dad/384289/.

year of working for her "has recalibrated the circadian rhythms of generations of her clerks."[9] After a full day of class and studying, Ginsburg would go home, relieve the nanny who had been taking care of Jane, entertain and care for her daughter—entailing play time, library time, dinner time, and bath time—and then sit down with Marty to help him with his assignments.[10] Marty would dictate papers to Ruth from midnight until two a.m., and then, from two to four a.m., she would finish studying for her own classes, which started at eight the next morning.[11]

The Ginsburgs both prevailed, even in the face of such difficulty. Marty healed and graduated from Harvard and into a good job at a New York law firm. To be with him, Ruth transferred to Columbia for her final year of law school, where she continued to set precedent: she became the first woman to serve on the Columbia Law Review (she had also been the first woman to serve on the Harvard Law Review) and graduated at the top of her class with glowing recommendations from her professors.[12]

Yet despite all her success, Ginsburg was unable to find a job. While Marty had easily found a position in a private firm, Ruth was turned down by each of the twelve firms with which she interviewed.[13] And despite receiving a personal recommendation from a renowned Harvard professor for a clerkship with Supreme Court Associate Justice Felix Frankfurter, the Justice refused to consider Ginsburg for the position, citing discomfort with having a woman in his chambers.[14] These experiences stung Ginsburg for their obvious gender-based discrimination—particularly potential employers' discomfort with her status as mother to a four-year-old—but, with characteristic tenacity, she kept interviewing.[15] She eventually found a job with U.S. District Judge Edmund Palmieri, for whom she clerked for two years before entering academia—joining Columbia University's Project on International Procedure. After becoming associate director of the project, she taught herself Swedish and headed to the University of Lund to study Sweden's legal structure.

While overseas, Ginsburg found confirmation that her incipient feelings about the unjust state of women's rights in the United States

---

[9] *Id.*

[10] Ginsburg, *supra* note 6.

[11] *Ruth Bader Ginsburg, supra* note 1, at 8:16.

[12] Colleen Walsh, *Ginsburg Holds Court*, HARV. GAZETTE (Feb. 6, 2013), https://news.harvard.edu/gazette/story/2013/02/ginsburg-holds-court/.

[13] *Ruth Bader Ginsburg*, ACAD. ACHIEVEMENT, https://www.achievement.org/achiever/ruth-bader-ginsburg/ (last updated Jan. 3, 2019).

[14] *Id.*

[15] Ginsburg, *supra* note 6.

(both within the legal profession and in general) were well-founded. She learned that women comprised nearly a quarter of Swedish law students; read op-eds in local newspapers about the injustice of expecting women to do all the housework and also work full-time; and saw that safe and legal abortions were saving women's lives.[16]

Ginsburg returned to the United States in 1963 and took a job at Rutgers University's law school with a year-to-year contract. When she became pregnant during her second year—which Marty's doctors had warned would be almost impossible—Ruth, while overjoyed that their family was growing, felt she had to hide the pregnancy from her coworkers and superiors until after she received a renewed contract for the following year. She dressed herself in her mother-in-law's oversized suits for the entire spring semester and, right before school broke for the summer, told her coworkers that by the time they saw each other again in the fall, her family would be four.[17]

Upon her return from abroad, Ginsburg decided to apply her considerable legal acumen in attempting to remedy gender-based discrimination of the type she had experienced her entire professional life. She began reviewing federal court decisions addressing gender discrimination and realized there was a dearth of such decisions defending or expanding women's rights.[18] This realization led Ginsburg to volunteer with the ACLU of New Jersey in the hopes of coming by a case that could make a difference in this area of law.[19]

Women came to the ACLU with all sorts of complaints: blue-collar workers who were denied health insurance for their families their male counterparts received; mothers whose daughters were not allowed to apply to Princeton's prestigious engineering programs because it only allowed men; teachers who became pregnant and were forced to take leave as soon as they were showing, so as not to confuse their young pupils.[20] Ginsburg worked on such cases and, in 1973, argued her first case before the United States Supreme Court.[21] That

---

[16] Ruth Bader Ginsburg, Gillian Metzger & Abbe Gluck, *A Conversation with Justice Ruth Bader Ginsburg*, 25 COLUM. J. GENDER & L 6, 8 (2013).

[17] *Ruth Bader Ginsburg, supra* note 1, at 20:14.

[18] Indeed, as Ginsburg herself has observed, "Until 1971, women did not prevail before the Supreme Court in any case charging unconstitutional sex discrimination." Ruth Bader Ginsburg, *Speaking in a Judicial Voice*, 67 N.Y.U. L. Rev. 1185, 1202–03 (1992).

[19] Ginsburg, Metzger & Gluck, *supra* note 16, at 8.

[20] *Id.*

[21] *Tribute: The Legacy of Ruth Bader Ginsburg and WRP Staff*, AM. C.L. UNION, https:/www.aclu.org/other/tribute-legacy-ruth-bader-ginsburg-and-wrp-staff (last visited Apr. 2, 2019).

case, *Frontiero v. Richardson*,[22] focused on a female lieutenant in the Air Force who was denied the same housing and family healthcare allowance given to male officers as a matter of course. Ginsburg argued that the Air Force should not be allowed to differentiate benefits based on gender. In an 8–1 decision, the Supreme Court agreed.[23]

In nearly ten years as a civil rights litigator, Ginsburg appeared in six cases before the Court, finishing with a 5–1 record and a well-honed aptitude for successful legal advocacy—including the skill of marrying public opinion with legal reasoning to advance the cause of gender equality.

In 1980, her reputation led President Jimmy Carter to appoint Ginsburg to what most legal scholars consider the second-highest court in the land: the United States Court of Appeals for the District of Columbia Circuit. Her reputation later made her a compelling choice in 1993 to succeed outgoing Supreme Court Justice Byron White. President Bill Clinton appointed her, and she was confirmed by the Senate 96–3, making Ginsburg the second-ever woman to join the high court.

On the court, Ginsburg attained renown for her cogent, didactic opinions, and especially for her dissents in cases where the Court's majority issued decisions which Ginsburg viewed as inimical to gender equality and the advancement of women's rights. Each of the four cases that follow feature dissents in which Ginsburg chides the majority in some way for setting back the cause of gender parity and equal rights for women.

The oldest, *Gonzales v. Carhart*,[24] castigated the majority for a "flimsy and transparent"[25] opinion which controverted the Court's own precedent in upholding restrictions on abortion rights and which Ginsburg charged "def[ied] the Court's longstanding precedent affirming the necessity of a health [of the mother] exception [to restrictions on abortion], with no carve-out for circumstances of medical uncertainty."[26] The next dissent, in *Ledbetter v. Goodyear Tire & Rubber Co.*,[27] is arguably Ginsburg's most effective, as it led to a change in a

---

[22] 411 U.S. 677 (1973).

[23] Ginsburg, Metzger & Gluck, *supra* note 16, at 11. In an interesting bit of historical irony, the Court's only dissenter, Associate Justice William Rehnquist, later served as Chief Justice upon Ginsburg's ascendance to the Court, and the two served as Justices together for more than twelve years until Rehnquist's death from thyroid cancer in 2005. JEFFREY TOOBIN, THE OATH: THE OBAMA WHITE HOUSE AND THE SUPREME COURT 138, 208 (2012).

[24] 550 U.S. 124 (2007).

[25] *Id.* at 181 (Ginsburg, J., dissenting).

[26] *Id.* at 179.

[27] 550 U.S. 618 (2007).

federal law which the majority had interpreted as denying an Alabama woman's claimed entitlement to back pay and damages for
years of underpayment compared with male employees in the same
job.[28] The dissent, issued in 2007, appealed directly to Congress to
remedy the injustice wrought by the majority.[29] In 2009, Congress
passed the Lilly Ledbetter Fair Pay Act of 2009 (the first bill President Obama signed) which effectively enshrined the approach advocated in Justice Ginsburg's dissent into law.

In the third case, *Coleman v. Court of Appeals of Maryland*,[30]
Ginsburg's dissent hearkened back to her days as a litigant before the
Court, when she was known for devising innovative legal strategies to
help effectuate her desired results. The dissent criticized the plurality
opinion for effectively curtailing the scope and efficacy of a portion of
the Family and Medical Leave Act ("FLMA"), the "overarching aim" of
which Ginsburg argued was "to make it feasible for women to work
while sustaining family life."[31] Ginsburg then traced the history of the
FMLA, demonstrating that it was designed in large part to remedy
gender discrimination in the workplace and ultimately concluded by
detailing multiple ways in which the FMLA's anti-discriminatory
aims were still achievable through legal or quasi-legal actions which
had not been proscribed by the Court—thereby effectively offering *pro
bono* legal advice to would-be plaintiffs seeking redress under the
statute.[32]

In the final dissent, Ginsburg criticizes the majority's holding in
Burwell v. Hobby Lobby Stores, Inc.,[33] that closely-held corporations
were not required to provide contraceptive coverage to their employees through the corporations' health insurance plans. Ginsburg faulted
the majority for finding that First Amendment "free exercise [of reli-
gion] rights pertain to for-profit corporations" because "the exercise of
religion is characteristic of natural persons, not artificial legal entities."[34] Ginsburg believed the majority's decision would ultimately
impede women's ability to access healthcare benefits (and, implicitly,
contraception) in ways that had not been intended by Congress.[35]

Ginsburg's dissents are redolent with the wisdom she gained from
firsthand experience facing adversity and discrimination at nearly
every stage of her career; indeed, her writing is especially emphatic

[28] *Ruth Bader Ginsburg, supra* note 13.
[29] *Ledbetter*, 550 U.S. at 661 (Ginsburg, J., dissenting).
[30] 566 U.S. 30 (2012).
[31] *Id.* at 65 (Ginsburg, J., dissenting).
[32] *Id.* at 64–65.
[33] 573 U.S. 682 (2014).
[34] *Id.* at 752 (Ginsburg, J., dissenting).
[35] *Id.* at 765–66.

when a plaintiffs' case serves to continue her quest for progress and equality. Yet Justice Ginsburg is a judicial realist and understands the limits of her institution's authority. She has maintained that the Court should only respond when shifts in popular sentiment support a reinterpretation of the law: "It has to be the people who want the change, and without them no change will be lasting."[36] Regardless, she also retains hope that popular sentiment is on her side: "I am optimistic," she has said, "that movement toward enlistment of the talent of all who compose 'We, the people,' will continue."[37]

---

[36] Walsh, *supra* note 12.
[37] Ruth Bader Ginsburg, *supra* note 1.

LEDBETTER

"Once again, the ball is in Congress' court. As in 1991, the Legislature may act to correct this Court's parsimonious reading of Title VII."

The Case

After working for Goodyear Tire & Rubber as a plant supervisor for nearly 19 years, Lilly Ledbetter received an anonymous note telling her she made thousands of dollars per year less than her male colleagues employed in similar positions doing the same work.[1] In March of 1998, Ledbetter submitted a "questionnaire" to the Equal Employment Opportunity Commission (EEOC) alleging certain acts of sex discrimination and, in July 1998, filed a formal "charge" of discrimination with the EEOC. She then sued in the United States District Court for the Northern District of Alabama asserting, among other allegations, a pay discrimination claim under Title VII of the Civil Rights Act of 1964.[2]

The District Court allowed Ledbetter's Title VII claim to proceed to a jury, which found in her favor and awarded over $3.5 million in damages. Goodyear appealed the case to the United States Court of Appeals for the Eleventh Circuit, arguing that Ledbetter's pay discrimination claim was time-barred with respect to all pay decisions made prior to September 26, 1997. That date was significant because it was 180 days before the filing of Ledbetter's EEOC "questionnaire." A formal complaint of discrimination—usually, the EEOC "charge," but here, the EEOC "questionnaire"[3]—must be filed with the EEOC

---

[1] "By the end of 1997, Ledbetter was the only woman working as an area manager and the pay discrepancy between Ledbetter and her 15 male counterparts was stark: Ledbetter was paid $3,727 per month; the lowest paid male area manager received $4,286 per month, the highest paid, $5,236." Ledbetter v. Goodyear Tire & Rubber Co., 550 U.S. 618, 643 (2007) (Ginsburg, J., dissenting).

[2] Title VII prohibits discrimination by covered employers on the basis of race, color, religion, sex or national origin. *See* 42 U.S.C. § 2000e-2. Title VII is violated when an employer takes an "adverse" employment action for discriminatory reasons. *See id.* An adverse employment action is one that materially affects the terms and conditions of employment, such as a termination, failure to promote, denial of transfer, suspension, or reduction in pay.

[3] Though an EEOC "questionnaire" and an EEOC "charge" are technically

"within a specified period (either 180 or 300 days, depending on the State) 'after the alleged unlawful employment practice occurred,' and if the employee does not submit a timely EEOC charge, the employee may not challenge that practice in court."[4] The 180-day period is generally referred to as the "charging period."

Deeming Ledbetter's EEOC questionnaire untimely filed, the Eleventh Circuit reversed the jury verdict. In doing so, the court explicitly rejected the claim that each unfair paycheck Ledbetter received was an independent act of discrimination, and instead held that an employee could reach outside the 180-day limitations period "no further . . . than the last affirmative decision directly affecting the employee's pay immediately preceding the start of the limitations period."[5] This decision effectively barred Ledbetter from any recovery because she could not prove that the last "affirmative decision" affecting her pay which was made prior to the limitations period was a result of discriminatory decision-making.[6] Accordingly, Ledbetter appealed to the Supreme Court.

Justice Alito's Majority Opinion

In a 5–4 opinion authored by Justice Alito, the majority considered its precedent in this area and concluded that the "EEOC charging period is triggered when a discrete unlawful practice takes place."[7] It further stated that "[a] new violation does not occur, and a new charging period does not commence, upon the occurrence of subsequent nondiscriminatory acts that entail adverse effects resulting from the past discrimination."[8] In other words, even if the ramifications of a past discriminatory act—such as a decision to pay women less than men—are still felt every time a woman received a smaller paycheck, the 180-day charging period began when the initial discriminatory

---

different things, the majority in *Ledbetter* "assume[d] for the sake of argument that the filing of the questionnaire, rather than the formal charge, is the appropriate date" for purposes of Ledbetter's claims. *Ledbetter*, 550 U.S. at 622 n.1.

[4] *Id.* at 623–24 (quoting § 2000e–5(f)(1)) (internal citation omitted).

[5] Ledbetter v. Goodyear Tire & Rubber Co., 421 F.3d 1169, 1183 (11th Cir. 2005).

[6] The last "affirmative decision" affecting Ledbetter's pay had been a decision by a female supervisor of Ledbetter not to recommend that she receive a raise—a decision the Eleventh Circuit found was "not one that any reasonable jury could find discriminatory." *Id.* at 1180, 1184.

[7] *Ledbetter*, 550 U.S. at 628.

[8] *Id.*

decision to pay her less was made.[9] This would be true even if the cited discrimination was the result of longstanding and reoccurring discriminatory action by the employer.

Notably, in reaching its decision, the majority rejected numerous arguments by analogy to "other statutory regimes" which Ledbetter cited to support what the majority called "her 'paycheck accrual rule.'"[10] The majority also declined to evaluate numerous policy arguments Ledbetter had advanced "in favor of giving the alleged victims of pay discrimination more time before they are required to file a charge with the EEOC."[11] The language of the majority's opinion made clear that it was concerned about expanding Title VII's 180-day charging period, which could conceivably allow plaintiffs to bring suit for wrongs committed decades in the past.[12] Instead, the majority stated it would "apply the statute as written, and this means that any unlawful employment practice, including those involving compensation, must be presented to the EEOC within the period prescribed by statute."[13]

Justice Ginsburg's Dissent

Noting that the majority's opinion was formalistic and technical in a case where there was essentially no dispute that Ledbetter had experienced pay discrimination, Justice Ginsburg's dissent assailed the majority's rationale as being out-of-touch with the functional realities of pay discrimination and inconsistent with the Court's most relevant applicable precedent. Its holding, she maintained, was in direct contravention to the purpose of Title VII.

Attacking the majority's logic, Ginsburg observed that when an employer discriminates against a woman by paying her less, "cause to suspect that discrimination is at work develops only over time," and "[c]omparative pay information" is frequently "hidden from the employee's view."[14]

She concluded that pay disparities "are thus significantly different from adverse actions" of the type found in the cases relied upon by the

---

[9] Or, in the majority's words, "current effects alone cannot breathe life into prior, uncharged discrimination; as we held [previously], such effects in themselves have 'no present legal consequences.'" *Id.* (quoting United Air Lines, Inc. v. Evans, 431 U.S. 553, 558 (1977)).

[10] *See id.* at 640–42.

[11] *Id.* at 642.

[12] *See id.* at 630–31.

[13] *Id.* at 642–43.

[14] *Id.* at 645 (Ginsburg, J., dissenting).

majority, "'such as termination, failure to promote, . . . or refusal to hire,' all involving fully communicated discrete acts, [which are] 'easy to identify' as discriminatory."[15] In contrast to these easily identifiable acts, it is only when a pay disparity "becomes apparent and sizable, [for example] through future raises calculated as a percentage of current salaries, that an employee in Ledbetter's situation is likely to comprehend her plight and, therefore, to complain."[16] Accordingly, such pay disparities "have a closer kinship to hostile work environment claims than to charges of a single episode of discrimination" because they rest "not on one particular paycheck, but on 'the cumulative effect of individual acts.'"[17] In short, in Ledbetter's case, "with each new paycheck, Goodyear contributed incrementally to the accumulating harm."[18]

Ginsburg then demonstrated that each case relied on by the majority involved "single," "discrete" acts of discrimination, and thus held "no sway" in circumstances such as Ledbetter's, which she believed should have been analyzed under the "cumulative effect" framework just described.[19] Underscoring this conclusion, Ginsburg pointed to numerous decisions by various Courts of Appeal which she believed heralded the proper course. In each case, the respective court in question recognized "the unlawful practice is the *current payment* of salaries infected by gender-based (or race-based) discrimination—a practice that occurs whenever a paycheck delivers less to a woman than to a similarly situated man."[20] Such approach, she observed, was also of accord with that of the EEOC, which "has interpreted [Title VII] to permit employees to challenge disparate pay each time it is received."[21] Ultimately, Ginsburg assessed the result of the majority's opinion to be that "[k]nowingly carrying past pay discrimination forward must be treated as lawful conduct," and asserted that the majority's "approbation of these consequences is totally at odds with the robust protection against workplace discrimination Congress intended Title VII to secure."[22]

---

[15] *Id.* (quoting Nat'l R.R. Passenger Corp. v. Morgan, 536 U.S. 101, 114 (2002)).

[16] *Id.*

[17] *Id.* at 648 (quoting *Morgan*, 536 U.S. at 115).

[18] *Id.* at 649.

[19] *See id.* at 651–52.

[20] *Id.* at 645.

[21] *Id.* at 655.

[22] *Id.* at 660.

The Real-World Effects of Justice Ginsburg's Dissent

Justice Ginsburg's dissent helped bring about tangible legislative action to remedy what she viewed as the majority's erroneous holding. Her dissent's conclusion warned that the last time the Court "ordered a cramped interpretation of Title VII," Congress rebuked the Justices by passing the Civil Rights Act of 1991—overturning the majority's decision. She then made what was effectively a direct appeal for the same result: "Once again, the ball is in Congress' court. As in 1991, the Legislature may act to correct this Court's parsimonious reading of Title VII."[23]

Congress did just that. In 2009 it passed, and President Barack Obama signed, the Lilly Ledbetter Fair Pay Act—effectively adopting as law the approach advocated by Justice Ginsburg. The Act amended the Civil Rights Act of 1964 specifically to state that the 180-day statute of limitations (discussed above as the EEOC "charging period") is reset upon the receipt of each new paycheck affected by an allegedly discriminatory action; accordingly, even if the decision to pay a woman less than a man took place twenty years ago, the limitations period for that woman to file a charge of discrimination is reset with each paycheck she receives. Though the Act could not apply retroactively to the case of Ledbetter herself, it applied to any future plaintiff fighting a similar case.

---

[23] *Id.* at 661.

LEDBETTER V. GOODYEAR TIRE & RUBBER COMPANY

JUSTICE GINSBURG, with whom JUSTICE STEVENS, JUSTICE SOUTER, and JUSTICE BREYER join, DISSENTING.

Lilly Ledbetter was a supervisor at Goodyear Tire and Rubber's plant in Gadsden, Alabama, from 1979 until her retirement in 1998. For most of those years, she worked as an area manager, a position largely occupied by men. Initially, Ledbetter's salary was in line with the salaries of men performing substantially similar work. Over time, however, her pay slipped in comparison to the pay of male area managers with equal or less seniority. By the end of 1997, Ledbetter was the only woman working as an area manager and the pay discrepancy between Ledbetter and her 15 male counterparts was stark: Ledbetter was paid $3,727 per month; the lowest paid male area manager received $4,286 per month, the highest paid, $5,236.[1]

Ledbetter launched charges of discrimination before the Equal Employment Opportunity Commission (EEOC) in March 1998. Her formal administrative complaint specified that, in violation of Title VII, Goodyear paid her a discriminatorily low salary because of her sex.[2] That charge was eventually tried to a jury, which found it "more likely than not that [Goodyear] paid [Ledbetter] a[n] unequal salary because of her sex."[3] In accord with the jury's liability determination, the District Court entered judgment for Ledbetter for backpay and damages, plus counsel fees and costs.

The Court of Appeals for the Eleventh Circuit reversed. Relying on Goodyear's system of annual merit-based raises, the court held that Ledbetter's claim, in relevant part, was time barred.[4] Title VII provides that a charge of discrimination "shall be filed within [180] days

---

[1] *See* Ledbetter v. Goodyear Tire & Rubber Co., 421 F.3d 1169, 1174 (11th Cir. 2005); Brief for Petitioner at 4, *Ledbetter*, 550 U.S. 618 (No. 05-1074).

[2] *See* 42 U.S.C. § 2000e–2(a)(1) (rendering it unlawful for an employer "to discriminate against any individual with respect to [her] compensation . . . because of such individual's . . . sex").

[3] Petition for Writ of Certiorari app. at 102, *Ledbetter*, 550 U.S. 618 (No.05-1074).

[4] *Ledbetter*, 421 F.3d at 1171, 1182–83.

after the alleged unlawful employment practice occurred."[5; 6] [FN 1]
Ledbetter charged, and proved at trial, that within the 180-day period,
her pay was substantially less than the pay of men doing the same
work. Further, she introduced evidence sufficient to establish that
discrimination against female managers at the Gadsden plant, not
performance inadequacies on her part, accounted for the pay differential.[7] That evidence was unavailing, the Eleventh Circuit held, and
the Court today agrees, because it was incumbent on Ledbetter to file
charges year-by-year, each time Goodyear failed to increase her salary
commensurate with the salaries of male peers. Any annual pay decision not contested immediately (within 180 days), the Court affirms,
becomes grandfathered, a fait accompli beyond the province of Title
VII ever to repair.

The Court's insistence on immediate contest overlooks common
characteristics of pay discrimination. Pay disparities often occur, as
they did in Ledbetter's case, in small increments; cause to suspect
that discrimination is at work develops only over time. Comparative
pay information, moreover, is often hidden from the employee's view.
Employers may keep under wraps the pay differentials maintained
among supervisors, no less the reasons for those differentials. Small
initial discrepancies may not be seen as meet for a federal case, particularly when the employee, trying to succeed in a nontraditional
environment, is averse to making waves.

Pay disparities are thus significantly different from adverse actions "such as termination, failure to promote, . . . or refusal to hire,"
all involving fully communicated discrete acts, "easy to identify" as
discriminatory.[8] It is only when the disparity becomes apparent and
sizable, e.g., through future raises calculated as a percentage of current salaries, that an employee in Ledbetter's situation is likely to
comprehend her plight and, therefore, to complain. Her initial readi-
ness to give her employer the benefit of the doubt should not preclude
her from later challenging the then current and continuing payment
of a wage depressed on account of her sex.

On questions of time under Title VII, we have identified as the critical inquiries: "What constitutes an 'unlawful employment practice'

---

[5] 42 U.S.C. § 2000e–5(e)(1).

[6] [FN 1] If the complainant has first instituted proceedings with a state or local
agency, the filing period is extended to 300 days or 30 days after the denial of
relief by the agency. 42 U.S.C. § 2000e–5(e)(1). Because the 180-day period
applies to Ledbetter's case, that figure will be used throughout. *See Ledbetter*,
550 U.S. 622–24.

[7] *See, e.g.*, Petition for Writ of Certiorari, *supra* note 3, app. at 36–47, 51–68,
82–87, 90–98, 112–113.

[8] *See* Nat'l R.R. Passenger Corp. v. Morgan, 536 U.S. 101, 114 (2002).

and when has that practice 'occurred'?"[9] Our precedent suggests, and lower courts have overwhelmingly held, that the unlawful practice is the current payment of salaries infected by gender-based (or race-based) discrimination—a practice that occurs whenever a paycheck delivers less to a woman than to a similarly situated man.[10]

I

Title VII proscribes as an "unlawful employment practice" discrimination "against any individual with respect to his compensation . . . because of such individual's race, color, religion, sex, or national origin."[11] An individual seeking to challenge an employment practice under this proscription must file a charge with the EEOC within 180 days "after the alleged unlawful employment practice occurred."[12]

Ledbetter's petition presents a question important to the sound application of Title VII: What activity qualifies as an unlawful employment practice in cases of discrimination with respect to compensation. One answer identifies the pay-setting decision, and that decision alone, as the unlawful practice. Under this view, each particular salary-setting decision is discrete from prior and subsequent decisions, and must be challenged within 180 days on pain of forfeiture. Another response counts both the pay-setting decision and the actual payment of a discriminatory wage as unlawful practices. Under this approach, each payment of a wage or salary infected by sex-based discrimination constitutes an unlawful employment practice; prior decisions, outside the 180-day charge-filing period, are not themselves actionable, but they are relevant in determining the lawfulness of conduct within the period. The Court adopts the first view,[13] but the second is more faithful to precedent, more in tune with the realities of the workplace, and more respectful of Title VII's remedial purpose.

A

In *Bazemore*, we unanimously held that an employer, the North Carolina Agricultural Extension Service, committed an unlawful employment practice each time it paid black employees less than similarly

---

[9] *Id.* at 110.

[10] *See* Bazemore v. Friday, 478 U.S. 385, 395 (1986) (Brennan, J., joined by all other Members of the Court, concurring in part).

[11] 42 U.S.C. § 2000e–2(a)(1).

[12] § 2000e–5(e)(1); *see* Ledbetter v. Goodyear Tire & Rubber Co., 550 U.S. 618, 623–24 (2007); *id.* 644 & n.1 (Ginsburg, J., dissenting).

[13] *See id.* at 621–25 (majority opinion).

situated white employees.[14] Before 1965, the Extension Service was divided into two branches: a white branch and a "Negro branch."[15] Employees in the "Negro branch" were paid less than their white counterparts. In response to the Civil Rights Act of 1964, which included Title VII, the State merged the two branches into a single organization, made adjustments to reduce the salary disparity, and began giving annual raises based on nondiscriminatory factors.[16] Nonetheless, "some pre-existing salary disparities continued to linger on."[17] We rejected the Court of Appeals' conclusion that the plaintiffs could not prevail because the lingering disparities were simply a continuing effect of a decision lawfully made prior to the effective date of Title VII.[18] Rather, we reasoned, "[e]ach week's paycheck that delivers less to a black than to a similarly situated white is a wrong actionable under Title VII."[19] Paychecks perpetuating past discrimination, we thus recognized, are actionable not simply because they are "related" to a decision made outside the charge-filing period,[20] but because they discriminate anew each time they issue.[21]

Subsequently, in *Morgan*, we set apart, for purposes of Title VII's timely filing requirement, unlawful employment actions of two kinds: "discrete acts" that are "easy to identify" as discriminatory, and acts that recur and are cumulative in impact.[22] "[A] [d]iscrete ac[t] such as termination, failure to promote, denial of transfer, or refusal to hire,"[23] we explained, "'occur[s]' on the day that it 'happen[s].' A party, therefore, must file a charge within . . . 180 . . . days of the date of the act or lose the ability to recover for it."[24]

"[D]ifferent in kind from discrete acts," we made clear, are "claims . . . based on the cumulative effect of individual acts."[25] The *Morgan* decision placed hostile work environment claims in that category.

---

[14] *Bazemore*, 478 U.S. at 395 (opinion of Brennan, J.)

[15] *Id.* at 390.

[16] *Id.* at 390–91, 394–95.

[17] *Id.* at 394 (internal quotation marks omitted).

[18] *See id.* at 395–96.

[19] *Id.* at 395.

[20] *Cf.* Ledbetter v. Goodyear Tire & Rubber Co., 550 U.S. 618, 636 (2007).

[21] *See Bazemore*, 478 U.S. at 395–96 & n.6; Nat'l R.R. Passenger Corp. v. Morgan, 536 U.S. 101, 111–12 (2002).

[22] *See Morgan*, 550 U.S. at 110, 113–15.

[23] *Id.* at 114.

[24] *Id.* at 110; *see id.* at 113 ("[D]iscrete discriminatory acts are not actionable if time barred, even when they are related to acts alleged in timely filed charges. Each discrete discriminatory act starts a new clock for filing charges alleging that act.").

[25] *Id.* at 115.

"Their very nature involves repeated conduct."[26] "The unlawful employment practice" in hostile work environment claims, "cannot be said to occur on any particular day. It occurs over a series of days or perhaps years and, in direct contrast to discrete acts, a single act of harassment may not be actionable on its own."[27] The persistence of the discriminatory conduct both indicates that management should have known of its existence and produces a cognizable harm.[28] Because the very nature of the hostile work environment claim involves repeated conduct, "[i]t does not matter, for purposes of the statute, that some of the component acts of the hostile work environment fall outside the statutory time period. Provided that an act contributing to the claim occurs within the filing period, the entire time period of the hostile environment may be considered by a court for the purposes of determining liability."[29]

Consequently, although the unlawful conduct began in the past, "a charge may be filed at a later date and still encompass the whole."[30]

Pay disparities, of the kind Ledbetter experienced, have a closer kinship to hostile work environment claims than to charges of a single episode of discrimination. Ledbetter's claim, resembling *Morgan*'s, rested not on one particular paycheck, but on "the cumulative effect of individual acts."[31] She charged insidious discrimination building up slowly but steadily.[32] Initially in line with the salaries of men performing substantially the same work, Ledbetter's salary fell 15 to 40 percent behind her male counterparts only after successive evaluations and percentage-based pay adjustments.[33] Over time, she alleged and proved, the repetition of pay decisions undervaluing her work gave rise to the current discrimination of which she complained. Though component acts fell outside the charge-filing period, with each new paycheck, Goodyear contributed incrementally to the accumulating harm.[34; 35] [FN 2]

---

[26] *Id.*

[27] *Id.* (internal quotation marks omitted).

[28] *Id.*

[29] *Id.* at 117.

[30] *Id.*

[31] *See id.* at 115; *see also* Brief for Petitioner at 13, 15–17, 17 n.9, Ledbetter v. Goodyear Tire & Rubber Co., 550 U.S. 618 (2007) (No. 05-1074) (analogizing Ledbetter's claim to the recurring and cumulative harm at issue in *Morgan*); Reply Brief for Petitioner at 13, *Ledbetter*, 550 U.S. 618 (No. 05-1074) (distinguishing pay discrimination from "easy to identify" discrete acts (internal quotation marks omitted)).

[32] *See* Brief for Petitioner, *supra* note 31, at 5–8.

[33] *See Ledbetter*, 550 U.S. at 643 (Ginsburg, J., dissenting).

[34] *See Morgan*, 536 U.S. at 117; Bazemore v. Friday, 478 U.S. 385, 395–96 (1986); *cf.* Hanover Shoe, Inc. v. United Shoe Mach. Corp., 392 U.S. 481,

B

The realities of the workplace reveal why the discrimination with respect to compensation that Ledbetter suffered does not fit within the category of singular discrete acts "easy to identify." A worker knows immediately if she is denied a promotion or transfer, if she is fired or refused employment. And promotions, transfers, hirings, and firings are generally public events, known to co-workers. When an employer makes a decision of such open and definitive character, an employee can immediately seek out an explanation and evaluate it for pretext. Compensation disparities, in contrast, are often hidden from sight. It is not unusual, decisions in point illustrate, for management to decline to publish employee pay levels, or for employees to keep private their own salaries.[36; 37] [FN 3] Tellingly, as the record in this case bears out, Goodyear kept salaries confidential; employees had only limited access to information regarding their colleagues' earnings.[38]

The problem of concealed pay discrimination is particularly acute where the disparity arises not because the female employee is flatly denied a raise but because male counterparts are given larger raises. Having received a pay increase, the female employee is unlikely to discern at once that she has experienced an adverse employment decision. She may have little reason even to suspect discrimination until a pattern develops incrementally and she ultimately becomes aware of the disparity. Even if an employee suspects that the reason for a

---

502 n.15 (1968).

[35] [FN 2] *National Railroad Passenger Corporation v. Morgan*, 536 U.S. 101, 117 (2002), the Court emphasizes, required that "an act contributing to the claim occu[r] within the [charge-]filing period." *Ledbetter*, 550 U.S. at 648, 638 n.7 (emphasis deleted; internal quotation marks omitted). Here, each paycheck within the filing period compounded the discrimination Ledbetter encountered, and thus contributed to the "actionable wrong," i.e., the succession of acts composing the pattern of discriminatory pay, of which she complained.

[36] *See, e.g.*, Goodwin v. General Motors Corp., 275 F.3d 1005, 1008–09 (10th Cir. 2002) (plaintiff did not know what her colleagues earned until a printout listing of salaries appeared on her desk, seven years after her starting salary was set lower than her co-workers' salaries); McMillan v. Mass. Soc. for the Prevention of Cruelty to Animals, 140 F.3d 288, 296 (1st Cir. 1998) (plaintiff worked for employer for years before learning of salary disparity published in a newspaper).

[37] [FN 3] *See also* Leonard Bierman & Rafael Gely, *"Love, Sex and Politics? Sure. Salary? No Way": Workplace Social Norms and the Law*, 25 BERKELEY J. EMP. & LAB. L. 167, 168, 171 (2004) (one-third of private sector employers have adopted specific rules prohibiting employees from discussing their wages with co-workers; only one in ten employers has adopted a pay openness policy).

[38] Petition for Writ of Certiorari, *supra* note 3, app. at 56–57, 89.

comparatively low raise is not performance but sex (or another protected ground), the amount involved may seem too small, or the employer's intent too ambiguous, to make the issue immediately actionable—or winnable.

Further separating pay claims from the discrete employment actions identified in *Morgan*, an employer gains from sex-based pay disparities in a way it does not from a discriminatory denial of promotion, hiring, or transfer. When a male employee is selected over a female for a higher level position, someone still gets the promotion and is paid a higher salary; the employer is not enriched. But when a woman is paid less than a similarly situated man, the employer reduces its costs each time the pay differential is implemented. Furthermore, decisions on promotions, like decisions installing seniority systems, often implicate the interests of third-party employees in a way that pay differentials do not.[39] Disparate pay, by contrast, can be remedied at any time solely at the expense of the employer who acts in a discriminatory fashion.

C

In light of the significant differences between pay disparities and discrete employment decisions of the type identified in *Morgan*, the cases on which the Court relies hold no sway.[40] *Evans* and *Ricks* both involved a single, immediately identifiable act of discrimination: in *Evans*, a constructive discharge;[41] in *Ricks*, a denial of tenure.[42] In each case, the employee filed charges well after the discrete discriminatory act occurred: When United Airlines forced Evans to resign because of its policy barring married female flight attendants, she filed no charge; only four years later, when Evans was rehired, did she allege that the airline's former no-marriage rule was unlawful and therefore should not operate to deny her seniority credit for her prior service.[43] Similarly, when Delaware State College denied Ricks tenure, he did not object until his terminal contract came to an end, one

---

[39] *Cf.* Int'l Bhd. of Teamsters v. United States, 431 U.S. 324, 352–53 (1977) (recognizing that seniority systems involve "vested . . . rights of employees" and concluding that Title VII was not intended to "destroy or water down" those rights).

[40] *See Ledbetter*, 550 U.S. at 5–10 (discussing United Air Lines, Inc. v. Evans, 431 U.S. 553 (1977), Del. State Coll. v. Ricks, 449 U.S. 250 (1980), and Lorance v. AT&T Techs., Inc., 490 U.S. 900 (1989)).

[41] *Evans*, 431 U.S. 553, 554 (1977).

[42] *Ricks*, 449 U.S. 250, 252 (1980).

[43] *See Evans*, 431 U.S. at 554–57.

year later.[44] No repetitive, cumulative discriminatory employment practice was at issue in either case.[45; 46 [FN 4]]

Lorance is also inapposite, for, in this Court's view, it too involved a one-time discrete act: the adoption of a new seniority system that "had its genesis in sex discrimination."[47] The Court's extensive reliance on *Lorance*,[48] moreover, is perplexing for that decision is no longer effective: In the 1991 Civil Rights Act, Congress superseded *Lorance*'s holding.[49] Repudiating our judgment that a facially neutral seniority system adopted with discriminatory intent must be challenged immediately, Congress provided:

> For purposes of this section, an unlawful employment practice occurs . . . when the seniority system is adopted, when an individual becomes subject to the seniority system, or when a person aggrieved is injured by the application of the seniority system or provision of the system.[50]

Congress thus agreed with the dissenters in *Lorance* that "the harsh reality of [that] decision," was "glaringly at odds with the purposes of Title VII."[51]

---

[44] *Ricks*, 449 U.S. at 253–54, 257–58.

[45] *See Evans*, 431 U.S. at 557–58; *Ricks*, 449 U.S. at 258.

[46] [FN 4] The Court also relies on *Machinists v. NLRB*, 362 U.S. 411 (1960), which like *Evans* and *Ricks*, concerned a discrete act: the execution of a collective bargaining agreement containing a union security clause. 362 U.S. at 412, 417. In *Machinists*, it was undisputed that under the National Labor Relations Act (NLRA), a union and an employer may not agree to a union security clause "if at the time of original execution the union does not represent a majority of the employees in the [bargaining] unit." *Id.* at 412–14, 417. The complainants, however, failed to file a charge within the NLRA's six-month charge filing period; instead, they filed charges 10 and 12 months after the execution of the agreement, objecting to its subsequent enforcement. *See id.* at 412, 414. Thus, as in *Evans* and *Ricks*, but in contrast to Ledbetter's case, the employment decision at issue was easily identifiable and occurred on a single day.

[47] *See* Lorance v. AT&T Techs., Inc., 490 U.S. 900, 902, 905 (1989) (internal quotation marks omitted).

[48] Ledbetter v. Goodyear Tire & Rubber Co., 550 U.S. 618, 626–29, 633, 636–37 (2007).

[49] Civil Rights Act of 1991 § 112, 105 Stat. 1079 (codified as amended at 42 U.S.C. § 2000e–5(e)(2)).

[50] *Id.*

[51] *Lorance*, 490 U.S. at 914 (Marshall, J., dissenting); *see also* Civil Rights Act of 1991 § 3, 105 Stat. 1071 (1991 Civil Rights Act was designed "to respond to recent decisions of the Supreme Court by expanding the scope of relevant civil rights statutes in order to provide adequate protection to victims of discrimination").

True, §112 of the 1991 Civil Rights Act directly addressed only seniority systems.[52] But Congress made clear (1) its view that this Court had unduly contracted the scope of protection afforded by Title VII and other civil rights statutes, and (2) its aim to generalize the ruling in *Bazemore*. As the Senate Report accompanying the proposed Civil Rights Act of 1990, the precursor to the 1991 Act, explained:

> Where, as was alleged in *Lorance*, an employer adopts a rule or decision with an unlawful discriminatory motive, each application of that rule or decision is a new violation of the law. In *Bazemore* . . ., for example, . . . the Supreme Court properly held that each application of th[e] racially motivated salary structure, i.e., each new paycheck, constituted a distinct violation of Title VII. Section 7(a)(2) generalizes the result correctly reached in *Bazemore*.[53; 54 [FN 5]]

Until today, in the more than 15 years since Congress amended Title VII, the Court had not once relied upon *Lorance*. It is mistaken to do so now. Just as Congress' "goals in enacting Title VII . . . never included conferring absolute immunity on discriminatorily adopted seniority systems that survive their first [180] days,"[55] Congress never intended to immunize forever discriminatory pay differentials unchallenged within 180 days of their adoption. This assessment gains weight when one comprehends that even a relatively minor pay disparity will expand exponentially over an employee's working life if raises are set as a percentage of prior pay.

A clue to congressional intent can be found in Title VII's backpay provision. The statute expressly provides that backpay may be awarded for a period of up to two years before the discrimination charge is filed.[56] This prescription indicates that Congress contemplated challenges to pay discrimination commencing before, but continuing

---

[52] *See Ledbetter*, 550 U.S. at 627 & n.2.

[53] S. REP. NO. 101-315, at 54 (1990); *see also* 137 CONG. REC. 29,046–47 (1991) (Sponsors' Interpretative Memorandum) ("This legislation should be interpreted as disapproving the extension of [*Lorance*] to contexts outside of seniority systems.") *But cf. Ledbetter*, 550 U.S. at 637 (relying on *Lorance* to conclude that "when an employer issues paychecks pursuant to a system that is facially nondiscriminatory and neutrally applied" a new Title VII violation does not occur (internal quotation marks omitted)).

[54] [FN 5] No Senate Report was submitted with the Civil Rights Act of 1991, which was in all material respects identical to the proposed 1990 Act.

[55] *Lorance*, 490 U.S. at 914 (Marshall, J., dissenting).

[56] 42 U.S.C. § 2000e–5(g)(1) ("Back pay liability shall not accrue from a date more than two years prior to the filing of a charge with the Commission.").

into, the 180-day filing period.[57] As we recognized in *Morgan*, "the fact that Congress expressly limited the amount of recoverable damages elsewhere to a particular time period [i.e., two years] indicates that the [180-day] timely filing provision was not meant to serve as a specific limitation . . . [on] the conduct that may be considered."[58]

D

In tune with the realities of wage discrimination, the Courts of Appeals have overwhelmingly judged as a present violation the payment of wages infected by discrimination: Each paycheck less than the amount payable had the employer adhered to a nondiscriminatory compensation regime, courts have held, constitutes a cognizable harm.[59]

Similarly in line with the real-world characteristics of pay discrimination, the EEOC—the federal agency responsible for enforcing Title VII[60]—has interpreted the Act to permit employees to challenge disparate pay each time it is received. The EEOC's Compliance Manual provides that "repeated occurrences of the same discriminatory

---

[57] *See* Nat'l R.R. Passenger Corp. v. Morgan, 536 U.S. 101, 119 (2002) ("If Congress intended to limit liability to conduct occurring in the period within which the party must file the charge, it seems unlikely that Congress would have allowed recovery for two years of backpay.").

[58] *Id.*

[59] *See, e.g.*, Forsyth v. Fed'n Employment & Guidance Serv., 409 F.3d 565, 573 (2d Cir. 2005) ("Any paycheck given within the [charge-filing] period . . . would be actionable, even if based on a discriminatory pay scale set up outside of the statutory period."); Shea v. Rice, 409 F.3d 448, 452–53 (D.C. Cir. 2005) ("[An] employer commit[s] a separate unlawful employment practice each time he pa[ys] one employee less than another for a discriminatory reason" (citing Bazemore v. Friday, 478 U.S. 385, 396 (1986))); Goodwin v. General Motors Corp., 275 F.3d 1005, 1009–10 (10th Cir. 2002) ("[*Bazemore*] has taught a crucial distinction with respect to discriminatory disparities in pay, establishing that a discriminatory salary is not merely a lingering effect of past discrimination—instead it is itself a continually recurring violation . . . . [E]ach race-based discriminatory salary payment constitutes a fresh violation of Title VII." (footnote omitted)); Anderson v. Zubieta, 180 F.3d 329, 335 (D.C. Cir. 1999) ("The Courts of Appeals have repeatedly reached the . . . conclusion" that pay discrimination is "actionable upon receipt of each paycheck."); *accord* Hildebrandt v. Ill. Dep't of Nat. Res., 347 F.3d 1014, 1025–29 (7th Cir. 2003); Cardenas v. Massey, 269 F.3d 251, 257 (3d Cir. 2001); Ashley v. Boyle's Famous Corned Beef Co., 66 F.3d 164, 167–68 (8th Cir. 1995) (en banc); Brinkley-Obu v. Hughes Training, Inc., 36 F.3d 336, 347–49 (4th Cir. 1994); Gibbs v. Pierce Cty. Law Enf't Support Agency, 785 F.2d 1396, 1399–1400 (9th Cir. 1986).

[60] *See, e.g.*, 42 U. S. C. §§ 2000e–5(f), 2000e–12(a).

employment action, such as discriminatory paychecks, can be challenged as long as one discriminatory act occurred within the charge filing period."[61]

The EEOC has given effect to its interpretation in a series of administrative decisions.[62] And in this very case, the EEOC urged the Eleventh Circuit to recognize that Ledbetter's failure to challenge any particular pay-setting decision when that decision was made "does not deprive her of the right to seek relief for discriminatory paychecks she received in 1997 and 1998."[63; 64 [FN 6]]

II

The Court asserts that treating pay discrimination as a discrete act, limited to each particular pay-setting decision, is necessary to "protec[t] employers from the burden of defending claims arising from

---

[61] U.S. EQUAL EMP. OPPORTUNITY COMM'N, 2 EEOC COMPLIANCE MANUAL § 2–IV–C(1)(a) (2006) at 605:0024 & n.183; cf. id. § 10–III at 633:0002 (Title VII requires an employer to eliminate pay disparities attributable to a discriminatory system, even if that system has been discontinued).

[62] See Joan Albritton, EEOC Appeal No. 01A44063, 2004 WL 2983682, at *2 (EEOC Office of Fed. Operations, Dec. 17, 2004) (although disparity arose and employee became aware of the disparity outside the charge-filing period, claim was not time barred because "[e]ach paycheck that complainant receives which is less than that of similarly situated employees outside of her protected classes could support a claim under Title VII if discrimination is found to be the reason for the pay discrepancy." (citing Bazemore, 478 U.S. at 396)); see also Pamela S. Bynum-Doles, EEOC Appeal No. 01A53973, 2006 WL 2096290 (EEOC Office of Fed. Operations, July 18, 2006); Rosie L. Ward, EEOC Appeal No. 01A60047, 2006 WL 721992 (EEOC Office of Fed. Operations, Mar. 10, 2006).

[63] Brief of EEOC in Support of Petition for Rehearing and Suggestion for Rehearing En Banc at 14, Ledbetter v. Goodyear Tire & Rubber Co., 421 F.3d 1169 (11th Cir. 2005) (No. 03-15264) [hereinafter EEOC Brief] (citing Nat'l R.R. Passenger Corp. v. Morgan, 536 U.S. 101, 113 (2002)).

[64 [FN 6]] The Court dismisses the EEOC's considerable "experience and informed judgment," Firefighters v. Cleveland, 478 U.S. 501, 518 (1986) (internal quotation marks omitted), as unworthy of any deference in this case, see Ledbetter v. Goodyear Tire & Rubber Co., 550 U.S. 618, 642 n.11 (2007). But the EEOC's interpretations mirror workplace realities and merit at least respectful attention. In any event, the level of deference due the EEOC here is an academic question, for the agency's conclusion that Ledbetter's claim is not time barred is the best reading of the statute even if the Court "were interpreting [Title VII] from scratch." See Edelman v. Lynchburg College, 535 U.S. 106, 114 (2002); see Ledbetter, 550 U.S. at 623–33 (Ginsburg, J., dissenting).

employment decisions that are long past."[65] But the discrimination of which Ledbetter complained is not long past. As she alleged, and as the jury found, Goodyear continued to treat Ledbetter differently because of sex each pay period, with mounting harm. Allowing employees to challenge discrimination "that extend[s] over long periods of time," into the charge-filing period, we have previously explained, "does not leave employers defenseless" against unreasonable or prejudicial delay.[66] Employers disadvantaged by such delay may raise various defenses.[67] Doctrines such as "waiver, estoppel, and equitable tolling" "allow us to honor Title VII's remedial purpose without negating the particular purpose of the filing requirement, to give prompt notice to the employer."[68; 69 [FN 7]]

In a last-ditch argument, the Court asserts that this dissent would allow a plaintiff to sue on a single decision made 20 years ago "even if the employee had full knowledge of all the circumstances relating to the . . . decision at the time it was made."[70] It suffices to point out that the defenses just noted would make such a suit foolhardy. No sensible judge would tolerate such inexcusable neglect.[71]

Ledbetter, the Court observes,[72] dropped an alternative remedy she could have pursued: Had she persisted in pressing her claim under the Equal Pay Act of 1963 (EPA),[73] she would not have encountered a time

---

[65] *Ledbetter*, 550 U.S. at 631 (quoting Del. State Coll. v. Ricks, 449 U.S. 250, 256–57 (1980)).

[66] *Morgan*, 536 U.S. at 121.

[67] *Id.* at 122.

[68] *Id.* at 121 (quoting Zipes v. Trans World Airlines, Inc., 455 U.S. 385, 398 (1982)); *see id.* at 121 (defense of laches may be invoked to block an employee's suit "if he unreasonably delays in filing [charges] and as a result harms the defendant"); EEOC Brief, *supra* note 63, at 15 ("[I]f Ledbetter unreasonably delayed challenging an earlier decision, and that delay significantly impaired Goodyear's ability to defend itself . . . Goodyear can raise a defense of laches . . . .").

[69] [FN 7] Further, as the EEOC appropriately recognized in its brief to the Eleventh Circuit, Ledbetter's failure to challenge particular pay raises within the charge-filing period "significantly limit[s] the relief she can seek. By waiting to file a charge, Ledbetter lost her opportunity to seek relief for any discriminatory paychecks she received between 1979 and late 1997." EEOC Brief, supra note 63, at 14; *see also Ledbetter*, 550 U.S. at 654–56 (Ginsburg, Jr., dissenting).

[70] *Ledbetter*, 550 U.S. at 639.

[71] *See Morgan*, 536 U.S. at 121 ("In such cases, the federal courts have the discretionary power . . . to locate a just result in light of the circumstances peculiar to the case." (internal quotation marks omitted)).

[72] *Ledbetter*, 550 U.S. at 640 n.9.

[73] 29 U.S.C. § 206(d).

bar.[74] [FN 8]; [75] Notably, the EPA provides no relief when the pay discrimination charged is based on race, religion, national origin, age, or disability. Thus, in truncating the Title VII rule this Court announced in *Bazemore*, the Court does not disarm female workers from achieving redress for unequal pay, but it does impede racial and other minorities from gaining similar relief.[76] [FN 9]

Furthermore, the difference between the EPA's prohibition against paying unequal wages and Title VII's ban on discrimination with regard to compensation is not as large as the Court's opinion might suggest.[77] The key distinction is that Title VII requires a showing of intent. In practical effect, "if the trier of fact is in equipoise about whether the wage differential is motivated by gender discrimination," Title VII compels a verdict for the employer, while the EPA compels a verdict for the plaintiff.[78] In this case, Ledbetter carried the burden of persuading the jury that the pay disparity she suffered was attributable to intentional sex discrimination.

III

To show how far the Court has strayed from interpretation of Title VII with fidelity to the Act's core purpose, I return to the evidence Ledbetter presented at trial. Ledbetter proved to the jury the following: She was a member of a protected class; she performed work substantially equal to work of the dominant class (men); she was

---

[74] [FN 8] Under the EPA 29 U.S.C. § 206(d), which is subject to the Fair Labor Standards Act's time prescriptions, a claim charging denial of equal pay accrues anew with each paycheck. 1 BARBARA LINDEMANN & PAUL GROSSMAN, EMPLOYMENT DISCRIMINATION LAW 529 (3d ed. 1996); *cf.* 29 U.S.C. § 255(a) (prescribing a two-year statute of limitations for violations generally, but a three-year limitation period for willful violations).

[75] *See Ledbetter*, 550 U.S. at 640 ("If Ledbetter had pursued her EPA claim, she would not face the Title VII obstacles that she now confronts."); *cf.* Corning Glass Works v. Brennan, 417 U.S. 188, 208–10 (1974).

[76] [FN 9] For example, under today's decision, if a black supervisor initially received the same salary as his white colleagues, but annually received smaller raises, there would be no right to sue under Title VII outside the 180-day window following each annual salary change, however strong the cumulative evidence of discrimination might be. The Court would thus force plaintiffs, in many cases, to sue too soon to prevail, while cutting them off as time barred once the pay differential is large enough to enable them to mount a winnable case.

[77] *See Ledbetter*, 550 U.S. at 640–41.

[78] 2 CHARLES A. SULLIVAN, MICHAEL J. ZIMMER, & REBECCA HANNER WHITE, EMPLOYMENT DISCRIMINATION: LAW AND PRACTICE § 7.08[F][3], at 532 (3d ed. 2002).

compensated less for that work; and the disparity was attributable to gender-based discrimination.[79]

Specifically, Ledbetter's evidence demonstrated that her current pay was discriminatorily low due to a long series of decisions reflecting Goodyear's pervasive discrimination against women managers in general and Ledbetter in particular. Ledbetter's former supervisor, for example, admitted to the jury that Ledbetter's pay, during a particular one-year period, fell below Goodyear's minimum threshold for her position.[80] Although Goodyear claimed the pay disparity was due to poor performance, the supervisor acknowledged that Ledbetter received a "Top Performance Award" in 1996.[81] The jury also heard testimony that another supervisor—who evaluated Ledbetter in 1997 and whose evaluation led to her most recent raise denial—was openly biased against women.[82] And two women who had previously worked as managers at the plant told the jury they had been subject to pervasive discrimination and were paid less than their male counterparts. One was paid less than the men she supervised.[83] Ledbetter herself testified about the discriminatory animus conveyed to her by plant officials. Toward the end of her career, for instance, the plant manager told Ledbetter that the "plant did not need women, that [women] didn't help it, [and] caused problems."[84; 85 [FN 10]] After weighing all the evidence, the jury found for Ledbetter, concluding that the pay disparity was due to intentional discrimination.

Yet, under the Court's decision, the discrimination Ledbetter proved is not redressable under Title VII. Each and every pay decision she did not immediately challenge wiped the slate clean. Consideration may not be given to the cumulative effect of a series of decisions that, together, set her pay well below that of every male area manager. Knowingly carrying past pay discrimination forward must be treated as lawful conduct. Ledbetter may not be compensated for the lower pay she was in fact receiving when she complained to the EEOC. Nor, were she still employed by Goodyear, could she gain, on the proof she presented at trial, injunctive relief requiring, prospectively, her receipt of the same compensation men

---

[79] *See Ledbetter*, 550 U.S. at 643–44 (Ginsburg, J., dissenting).

[80] Petition for Writ of Certiorari, *supra* note 3, app. at 93–97.

[81] *Id.* at 90–93.

[82] *Id.* at 46, 77–82.

[83] *Id.* at 51–68.

[84] *Id.* at 36.

[85] [FN 10] Given this abundant evidence, the Court cannot tenably maintain that Ledbetter's case "turned principally on the misconduct of a single Goodyear supervisor." *See* Ledbetter v. Goodyear Tire & Rubber Co., 550 U.S. 618, 632 n.4.

receive for substantially similar work. The Court's approbation of these consequences is totally at odds with the robust protection against workplace discrimination Congress intended Title VII to secure.[86]

This is not the first time the Court has ordered a cramped interpretation of Title VII, incompatible with the statute's broad remedial purpose.[87] Once again, the ball is in Congress' court. As in 1991, the Legislature may act to correct this Court's parsimonious reading of Title VII.

*   *   *

For the reasons stated, I would hold that Ledbetter's claim is not time barred and would reverse the Eleventh Circuit's judgment.

---

[86] *See, e.g.*, Int'l Bhd. of Teamsters v. United States, 431 U.S. 324, 348 (1977) ("The primary purpose of Title VII was to assure equality of employment opportunities and to eliminate . . . discriminatory practices and devices . . . ." (internal quotation marks omitted)); Albemarle Paper Co. v. Moody, 422 U.S. 405, 418 (1975) ("It is . . . the purpose of Title VII to make persons whole for injuries suffered on account of unlawful employment discrimination.").

[87] *See Ledbetter*, 550 U.S. at 652–54 (Ginsburg, J., dissenting); *see also* Wards Cove Packing Co. v. Atonio, 490 U.S. 642 (1989) (superseded in part by the Civil Rights Act of 1991); Price Waterhouse v. Hopkins, 490 U.S. 228 (1989) (plurality opinion) (superseded in part by the Civil Rights Act of 1991); 1 LINDEMANN & GROSSMAN, supra note 74, at 2 ("A spate of Court decisions in the late 1980s drew congressional fire and resulted in demands for legislative change[,]" culminating in the 1991 Civil Rights Act (footnote omitted)).

HOBBY LOBBY

"The Court, I fear, has ventured into a minefield."

The Case

In *Burwell v. Hobby Lobby Stores, Inc.*, the Court reviewed a dispute over a provision of the Patient Protection and Affordable Care Act ("ACA"), commonly known as "Obamacare," requiring business-provided health insurance plans to include coverage for contraception. Hobby Lobby was an arts-and-crafts chain store with over 500 locations across the U.S. The company was owned and exclusively controlled by the Green family, whose members claimed—according to their Christian religious beliefs—life begins at conception, and that it would violate their religion to facilitate access to contraceptive drugs or devices that operate after that point.

The ACA requires employers with 50 or more full-time employees either to offer a group health plan or group health insurance or to pay a substantial penalty. The ACA also requires the provision of preventive care for women which encompasses preventive pregnancy care, including FDA-approved contraception devices. There were exemptions to this mandate for religious, non-profit and church organizations. However, the ACA did not exempt for-profit organizations such as Hobby Lobby even if the owners held sincere religious beliefs against the use of contraception.

Once the ACA took effect, Hobby Lobby was forced to offer its employees health insurance that complied with the law's mandates. The Greens had religious objections to abortion and contended that four of the contraceptive methods of the ACA were abortifacients. As a result, the Greens and Hobby Lobby sued the Department of Health and Human Services ("HHS") and other federal agencies and officials to challenge the contraceptive mandate under the First Amendment's Free Exercise Clause and the Religious Freedom Restoration Act of 1993 ("RFRA").[1] The lawsuit sought injunctive relief in the United

---

[1] Congress enacted RFRA in 1993 in order to provide very broad protections for religious liberty. To do so, RFRA provides that "Government shall not substantially burden a person's exercise of religion even if the burden results from a rule of general applicability." 42 U.S.C. § 2000bb-1(a). In this context, a "rule of general applicability" is a rule that is designed to affect all people in

States District Court for the Western District of Oklahoma, which was denied. That decision was appealed to the United States Court of Appeals for the Tenth Circuit, which held, among other things, that the Greens' businesses were "persons" within the meaning of RFRA and could therefore bring suit under the law.

Justice Alito's Majority Opinion

The Court's majority, in an opinion by Justice Alito, addressed three major issues in concluding that Hobby Lobby was not required to provide contraceptive coverage to its employees.

First, the Court held that closely-held corporations, such as Hobby Lobby, are "persons" under RFRA and as such are entitled to RFRA's protections governing the "exercise of religion."[2] The Court observed that in other contexts, the concept of corporate "personhood" is a well-established "legal fiction," and that "the purpose of this fiction is to provide protection for human beings. A corporation is simply a form of organization used by human beings to achieve desired ends."[3] The Court also noted that HHS already treated nonprofit corporations as "persons" within the meaning of RFRA, and that "no conceivable definition of the term includes [both] natural persons and nonprofit corporations, but not for-profit corporations."[4] Accordingly, the Court observed that furthering the religious freedom of for-profit corporations by deeming them "persons" under RFRA was justifiable because it also "furthers individual religious freedom."[5]

Second, the majority held that the ACA's contraceptive mandate did in fact substantially burden Hobby Lobby's "exercise of religion" under RFRA. The Court found that by requiring the Greens to facilitate the provision of contraceptive coverage which could result in the destruction of embryos, the ACA forced them to engage in conduct which violated their sincerely-held religious beliefs.[6] Though Hobby

---

the same way regardless of their religious beliefs. If the Government substantially burdens a person's exercise of religion, then under RFRA that person is entitled to an exemption from the rule unless the Government demonstrates that application of the burden to the person "(1) is in furtherance of a compelling governmental interest; and (2) is the least restrictive means of furthering that compelling governmental interest." 42 U.S.C. § 2000bb-1(b).

[2] Because it held that RFRA was applicable, the majority did not address Hobby Lobby's claims under the Free Exercise Clause of the First Amendment.

[3] Burwell v. Hobby Lobby Stores, Inc., 573 U.S. 682, 706 (2014).

[4] *Id.* at 708.

[5] *Id.*

[6] *Id.* at 720.

Lobby could choose not to provide contraceptive coverage and instead pay a penalty, the Court was especially concerned about the financial burden that Hobby Lobby would face under the ACA for such refusal: payment of a penalty totaling about $475 million per year.[7]

Third, the Court found that the contraceptive mandate was not the least restrictive means of furthering the compelling government interest of access to contraceptive coverage.[8] Specifically, the majority determined that less restrictive options were available to Congress or HHS to ensure "that every woman has cost-free access to the particular contraceptives at issue here and, indeed, to all FDA-approved contraceptives," pointing to the fact that HHS had already established an accommodation for nonprofit organizations with religious objections, and could easily do the same for for-profit corporations.[9] The Court therefore held that the ACA's contraceptive mandate violated RFRA because it substantially burdened the exercise of religion of "persons," including for-profit corporations, protected by RFRA and was not the least restrictive means of serving the compelling government interest of guaranteeing cost-free access to contraceptives.[10]

Justice Ginsburg's Dissent

Justice Ginsburg was most concerned with the "startling" implications of the majority's ruling regarding corporate personhood, which she opined were "that commercial enterprises, including corporations, along with partnerships and sole proprietorships, c[ould] opt out of any law (saving only tax laws) they judge incompatible with their sincerely held religious beliefs."[11] Ginsburg believed the Court had misconstrued the purpose of RFRA, citing that law's legislative history to argue the scope of RFRA was limited to returning the Court's Free-Exercise-Clause analysis to where it was prior to several recent Court decisions.[12] Under that older analysis, Ginsburg argued—and, therefore, under RFRA as properly construed—the Court could never have found that "free exercise rights pertain to for-profit corporations" because "the exercise of religion is characteristic of natural persons, not

---

[7] See id.

[8] The Court assumed, without deciding, that "the interest in guaranteeing cost-free access to the four challenged contraceptive methods is compelling within the meaning of RFRA." Id. at 728.

[9] Id. at 692.

[10] Id. at 728.

[11] Id. at 739–40 (Ginsburg, J., dissenting).

[12] See id. at 746–50.

artificial legal entities."[13] Ginsburg was equally unimpressed with the majority's reliance on the existence of free-exercise exemptions for churches and other nonprofit religious organizations, citing a history of such cabined exemptions dating back centuries which had long been justifiable because religious entities exist specifically to perpetuate religious values and not, as for-profit corporations do, simply to make a profit.[14]

Regardless, Justice Ginsburg also took issue with the notion that the ACA substantially burdened Hobby Lobby's free exercise of religion. In her estimation, the majority viewed the simple fact that a religious belief might be implicated by a law as evidence that the law placed a burden on free exercise of that belief—a view which "elides entirely the distinction between the sincerity of a challenger's religious belief and the substantiality of the burden placed on the challenger."[15] Ginsburg also believed that the Government had shown that the contraceptive coverage mandated by the ACA furthers compelling interests in public health and women's well-being. As in so many other dissents, Ginsburg here addressed the numerous disadvantages posed to women by the implications of the majority opinion, citing numerous statistical and social-science analyses in support of her argument.[16] She also disputed the majority's assertion of less restrictive means by which the government could have effectuated the same result, observing that such means would again, and inevitably, shift the burden from the government onto individual women: "Impeding women's receipt of benefits 'by requiring them to take steps to learn about, and to sign up for, a new [government funded and administered] health benefit' was scarcely what Congress contemplated" in passing the ACA.[17] Ultimately, Ginsburg concluded, the Court could have avoided all these issues by narrowly confining the availability of religious exemptions under RFRA to religious organizations, where she believed they belong.[18]

---

[13] *Id.* at 751–52.

[14] *See id.* at 755–56,

[15] *Id.* at 760.

[16] *See id.* at 761–64.

[17] *Id.* at 765–66 (quoting Coverage of Certain Preventive Services Under the Affordable Care Act, 78 Fed. Reg. 39,870, 39,888 (July 2, 2013) (to be codified at 26 C.F.R. pt. 54)).

[18] *Id.* at 771–72.

BURWELL V. HOBBY LOBBY STORES, INC.

JUSTICE GINSBURG, with whom JUSTICE SOTOMAYOR joins, and with whom JUSTICE BREYER and JUSTICE KAGAN join as to all but Part III–C–1, DISSENTING.

In a decision of startling breadth, the Court holds that commercial enterprises, including corporations, along with partnerships and sole proprietorships, can opt out of any law (saving only tax laws) they judge incompatible with their sincerely held religious beliefs.[1] Compelling governmental interests in uniform compliance with the law, and disadvantages that religion-based opt-outs impose on others, hold no sway, the Court decides, at least when there is a "less restrictive alternative." And such an alternative, the Court suggests, there always will be whenever, in lieu of tolling an enterprise claiming a religion-based exemption, the government, i.e., the general public, can pick up the tab.[2; 3 [FN 1]]

The Court does not pretend that the First Amendment's Free Exercise Clause demands religion-based accommodations so extreme, for our decisions leave no doubt on that score.[4] Instead, the Court holds that Congress, in the Religious Freedom Restoration Act of 1993 (RFRA),[5] dictated the extraordinary religion-based exemptions today's decision endorses. In the Court's view, RFRA demands accommodation of a for-profit corporation's religious beliefs no matter the impact that accommodation may have on third parties who do not

---

[1] *See id.* at 705–36 (majority opinion).

[2] *See id.* at 728–30.

[3] [FN 1] The Court insists it has held none of these things, for another less restrictive alternative is at hand: extending an existing accommodation, currently limited to religious nonprofit organizations, to encompass commercial enterprises. *See id.* at 692–93. With that accommodation extended, the Court asserts, "women would still be entitled to all [Food and Drug Administration]-approved contraceptives without cost sharing." *Id.* at 693. In the end, however, the Court is not so sure. In stark contrast to the Court's initial emphasis on this accommodation, it ultimately declines to decide whether the highlighted accommodation is even lawful. *See id.* at 731 ("We do not decide today whether an approach of this type complies with RFRA . . . .").

[4] *See id.* at 744–46 (Ginsburg, J., dissenting).

[5] 42 U.S.C. §§ 2000bb to 2000bb-4.

share the corporation owners' religious faith—in these cases, thousands of women employed by Hobby Lobby and Conestoga or dependents of persons those corporations employ. Persuaded that Congress enacted RFRA to serve a far less radical purpose, and mindful of the havoc the Court's judgment can introduce, I dissent.

I

"The ability of women to participate equally in the economic and social life of the Nation has been facilitated by their ability to control their reproductive lives."[6] Congress acted on that understanding when, as part of a nationwide insurance program intended to be comprehensive, it called for coverage of preventive care responsive to women's needs. Carrying out Congress' direction, the Department of Health and Human Services (HHS), in consultation with public health experts, promulgated regulations requiring group health plans to cover all forms of contraception approved by the Food and Drug Administration (FDA). The genesis of this coverage should enlighten the Court's resolution of these cases.

A

The Affordable Care Act (ACA), in its initial form, specified three categories of preventive care that health plans must cover at no added cost to the plan participant or beneficiary.[7] [FN 2] Particular services were to be recommended by the U. S. Preventive Services Task Force, an independent panel of experts. The scheme had a large gap, however; it left out preventive services that "many women's health advocates and medical professionals believe are critically important."[8] To correct this oversight, Senator Barbara Mikulski introduced the Women's Health Amendment, which added to the ACA's minimum coverage requirements a new category of preventive services specific to women's health.

---

[6] Planned Parenthood of Se. Pa. v. Casey, 505 U.S. 833, 856 (1992).

[7] [FN 2] See 42 U.S.C. § 300gg-13(a)(1) to (3) (group health plans must provide coverage, without cost sharing, for (1) certain "evidence-based items or services" recommended by the U. S. Preventive Services Task Force; (2) immunizations recommended by an advisory committee of the Centers for Disease Control and Prevention; and (3) "with respect to infants, children, and adolescents, evidence-informed preventive care and screenings provided for in the comprehensive guidelines supported by the Health Resources and Services Administration").

[8] 155 CONG. REC. 28,841 (2009) (statement of Sen. Boxer).

Women paid significantly more than men for preventive care, the amendment's proponents noted; in fact, cost barriers operated to block many women from obtaining needed care at all.[9] And increased access to contraceptive services, the sponsors comprehended, would yield important public health gains.[10]

As altered by the Women's Health Amendment's passage, the ACA requires new insurance plans to include coverage without cost sharing of "such additional preventive care and screenings . . . as provided for in comprehensive guidelines supported by the Health Resources and Services Administration [(HRSA)]," a unit of HHS.[11] Thus charged, the HRSA developed recommendations in consultation with the Institute of Medicine (IOM).[12; 13 [FN 3]] The IOM convened a group of independent experts, including "specialists in disease prevention [and] women's health"; those experts prepared a report evaluating the efficacy of a number of preventive services.[14] Consistent with the findings of "[n]umerous health professional associations" and other organizations, the IOM experts determined that preventive coverage should include the "full range" of FDA-approved contraceptive methods.[15]

In making that recommendation, the IOM's report expressed concerns similar to those voiced by congressional proponents of the Women's Health Amendment. The report noted the disproportionate burden women carried for comprehensive health services and the adverse health consequences of excluding contraception from preventive care available to employees without cost sharing.[16]

---

[9] See, e.g., id. at 29,070 (statement of Sen. Feinstein) ("Women of childbearing age spend 68 percent more in out-of-pocket health care costs than men."); id. at 29,302 (statement of Sen. Mikulski) ("copayments are [often] so high that [women] avoid getting [preventive and screening services] in the first place").

[10] See, e.g., id. at 29,768 (statement of Sen. Durbin) ("This bill will expand health insurance coverage to the vast majority of [the 17 million women of reproductive age in the United States who are uninsured] . . . . This expanded access will reduce unintended pregnancies.").

[11] 42 U.S.C. § 300gg-13(a)(4).

[12] See Group Health Plans and Health Insurance Issuers Relating to Coverage of Preventive Services Under the Patient Protection and Affordable Care Act, 77 Fed. Reg. 8,725, 8,725–26 (Feb. 15, 2012) (to be codified at 26 C.F.R. pt. 54).

[13] [FN 3] The IOM is an arm of the National Academy of Sciences, an organization Congress established "for the explicit purpose of furnishing advice to the Government." Pub. Citizen v. U.S. Dep't of Justice, 491 U.S. 440, 460 n.11 (1989) (internal quotation marks omitted).

[14] INST. OF MED., CLINICAL PREVENTION SERVICES FOR WOMEN: CLOSING THE GAPS 2 (2011).

[15] Id. at 10; see also id. at 102–10.

[16] See, e.g., id. at 19 ("[W]omen are consistently more likely than men to report

In line with the IOM's suggestions, the HRSA adopted guidelines recommending coverage of "[a]ll [FDA-]approved contraceptive methods, sterilization procedures, and patient education and counseling for all women with reproductive capacity."[17] [FN 4] Thereafter, HHS, the Department of Labor, and the Department of Treasury promulgated regulations requiring group health plans to include coverage of the contraceptive services recommended in the HRSA guidelines, subject to certain exceptions, described infra.[18; 19] [FN 5] This opinion refers to these regulations as the contraceptive coverage requirement.

B

While the Women's Health Amendment succeeded, a countermove proved unavailing. The Senate voted down the so-called "conscience amendment," which would have enabled any employer or insurance provider to deny coverage based on its asserted "religious beliefs or moral convictions."[20; 21] [FN 6] That amendment, Senator Mikulski observed, would have "pu[t] the personal opinion of employers and insurers over the practice of medicine."[22] Rejecting the "conscience amendment," Congress left health care decisions—including the

---

a wide range of cost-related barriers to receiving . . . medical tests and treatments and to filling prescriptions for themselves and their families."); *id.* at 103–04, 107 (pregnancy may be contraindicated for women with certain medical conditions, for example, some congenital heart diseases, pulmonary hypertension, and Marfan syndrome, and contraceptives may be used to reduce risk of endometrial cancer, among other serious medical conditions); *id.* at 103 (women with unintended pregnancies are more likely to experience depression and anxiety, and their children face "increased odds of preterm birth and low birth weight").

[17] [FN 4] *Women's Preventive Services Guidelines*, Health Res. & Servs. Admin., http://www.hrsa.gov/womensguidelines/ (last visited June 27, 2014), reprinted in Brief for Petitioners, App. at 43–44a, Burwell v. Hobby Lobby Stores, Inc., 573 U.S. 682 (2014) (No. 13-354); *see also* Group Health Plans, 77 Fed. Reg. at 8,725–26.

[18] *Burwell*, 573 U.S. at 763–64 (Ginsburg, J., dissenting).

[19] [FN 5] 45 C.F.R. § 147.130(a)(1)(iv) (2013) (HHS); 29 C.F.R. § 2590.715-2713(a)(1)(iv) (2013) (Labor); 26 C.F.R. § 54.9815-2713(a)(1)(iv) (2013) (Treasury).

[20] 158 Cong. Rec. S539 (daily ed. Feb. 9, 2012); *see* 158 Cong. Rec. S1,162–S1,173 (daily ed. Mar. 1, 2012) (debate and vote).

[21] [FN 6] Separating moral convictions from religious beliefs would be of questionable legitimacy. *See* Welsh v. United States, 398 U.S. 333, 357–58 (1970) (Harlan, J., concurring in result).

[22] 158 Cong. Rec. S1,127 (daily ed. Feb. 29, 2012).

choice among contraceptive methods—in the hands of women, with the aid of their health care providers.

II

Any First Amendment Free Exercise Clause claim Hobby Lobby or Conestoga[23] [FN 7] might assert is foreclosed by this Court's decision in *Employment Div., Dept. of Human Resources of Ore. v. Smith*.[24] In *Smith*, two members of the Native American Church were dismissed from their jobs and denied unemployment benefits because they ingested peyote at, and as an essential element of, a religious ceremony. Oregon law forbade the consumption of peyote, and this Court, relying on that prohibition, rejected the employees' claim that the denial of unemployment benefits violated their free exercise rights. The First Amendment is not offended, *Smith* held, when "prohibiting the exercise of religion . . . is not the object of [governmental regulation] but merely the incidental effect of a generally applicable and otherwise valid provision."[25] The ACA's contraceptive coverage requirement applies generally, it is "otherwise valid," it trains on women's wellbeing, not on the exercise of religion, and any effect it has on such exercise is incidental.

Even if *Smith* did not control, the Free Exercise Clause would not require the exemption Hobby Lobby and Conestoga seek. Accommodations to religious beliefs or observances, the Court has clarified, must not significantly impinge on the interests of third parties.[26] [FN 8]

---

23 [FN 7] As the Court explains, *see Burwell*, 573 U.S. at 700–05, these cases arise from two separate lawsuits, one filed by Hobby Lobby, its affiliated business (Mardel), and the family that operates these businesses (the Greens); the other filed by Conestoga and the family that owns and controls that business (the Hahns). Unless otherwise specified, this opinion refers to the respective groups of plaintiffs as Hobby Lobby and Conestoga.

24 494 U.S. 872 (1990).

25 *Id.* at 878; *see id.* at 878–79 ("an individual's religious beliefs [do not] excuse him from compliance with an otherwise valid law prohibiting conduct that the State is free to regulate").

26 [FN 8] See Wisconsin v. Yoder, 406 U.S. 205, 230 (1972) ("This case, of course, is not one in which any harm to the physical or mental health of the child or to the public safety, peace, order, or welfare has been demonstrated or may be properly inferred."); Estate of Thornton v. Caldor, Inc., 472 U.S. 703 (1985) (invalidating state statute requiring employers to accommodate an employee's Sabbath observance where that statute failed to take into account the burden such an accommodation would impose on the employer or other employees). Notably, in construing the Religious Land Use and Institutionalized Persons Act of 2000 (RLUIPA), 42 U.S.C. §§ 2000cc to 2000cc-5, the Court has cautioned that "adequate account" must be taken of "the burdens a requested

The exemption sought by Hobby Lobby and Conestoga would override significant interests of the corporations' employees and covered dependents. It would deny legions of women who do not hold their employers' beliefs access to contraceptive coverage that the ACA would otherwise secure.[27] In sum, with respect to free exercise claims no less than free speech claims, "'[y]our right to swing your arms ends just where the other man's nose begins.'"[28]

III

A

Lacking a tenable claim under the Free Exercise Clause, Hobby Lobby and Conestoga rely on RFRA, a statute instructing that "[g]overnment shall not substantially burden a person's exercise of religion even if the burden results from a rule of general applicability" unless the government shows that application of the burden is "the least restrictive means" to further a "compelling governmental interest."[29] In RFRA, Congress "adopt[ed] a statutory rule comparable to the constitutional rule rejected in Smith."[30]

RFRA's purpose is specific and written into the statute itself. The Act was crafted to "restore the compelling interest test as set forth in *Sherbert v. Verner*[31] and *Wisconsin v. Yoder*,[32] and to guarantee its application in all cases where free exercise of religion is substantially burdened."[33; 34 [FN 9]]

---

accommodation may impose on nonbeneficiaries." Cutter v. Wilkinson, 544 U.S. 709, 720 (2005); *see id.* at 722 ("an accommodation must be measured so that it does not override other significant interests"). A balanced approach is all the more in order when the Free Exercise Clause itself is at stake, not a statute designed to promote accommodation to religious beliefs and practices.

[27] *See* Catholic Charities of Sacramento, Inc. v. Superior Court, 85 P.3d 67, 93 (Cal. 2004) ("We are unaware of any decision in which . . . [the U. S. Supreme Court] has exempted a religious objector from the operation of a neutral, generally applicable law despite the recognition that the requested exemption would detrimentally affect the rights of third parties.").

[28] Zechariah Chafee, Jr., *Freedom of Speech in War Time*, 32 Harv. L. Rev. 932, 957 (1919).

[29] 42 U.S.C. § 2000bb-1(a), (b)(2).

[30] Gonzales v. O Centro Espírita Beneficente União do Vegetal, 546 U.S. 418, 424 (2006).

[31] 374 U.S. 398 (1963).

[32] 406 U.S. 205 (1972).

[33] 42 U.S.C. § 2000bb(b)(1); *see also* 42 U.S.C. § 2000bb(a)(5) ("[T]he compelling interest test as set forth in prior Federal court rulings is a workable test for striking sensible balances between religious liberty and competing prior

The legislative history is correspondingly emphatic on RFRA's aim.[35] In line with this restorative purpose, Congress expected courts considering RFRA claims to "look to free exercise cases decided prior to Smith for guidance."[36] In short, the Act reinstates the law as it was prior to Smith, without "creat[ing] . . . new rights for any religious practice or for any potential litigant."[37] Given the Act's moderate purpose, it is hardly surprising that RFRA's enactment in 1993 provoked little controversy.[38]

B

Despite these authoritative indications, the Court sees RFRA as a bold initiative departing from, rather than restoring, pre-*Smith* jurisprudence.[39] To support its conception of RFRA as a measure detached from this Court's decisions, one that sets a new course, the Court points first to the Religious Land Use and Institutionalized Persons Act of 2000 (RLUIPA),[40] which altered RFRA's definition of the term "exercise of religion." RFRA, as originally enacted, defined that term to mean "the exercise of religion under the First Amendment to the Constitution."[41] As amended by RLUIPA, RFRA's definition now includes "any exercise of religion, whether or not compelled by, or central to, a

---

governmental interests."); Burwell v. Hobby Lobby Stores, Inc., 573 U.S. 682, 735–36 (2014) (agreeing that the pre-*Smith* compelling interest test is "workable" and "strike[s] sensible balances").

[34] [FN 9] Under *Sherbert* and *Yoder*, the Court "requir[ed] the government to justify any substantial burden on religiously motivated conduct by a compelling state interest and by means narrowly tailored to achieve that interest." Emp't Div., Dep't of Human Res. of Or. v. Smith, 494 U.S. 872, 894 (1990) (O'Connor, J., concurring in judgment).

[35] *See, e.g.,* S. REP. NO. 103-111, at 12 (1993) [hereinafter Senate Report] (RFRA's purpose was "only to overturn the Supreme Court's decision in Smith," not to "unsettle other areas of the law."); 139 CONG. REC. 26,178 (1993) (statement of Sen. Kennedy) (RFRA was "designed to restore the compelling interest test for deciding free exercise claims.").

[36] Senate Report, *supra* note 35, at 8; *see also* H.R. REP. NO. 103-88, at 6–7 (1993) [hereinafter House Report] (same).

[37] 139 CONG. REC. 26,178 (1993) (statement of Sen. Kennedy).

[38] *See* Brief for Senator Murray et al. as Amici Curiae at 8, Burwell v. Hobby Lobby Stores, Inc., 573 U.S. 682 (2014) (Nos. 13-354, 13-356) [hereinafter Senators Brief] (RFRA was approved by a 97-to-3 vote in the Senate and a voice vote in the House of Representatives).

[39] *See Burwell*, 573 U.S. at 695 n.3, 696, 706, 713–16.

[40] 42 U.S.C. §§ 2000cc to 2000cc-5.

[41] 42 U.S.C. § 2000bb-2(4) (1994 ed.); *see Burwell*, 573 U.S. at 695–96.

system of religious belief."[42] That definitional change, according to the Court, reflects "an obvious effort to effect a complete separation from First Amendment case law."[43]

The Court's reading is not plausible. RLUIPA's alteration clarifies that courts should not question the centrality of a particular religious exercise. But the amendment in no way suggests that Congress meant to expand the class of entities qualified to mount religious accommodation claims, nor does it relieve courts of the obligation to inquire whether a government action substantially burdens a religious exercise.[44; 45 [FN 10]]

Next, the Court highlights RFRA's requirement that the government, if its action substantially burdens a person's religious observance, must demonstrate that it chose the least restrictive means for furthering a compelling interest. "[B]y imposing a least-restrictive-means test," the Court suggests, RFRA "went beyond what was required by our pre-Smith decisions."[46] But as RFRA's statements of purpose and legislative history make clear, Congress intended only to restore, not to scrap or alter, the balancing test as this Court had applied it pre-Smith.[47]

The Congress that passed RFRA correctly read this Court's pre-Smith case law as including within the "compelling interest test" a

---

[42] 42 U.S.C. § 2000bb-2(4) (2012 ed.) (cross-referencing § 2000cc-5).

[43] *Burwell*, 573 U.S. at 696.

[44] *See* Rasul v. Myers, 563 F.3d 527, 535 (D.C. Cir. 2009) (Brown, J., concurring) ("There is no doubt that RLUIPA's drafters, in changing the definition of 'exercise of religion,' wanted to broaden the scope of the kinds of practices protected by RFRA, not increase the universe of individuals protected by RFRA."); H.R. REP. NO. 106-219, at 30 (1999); *see also* Gilardi v. U.S. Dep't of Health & Human Servs., 733 F.3d 1208, 1211 (D.C. Cir. 2013) (RFRA, as amended, "provides us with no helpful definition of 'exercise of religion.'"); Henderson v. Kennedy, 265 F.3d 1072, 1073 (D.C. Cir. 2001) ("The [RLUIPA] amendments did not alter RFRA's basic prohibition that the '[g]overnment shall not substantially burden a person's exercise of religion.'").

[45 [FN 10]] RLUIPA, the Court notes, includes a provision directing that "[t]his chapter [*i.e.*, RLUIPA] shall be construed in favor of a broad protection of religious exercise, to the maximum extent permitted by the terms of [the Act] and the Constitution." 42 U.S.C. § 2000cc-3(g); *see Burwell*, 573 U.S. at 695–96, 714. RFRA incorporates RLUIPA's definition of "exercise of religion," as RLUIPA does, but contains no omnibus rule of construction governing the statute in its entirety.

[46] *Burwell*, 573 U.S. at 706 n.18 (citing City of Boerne v. Flores, 521 U.S. 507 (1997)); *see also id.* at 695 n.3.

[47] *See id.* at 746–47 (Ginsburg, J., dissenting); *see also* Senate Report, *supra* note 35, at 9 (RFRA's "compelling interest test generally should not be construed more stringently or more leniently than it was prior to Smith."); House Report, *supra* note 35, at 7 (same).

"least restrictive means" requirement.[48] And the view that the pre-Smith test included a "least restrictive means" requirement had been aired in testimony before the Senate Judiciary Committee by experts on religious freedom.[49]

Our decision in City of Boerne, it is true, states that the least restrictive means requirement "was not used in the pre-Smith jurisprudence RFRA purported to codify."[50] As just indicated, however, that statement does not accurately convey the Court's pre-Smith jurisprudence.[51; 52 [FN 11]]

C

With RFRA's restorative purpose in mind, I turn to the Act's application to the instant lawsuits. That task, in view of the positions taken by the Court, requires consideration of several questions, each potentially dispositive of Hobby Lobby's and Conestoga's claims: Do for-profit corporations rank among "person[s]" who "exercise . . . religion"? Assuming that they do, does the contraceptive coverage requirement "substantially burden" their religious exercise? If so, is the requirement "in furtherance of a compelling government interest"?

---

[48] *See, e.g.,* Senate Report, *supra* note 35, at 5 ("Where [a substantial] burden is placed upon the free exercise of religion, the Court ruled [in Sherbert], the Government must demonstrate that it is the least restrictive means to achieve a compelling governmental interest.").

[49] *See, e.g., Hearing on S. 2969 before the Senate Committee on the Judiciary,* 102d Cong., 2d Sess., 78–79 (1993) (statement of Prof. Douglas Laycock).

[50] *See Burwell,* 573 U.S. at 695 n.3, 706 n.18.

[51] *See* Sherbert v. Verner, 374 U.S. 398, 407 (1963) ("[I]t would plainly be incumbent upon the [government] to demonstrate that no alternative forms of regulation would combat [the problem] without infringing First Amendment rights."); Thomas v. Review Bd. of Ind. Emp't Sec. Div., 450 U.S. 707, 718 (1981) ("The state may justify an inroad on religious liberty by showing that it is the least restrictive means of achieving some compelling state interest."); *see also* Thomas C. Berg, *The New Attacks on Religious Freedom Legislation and Why They Are Wrong,* 21 CARDOZO L. REV. 415, 424 (1999) ("In Boerne, the Court erroneously said that the least restrictive means test 'was not used in the pre-Smith jurisprudence.'").

[52 [FN 11]] The Court points out that I joined the majority opinion in and did not then question the statement that "least restrictive means . . . was not used [pre-*Smith*]." *Burwell,* 573 U.S. at 706 n.18. Concerning that observation, I remind my colleagues of Justice Jackson's sage comment: "I see no reason why I should be consciously wrong today because I was unconsciously wrong yesterday." Massachusetts v. United States, 331 U.S. 611, 639–40 (1948) (Jackson, J., dissenting).

And last, does the requirement represent the least restrictive means for furthering that interest?

Misguided by its errant premise that RFRA moved beyond the pre-Smith case law, the Court falters at each step of its analysis.

1

RFRA's compelling interest test, as noted,[53] applies to government actions that "substantially burden a person's exercise of religion."[54] This reference, the Court submits, incorporates the definition of "person" found in the Dictionary Act,[55] which extends to "corporations, companies, associations, firms, partnerships, societies, and joint stock companies, as well as individuals."[56] The Dictionary Act's definition, however, controls only where "context" does not "indicat[e] otherwise."[57] Here, context does so indicate. RFRA speaks of "a person's exercise of religion."[58; 59 [FN 12]] Whether a corporation qualifies as a "person" capable of exercising religion is an inquiry one cannot answer without reference to the "full body" of pre-Smith "free-exercise caselaw."[60] There is in that case law no support for the notion that free exercise rights pertain to for-profit corporations.

Until this litigation, no decision of this Court recognized a for-profit corporation's qualification for a religious exemption from a generally applicable law, whether under the Free Exercise Clause or RFRA.[61 [FN 13]] The absence of such precedent is just what one would

---

[53] *See Burwell*, 573 U.S. at 746 (Ginsburg, J., dissenting).
[54] 42 U.S.C. § 2000bb-1(a) (emphasis added).
[55] 1 U.S.C. § 1.
[56] *See Burwell*, 573 U.S. at 707–08.
[57] 1 U.S.C. § 1.
[58] 42 U.S.C. § 2000bb-1(a) (emphasis added); *see also* 42 U.S.C. §§ 2000bb-2(4), 2000cc-5(7)(a).
[59] [FN 12] As earlier explained, see *Burwell*, 573 U.S. at 747–48 (Ginsburg, J., dissenting), RLUIPA's amendment of the definition of "exercise of religion" does not bear the weight the Court places on it. Moreover, it is passing strange to attribute to RLUIPA any purpose to cover entities other than "religious assembl[ies] or institution[s]." 42 U.S.C. § 2000cc(a)(1). *But cf. Burwell*, 573 U.S. at 714. That law applies to land-use regulation. 42 U.S.C. § 2000cc(a)(1). To permit commercial enterprises to challenge zoning and other land-use regulations under RLUIPA would "dramatically expand the statute's reach" and deeply intrude on local prerogatives, contrary to Congress' intent. Brief for National League of Cities et al. as Amici Curiae at 26, *Burwell*, 573 U.S. 682 (Nos. 13-354, 13-356).
[60] Gilardi v. U.S. Dep't of Health & Human Servs., 733 F.3d 1208, 1212 (D.C. Cir. 2013).
[61] [FN 13] The Court regards *Gallagher v. Crown Kosher Super Market of Mass.*,

expect, for the exercise of religion is characteristic of natural persons, not artificial legal entities. As Chief Justice Marshall observed nearly two centuries ago, a corporation is "an artificial being, invisible, intangible, and existing only in contemplation of law."[62] Corporations, Justice Stevens more recently reminded, "have no consciences, no beliefs, no feelings, no thoughts, no desires."[63]

The First Amendment's free exercise protections, the Court has indeed recognized, shelter churches and other nonprofit religion-based organizations.[64] [FN 14] "For many individuals, religious activity derives meaning in large measure from participation in a larger religious community," and "furtherance of the autonomy of religious organizations often furthers individual religious freedom as well."[65] The Court's "special solicitude to the rights of religious organizations,"[66] however, is just that. No such solicitude is traditional for commercial organizations.[67] [FN 15] Indeed, until today, religious exemptions had

---

Inc., 366 U.S. 617 (1961), as "suggest[ing] . . . that for-profit corporations possess [free-exercise] rights." *Burwell*, 573 U.S. at 714–15; *see also id.* at 709 n.21. The suggestion is barely there. True, one of the five challengers to the Sunday closing law assailed in was a corporation owned by four Orthodox Jews. The other challengers were human individuals, not artificial, law-created entities, so there was no need to determine whether the corporation could institute the litigation. Accordingly, the plurality stated it could pretermit the question "whether appellees ha[d] standing" because *Braunfeld v. Brown*, 366 U.S. 599 (1961), which upheld a similar closing law, was fatal to their claim on the merits. 366 U.S. at 631.

[62] Trs. of Dartmouth Coll. v. Woodward, 17 U.S. (4 Wheat.) 518, 636 (1819).

[63] Citizens United v. Fed. Election Comm'n, 558 U.S. 310, 466 (2010) (Stevens, J., concurring in part and dissenting in part).

[64] [FN 14] *See, e.g.*, Hosanna-Tabor Evangelical Lutheran Church & Sch. v. Equal Emp't Opportunity Comm'n, 565 U.S. 171 (2012); Gonzales v. O Centro Espírita Beneficente União do Vegetal, 546 U.S. 418 (2006); Church of the Lukumi Babalu Aye, Inc. v. City of Hialeah, 508 U.S. 520 (1993); Jimmy Swaggart Ministries v. Bd. of Equalization of Cal., 493 U.S. 378 (1990).

[65] Corp. of the Presiding Bishop of the Church of Jesus Christ of Latter-Day Saints v. Amos, 483 U.S. 327, 342 (1987) (Brennan, J., concurring in judgment).

[66] *Hosanna-Tabor*, 565 U.S. at 189.

[67] [FN 15] Typically, Congress has accorded to organizations religious in character religion-based exemptions from statutes of general application. *E.g.*, 42 U.S.C. § 2000e-1(a) (Title VII exemption from prohibition against employment discrimination based on religion for "a religious corporation, association, educational institution, or society with respect to the employment of individuals of a particular religion to perform work connected with the carrying on . . . of its activities"); 42 U.S.C. § 12113(d)(1) (parallel exemption in Americans With Disabilities Act of 1990). It can scarcely be maintained that RFRA enlarges these exemptions to allow Hobby Lobby and Conestoga to hire

never been extended to any entity operating in "the commercial, profit-making world."[68; 69 [FN 16]]

The reason why is hardly obscure. Religious organizations exist to foster the interests of persons subscribing to the same religious faith. Not so of for-profit corporations. Workers who sustain the operations of those corporations commonly are not drawn from one religious community. Indeed, by law, no religion-based criterion can restrict the work force of for-profit corporations.[70] The distinction between a community made up of believers in the same religion and one embracing persons of diverse beliefs, clear as it is, constantly escapes the Court's attention.[71 [FN 17]] One can only wonder why the Court shuts this key difference from sight.

Reading RFRA, as the Court does, to require extension of religion-based exemptions to for-profit corporations surely is not grounded in the pre-Smith precedent Congress sought to preserve. Had Congress intended RFRA to initiate a change so huge, a clarion statement to that effect likely would have been made in the legislation.[72] The text of RFRA makes no such statement and the legislative history does not so much as mention for-profit corporations.[73]

---

only persons who share the religious beliefs of the Greens or Hahns. Nor does the Court suggest otherwise. *Cf.* Burwell v. Hobby Lobby Stores, Inc., 573 U.S. 682, 716–17 (2014).

[68] *Amos*, 483 U.S. at 337.

[69 [FN 16]] That is not to say that a category of plaintiffs, such as resident aliens, may bring RFRA claims only if this Court expressly "addressed their [free-exercise] rights before *Smith*." *Burwell*, 573 U.S. at 715–16. Continuing with the Court's example, resident aliens, unlike corporations, are flesh-and-blood individuals who plainly count as persons sheltered by the First Amendment, *see* United States v. Verdugo-Urquidez, 494 U.S. 259, 271 (1990) (citing Bridges v. Wixon, 326 U.S. 135, 148 (1945)), and *a fortiori*, RFRA.

[70] See 42 U.S.C. §§ 2000e(b), 2000e-1(a), 2000e-2(a); *cf.* Trans World Airlines, Inc. v. Hardison, 432 U.S. 63, 80–81 (1977) (Title VII requires reasonable accommodation of an employee's religious exercise, but such accommodation must not come "at the expense of other[employees]").

[71 [FN 17]] I part ways with Justice KENNEDY on the context relevant here. He sees it as the employers' "exercise [of] their religious beliefs within the context of their own closely held, for-profit corporations." *Burwell*, 573 U.S. at 737 (Kennedy, J., concurring); *see also id.* at 773 (majority opinion) (similarly concentrating on religious faith of employers without reference to the different beliefs and liberty interests of employees). I see as the relevant context the employers' asserted right to exercise religion within a nationwide program designed to protect against health hazards employees who do not subscribe to their employers' religious beliefs.

[72] *See* Whitman v. Am. Trucking Ass'ns, Inc., 531 U.S. 457, 468 (2001) (Congress does not "hide elephants in mouseholes").

[73] *See* Hobby Lobby Stores, Inc. v. Sebelius, 723 F.3d 1114, 1169 (10th Cir.

The Court notes that for-profit corporations may support charitable causes and use their funds for religious ends, and therefore questions the distinction between such corporations and religious nonprofit organizations.[74; 75 [FN 18]] Again, the Court forgets that religious organizations exist to serve a community of believers. For-profit corporations do not fit that bill. Moreover, history is not on the Court's side. Recognition of the discrete characters of "ecclesiastical and lay" corporations dates back to Blackstone,[76] and was reiterated by this Court centuries before the enactment of the Internal Revenue Code.[77] To reiterate, "for-profit corporations are different from religious non-profits in that they use labor to make a profit, rather than to perpetuate [the] religious value[s] [shared by a community of believers]."[78]

Citing Braunfeld v. Brown,[79] the Court questions why, if "a sole proprietorship that seeks to make a profit may assert a free-exercise

---

2013) (Briscoe, C.J., concurring in part and dissenting in part) (legislative record lacks "any suggestion that Congress foresaw, let alone intended that, RFRA would cover for-profit corporations"); *see also* Senators Brief, *supra* note 38, at 10–13 (none of the cases cited in House or Senate Judiciary Committee reports accompanying RFRA, or mentioned during floor speeches, recognized the free exercise rights of for-profit corporations).

[74] *See Burwell*, 573 U.S. at 709–713; *see also id.* at 738 (Kennedy, J., concurring) (criticizing the Government for "distinguishing between different religious believers—burdening one while accommodating the other—when it may treat both equally by offering both of them the same accommodation").

[75] [FN 18] According to the Court, the Government "concedes" that "nonprofit corporation[s]" are protected by RFRA. *Id.* at 708 (majority opinion); *see also id.* at 709, 712, 718. That is not an accurate description of the Government's position, which encompasses only "churches," " institutions," and " nonprofits." Brief for Respondents at 28, *Burwell*, 573 U.S. 682 (No. 13-356) (emphasis added); *see also* Reply Brief at 8, *Burwell*, 573 U.S. 682 (No. 13-354) ("RFRA incorporates the longstanding and common-sense distinction between religious organizations, which sometimes have been accorded accommodations under generally applicable laws in recognition of their accepted religious character, and for-profit corporations organized to do business in the commercial world.").

[76] *See* 1 WILLIAM BLACKSTONE, COMMENTARIES 458 (1765).

[77] *See* Terrett v. Taylor, 13 U.S. (9 Cranch) 43, 49 (1815) (describing religious corporations); Trs. of Dartmouth College v. Woodward, 17 U.S. (4 Wheat.) 518, 645 (1819) (discussing "eleemosynary" corporations, including those "created for the promotion of religion").

[78] Gilardi v. U.S. Dep't of Health & Human Servs., 733 F.3d 1208, 1242 (D.C. Cir. 2013) (Edwards, J., concurring in part and dissenting in part) (emphasis deleted).

[79] 366 U.S. 599 (1961).

claim, [Hobby Lobby and Conestoga] can't . . . do the same?"[80] But even accepting, arguendo, the premise that unincorporated business enterprises may gain religious accommodations under the Free Exercise Clause, the Court's conclusion is unsound. In a sole proprietorship, the business and its owner are one and the same. By incorporating a business, however, an individual separates herself from the entity and escapes personal responsibility for the entity's obligations. One might ask why the separation should hold only when it serves the interest of those who control the corporation. In any event, Braunfeld is hardly impressive authority for the entitlement Hobby Lobby and Conestoga seek. The free exercise claim asserted there was promptly rejected on the merits.

The Court's determination that RFRA extends to for-profit corporations is bound to have untoward effects. Although the Court attempts to cabin its language to closely held corporations, its logic extends to corporations of any size, public or private.[81] [FN 19] Little doubt that RFRA claims will proliferate, for the Court's expansive notion of corporate personhood—combined with its other errors in construing RFRA—invites for-profit entities to seek religion-based exemptions from regulations they deem offensive to their faith.

2

Even if Hobby Lobby and Conestoga were deemed RFRA "person[s]," to gain an exemption, they must demonstrate that the contraceptive coverage requirement "substantially burden[s] [their] exercise of religion."[82] Congress no doubt meant the modifier "substantially" to carry weight. In the original draft of RFRA, the word "burden" appeared unmodified. The word "substantially" was inserted pursuant

---

[80] *Burwell*, 573 U.S. at 710 (footnote omitted); *see also id.* at 705–06.

[81] [FN 19] The Court does not even begin to explain how one might go about ascertaining the religious scruples of a corporation where shares are sold to the public. No need to speculate on that, the Court says, for "it seems unlikely" that large corporations "will often assert RFRA claims." *Id.* at 717. Perhaps so, but as Hobby Lobby's case demonstrates, such claims are indeed pursued by large corporations, employing thousands of persons of different faiths, whose ownership is not diffuse. "Closely held" is not synonymous with "small." Hobby Lobby is hardly the only enterprise of sizable scale that is family owned or closely held. For example, the family-owned candy giant Mars, Inc., takes in $33 billion in revenues and has some 72,000 employees, and closely held Cargill, Inc., takes in more than $136 billion in revenues and employs some 140,000 persons. *See America's Largest Private Companies 2013*, FORBES, http://www.forbes.com/largest-private-companies/.

[82] 42 U.S.C. § 2000bb-1(a).

to a clarifying amendment offered by Senators Kennedy and Hatch.[83] In proposing the amendment, Senator Kennedy stated that RFRA, in accord with the Court's pre-*Smith* case law, "does not require the Government to justify every action that has some effect on religious exercise."[84]

The Court barely pauses to inquire whether any burden imposed by the contraceptive coverage requirement is substantial. Instead, it rests on the Greens' and Hahns' "belie[f] that providing the coverage demanded by the HHS regulations is connected to the destruction of an embryo in a way that is sufficient to make it immoral for them to provide the coverage."[85; 86 [FN 20]] I agree with the Court that the Green and Hahn families' religious convictions regarding contraception are sincerely held.[87; 88 [FN 21]] But those beliefs, however deeply held, do not suffice to sustain a RFRA claim. RFRA, properly understood, distinguishes between "factual allegations that [plaintiffs'] beliefs are sincere and of a religious nature," which a court must accept as true, and the "legal conclusion . . . that [plaintiffs'] religious exercise is substantially burdened," an inquiry the court must undertake.[89]

That distinction is a facet of the pre-*Smith* jurisprudence RFRA incorporates. *Bowen v. Roy*,[90] is instructive. There, the Court rejected

---

[83] *See* 139 CONG. REC. 26,180 (1993).

[84] *Id.*

[85] *Burwell*, 573 U.S. at 724.

[86] [FN 20] The Court dismisses the argument, advanced by some, that the $2,000-per-employee tax charged to certain employers that fail to provide health insurance is less than the average cost of offering health insurance, noting that the Government has not provided the statistics that could support such an argument. *See id.* at 720–22. The Court overlooks, however, that it is not the Government's obligation to prove that an asserted burden is substantial. Instead, it is incumbent upon plaintiffs to demonstrate, in support of a RFRA claim, the substantiality of the alleged burden.

[87] *See* Thomas v. Review Bd. of Ind. Emp't Sec. Div., 450 U.S. 707, 715 (1981) (courts are not to question where an individual "dr[aws] the line" in defining which practices run afoul of her religious beliefs); *see also* 42 U.S.C. §§ 2000bb-1(a), 2000bb-2(4), 2000cc-5(7)(A).

[88] [FN 21] The Court levels a criticism that is as wrongheaded as can be. In no way does the dissent "tell the plaintiffs that their beliefs are flawed." *Burwell*, 573 U.S. at 724. Right or wrong in this domain is a judgment no Member of this Court, or any civil court, is authorized or equipped to make. What the Court must decide is not "the plausibility of a religious claim," *id.* (internal quotation marks omitted), but whether accommodating that claim risks depriving others of rights accorded them by the laws of the United States. *See id.* at 745–46, 764 (Ginsburg, J., dissenting).

[89] Kaemmerling v. Lappin, 553 F.3d 669, 679 (D.C. Cir. 2008).

[90] 476 U.S. 693 (1986).

a free exercise challenge to the Government's use of a Native American child's Social Security number for purposes of administering benefit programs. Without questioning the sincerity of the father's religious belief that "use of [his daughter's Social Security] number may harm [her] spirit," the Court concluded that the Government's internal uses of that number "place[d] [no] restriction on what [the father] may believe or what he may do."[91] Recognizing that the father's "religious views may not accept" the position that the challenged uses concerned only the Government's internal affairs, the Court explained that "for the adjudication of a constitutional claim, the Constitution, rather than an individual's religion, must supply the frame of reference."[92] Inattentive to this guidance, today's decision elides entirely the distinction between the sincerity of a challenger's religious belief and the substantiality of the burden placed on the challenger.

Undertaking the inquiry that the Court forgoes, I would conclude that the connection between the families' religious objections and the contraceptive coverage requirement is too attenuated to rank as substantial. The requirement carries no command that Hobby Lobby or Conestoga purchase or provide the contraceptives they find objectionable. Instead, it calls on the companies covered by the requirement to direct money into undifferentiated funds that finance a wide variety of benefits under comprehensive health plans. Those plans, in order to comply with the ACA,[93] must offer contraceptive coverage without cost sharing, just as they must cover an array of other preventive services.

Importantly, the decisions whether to claim benefits under the plans are made not by Hobby Lobby or Conestoga, but by the covered employees and dependents, in consultation with their health care providers. Should an employee of Hobby Lobby or Conestoga share the religious beliefs of the Greens and Hahns, she is of course under no compulsion to use the contraceptives in question. But "[n]o individual decision by an employee and her physician—be it to use contraception, treat an infection, or have a hip replaced—is in any meaningful sense [her employer's] decision or action."[94] It is doubtful

---

[91] *Id.* at 699.

[92] *Id.* at 700 n.6; *see also* Hernandez v. Comm'r of Internal Revenue, 490 U.S. 680, 699 (1989) (distinguishing between, on the one hand, "question[s] [of] the centrality of particular beliefs or practices to a faith, or the validity of particular litigants' interpretations of those creeds," and, on the other, "whether the alleged burden imposed [by the challenged government action] is a substantial one").

[93] *See Burwell*, 573 U.S. at 741–44.

[94] Grote v. Sebelius, 708 F.3d 850, 865 (7th Cir. 2013) (Rovner, J., dissenting).

that Congress, when it specified that burdens must be "substantia[l]," had in mind a linkage thus interrupted by independent decisionmakers (the woman and her health counselor) standing between the challenged government action and the religious exercise claimed to be infringed. Any decision to use contraceptives made by a woman covered under Hobby Lobby's or Conestoga's plan will not be propelled by the Government, it will be the woman's autonomous choice, informed by the physician she consults.

3

Even if one were to conclude that Hobby Lobby and Conestoga meet the substantial burden requirement, the Government has shown that the contraceptive coverage for which the ACA provides furthers compelling interests in public health and women's wellbeing. Those interests are concrete, specific, and demonstrated by a wealth of empirical evidence. To recapitulate, the mandated contraception coverage enables women to avoid the health problems unintended pregnancies may visit on them and their children.[95] The coverage helps safeguard the health of women for whom pregnancy may be hazardous, even life threatening.[96] And the mandate secures benefits wholly unrelated to pregnancy, preventing certain cancers, menstrual disorders, and pelvic pain.[97]

That Hobby Lobby and Conestoga resist coverage for only 4 of the 20 FDA-approved contraceptives does not lessen these compelling interests. Notably, the corporations exclude intrauterine devices (IUDs), devices significantly more effective, and significantly more expensive than other contraceptive methods.[98; 99 [FN 22]] Moreover, the Court's

---

[95] *See* INST. OF MED., *supra* note 14, at 102–07.

[96] *See* Brief for American College of Obstetricians and Gynecologists et al. as Amici Curiae at 14–15, *Burwell*, 573 U.S. 682 (Nos. 13-354, 13-356).

[97] Brief for Ovarian Cancer National Alliance et al. as Amici Curiae at 4, 6–7, 15–16, *Burwell*, 573 U.S. 682 (Nos. 13-354, 13-356); Coverage of Certain Preventative Services Under the Affordable Care Act, 78 Fed. Reg. 39,870, 39,872 (July 2, 2013) (to be codified at 26 C.F.R. pt. 54); INST. OF MED., *supra* note 14, at 107.

[98] *See* INST. OF MED., *supra* note 14, at 105.

[99 [FN 22]] IUDs, which are among the most reliable forms of contraception, generally cost women more than $1,000 when the expenses of the office visit and insertion procedure are taken into account. *See* David Eisenberg, Colleen McNicholas & Jeffrey F. Peipert, *Cost as a Barrier to Long-Acting Reversible Contraceptive (LARC) Use in Adolescents*, 52 J. ADOLESCENT HEALTH S59, S60 (2013); *see also* Brooke Winner et al., *Effectiveness of Long-Acting Reversible Contraception*, 366 NEW ENG. J. MED. 1998, 1999 (2012).

reasoning appears to permit commercial enterprises like Hobby Lobby and Conestoga to exclude from their group health plans all forms of contraceptives.[100]

Perhaps the gravity of the interests at stake has led the Court to assume, for purposes of its RFRA analysis, that the compelling interest criterion is met in these cases.[101; 102 [FN 23]] It bears note in this regard that the cost of an IUD is nearly equivalent to a month's full-time pay for workers earning the minimum wage;[103] that almost one-third of women would change their contraceptive method if costs were not a factor;[104] and that only one-fourth of women who request an IUD actually have one inserted after finding out how expensive it would be.[105]

Stepping back from its assumption that compelling interests support the contraceptive coverage requirement, the Court notes that small employers and grandfathered plans are not subject to the requirement. If there is a compelling interest in contraceptive coverage, the Court suggests, Congress would not have created these exclusions.[106]

---

[100] *See* Transcript of Oral Argument at 38–39, *Burwell*, 573 U.S. 682 (Nos. 13-354, 13-356) (counsel for Hobby Lobby acknowledged that his "argument . . . would apply just as well if the employer said 'no contraceptives'" (internal quotation marks added)).

[101] *See Burwell*, 573 U.S. at 728.

[102] [FN 23] Although the Court's opinion makes this assumption grudgingly, *see id.* at 726–28, one Member of the majority recognizes, without reservation, that "the [contraceptive coverage] mandate serves the Government's compelling interest in providing insurance coverage that is necessary to protect the health of female employees." *Id.* at 737 (Kennedy, J., concurring).

[103] Brief for Guttmacher Institute et al. as Amici Curiae at 16, *Burwell*, 573 U.S. 682 (Nos. 13-354, 13-356).

[104] Jennifer J. Frost & Jacqueline E. Darroch, *Factors Associated With Contraceptive Choice and Inconsistent Method Use, United States, 2004*, 40 PERSP. ON SEXUAL & REPROD. HEALTH 94, 98 (2008).

[105] Aileen M. Gariepy, Erica J. Simon, Divya A. Patel, Mitchell D. Creinin & Eleanor B. Schwarz, *The Impact of Out-of-Pocket Expense on IUD Utilization Among Women with Private Insurance*, 84 CONTRACEPTION e39, e40 (2011); *see also* Eisenberg, McNicholas & Peipert, *supra* note 99, at S60 (recent study found that women who face out-of-pocket IUD costs in excess of $50 were "11-times less likely to obtain an IUD than women who had to pay less than $50"); Debbie Postlethwaite, James Trussell, Anthony Zoolakis, Ruth Shabear & Diana Petitti, *A Comparison of Contraceptive Procurement Pre- and Post-Benefit Change*, 76 CONTRACEPTION 360, 361–62 (2007) (when one health system eliminated patient cost sharing for IUDs, use of this form of contraception more than doubled).

[106] *See Burwell*, 573 U.S. at 726–28.

Federal statutes often include exemptions for small employers, and such provisions have never been held to undermine the interests served by these statutes.[107]

The ACA's grandfathering provision[108] allows a phasing-in period for compliance with a number of the Act's requirements (not just the contraceptive coverage or other preventive services provisions). Once specified changes are made, grandfathered status ceases.[109] Hobby Lobby's own situation is illustrative. By the time this litigation commenced, Hobby Lobby did not have grandfathered status. Asked why by the District Court, Hobby Lobby's counsel explained that the "grandfathering requirements mean that you can't make a whole menu of changes to your plan that involve things like the amount of co-pays, the amount of co-insurance, deductibles, that sort of thing."[110] Counsel acknowledged that, "just because of economic realities, our plan has to shift over time. I mean, insurance plans, as everyone knows, shif[t] over time."[111; 112 [FN 24]] The percentage of employees in grandfathered plans is steadily declining, having dropped from 56% in 2011 to 48% in 2012 to 36% in 2013.[113] In short, far from ranking as a categorical exemption, the grandfathering provision is "temporary, intended to be a means for gradually transitioning employers into mandatory coverage."[114]

---

[107] *See, e.g.,* Family and Medical Leave Act of 1993, 29 U.S.C. § 2611(4)(A)(i) (applicable to employers with 50 or more employees); Age Discrimination in Employment Act of 1967, 29 U.S.C. § 630(b) (originally exempting employers with fewer than 50 employees, 81 Stat. 605, the statute now governs employers with 20 or more employees); Americans With Disabilities Act, 42 U.S.C. § 12111(5)(A) (applicable to employers with 15 or more employees); Title VII, 42 U.S.C. § 2000e(b) (originally exempting employers with fewer than 25 employees, *see* Arbaugh v. Y & H Corp., 546 U.S. 500, 505 n.2 (2006), the statute now governs employers with 15 or more employees).

[108] 42 U.S.C. § 18011.

[109] *See* 45 C.F.R. § 147.140(g).

[110] App. at 39–40, *Burwell*, 573 U.S. 682 (No. 13-354).

[111] *Id.* at 40.

[112] [FN 24] Hobby Lobby's *amicus* National Religious Broadcasters similarly states that, "[g]iven the nature of employers' needs to meet changing economic and staffing circumstances, and to adjust insurance coverage accordingly, the actual benefit of the 'grandfather' exclusion is and transitory at best." Brief for National Religious Broadcasters as Amicus Curiae at 28, *Burwell*, 573 U.S. 682 (No. 13-354).

[113] THE KAISER FAMILY FOUND. & HEALTH RESEARCH & EDUC. TR., EMPLOYER HEALTH BENEFITS: 2013 ANNUAL SURVEY 7, 196.

[114] Gilardi v. U.S. Dep't of Health & Human Servs., 733 F.3d 1208, 1241 (D.C. Cir. 2013) (Edwards, J., concurring in part and dissenting in part).

The Court ultimately acknowledges a critical point: RFRA's application "*must* take adequate account of the burdens a requested accommodation may impose on nonbeneficiaries."[115] No tradition, and no prior decision under RFRA, allows a religion-based exemption when the accommodation would be harmful to others—here, the very persons the contraceptive coverage requirement was designed to protect.[116]

4

After assuming the existence of compelling government interests, the Court holds that the contraceptive coverage requirement fails to satisfy RFRA's least restrictive means test. But the Government has shown that there is no less restrictive, equally effective means that would both (1) satisfy the challengers' religious objections to providing insurance coverage for certain contraceptives (which they believe cause abortions); and (2) carry out the objective of the ACA's contraceptive coverage requirement, to ensure that women employees receive, at no cost to them, the preventive care needed to safeguard their health and wellbeing. A "least restrictive means" cannot require employees to relinquish benefits accorded them by federal law in order to ensure that their commercial employers can adhere unreservedly to their religious tenets.[117; 118 [FN 25]]

Then let the government pay (rather than the employees who do not share their employer's faith), the Court suggests. "The most straightforward [alternative]," the Court asserts, "would be for the Government to assume the cost of providing . . . contraceptives . . . to any women who are unable to obtain them under their health-

---

[115] *Burwell*, 573 U.S. at 729 n.37 (emphasis added) (quoting Cutter v. Wilkinson, 544 U.S. 709, 720 (2005)).

[116] *Cf. Burwell*, 573 U.S. at 745–46 (Ginsburg, J., dissenting); Prince v. Massachusetts, 321 U.S. 158, 177 (1944) (Jackson, J., dissenting) ("[The] limitations which of necessity bound religious freedom . . . begin to operate whenever activities begin to affect or collide with liberties of others or of the public.").

[117] *See Burwell*, 573 U.S. at 746, 764–65 (Ginsburg, J., dissenting).

[118] [FN 25] As the Court made clear in *Cutter*, the government's license to grant religion-based exemptions from generally applicable laws is constrained by the Establishment Clause. Cutter v. Wilkinson, 544 U.S. 709, 720–22 (2005). "[W]e are a cosmopolitan nation made up of people of almost every conceivable religious preference," Braunfeld v. Brown, 366 U.S. 599, 606 (1961), a "rich mosaic of religious faiths," Town of Greece v. Galloway, 572 U.S. 565, 628 (2014) (Kagan, J., dissenting). Consequently, one person's right to free exercise must be kept in harmony with the rights of her fellow citizens, and "some religious practices [must] yield to the common good." United States v. Lee, 455 U.S. 252, 259 (1982).

insurance policies due to their employers' religious objections."[119] The ACA, however, requires coverage of preventive services through the existing employer-based system of health insurance "so that [employees] face minimal logistical and administrative obstacles."[120] Impeding women's receipt of benefits "by requiring them to take steps to learn about, and to sign up for, a new [government funded and administered] health benefit" was scarcely what Congress contemplated.[121] Moreover, Title X of the Public Health Service Act[122] "is the nation's only dedicated source of federal funding for safety net family planning services."[123] "Safety net programs like Title X are not designed to absorb the unmet needs of . . . insured individuals."[124] Note, too, that Congress declined to write into law the preferential treatment Hobby Lobby and Conestoga describe as a less restrictive alternative.[125]

And where is the stopping point to the "let the government pay" alternative? Suppose an employer's sincerely held religious belief is offended by health coverage of vaccines, or paying the minimum wage,[126] or according women equal pay for substantially similar work?[127] Does it rank as a less restrictive alternative to require the government to provide the money or benefit to which the employer has a religion-based objection?[128] [FN 26] Because the Court cannot easily answer that question, it proposes something else: Extension to commercial enterprises of the accommodation already afforded to nonprofit religion-based organizations.[129] "At a minimum," according to the Court, such an approach would not "impinge on [Hobby Lobby's and Conestoga's] religious belief."[130] I have already discussed the "special solicitude" generally accorded nonprofit religion-based organizations that exist to

---

[119] *Burwell*, 573 U.S. at 728.

[120] Coverage of Certain Preventative Services Under the Affordable Care Act, 78 Fed. Reg. 39,870, 39,888 (July 2, 2013) (to be codified at 26 C.F.R. pt. 54).

[121] *Id.*

[122] 42 U.S.C. §§ 300 to 300a-6.

[123] Brief for National Health Law Program et al. as Amici Curiae at 23, *Burwell*, 573 U.S. 682 (Nos. 13-354, 13-356).

[124] *Id.* at 24.

[125] *See Burwell*, 573 U.S. at 744 (Ginsburg, J., dissenting).

[126] *See* Tony & Susan Alamo Found. v. Sec'y of Labor, 471 U.S. 290, 303 (1985).

[127] *See* Dole v. Shenandoah Baptist Church, 899 F.2d 1389, 1392 (4th Cir. 1990).

[128] [FN 26] *Cf.* Ashcroft v. Am. Civil Liberties Union, 542 U.S. 656, 666 (2004) (in context of Speech Clause challenge to a content-based speech restriction, courts must determine "whether the challenged regulation is the least restrictive means among , effective alternatives" (emphasis added)).

[129] *See Burwell*, 573 U.S. at 692–93, 698–99, 730–32.

[130] *Id.* at 731.

serve a community of believers, solicitude never before accorded to commercial enterprises comprising employees of diverse faiths.[131]

Ultimately, the Court hedges on its proposal to align for-profit enterprises with nonprofit religion-based organizations. "We do not decide today whether [the] approach [the opinion advances] complies with RFRA for purposes of all religious claims."[132] Counsel for Hobby Lobby was similarly noncommittal. Asked at oral argument whether the Court-proposed alternative was acceptable,[133] [FN 27] counsel responded: "We haven't been offered that accommodation, so we haven't had to decide what kind of objection, if any, we would make to that."[134]

Conestoga suggests that, if its employees had to acquire and pay for the contraceptives (to which the corporation objects) on their own, a tax credit would qualify as a less restrictive alternative.[135] A tax credit, of course, is one variety of "let the government pay." In addition to departing from the existing employer-based system of health insurance, Conestoga's alternative would require a woman to reach into her own pocket in the first instance, and it would do nothing for the woman too poor to be aided by a tax credit.

In sum, in view of what Congress sought to accomplish, i.e., comprehensive preventive care for women furnished through employer-based health plans, none of the proffered alternatives would satisfactorily serve the compelling interests to which Congress responded.

---

[131] *See id.* at 752–55 (Ginsburg, J., dissenting).

[132] *Id.* at 731 (majority opinion).

[133] [FN 27] On brief, Hobby Lobby and Conestoga barely addressed the extension solution, which would bracket commercial enterprises with nonprofit religion-based organizations for religious accommodations purposes. The hesitation is understandable, for challenges to the adequacy of the accommodation accorded religious nonprofit organizations are currently *sub judice. See, e.g.,* Little Sisters of the Poor Home for the Aged v. Sebelius, 6 F. Supp. 2d 1225 (D. Colo. 2013), *vacated and remanded* Zubik v. Burwell, 136 S. Ct. 1557 (2016). At another point in today's decision, the Court refuses to consider an argument neither "raised below [nor] advanced in this Court by any party," giving Hobby Lobby and Conestoga "[no] opportunity to respond to [that] novel claim." *Burwell,* 573 U.S. at 721. Yet the Court is content to decide this case (and this case only) on the ground that HHS could make an accommodation never suggested in the parties' presentations. RFRA cannot sensibly be read to "requir[e] the government to . . . refute each and every conceivable alternative regulation," United States v. Wilgus, 638 F.3d 1274, 1289 (10th Cir. 2011), especially where the alternative on which the Court seizes was not pressed by any challenger.

[134] Transcript of Oral Argument, *supra* note 110, at 86–87.

[135] *See* Brief for Petitioners at 64, *Burwell,* 573 U.S. 682 (No. 13-356).

IV

Among the path marking pre-Smith decisions RFRA preserved is United States v. Lee.[136] Lee, a sole proprietor engaged in farming and carpentry, was a member of the Old Order Amish. He sincerely believed that withholding Social Security taxes from his employees or paying the employer's share of such taxes would violate the Amish faith. This Court held that, although the obligations imposed by the Social Security system conflicted with Lee's religious beliefs, the burden was not unconstitutional.[137; 138 [FN 28]] The Government urges that Lee should control the challenges brought by Hobby Lobby and Conestoga.[139] In contrast, today's Court dismisses Lee as a tax case.[140] Indeed, it was a tax case and the Court in Lee homed in on "[t]he difficulty in attempting to accommodate religious beliefs in the area of taxation."[141]

But the Lee Court made two key points one cannot confine to tax cases. "When followers of a particular sect enter into commercial activity as a matter of choice," the Court observed, "the limits they accept on their own conduct as a matter of conscience and faith are not to be superimposed on statutory schemes which are binding on others in that activity."[142] The statutory scheme of employer-based comprehensive health coverage involved in these cases is surely binding on others engaged in the same trade or business as the corporate challengers here, Hobby Lobby and Conestoga. Further, the Court recognized in Lee that allowing a religion-based exemption to a commercial employer would "operat[e] to impose the employer's religious faith on the employees."[143; 144 [FN 29]] No doubt the Greens and Hahns and all

---

[136] 455 U.S. 252 (1982).

[137] *Id.* at 260–61; *see also id.* at 258 (recognizing the important governmental interest in providing a "nationwide . . . comprehensive insurance system with a variety of benefits available to all participants, with costs shared by employers and employees").

[138] [FN 28] As a sole proprietor, Lee was subject to personal liability for violating the law of general application he opposed. His claim to a religion-based exemption would have been even thinner had he conducted his business as a corporation, thus avoiding personal liability.

[139] *See* Brief for Respondents, supra note 75, at 18.

[140] *See Burwell,* 573 U.S. at 733–35.

[141] *Lee,* 455 U.S. at 259.

[142] *Id.* at 261.

[143] *Id.*

[144] [FN 29] Congress amended the Social Security Act in response to *Lee.* The amended statute permits Amish sole proprietors and partnerships (but not Amish-owned corporations) to obtain an exemption from the obligation to pay Social Security taxes only for employees who are co-religionists and who

who share their beliefs may decline to acquire for themselves the contraceptives in question. But that choice may not be imposed on employees who hold other beliefs. Working for Hobby Lobby or Conestoga, in other words, should not deprive employees of the preventive care available to workers at the shop next door,[145] [FN 30] at least in the absence of directions from the Legislature or Administration to do so.

Why should decisions of this order be made by Congress or the regulatory authority, and not this Court? Hobby Lobby and Conestoga surely do not stand alone as commercial enterprises seeking exemptions from generally applicable laws on the basis of their religious beliefs.[146] Would RFRA require exemptions in cases of this ilk? And if not, how does the Court divine which religious beliefs are worthy of accommodation, and which are not? Isn't the Court disarmed from making such a judgment given its recognition that "courts must not presume to determine . . . the plausibility of a religious claim"?[147]

Would the exemption the Court holds RFRA demands for employers with religiously grounded objections to the use of certain contraceptives extend to employers with religiously grounded objections to

---

likewise seek an exemption and agree to give up their Social Security benefits. *See* 26 U.S.C. § 3127(a)(2), (b)(1). Thus, employers with sincere religious beliefs have no right to a religion-based exemption that would deprive employees of Social Security benefits without the employee's consent—an exemption analogous to the one Hobby Lobby and Conestoga seek here.

[145] [FN 30] *Cf.* Tony & Susan Alamo Found. v. Sec'y of Labor, 471 U.S. 290, 299 (1985) (disallowing religion-based exemption that "would undoubtedly give [the commercial enterprise seeking the exemption] and similar organizations an advantage over their competitors").

[146] *See, e.g.*, Newman v. Piggie Park Enters., Inc., 256 F. Supp. 941, 945 (D.S.C. 1966) (owner of restaurant chain refused to serve black patrons based on his religious beliefs opposing racial integration), *aff'd in relevant part and rev'd in part on other grounds*, 377 F.2d 433 (4th Cir. 1967), *aff'd and modified on other grounds*, 390 U.S. 400 (1968); *In re* Minnesota *ex rel.* McClure, 370 N.W.2d 844, 847 (Minn. 1985) (born-again Christians who owned closely held, for-profit health clubs believed that the Bible proscribed hiring or retaining an "individua[l] living with but not married to a person of the opposite sex," "a young, single woman working without her father's consent or a married woman working without her husband's consent," and any person "antagonistic to the Bible," including "fornicators and homosexuals" (internal quotation marks omitted)), *appeal dismissed*, 478 U.S. 1015 (1986); Elane Photography, LLC v. Willock, 2013–NMSC–040, 309 P.3d 53 (2013) (for-profit photography business owned by a husband and wife refused to photograph a lesbian couple's commitment ceremony based on the religious beliefs of the company's owners), *cert. denied*, 572 U.S. 1046 (2014).

[147] Burwell v. Hobby Lobby Stores, Inc., 573 U.S. 682, 724 (2014).

blood transfusions (Jehovah's Witnesses); antidepressants (Scientologists); medications derived from pigs, including anesthesia, intravenous fluids, and pills coated with gelatin (certain Muslims, Jews, and Hindus); and vaccinations (Christian Scientists, among others)?[148] [FN 31] According to counsel for Hobby Lobby, "each one of these cases . . . would have to be evaluated on its own . . . apply[ing] the compelling interest-least restrictive alternative test."[149] Not much help there for the lower courts bound by today's decision.

The Court, however, sees nothing to worry about. Today's cases, the Court concludes, are "concerned solely with the contraceptive mandate. Our decision should not be understood to hold that an insurance-coverage mandate must necessarily fall if it conflicts with an employer's religious beliefs. Other coverage requirements, such as immunizations, may be supported by different interests (for example, the need to combat the spread of infectious diseases) and may involve different arguments about the least restrictive means of providing them."[150] But the Court has assumed, for RFRA purposes, that the interest in women's health and wellbeing is compelling and has come up with no means adequate to serve that interest, the one motivating Congress to adopt the Women's Health Amendment.

There is an overriding interest, I believe, in keeping the courts "out of the business of evaluating the relative merits of differing religious claims,"[151] or the sincerity with which an asserted religious belief is held. Indeed, approving some religious claims while deeming others unworthy of accommodation could be "perceived as favoring one religion over another," the very "risk the Establishment Clause was designed to preclude."[152] The Court, I fear, has ventured into a minefield[153] by its immoderate reading of RFRA. I would confine religious exemptions under that Act to organizations formed "for a religious purpose," "engage[d] primarily in carrying out that religious

---

[148] [FN 31] Religious objections to immunization programs are not hypothetical. *See* Phillips v. New York, 27 F. Supp. 2d 310 (E.D.N.Y. 2014) (dismissing free exercise challenges to New York's vaccination practices); *Compulsory Vaccinations Threaten Religious Freedom*, LIBERTY COUNSEL (2007), http://www.lc.org/media/9980/attachments/memo_vaccination.pdf.

[149] Transcript of Oral Argument, *supra* note 110, at 6.

[150] *Burwell*, 573 U.S. at 733.

[151] United States v. Lee, 455 U.S. 252, 263 n.2 (Stevens, J., concurring in judgment).

[152] *Id.*

[153] *Cf.* Spencer v. World Vision, Inc., 633 F.3d 723, 730 (9th Cir. 2010) (O'Scannlain, J., concurring).

purpose," and not "engaged . . . substantially in the exchange of goods or services for money beyond nominal amounts."[154]

*   *   *

For the reasons stated, I would reverse the judgment of the Court of Appeals for the Tenth Circuit and affirm the judgment of the Court of Appeals for the Third Circuit.

---

[154] *See id.* at 748 (Kleinfeld, J., concurring).

COLEMAN

"[D]enial or curtailment of women's employment opportunities has been traceable directly to the pervasive presumption that women are mothers first, and workers second."

The Case

In *Coleman v. Court of Appeals of Maryland*,[1] the Court took up the case of an employee who sued his employer for violating the Family Medical Leave Act ("FMLA" or "the Act") by failing to provide him with self-care leave. The FMLA is a federal law requiring employers (including public employers) to provide their employees unpaid leave without penalty for certain legally-defined family and medical reasons. Specifically, the FMLA entitles eligible employees to take up to twelve work weeks of unpaid leave per year for the birth of a child; to facilitate adoption or foster-care placement; for the care of a "spouse . . . son, daughter, or parent" with "a serious health condition;" and for the employee's own "serious health condition" which "interferes with the employee's ability to perform at work."[2] The first three provisions are called the "family-care provisions" and the last provision is called the "self-care provision." The FMLA creates a private right to sue "any employer," including a State government or agency, which violates the Act's provisions.[3]

In *Coleman*, the Plaintiff, Daniel Coleman, was an employee of the Court of Appeals of Maryland. When Coleman requested sick leave under the FMLA's self-care provision, he was informed he would be terminated if he did not resign. Coleman then sued the state court in the United States District Court for the District of Maryland, claiming his employer had violated the FMLA by failing to provide him with self-care leave. Both the District Court and, subsequently, the United States Court of Appeals for the Fourth Circuit ruled against Coleman, finding that the Maryland Court of Appeals, as an entity of a sovereign state, was immune from a suit for money damages. Key to both courts' analysis was their finding that the FMLA's self-care provision did not validly abrogate the State's immunity from suit.

---

[1] 566 U.S. 30 (2012).

[2] 29 U.S.C. § 2612(a)(1) (2012).

[3] 29 U.S.C. § 2617(a)(2) (2012).

A Brief Explanation of Sovereign Immunity

The critical legal concept at issue in Coleman was sovereign immunity. Under the United States' federal system, States, as sovereigns, are immune from suits for damages unless they elect to waive that defense. Both the federal government and all of the state governments have passed laws consenting to suit in certain limited circumstances. These laws are known as limited "waivers" of sovereign immunity.

Separately, under Section 5 of the Fourteenth Amendment to the U.S. Constitution, Congress has the authority to pass laws that abrogate a state's sovereign immunity in order to enforce the substantive guarantees of Section 1 of that Amendment, which include due process and equal protection. To do so, however, Congress "must identify a pattern of constitutional violations and tailor a remedy congruent and proportional to the documented violations."[4] As well, the Supreme Court previously held, in *Nevada Department of Human Resources v. Hibbs*, that the intent to abrogate must be "unmistakably clear in the language of the statute."[5]

Justice Kennedy's Majority Opinion

Along with a plurality opinion[6] written by Justice Kennedy, a majority of the Court affirmed the judgment of the lower courts that the self-care provisions of the FMLA *did not* validly abrogate state sovereign immunity under Section 5 of the Fourteenth Amendment. The plurality opinion began by drawing a distinction between the FMLA's self-care provisions and its family-care provision. It noted that in *Hibbs*, discussed above, the majority found that one of the family-care provisions of the FMLA—the provision pertaining to leave for the care of a spouse, child, or parent with a serious health condition—was a valid abrogation of state sovereign immunity because Congress found evidence of "a well-documented pattern of sex-based discrimination in family-leave policies"—that generally favored women to the detriment

---

[4] *Coleman*, 566 U.S. at 43.
[5] 538 U.S. 721, 726 (2003).
[6] In *Coleman*, Justice Scalia concurred only in the result, but did not adopt the reasoning of the Court as set forth in Justice Kennedy's opinion. Accordingly, while the result of the case was binding (a majority voted to affirm the Court of Appeals below), the plurality opinion in *Coleman* is of limited precedential value because it did not set forth the views of a majority of the Court's members.

of men—and narrowly tailored its solution to remedy that discrimination by requiring state employers to give all employees the opportunity to take family-care leave equally.[7] By contrast, on the facts presented in *Coleman*, the plurality found an absence of "evidence of a pattern of state constitutional violations accompanied by a remedy drawn in narrow terms to address or prevent those violations," which the plurality found necessary for the self-care provision to be "a valid abrogation" of the States' immunity from suit under Section 5 of the Fourteenth Amendment.[8]

In reaching this conclusion, the plurality employed the so-called "congruence and proportionality" test, which asks whether there is a relationship between the type of injury suffered (here, gender-based discrimination in the workplace) and the means adopted to remedy that harm (the FMLA self-care provisions), and requires that such means be congruent and proportional to the harms to be rectified. Ultimately, the plurality found no evidence of discrimination in either the language or implementation of state leave policies, such that "abrogating the States' immunity from suits for damages for failure to give self-care leave" was not "a congruent and proportional remedy" because "the existing state leave policies would have sufficed."[9]

Justice Ginsburg's Dissent

Justice Ginsburg's dissent was focused on showing the self-care provision did, indeed, pass muster under the "congruence and proportionality" test, and that in opining otherwise, the "plurality pa[id] scant attention to the overarching aim of the FMLA: to make it feasible for women to work while sustaining family life."[10] Ginsburg would have held that the self-care provision "validly enforces the right to be free from gender discrimination in the workplace."[11] To support this conclusion, Ginsburg engaged in an extremely detailed discussion of the California law on which the FMLA was based and its influence on the creation of the FMLA.[12] Ginsburg convincingly demonstrated that the foundational purpose of the FMLA was to remedy historical discrimination against women who required leave due to childcare concerns, and that such discrimination abounded in the years prior to the

---

[7] *Coleman*, 566 U.S. at 36–37 (discussing *Hibbs*, 538 U.S. at 729–35).

[8] *Id.* at 37.

[9] *Id.* at 39.

[10] *Id.* at 65 (Ginsburg, J., dissenting).

[11] *Id.* at 46.

[12] *See id.* at 47–50.

passage of the Act.[13] Accordingly, Ginsburg asserted that "the plurality undervalue[d] the language, purpose, and history of the FMLA, and the self-care provision's important role in the statutory scheme."[14]

Ginsburg's historical survey revealed that women were a primary concern for the drafters of the FMLA self-care provisions. She first highlighted the historical use of extended medical leave time as an excuse for employers to fire women after pregnancy.[15] Second, Ginsburg showed that male employers were still ambivalent about the notion that men and women occupied equal positions in the workforce and described how many employers used women's tendency to take medical leave time as an excuse either to push them out of the workforce or not to hire them at all.[16] Third, she argued that self-care leave was "a key part of Congress' endeavor to make it feasible for women to work and have families."[17] By liberally peppering her arguments with citations to the evidence that Congress relied upon when drafting the FMLA, Ginsburg demonstrated that Congress intended the FMLA's self-care provisions to remedy gender discrimination in the workplace, and thus presented a convincing argument that the self-care provision withstood the "congruent and proportional" test. Accordingly, Ginsburg would have held that the FMLA's "purpose and legislative history reinforce[d] the conclusion that the [Act], in its entirety, is directed at sex discrimination. Indeed, the FMLA was originally envisioned as a way to guarantee—without singling out women or pregnancy—that pregnant women would not lose their jobs when they gave birth. The self-care provision achieves that aim."[18]

Notably, Justice Ginsburg concluded her dissent by setting forth multiple ways in which the FMLA's anti-discriminatory aims were still achievable through actions which had not been proscribed by the Court. She reminded her readers that the FMLA still technically applied to state government agencies, even if they could not be sued for money damages because of sovereign immunity.[19] The majority did not contradict this point. In effect, Justice Ginsburg used her closing words to offer a bit of *pro bono* legal advice to would-be plaintiffs, explaining that they could still seek injunctive relief to prevent termination, or even complain directly to the U.S. Department of Labor, which could take on the state agency on their behalf.[20]

---

[13] *See id.* at 47–54.

[14] *Id.* at 47.

[15] *See id.* at 51–54, 61–64.

[16] *See id.*

[17] *Id.* at 63.

[18] *Id.* at 47.

[19] *See id.* at 64–65.

[20] *See id.* at 65.

COLEMAN V. COURT OF APPEALS OF MARYLAND

JUSTICE GINSBURG, with whom JUSTICE BREYER joins, and with whom JUSTICE SOTOMAYOR and JUSTICE KAGAN join as to all but footnote 1, DISSENTING.

Section 1 of the Fourteenth Amendment provides: "No State shall . . . deny to any person within its jurisdiction the equal protection of the laws." Section 5 grants Congress the "power to enforce, by appropriate legislation, the provisions of this article." Congress' §5 enforcement power includes the authority to remedy and deter violations of §1's substantive guarantees by prohibiting conduct "not itself forbidden by the Amendment's text."[1] "In other words, Congress may enact so-called prophylactic legislation that proscribes facially constitutional conduct, in order to prevent and deter unconstitutional conduct."[2]

The Family and Medical Leave Act of 1993 (FMLA or Act) entitles eligible employees to 12 weeks of job-secured leave during any 12-month period: (A) to care for a newborn son or daughter; (B) to care for a newly adopted son or daughter; (C) to care for a spouse, child, or parent with a serious health condition; or (D) because the employee has a serious health condition that makes her unable to perform the functions of her position.[3]

Even accepting this Court's view of the scope of Congress' power under §5 of the Fourteenth Amendment, I would hold that the self-care provision, § 2612(a)(1)(D), validly enforces the right to be free from gender discrimination in the workplace.[4] [FN 1]

---

[1] Kimel v. Fla. Bd. of Regents, 528 U.S. 62, 81 (2000).
[2] Nev. Dep't. of Human Resources v. Hibbs, 538 U.S. 721, 721–728 (2003).
[3] 29 U.S.C. § 2612(a)(1) (2012).
[4] [FN 1] I remain of the view that Congress can abrogate state sovereign immunity pursuant to its Article I Commerce Clause power. See Seminole Tribe of Fla. v. Florida, (Souter, J., dissenting). Beyond debate, is valid Commerce Clause legislation. See infra, at 21. I also share the view that Congress can abrogate state immunity pursuant to §5 where Congress could reasonably conclude that legislation "constitutes an appropriate way to enforce [a] basic equal protection requirement." Board of Trustees of Univ. of Ala. v. Garrett,

I

Section 5 legislation "must be targeted at conduct transgressing the Fourteenth Amendment's substantive provisions,"[5] "[a]nd '[t]here must be a congruence and proportionality between the injury to be prevented or remedied and the means adopted to that end.'"[6] The first step of the now-familiar *Boerne* inquiry calls for identification of the constitutional right Congress sought to enforce.[7] The FMLA's self-care provision, Maryland asserts, trains not on the right to be free from gender discrimination, but on an "equal protection right to be free from irrational state employment discrimination based on a medical condition."[8] The plurality agrees, concluding that the self-care provision reveals "a concern for discrimination on the basis of illness, not sex."[9] In so declaring, the plurality undervalues the language, purpose, and history of the FMLA, and the self-care provision's important role in the statutory scheme. As well, the plurality underplays the main theme of our decision in *Hibbs*: "The FMLA aims to protect the right to be free from gender-based discrimination in the workplace."[10]

I begin with the text of the statute, which repeatedly emphasizes gender discrimination. One of the FMLA's stated purposes is to "entitle employees to take reasonable leave,"[11] "in a manner that, consistent with the Equal Protection Clause of the Fourteenth Amendment, minimizes the potential for employment discrimination on the basis of sex by ensuring generally that leave is available for eligible medical reasons (including maternity-related disability) and for compelling family reasons, on a gender-neutral basis."[12] Another identified aim is "to promote the goal of equal employment opportunity for women and men, pursuant to [the Equal Protection Clause]."[13] "[E]mployment standards that apply to one gender only," Congress expressly found, "have serious potential for encouraging employers to discriminate against employees and applicants for employment who are of that gender."[14]

(Breyer, J., dissenting) (internal quotation marks omitted).

[5] *Ante*, at 5 (internal quotation marks omitted).

[6] *Id.* (quoting City of Boerne v. Flores, 521 U.S. 507, 520 (1997)).

[7] *See, e.g.*, Tennessee v. Lane, 541 U.S. 509, 522 (2004).

[8] Brief for Respondents at 14.

[9] *Ante*, at 7.

[10] Nev. Dep't. of Human Resources v. Hibbs, 538 U.S. 721, 728 (2003).

[11] 29 U.S.C. § 2601(b)(2) (2012).

[12] § 2601(b)(4).

[13] § 2601(b)(5).

[14] § 2601(a)(6).

The FMLA's purpose and legislative history reinforce the conclusion that the FMLA, in its entirety, is directed at sex discrimination. Indeed, the FMLA was originally envisioned as a way to guarantee—without singling out women or pregnancy—that pregnant women would not lose their jobs when they gave birth. The self-care provision achieves that aim.

A brief history is in order. In his 1982 congressional campaign, then-candidate Howard Berman pledged to introduce legislation similar to the California law challenged in *California Federal Savings & Loan Ass'n. v. Guerra.*[15] California's law, enacted in 1978, made it unlawful for an employer to refuse to grant female employees disabled by pregnancy or childbirth up to four months' unpaid, job-protected leave.[16]

The California law sharply divided women's rights advocates. "Equal-treatment" feminists asserted it violated the Pregnancy Discrimination Act's (PDA) commitment to treating pregnancy the same as other disabilities.[17] [FN 2] It did so by requiring leave only for disability caused by pregnancy and childbirth, thereby treating pregnancy as *sui generis.*[18] "Equal-opportunity" feminists disagreed, urging that the California law was consistent with the PDA because it remedied the discriminatory burden that inadequate leave policies placed on a woman's right to procreate.[19]

While *California Fed.* moved through the lower federal courts, equal-treatment feminists began work on a gender-neutral leave

---

[15] 479 U.S. 272 (1987); *see also* STEVEN WISENSALE, FAMILY LEAVE POLICY: THE POLITICAL ECONOMY OF WORK AND FAMILY IN AMERICA 134 (2001).

[16] *See* 1978 Cal. Stat. ch. 1321, §1, now codified at CAL. GOV'T. CODE§ 12945(a)(1) (West 2012).

[17] [FN 2] Enacted as an addition to the section defining terms used in Title VII of the Civil Rights Act of 1964, the Pregnancy Discrimination Act of 1978 (PDA) provides: "The terms 'because of sex' or 'on the basis of sex' include, but are not limited to, because of or on the basis of pregnancy, childbirth, or related medical conditions; and women affected by pregnancy, childbirth, or related medical conditions shall be treated the same for all employment-related purposes, including receipt of benefits under fringe benefit programs, as other persons not so affected but similar in their ability or inability to work . . . ." 92 Stat. 2076, 42 U.S.C. §2000e(k) (2012).

[18] *See* Brief for American Civil Liberties Union et al. as Amici Curiae at 5–10 in Cal. Fed. Sav. & Loan Ass'n v. Guerra, 479 U.S. 272 (1987) (No. 85–494).

[19] *See* Brief for Coalition for Reproductive Equality in the Workplace et al. as Amici Curiae at 2–6 in *Cal. Fed.* 479 U.S. 272 (No. 85–494); *see also* Williams, *Equality's Riddle: Pregnancy and the Equal Treatment/Special Treatment Debate,* 13 N.Y.U. REV. L. & SOC. CHANGE 325, 326–328 (1984–1985)] (discussing disagreement).

model, which eventually became the FMLA.[20] Then-Congressman Berman met with the Women's Legal Defense Fund's Donna Lenhoff, a drafter of the first FMLA bill.[21; 22 [FN 3]] They agreed that any national bill would focus not only on pregnancy, but on equal treatment for all workers.[23]

Though this Court, in *California Fed.*, eventually upheld California's pregnancy-only leave policy as not preempted by the PDA, equal-treatment feminists continued to believe that viewing pregnancy as *sui generis* perpetuated widespread discrimination against women.[24 [FN 4]] They therefore maintained their commitment to gender-neutral leave.[25]

---

[20] *See* Ross, *Legal Aspects of Parental Leave, in* PARENTAL LEAVE AND CHILD CARE 97 (J. Hyde & M. Essex eds. 1991).

[21] *Id.*, at 114–115, n.27; WISENSALE, *supra* note 1, at 136.

[22] [FN 3] Lenhoff advanced The Parental and Disability Act of 1985, introduced by Rep. Patricia Schroeder. *See* STEVEN WISENSALE, FAMILY LEAVE POLICY: THE POLITICAL ECONOMY OF WORK AND FAMILY IN AMERICA 136–138 (2001). She was later named Vice Chair of the Commission on Leave, created by the FMLA to study family and medical leave policies. See 29 U.S.C. §§ 2631–2632 (2012); U.S. COMMISSION ON FAMILY AND MEDICAL LEAVE, A WORKABLE BALANCE: REPORT TO CONGRESS ON FAMILY AND MEDICAL LEAVE POLICIES 210 (Apr. 30, 1996).

[23] Ross, *supra* note 6, at 114–115, n.27; *see also* Kazmier v. Widmann, 225 F.3d 519, 547 (5th Cir. 2000) (Dennis, J., dissenting) ("Perceiving that enacting the PDA had not achieved the intended result of preventing discrimination against either women or men in the granting of leave time in that the States felt it necessary to affirmatively grant pregnancy leave to women and not men, in 1985 Congress began considering the issue of family and medical leave.").

[24] [FN 4] For example, in addition to mandating pregnancy leave, the California statute allowed employers to discriminate against pregnant workers. Employers could refuse to select a pregnant woman for a training program if she would not finish the program at least three months before giving birth. *See* 1978 Cal. Stats. ch. 1321, §1. The law limited pregnancy disability leave to six weeks, §1, and provided that women were to receive paid disability benefits for only three weeks after childbirth, §2, even if a particular woman remained disabled beyond the three-week period, and even if a man received paid disability benefits throughout his disability. Finally, although it prohibited employers from refusing to promote a woman because of pregnancy, it did not forbid refusing to hire a woman on that basis. *See* §1; *see also* Brief for National Organization for Women et al. as Amici Curiae at 14–15, in Cal. Fed. Sav. & Loan Ass'n. v. Guerra, 479 U.S. 272 (1987) (No. 85–494). These provisions were all expressly made inapplicable to employers covered by Title VII, "[i]n the event Congress enacts legislation amending Title VII . . . to prohibit sex discrimination on the basis of pregnancy," namely, the PDA. *See* 1978 Cal. Stats. ch. 1321, §4.

[25] See *Joint Hearing on H.R. 925 before the Subcomm. on Civil Service and*

Congress agreed.[26] Adhering to equal-treatment feminists' aim, the self-care provision,[27] prescribes comprehensive leave for women disabled during pregnancy or while recuperating from childbirth—without singling out pregnancy or childbirth.[28] In view of this history, it is impossible to conclude that "nothing in particular about self-care leave . . . connects it to gender discrimination."[29]

II

A

Boerne next asks "whether Congress had evidence of a pattern of constitutional violations on the part of the States."[30] Beyond question, Congress had evidence of a well-documented pattern of workplace discrimination against pregnant women. Section 2612(a)(1)(D) can therefore "be understood as responsive to, or designed to prevent, unconstitutional behavior."[31]

Although the PDA proscribed blatant discrimination on the basis of pregnancy,[32] the Act is fairly described as a necessary, but not a sufficient measure. FMLA hearings conducted between 1986 and

---

the Subcomm. on Compensation and Employee Benefits of the H. Comm. on Post Office and Civil Service, 100th Cong., 1st Sess., 36 (1987) [hereinafter *1987 House Hearing*] (statement of Prof. Eleanor Holmes Norton, Georgetown University Law Center) ("[If *California Fed.*] becomes the model, employers will provide something for women affected by pregnancy that they are not required to provide for other employees. This gives fodder to those who seek to discriminate against women in employment. . . . In the [*California Fed.*] case, I would have preferred the interpretation urged by the [equal-treatment feminists].").

[26] *See infra*, at 14–15.

[27] 29 U.S.C. § 2612(a)(1)(D) (2012).

[28] *See* S. REP. NO. 101–77, at 32 (1989) ("[A] significant benefit of the temporary medical leave provided by this legislation is the form of protection it offers women workers who bear children. Because the bill treats all employees who are temporarily unable to work due to serious health conditions in the same fashion, it does not create the risk of discrimination against pregnant women posed by legislation which provides job protection only for pregnancy-related disability. Legislation solely protecting pregnant women gives employers an economic incentive to discriminate against women in hiring policies; legislation helping all workers equally does not have this effect.").

[29] *Ante*, at 10.

[30] Nev. Dep't. of Human Resources v. Hibbs, 538 U.S. 721, 729 (2003); *see also* City of Boerne v. Flores, 521 U.S. 507, 530–532 (1997).

[31] *Id.*, at 532.

[32] *See* 42 U.S.C. §§ 2000e(k), 2000e–2 (2012), *supra*, at 4, n.2.

1993 included illustrative testimony from women fired after becoming pregnant or giving birth. For example, Beverly Wilkenson was granted seven weeks of leave upon the birth of her child. On the eve of her return to work, a superior informed her that her job had been eliminated. He stated: "Beverly, the best thing for you to do is stay home and take care of your baby and collect your unemployment."[33] Similarly, Linda Pillsbury was notified that she no longer had a job three weeks after her daughter was born.[34] [FN 5] Three secretaries at the same workplace were also forced out of their jobs when they returned to work within weeks of giving birth.[35]

These women's experiences, Congress learned, were hardly isolated incidents. A spokeswoman for the Mayor's Commission on Women's Affairs in Chicago testified: "The lack of uniform parental and medical leave policies in the workplace has created an environment where discrimination is rampant. Very often we are contacted by women workers who are at risk of losing their jobs or have lost them because they are pregnant, [or have] given birth."[36] As summarized by the American Bar Association:

---

[33] *Hearing on H.R. 770 before the Subcomm. on Labor-Management Relations of the H. Comm. on Education and Labor*, 101st Cong., 1st Sess., 12 (1989) [hereinafter *1989 House Hearing*)] (statement of Beverly Wilkenson); *see also* S. *Rep. No.* 102–68, p. 27 (1991) [hereinafter *1991 Senate Report*] (describing Ms. Wilkenson's testimony).

[34] [FN 5] The medical recovery period for a normal childbirth is four to eight weeks. See Nev. Dep't. of Human Resources v. Hibbs, 538 U.S. 721, 731, n.4 (2003).

[35] *See Hearings on S. 249 before the Subcomm. on Children, Family, Drugs and Alcoholism of the S. Comm. on Labor and Human Resources*, 100th Cong., 1st Sess., pt. 2, pp. 16, 23 (1987) [hereinafter *1987 Senate Hearings*] (statement of Linda Pillsbury).

[36] *Id.*, at 170 (statement of Peggy Montes); *see also Joint Hearing on The Parental and Medical Leave Act of 1986 before the Subcomm. on Labor-Management Relations and the Subcomm. on Labor Standards of the H. Comm. on Education and Labor*, 99th Cong., 2d Sess., 110, n.18 (1986) [hereinafter *1986 House Hearing*] (statement of Women's Legal Defense Fund) ("[W]omen who are temporarily unable to work due to pregnancy, child-birth, and related medical conditions such as morning sickness, threatened miscarriage, or complications arising from childbirth, often lose their jobs because of the inadequacy of their employers' leave policies."); S. REP. NO. 28 (1991) (recording that an Atlanta-based job counseling hotline received approximately 100 calls each year from women who were fired, harassed, or forced out of their jobs due to pregnancy or maternity-disability leave); 139 CONG. REC. 1826 (1993) (remarks of Sen. Edward Kennedy) ("[W]omen who are pregnant are discriminated against as a general rule in our society and have difficulty retaining their jobs.").

Historically, denial or curtailment of women's employment opportunities has been traceable directly to the pervasive presumption that women are mothers first, and workers second. This prevailing ideology about women's roles has in turn justified discrimination against women when they are mothers or mothers-to-be.[37]

"Many pregnant women have been fired when their employer refused to provide an adequate leave of absence," Congress had ample cause to conclude.[38] Pregnancy, Congress also found, has a marked impact on women's earnings. One year after childbirth, mothers' earnings fell to $1.40 per hour less than those of women who had not given birth.[39]

Congress heard evidence tying this pattern of discrimination to the States. A 50-state survey by the Yale Bush Center Infant Care Leave Project concluded that "[t]he proportion and construction of leave policies available to public sector employees differs little from those offered private sector employees."[40] Roughly 28% of women employed in the public sector did not receive eight weeks of job-protected medical leave to recover from childbirth.[41] A South Carolina state legislator testified: "[I]n South Carolina, as well as in other states . . . no unemployment compensation is paid to a woman who is necessarily absent from her place of employment because of pregnancy or maternity."[42] According to an employee of the State of Georgia, if state employees took leave, it was held against them when they were considered for promotions: "It is common practice for my Department to compare the balance sheets of workers who have and have not used [leave] benefits in determining who should and should not be promoted."[43] In

---

[37] *1989 House Hearing, supra* note 19, at 248 (American Bar Association Background Report); *see also Hibbs,* 538 U.S., at 736 (quoting same language).

[38] *See* H.R. REP. NO. 99–699, pt. 2, p. 22 (1986).

[39] *See 1991 Senate Report, supra* note 19, at 28; *see also 1989 House Hearing, supra* note 19, at 356–357 (Report of 9to5, National Association of Working Women (citing same study)).

[40] *Hibbs,* 538 U.S., at 730, n.3 (quoting *1986 House Hearing, supra* note 19, at 33 (statement of Meryl Frank)).

[41] *See 1987 Senate Hearings, supra* note 21, pt. 1, pp. 31, 35, 39 (statement of James T. Bond, National Counsel of Jewish Women).

[42] *See id.,* pt. 2, p. 361 (statement of Rep. Irene Rudnick).

[43] *Hearing on H.R. 2 before the Subcomm. on Labor-Management Relations of the H. Comm. on Education and Labor,* 102d Cong., 1st Sess., 36 (1991) (statement of Robert E. Dawkins); *see also id.,* at 33 (One type of leave for Georgia state employees "boils down to whether your supervisor wants you to come back or not").

short, Congress had every reason to believe that a pattern of workplace discrimination against pregnant women existed in public-sector employment, just as it did in the private sector.

B

"[A] state's refusal to provide pregnancy leave to its employees," Maryland responds, is "not unconstitutional."[44] *Aiello*'s footnote 20 proclaimed that discrimination on the basis of pregnancy is not discrimination on the basis of sex. In my view, this case is a fit occasion to revisit that conclusion. Footnote 20 reads:

> "The dissenting opinion to the contrary, this case is
> . . . a far cry from cases like *Reed v. Reed*, 404 U.S. 71
> (1971), and *Frontiero v. Richardson*, 411 U.S. 677
> (1973), involving discrimination based upon gender as
> such. The California insurance program does not exclude anyone from benefit eligibility because of gender
> but merely removes one physical condition—
> pregnancy—from the list of compensable disabilities.
> While it is true that only women can become pregnant, it does not follow that every legislative classification concerning pregnancy is a sex-based
> classification . . . .
> "The lack of identity between the excluded disability and gender as such under this insurance program
> becomes clear upon the most cursory analysis. The
> program divides potential recipients into two groups—
> pregnant women and nonpregnant persons. While the
> first group is exclusively female, the second includes
> members of both sexes. The fiscal and actuarial benefits of the program thus accrue to members of both
> sexes."[45]

First, "[a]s an abstract statement," it is "simply false" that "a classification based on pregnancy is gender-neutral."[46] Rather, discriminating on the basis of pregnancy "[b]y definition . . . discriminates on

---

[44] Brief for Respondents 23 (citing Geduldig v. Aiello, 417 U.S. 484, 495 (1974)).
[45] *Aiello*, 417 U.S., at 496, n.20.
[46] Bray v. Alexandria Women's Health Clinic, 506 U.S. 263, 327 (1993) (Stevens, J., dissenting).

account of sex; for it is the capacity to become pregnant which primarily differentiates the female from the male."[47]

This reality is well illustrated by the facts of *Aiello*. The California disability-insurance program at issue granted disability benefits for virtually any conceivable work disability, including those arising from cosmetic surgery, skiing accidents, and alcoholism.[48] It also compensated men for disabilities caused by ailments and procedures that affected men alone: for example, vasectomies, circumcision, and prostatectomies.[49] Only pregnancy was excluded from the definition of disability.[50] As Justice Brennan insightfully concluded in dissent, "a limitation is imposed upon the disabilities for which women workers may recover, while men receive full compensation for all disabilities suffered . . . . Such dissimilar treatment of men and women, on the basis of physical characteristics inextricably linked to one sex, inevitably constitutes sex discrimination."[51]

Second, pregnancy provided a central justification for the historic discrimination against women this Court chronicled in *Hibbs*.[52] Relatedly, discrimination against pregnant employees was often "based not on the pregnancy itself but on predictions concerning the future behavior of the pregnant woman when her child was born or on views about what her behavior should be."[53]

---

[47] General Elec. Co. v. Gilbert, 429 U.S. 125, 162 (1976) (Stevens, J., dissenting). See also Issacharoff & Rosenblum, *Women and the Workplace: Accommodating the Demands of Pregnancy*, 94 COLUM. L. REV. 2154, 2180 (1994) ("[I]t is precisely because pregnancy is a condition unique to women that the exclusion of pregnancy from disability coverage is a sex-based classification.").

[48] *See* Brief for EEOC as Amicus Curiae at 7, *Aiello*, 417, U.S. 484 (1974), (No. 73–640).

[49] *See* Brief for American Civil Liberties Union et al. as Amici Curiae at 17–18, *Aiello*, 417, U.S. 484 (1974), (No. 73–640).

[50] *See* CAL. UNEMP. INS. CODE § 2626 (West 1972); *Aiello*, 417 U.S., at 489.

[51] *Aiello*, 417 U.S., at 501.

[52] *See* Nev. Dep't. of Human Resources v. Hibbs, 538 U.S., 721, 729 (2003) ("[A] proper discharge of [a woman's] maternal functions—having in view not merely her own health, but the well-being of the race—justif[ies] legislation to protect her from the greed as well as the passion of man.") (quoting Muller v. Oregon, 208 U.S. 412, 422 (1908)) (2d and 3d alterations in *Hibbs*); *see also* Siegel, *Employment Equality Under the Pregnancy Discrimination Act of 1978*, 94 YALE L.J. 929, 942 (1985) ("[Pregnancy] is a biological difference central to the definition of gender roles, one traditionally believed to render women unfit for employment.").

[53] Williams, *supra* note 5, at 355. See also S. REP. NO. 95–331, p. 3 (1977) ("[T]he assumption that women will become pregnant and leave the labor market is at the core of the sex stereotyping resulting in unfavorable disparate treatment of women in the workplace.").

In sum, childbearing is not only a biological function unique to women. It is also inextricably intertwined with employers' "stereotypical views about women's commitment to work and their value as employees."[54] Because pregnancy discrimination is inevitably sex discrimination, and because discrimination against women is tightly interwoven with society's beliefs about pregnancy and motherhood, I would hold that *Aiello* was egregiously wrong to declare that discrimination on the basis of pregnancy is not discrimination on the basis of sex.

C

Boerne's third step requires "'a congruence and proportionality between the injury to be prevented or remedied and the means adopted to that end.'"[55] Section 2612(a)(1)(D), I would conclude, is an appropriate response to pervasive discriminatory treatment of pregnant women. In separating self-care leave for the physical disability following childbirth,[56] which affects only women, from family-care leave for parenting a newborn baby,[57] for which men and women are equally suited, Congress could attack gender discrimination and challenge stereotypes of women as lone childrearers.[58]

It would make scant sense to provide job-protected leave for a woman to care for a newborn, but not for her recovery from delivery, a miscarriage, or the birth of a stillborn baby. And allowing States to provide no pregnancy-disability leave at all, given that only women can become pregnant, would obviously "exclude far more women than men from the workplace."[59]

The plurality's statement that Congress lacked "widespread evidence of sex discrimination . . . in the administration of sick leave,"[60] misses the point. So too does the plurality's observation that state employees likely "could take leave for pregnancy-related illnesses"— presumably severe morning sickness, toxemia, etc.—under paid sick-leave plans.[61] Congress heard evidence that existing sick-leave plans

---

[54] *Hibbs*, 538 U.S., at 736.
[55] *Ante*, at 5 (quoting City of Boerne v. Flores, 521 U.S. 507, 520 (1997)).
[56] 29 U.S.C. § 2612(a)(1)(D) (2012).
[57] § 2612(a)(1)(A).
[58] *Cf. Hibbs*, 538 U.S., at 731 (States' extended "maternity" leaves, far exceeding a woman's physical disability following childbirth, were attributable "to the pervasive sex-role stereotype that caring for family members is women's work").
[59] *Id.*, at 738.
[60] *Ante*, at 6.
[61] *Ante*, at 7.

were inadequate to ensure that women were not fired when they needed to take time out to recover their strength and stamina after childbirth. The self-care provision responds to that evidence by requiring employers to allow leave for "ongoing pregnancy, miscarriages, . . . the need for prenatal care, childbirth, and recovery from childbirth."[62]

That §2612(a)(1)(D) entitles all employees to up to 12 weeks of unpaid, job-protected leave for a serious health condition, rather than singling out pregnancy or childbirth, does not mean that the provision lacks the requisite congruence and proportionality to the identified constitutional violations. As earlier noted,[63] Congress made plain its rationale for the prescription's broader compass: Congress sought to ward off the unconstitutional discrimination it believed would attend a pregnancy-only leave requirement. Under the caption "Equal protection and non-discrimination," Congress explained:

> "The FMLA addresses the basic leave needs of all employees. . . . This is an important principle reflected in the bill.
> "A law providing special protection to women . . . , in addition to being inequitable, runs the risk of causing discriminatory treatment. Employers might be less inclined to hire women . . . . For example, legislation addressing the needs of pregnant women only might encourage discriminatory hiring practices against women of child bearing age. Legislation addressing the needs of all workers equally does not have this effect. By addressing the serious leave needs of all employees, the FMLA avoids providing employers the temptation to discriminate [against women].

"The legislation is [thus] based not only on the Commerce Clause, but also on the guarantees of equal protection . . . embodied in the Fourteenth Amendment."[64]

Congress' concern was solidly grounded in workplace realities. After this Court upheld California's pregnancy-only leave policy in *California Fed.*, Don Butler, President of the Merchants and Manufacturers Association, one of the plaintiffs in that case, told National Public Radio reporter Nina Totenberg that, as a result of the

---

[62] S. REP. NO. 103–3, p. 29 (1993).

[63] *Supra*, at 6–7.

[64] H.R. REP. NO. 102–135, pt. 1, pp. 27–28 (1991) [hereinafter 1991 HOUSE REPORT].

decision, "many employers will be prone to discriminate against women in hiring and hire males instead."[65]

Finally, as in *Hibbs*, it is important to note the moderate cast of the FMLA, in particular, the considerable limitations Congress placed on §§2612(a)(1)(A)–(D)'s leave requirement.[66] FMLA leave is unpaid. It is limited to employees who have worked at least one year for the employer and at least 1,250 hours during the past year.[67] High-ranking employees, including state elected officials and their staffs, are not within the Act's compass.[68] Employees must provide advance notice of foreseeable leaves.[69] Employers may require a doctor's certification of a serious health condition.[70] And, if an employer violates the FMLA, the employees' recoverable damages are "strictly defined and measured by actual monetary losses."[71] The self-care provision, I would therefore hold, is congruent and proportional to the injury to be prevented.

III

But even if *Aiello* senselessly holds sway, and impedes the conclusion that §2612(a)(1)(D) is an appropriate response to the States' unconstitutional discrimination against pregnant women,[72] [FN 6] I would

---

[65] *1987 House Hearing, supra* note 11, at 36. Totenberg replied, "But that is illegal, too"—to which Butler responded, "Well, that is illegal, but try to prove it." *Id.*

[66] *See* Nev. Dep't. of Human Resources v. Hibbs, 538 U.S. 721, 738–739 (2003).

[67] 29 U.S.C. §§ 2611(2)(A), 2612(c)(1) (2012).

[68] §§ 203(e)(2)(C), 2611(3).

[69] § 2612(e).

[70] § 2613(a).

[71] *Hibbs*, 538 U.S., at 740 (citing §§2617(a)(1)(A)(i)–(iii)).

[72] [FN 6] Notably, the plurality does not cite or discuss *Geduldig v. Aiello*, perhaps embarrassed by that opinion's widely criticized conclusion that discrimination based on pregnancy does not involve "discrimination based upon gender as such," *id.*, at 496, n.20. *See supra*, at 10–13; E. CHEMERINSKY, CONSTITUTIONAL LAW 759 (3d ed. 2006) ("It is hard to imagine a clearer sex-based distinction" than the one at issue in *Aiello*.); Kay, *Equality and Difference: The Case of Pregnancy*, 1 BERKELEY WOMEN'S L.J. 1, 31 (1985) ("[*Aiello*] results in unequal treatment of similarly situated women and men who have engaged respectively in reproductive conduct [and wish to continue working]. It should be overruled."); Law, *Rethinking Sex and the Constitution*, 132 U. PA. L. REV. 955, 983–984 (1984) ("Criticizing [*Aiello*] has . . . become a cottage industry. Over two dozen law review articles have condemned both the Court's approach and the result. . . . Even the principal scholarly defense of [*Aiello*] admits that the Court was wrong in refusing to recognize that the

nevertheless conclude that the FMLA is valid §5 legislation. For it is a meet response to "the States' record of unconstitutional participation in, and fostering of, gender-based discrimination in the administration of [parental and family-care] leave benefits."[73]

Requiring States to provide gender-neutral parental and family-care leave alone, Congress was warned, would promote precisely the type of workplace discrimination Congress sought to reduce. The "pervasive sex-role stereotype that caring for family members is women's work,"[74] Congress heard, led employers to regard required parental and family-care leave as a woman's benefit. Carol Ball, speaking on behalf of the U.S. Chamber of Commerce, testified that she did not think "there are going to be many men that take up . . . parental leave."[75] She frankly admitted that she herself would choose to hire a man over an equally qualified woman if parental leave was required by law.[76]

Others similarly testified that mandating gender-neutral parental leave would lead to discrimination against women. A representative of the National Federal of Independent Business stated: "Requiring employers to provide parental leave benefits creates clear pressures for subtle discrimination based on . . . sex. When choosing between two equally qualified candidates, an employer may be more likely to hire the candidate least likely to take the leave. It is the wage levels and jobs of women of childbearing years which are most at risk in such a situation."[77]

---

classification was sex-based."); Karst, *The Supreme Court 1976 Term Foreword: Equal Citizenship under the Fourteenth Amendment*, 91 HARV. L. REV. 1, 54, n.304 (1977) ("[T]he constitutional sport of [*Aiello*] and last Term's even sillier statutory counterpart, *General Elec. Co. v. Gilbert*, , with their Alice-in-Wonderland view of pregnancy as a sex-neutral phenomenon, are good candidates for early retirement. These decisions are textbook examples of the effects of underrepresentation on 'legislative' insensitivity. Imagine what the presence of even one woman Justice would have meant to the Court's conferences.").

[73] *Hibbs*, 538 U.S., at 735; *see also id.*, at 729–731, and n.5 (Congress adduced evidence "of a pattern of constitutional violations on the part of the States" in granting parental and family-care leave).

[74] *Id.*, at 731.

[75] *See Hearing on S. 345 before the Subcomm. on Children, Family, Drugs, and Alcoholism of the S. Comm. on Labor and Human Resources*, 101st Cong., 1st Sess., 39 (1989) (statement of Carol Ball).

[76] *Id.*, at 30.

[77] *Hearing on H.R. 1 before the Subcomm. on Labor-Management Relations of the H. Comm. on Education and Labor*, 103d Cong., 1st Sess., 95 (1993); *see also 1989 House Hearing, supra* note 19, at 169 (statement of Cynthia Simpler, American Society for Personnel Administration) ("Since working women

Conversely—unlike perceptions surrounding who takes parental and family-care leave—Congress was told that men and women take medical leave approximately equally. According to one study, male workers missed an average of 4.9 days of work per year due to illness or injury; female workers missed 5.1 days.[78] "[T]he incidence of serious medical conditions that would be covered by medical leave under the bill," Congress determined, "is virtually the same for men and women. Employers will find that women and men will take medical leave with equal frequency."[79] "[P]arental and medical leave," Congress was thus alerted, "are inseparable":

"In the words of an old song, 'You can't have one without the other.'

"Adoption of parental leave protections without medical leave would . . . encourage discrimination against women of child-bearing age, who constitute approximately 73 percent of all the women in the labor force.

"Employers would tend to hire men, who are much less likely to claim [the parental leave] benefit. . . .

"Parental leave without medical leave would be the modern version of protective labor laws."[80]

Congress therefore had good reason to conclude that the self-care provision—which men no doubt would use—would counter employers' impressions that the FMLA would otherwise install female leave. Providing for self-care would thus reduce employers' corresponding incentive to discriminate against women in hiring and promotion. In other words, "[t]he availability of self-care leave to men serves to blunt the force of stereotypes of women as primary caregivers by increasing the odds that men and women will invoke the FMLA's leave provisions in near-equal numbers."[81] As Judge Lipez explained:

"If Congress had drawn a line at leave for caring for other family members, there is greater likelihood that the FMLA

---

will be viewed as the most likely candidates for parental leave, hidden discrimination will occur if this bill becomes law. Women of child-bearing age will be viewed as risks, potentially disrupting operations through an untimely leave.").

[78] See 1991 HOUSE REPORT, *supra* note 50 pt. 1, p. 28.

[79] *Id.*

[80] *1986 House Hearing, supra* note 22, at 33–34 (Statement of Irene Natividad, National Women's Political Caucus).

[81] *See* Brief for National Partnership for Women & Families et al. as Amici Curiae 26.

would have been perceived as further reason to avoid granting employment opportunities to women. Heretofore, women have provided most of the child and elder care, and legislation that focused on these duties could have had a deleterious impact because of the prevalent notion that women take more advantage of such leave policies. The inclusion of personal medical leave in the scheme, unrelated to any need to care for another person, undermines the assumption that women are the only ones taking leave because men, presumably, are as likely as women to get sick."[82]

Senator Barbara Boxer advanced a similar point. Responding to assertions that the FMLA would lead employers to discriminate against women, Senator Boxer stated: "[T]o say that women will not be hired by business is a specious argument . . . . Men also get sick. They get cancer. They get heart disease. They have ailments. And this bill applies to men and women."[83]

The plurality therefore gets it wrong in concluding that "[o]nly supposition and conjecture support the contention that the self-care provision is necessary to make the family-care provisions effective."[84] Self-care leave, I would hold, is a key part of Congress' endeavor to make it feasible for women to work and have families.[85] By reducing an employer's perceived incentive to avoid hiring women, §2612(a)(1)(D) lessens the risk that the FMLA as a whole would give rise to the very sex discrimination it was enacted to thwart. The plurality offers no legitimate ground to dilute the force of the Act.

---

[82] Laro v. New Hampshire, 259 F. 3d 1, 21 (1st Cir. 2001) (dissenting opinion).
[83] 139 CONG. REC. 1697 (1993); *see also 1987 Senate Hearings, supra* note 21, pt. 2, p. 536 (statement of Prof. Susan Deller Ross, Georgetown University Law Center) ("I just think it's wrong that there will be a perception that this is something that only women will take and they are, therefore, more expensive. Both men and women have medical conditions.").
[84] *Ante*, at 9.
[85] See *1991 Senate Report, supra* note 19, at 25–26 ("This legislation is essential if the nation is to address the dramatic changes that have occurred in the American workforce in recent years. . . . The once-typical American family, where the father worked for pay and the mother stayed at home with the children, is vanishing. . . . Today, more than one-half of all mothers with infants under one year of age work outside the home. That figure has doubled since 1970 . . . . By the year 2000, about three out of every four American children will have mothers in the workforce.").

IV

Two additional points. First, this Court reached a different conclusion than the one I reach here in *Board of Trustees of Univ. of Ala. v. Garrett*,[86] and *Kimel*.[87] In those cases, as we observed in *Hibbs*, we reviewed statutes targeting disability and age discrimination, respectively. Neither disability nor age is a suspect classification under this Court's Equal Protection Clause jurisprudence; States may discriminate on the basis of disability or age as long as the classification is rationally related to a legitimate state interest.[88] Therefore, for the statutes to be responsive to or designed to prevent unconstitutional discrimination, Congress needed to rely on a pattern of irrational state discrimination on the basis of disability or age.[89] Here, however, Congress homed in on gender discrimination, which triggers heightened review.[90] "[I]t was [therefore] easier for Congress to show a pattern of state constitutional violations."[91]

Finally, the plurality's opinion does not authorize state employers to violate the FMLA, although it does block injured employees from suing for monetary relief. The self-care provision remains valid Commerce Clause legislation, Maryland concedes, and consequently binds the states, as well as the private sector.[92] An employee wrongly denied self-care leave, Maryland also acknowledges, may, pursuant to *Ex parte Young*,[93] seek injunctive relief against the responsible state official.[94] Moreover, the U.S. Department of Labor may bring an action against a state for violating the self-care provision and may recover monetary relief on an employee's behalf.[95]

V

The plurality pays scant attention to the overarching aim of the FMLA: to make it feasible for women to work while sustaining family life. Over the course of eight years, Congress considered the problem

---

[86] 531 U.S. 356 (2001).

[87] 528 U.S. 62 (2000).

[88] *See Garrett*, 531 U.S., at 366–367; *Kimel*, 528 U.S., at 83–84.

[89] *See Garrett*, 531 U.S., at 368; *Kimel*, 528 U.S., at 89.

[90] See *United States v. Virginia*, 518 U.S. 515, 531 (1996) ("Parties who seek to defend gender-based government action must demonstrate an exceedingly persuasive justification for that action.") (internal quotation marks omitted).

[91] Nev. Dep't. of Human Resources v. Hibbs, 538 U.S. 721, 736 (2003).

[92] Tr. of Oral Arg. 25; Brief for Respondents 32–33.

[93] 209 U.S. 123 (1908).

[94] *See* Brief for Respondents 33.

[95] 29 U.S.C. §§ 2617(b)(2)–(3), (d) (2012).

of workplace discrimination against women, and devised the FMLA to reduce sex-based inequalities in leave programs. Essential to its design, Congress assiduously avoided a legislative package that, overall, was or would be seen as geared to women only. Congress thereby reduced employers' incentives to prefer men over women, advanced women's economic opportunities, and laid the foundation for a more egalitarian relationship at home and at work. The self-care provision is a key part of that endeavor, and, in my view, a valid exercise of congressional power under §5 of the Fourteenth Amendment. I would therefore reverse the judgment of the U.S. Court of Appeals for the Fourth Circuit.

CARHART

"As Casey comprehended, at stake in cases challenging abortion restrictions is a woman's control over her own destiny."

The Case

In 2003, Congress passed the Partial-Birth Abortion Ban Act, which prohibited an abortion procedure called "intact dilation and extraction" ("intact D&E") after the first trimester of pregnancy.[1] Many in the medical community considered this an inappropriate restriction on an accepted method of performing abortions. After the Act's passage, four doctors who practiced this procedure in Nebraska, including LeRoy Carhart, filed suit in the United States District Court for the District of Nebraska challenging the constitutionality of the Act and seeking a permanent injunction against its enforcement. The district court sided with the plaintiffs and enjoined enforcement of the Act. The Eighth Circuit Court of Appeals affirmed, finding the Act unconstitutional because it did not contain an exception for protecting the health of the mother.

Meanwhile, the San Francisco branch of Planned Parenthood filed a second, similar federal lawsuit in California. The district court there also found the Act unconstitutional and enjoined its enforcement. On appeal, the Ninth Circuit Court of Appeals affirmed. Finally, the constitutionality of the Act was challenged in the United States District Court for the Southern District of New York, which also found it unconstitutional. That decision was subsequently affirmed by the Second Circuit Court of Appeals.

Justice Kennedy's Majority Opinion

Prior to his retirement, Justice Anthony Kennedy developed a reputation as the Court's "swing Justice" because he frequently provided the deciding vote in various decisions that otherwise saw an even split between the Court's conservative and liberal wings. As the

---

[1] "Intact D&E" is one of several clinical terms used for abortions of this type; the term "partial-birth abortion" is non-medical colloquial terminology used to describe the same procedure.

crucial fifth vote, Justice Kennedy authored the majority opinion in *Planned Parenthood v. Casey*—arguably now more important than *Roe v. Wade,* though less well known— in which a 5-4 plurality[2] of the Court reaffirmed the central holding of *Roe,* stating that "matters [including abortion] involving the most intimate and personal choices a person may make in a lifetime, choices central to personal dignity and autonomy, are central to the liberty protected by the Fourteenth Amendment," thereby preserving the constitutional right to abortion enshrined by *Roe.*[3] In *Carhart,* by contrast, Justice Kennedy swung the other way and sided with the Court's conservatives in upholding a law designed to restrict abortion rights.

Notably, the majority in *Carhart* did not begin by reaffirming the original holding of *Roe,* as augmented by *Casey*; instead, the majority referenced those cases as "precedents we here assume to be controlling."[4] That distinction is subtle, but critical: the majority was assuming that *Roe* and *Casey* controlled, but not stating outright that they were correctly decided. This represented a landmark shift in Supreme Court jurisprudence toward a more favorable approach to restrictions on abortion rights. Nonetheless, the majority in *Carhart* did purport to reach its decision in line with the "principle" affirmed in *Casey* that "a State 'may not prohibit any woman from making the ultimate decision to terminate her pregnancy'"[5] and "may not impose upon this right an undue burden, which exists if a regulation's 'purpose or effect is to place a substantial obstacle in the path of a woman seeking an abortion before the fetus attains viability.'"[6] Ultimately, *Carhart* probed the parameters of *Roe* and *Casey* and placed implied restrictions on their extension, but did not explicitly undermine their precedential authority.

Reaching the substance of the Act, the majority upheld it as constitutional. Specifically, the majority addressed two issues: whether the Ban's language was too vague to be enforceable, and whether it was unduly burdensome to women seeking an abortion because its restrictions on abortion were overly broad—to include whether or not the law could possibly endanger women's health. The majority easily dispensed with the first issue. Relying on the plain language of the Act, it concluded the language was sufficiently specific and objective

---

[2] Two of the Justices in *Casey* agreed with the result but did not join Justice Kennedy's opinion, such that the opinion itself was only for a plurality of the Court.

[3] Planned Parenthood of Se. Pa. v. Casey, 505 U.S. 833, 851 (1992).

[4] Gonzales v. Carhart, 550 U.S. 124, 161 (2007).

[5] *Id.* (quoting *Casey,* 505 U.S. at 879).

[6] *Id.* (quoting *Casey,* 505 U.S. at 878).

to ensure the medical community understood what was proscribed and what was not.[7]

The second issue required more exacting analysis. The majority found that the objectives which Congress expounded in justifying the Act—which it articulated as "respect for the dignity of human life" and "protecting the integrity and ethics of the medical profession"[8]— to be legitimate, and concluded the "Act's ban on abortions that involve partial delivery of a living fetus furthers [those] objectives."[9] The majority seemed particularly concerned with the brutality of certain procedures utilized during partial birth abortion, and even quoted graphic testimony from the record, which included harsh, almost violent descriptions of the procedure.[10]

The majority then took up the issue of medical necessity, and whether the Act unconstitutionally burdened abortion rights by disallowing intact D&E when the procedure was necessary for the health of the mother. The majority observed that medical arguments existed both for and against such medical necessity, examining some of both, and ultimately asked "whether the Act can stand when this medical uncertainty persists."[11] The Court answered this question in the affirmative, observing that both state and federal legislatures retained "wide discretion to pass legislation in areas where there is medical and scientific uncertainty."[12] Notably, the majority appeared to hedge when attempting to justify the constitutionality of the Act; it did not offer a blanket assertion that the Act was unconstitutional, instead observing only that it was not "invalid on its face where there is uncertainty over whether the barred procedure is ever necessary to preserve a woman's health, given the availability of other abortion procedures that are considered to be safe alternatives."[13] The majority also explicitly stated that the Act remained open to a constitutional "as-applied challenge," meaning it would still be possible for an individual in unique circumstances to demonstrate that the act was unconstitutional "as applied" to those particular circumstances.[14]

---

[7] *See id.* at 146–50.

[8] *Id.* at 157.

[9] *Id.* at 158.

[10] *See id.* at 134–40, 158–60.

[11] *Id.* at 161–163.

[12] *Id.* at 163.

[13] *Id.* at 166–67.

[14] *Id.* at 167.

Justice Thomas's Concurring Opinion

Justice Thomas' concurring opinion, which was joined by Justice Scalia, was one paragraph long. It simply reiterated his view, long held, that "the Court's abortion jurisprudence, including" *Casey* and *Roe*, "has no basis in the Constitution," thereby implying his belief that the entirety of that jurisprudence should be overturned.[15] His concurrence is nonetheless important because it signals the desire of two members of the Court to extirpate the constitutional right to abortion entirely. This point is revelatory because it adumbrates that when conservative political activists call for the appointment of more judges in the mold of Thomas, they are often explicitly asking for judges who are willing to overturn *Roe* and its progeny.

Justice Ginsburg's Dissent

Prior to her appointment to the Supreme Court, Ruth Bader Ginsburg was a nationally-renowned women's rights advocate and a vocal supporter of abortion rights—she had even offered her endorsement of abortion rights during her confirmation hearings. Accordingly, Justice Ginsburg's dissent situated the issue before the Court in *Carhart* not in the context of the right to privacy (the grounds on which *Roe* had validated abortion), but of the personal autonomy and equal citizenship to which she believed all women are entitled: "legal challenges to undue restrictions on abortion procedures do not seek to vindicate some generalized notion of privacy; rather, they center on a woman's autonomy to determine her life's course, and thus to enjoy equal citizenship stature."[16]

Noting that the Court's prior abortion decisions had uniformly indicated that regulations of abortion must protect the health of the woman to survive constitutional scrutiny, Ginsburg believed that the majority had abandoned these precedents without justification. In an especially damning feat of tactical analysis, she applied the reasoning of the majority in *Casey*—an opinion which Justice Kennedy had also authored, and which the *Carhart* majority had indicated was controlling—and demonstrated that under *Casey's* rationale, the majority should have reached the exact opposite conclusion—finding the Act to be unconstitutional because "as long as 'substantial medical authority supports the proposition that banning a particular abortion procedure

---

[15] *See id.* at 169 (Thomas, J., concurring).
[16] *Id.* at 172 (Ginsburg, J., dissenting).

could endanger women's health, *Casey* requires the statute to include a health exception."' [17]

Next, Justice Ginsburg assailed the validity of the evidence upon which the majority so heavily relied. She first demonstrated that the Congressional findings cited by the majority in upholding the Act were not only one-sided and inaccurate, but intentionally so: "'[T]he oral testimony before Congress was not only unbalanced, but intentionally polemic.'"[18] She then analyzed the opinions of various District Courts which had previously considered bans on intact D&E, finding that those courts had heard from numerous well-qualified medical experts who had "explained that in certain circumstances and for certain women, intact D&E is safer than alternative procedures and necessary to protect women's health."[19] She provided an exhaustive accounting of the substantive bases for these opinions before observing that "each of the District Courts to consider the issue rejected Congress' findings as unreasonable and not supported by the evidence."[20] Noting that the majority "supplie[d] no reason to reject those findings," Ginsburg found the majority's assertion that the Act could survive when medical uncertainty persisted to be "bewildering" because it "def[ied] the Court's longstanding precedent affirming the necessity of a health exception, with no carve-out for circumstances of medical uncertainty."[21]

In other words, through careful and exacting analysis which parsed the record and the wording of the Court's prior decisions, Ginsburg implicitly demonstrated that Justice Kennedy was guilty of pretense. The weight of his own reasoning in *Casey* should have compelled him to reach the conclusion reached by Justice Ginsburg and the minority in *Carhart*. Yet he did not, causing Justice Ginsburg to levy an unusually personal (and poignant) jab at Kennedy by calling the reasoning of his majority opinion "flimsy and transparent."[22] She hinted that the majority's opinion was, instead, results-driven: the majority simply did not like the practice of intact D&E ("Ultimately, the Court admits that 'moral concerns' are at work . . ."),[23] and was therefore determined to find whatever justifications it could, no matter how inconsistent, biased, or strained, to let the Act stand.

---

[17] *Id.* at 174 (quoting Stenberg v. Carhart, 530 U.S. 914, 938 (2000)).
[18] *Id.* at 175 (quoting Planned Parenthood Fed'n of Am. v. Ashcroft, 320 F. Supp. 2d 957, 1019 (N.D. Cal. 2004)).
[19] *Id.* at 177.
[20] *Id.* at 178–79.
[21] *Id.* at 179.
[22] *Id.* at 181.
[23] *Id.*at 182.

Justice Ginsburg concluded with a brief discussion that was especially critical of the majority's failure to reaffirm *Roe* and *Casey*, instead of only "assum[ing]" their applicability.[24] She accused the
majority of infidelity to the Court's "earlier invocations of 'the rule of
law' and the 'principles of *stare decisis*,'"[25] which is a doctrine dictat-
ing that the Court should generally honor its prior precedents and not
flout or contravene them. For that reason, Ginsburg was of the firm
belief that a "decision so at odds with our jurisprudence should not
have staying power."[26]

---

[24] *See id.* at 161 (majority opinion).
[25] *Id.* at 191 (Ginsburg, J., dissenting).
[26] *Id.*

GONZALES V. CARHART

JUSTICE GINSBURG, with whom JUSTICE STEVENS, JUSTICE SOUTER, and JUSTICE BREYER join, Dissenting.

In *Planned Parenthood of Southeastern Pa. v. Casey*, the Court declared that "[l]iberty finds no refuge in a jurisprudence of doubt."[1] There was, the Court said, an "imperative" need to dispel doubt as to "the meaning and reach" of the Court's 7-to-2 judgment, rendered nearly two decades earlier in *Roe v. Wade*.[2] Responsive to that need, the Court endeavored to provide secure guidance to "[s]tate and federal courts as well as legislatures throughout the Union," by defining "the rights of the woman and the legitimate authority of the State respecting the termination of pregnancies by abortion procedures."[3]

Taking care to speak plainly, the *Casey* Court restated and reaffirmed *Roe's* essential holding.[4] First, the Court addressed the type of abortion regulation permissible prior to fetal viability. It recognized "the right of the woman to choose to have an abortion before viability and to obtain it without undue interference from the State."[5] Second, the Court acknowledged "the State's power to restrict abortions after fetal viability, if the law contains exceptions for pregnancies which endanger the woman's life or health."[6] Third, the Court confirmed that "the State has legitimate interests from the outset of the pregnancy in protecting the health of the woman and the life of the fetus that may become a child."[7]

In reaffirming *Roe*, the *Casey* Court described the centrality of "the decision whether to bear . . . a child,"[8] to a woman's "dignity and autonomy," her "personhood" and "destiny," her "conception of . . . her place in society."[9] Of signal importance here, the *Casey* Court

---

[1] 505 U.S. 833, 844 (1992).

[2] *Id.* at 845 (citing Roe v. Wade, 505 U.S. 113, 845 (1973)).

[3] *Id.*

[4] *Id.* at 845–46.

[5] *Id.* at 846.

[6] *Id.* (emphasis added).

[7] *Id.* (emphasis added).

[8] Eisenstadt v. Baird, 405 U.S. 438, 453 (1972).

[9] *Casey*, 505 U.S. at 851–52.

stated with unmistakable clarity that state regulation of access to abortion procedures, even after viability, must protect "the health of the woman."[10]

Seven years ago, in *Stenberg v. Carhart*,[11] the Court invalidated a Nebraska statute criminalizing the performance of a medical procedure that, in the political arena, has been dubbed "partial-birth abortion."[12] [FN1] With fidelity to the *Roe-Casey* line of precedent, the Court held the Nebraska statute unconstitutional in part because it lacked the requisite protection for the preservation of a woman's health.[13]

Today's decision is alarming. It refuses to take *Casey* and *Stenberg* seriously. It tolerates, indeed applauds, federal intervention to ban nationwide a procedure found necessary and proper in certain cases by the American College of Obstetricians and Gynecologists (ACOG). It blurs the line, firmly drawn in *Casey*, between previability and postviability abortions. And, for the first time since *Roe*, the Court blesses a prohibition with no exception safeguarding a woman's health.

I dissent from the Court's disposition. Retreating from prior rulings that abortion restrictions cannot be imposed absent an exception safeguarding a woman's health, the Court upholds an Act that surely would not survive under the close scrutiny that previously attended state-decreed limitations on a woman's reproductive choices.

I

A

As *Casey* comprehended, at stake in cases challenging abortion restrictions is a woman's "control over her [own] destiny."[14; 15] [FN2]

---

[10] *Id.* at 846.

[11] 530 U.S. 914 (2000).

[12] [FN1] The term "partial-birth abortion" is neither recognized in the medical literature nor used by physicians who perform second-trimester abortions. *See* Planned Parenthood Fed'n of Am. v. Ashcroft, 320 F. Supp. 2d 957, 964 (N.D. Cal. 2004), *aff'd*, 435 F.3d 1163 (9th Cir. 2006). The medical community refers to the procedure as either dilation & extraction (D&X) or intact dilation and evacuation (intact D&E). *See, e.g.*, Gonzales v. Carhart, 550 U.S. 124, 136 (2007); Stenberg v. Carhart, 530 U.S. 914, 927 (2000).

[13] *Stenberg*, 530 U.S. at 930; *cf.* Ayotte v. Planned Parenthood of N. New England, 546 U.S. 320, 327 (2006).

[14] *Casey*, 505 U.S. at 869 (plurality opinion); *see also id.* at 852 (majority opinion).

[15] [FN2] *Planned Parenthood of Southeastern Pennsylvania v. Casey*, 505 U.S. 833, 851–52 (1992), described more precisely than did *Roe v. Wade*, 410 U.S.

"There was a time, not so long ago," when women were "regarded as the center of home and family life, with attendant special responsibilities that precluded full and independent legal status under the Constitution."[16] Those views, this Court made clear in *Casey*, "are no longer consistent with our understanding of the family, the individual, or the Constitution."[17] Women, it is now acknowledged, have the talent, capacity, and right "to participate equally in the economic and social life of the Nation."[18] Their ability to realize their full potential, the Court recognized, is intimately connected to "their ability to control their reproductive lives."[19] Thus, legal challenges to undue restrictions on abortion procedures do not seek to vindicate some generalized notion of privacy; rather, they center on a woman's autonomy to determine her life's course, and thus to enjoy equal citizenship stature.[20]

In keeping with this comprehension of the right to reproductive choice, the Court has consistently required that laws regulating abortion, at any stage of pregnancy and in all cases, safeguard a woman's health.[21]

We have thus ruled that a State must avoid subjecting women to health risks not only where the pregnancy itself creates danger, but also where state regulation forces women to resort to less safe methods of abortion.[22] Indeed, we have applied the rule that abortion regulation

---

113 (1973), the impact of abortion restrictions on women's liberty. *Roe*'s focus was in considerable measure on "vindicat[ing] the right of the physician to administer medical treatment according to his professional judgment." *Id.* at 165.

[16] *Casey*, 505 U.S. at 896–97 (quoting Hoyt v. Florida, 368 U.S. 57, 62 (1961)).

[17] *Id.* at 897.

[18] *Id.* at 856.

[19] *Id.*

[20] *See, e.g.*, Reva Siegel, *Reasoning from the Body: A Historical Perspective on Abortion Regulation and Questions of Equal Protection*, 44 STAN. L. REV. 261 (1992); Sylvia A. Law, *Rethinking Sex and the Constitution*, 132 U. PA. L. REV. 955, 1002–28 (1984).

[21] *See, e.g.*, Ayotte v. Planned Parenthood of N. New England, 546 U.S. 320, 327–28 (2006) (quoting *Casey*, 505 U.S. at 879 (plurality opinion) ("[O]ur precedents hold . . . that a State may not restrict access to abortions that are necessary, in appropriate medical judgment, for preservation of the life or health of the [woman]."); Stenberg v. Carhart, 530 U.S. 914, 930 (2000) ("Since the law requires a health exception in order to validate even a postviability abortion regulation, it at a minimum requires the same in respect to previability regulation."); *see also* Thornburgh v. Am. Coll. of Obstetricians and Gynecologists, 476 U.S. 747, 768–69 (1986) (invalidating a post-viability abortion regulation for "fail[ure] to require that [a pregnant woman's] health be the physician's paramount consideration").

[22] *See* Planned Parenthood of Cent. Mo. v. Danforth, 428 U.S. 52, 79 (1976)

must safeguard a woman's health to the particular procedure at issue here—intact dilation and evacuation (D&E).[23 [FN3]]

In *Stenberg*, we expressly held that a statute banning intact D&E was unconstitutional in part because it lacked a health exception.[24] We noted that there existed a "division of medical opinion" about the relative safety of intact D&E,[25] but we made clear that as long as "substantial medical authority supports the proposition that banning

---

(holding unconstitutional a ban on a method of abortion that "force[d] a woman . . . to terminate her pregnancy by methods more dangerous to her health"); *see also Stenberg*, 530 U.S. at 931 ("[Our cases] make clear that a risk to . . . women's health is the same whether it happens to arise from regulating a particular method of abortion, or from barring abortion entirely.").

[23] [FN3] Dilation and evacuation (D&E) is the most frequently used abortion procedure during the second trimester of pregnancy; intact D&E is a variant of the D&E procedure. *See* Gonzales v. Carhart, 550 U.S. 124, 135, 137 (2007); *Stenberg*, 530 U.S. at 924, 927; Planned Parenthood Fed'n of Am. v. Ashcroft, 320 F. Supp. 2d 957, 966 (2004). Second-trimester abortions (i.e., midpregnancy, previability abortions) are, however, relatively uncommon. Between 85 and 90 percent of all abortions performed in the United States take place during the first three months of pregnancy. *Gonzales*, 550 U.S. at 134; *see also Stenberg*, 530 U.S. at 923–27; Nat'l Abortion Fed'n v. Ashcroft, 330 F. Supp. 2d 436, 464 (S.D.N.Y. 2004), *aff'd sub nom.* Nat'l Abortion Fed'n v. Gonzales, 437 F.3d 278 (2d Cir. 2006); *Planned Parenthood Fed'n of Am.*, 320 F. Supp. 2d at 960 & n.4.

Adolescents and indigent women, research suggests, are more likely than other women to have difficulty obtaining an abortion during the first trimester of pregnancy. Minors may be unaware they are pregnant until relatively late in pregnancy, while poor women's financial constraints are an obstacle to timely receipt of services. *See* Lawrence B. Finer, Lori F. Frohwirth, Lindsay A. Dauphinee, Shusheela Singh & Ann M. Moore, *Timing of Steps and Reasons for Delays in Obtaining Abortions in the United States*, 74 CONTRACEPTION 334, 341–43 (2006); *see also* Eleanor A. Drey et al., *Risk Factors Associated with Presenting for Abortion in the Second Trimester*, 107 OBSTETRICS & GYNECOLOGY 128, 133 (2006) (concluding that women who have second-trimester abortions typically discover relatively late that they are pregnant). Severe fetal anomalies and health problems confronting the pregnant woman are also causes of second-trimester abortions; many such conditions cannot be diagnosed or do not develop until the second trimester. *See, e.g.*, Finer, Frohwirth, Dauphinee, Singh & Moore, *supra*, at 344; F. CUNNINGHAM ET AL., WILLIAMS OBSTETRICS 242, 290, 328–29, (22d ed. 2005); *cf.* Kenneth B. Schechtman, Diana L. Gray, Jack D. Baty & Steven M. Rothman, *Decision-Making for Termination of Pregnancies with Fetal Anomalies: Analysis of 53,000 Pregnancies*, 99 OBSTETRICS & GYNECOLOGY 216, 220–21 (2002) (nearly all women carrying fetuses with the most serious central nervous system anomalies chose to abort their pregnancies).

[24] *Stenberg*, 530 U.S. at 930, 937.

[25] *Id.* at 937.

a particular abortion procedure could endanger women's health," a health exception is required.[26] We explained:

> The word 'necessary' in *Casey's* phrase 'necessary, in appropriate medical judgment, for the preservation of the life or health of the [pregnant woman],' cannot refer to an absolute necessity or to absolute proof. Medical treatments and procedures are often considered appropriate (or inappropriate) in light of estimated comparative health risks (and health benefits) in particular cases. Neither can that phrase require unanimity of medical opinion. Doctors often differ in their estimation of comparative health risks and appropriate treatment. And *Casey's* words 'appropriate medical judgment' must embody the judicial need to tolerate responsible differences of medical opinion . . . .[27]

Thus, we reasoned, division in medical opinion "at most means uncertainty, a factor that signals the presence of risk, not its absence."[28] "[A] statute that altogether forbids [intact D&E] . . . consequently must contain a health exception."[29]

B

In 2003, a few years after our ruling in *Stenberg*, Congress passed the Partial-Birth Abortion Ban Act—without an exception for women's health.[30; 31 [FN4]] The congressional findings on which the Partial-Birth Abortion Ban Act rests do not withstand inspection, as the lower courts have determined and this Court is obliged to concede.[32]

---

[26] *Id.* at 938.

[27] *Id.* at 937 (citation omitted).

[28] *Id.*

[29] *Id.* at 938. *See also id.* at 948 (O'Connor, J., concurring) ("Th[e] lack of a health exception necessarily renders the statute unconstitutional.").

[30] *See* 18 U.S.C. § 1531(a) (2000 ed., Supp. IV).

[31] [FN4] The Act's sponsors left no doubt that their intention was to nullify our ruling in *Stenberg*, 530 U.S. 914. *See, e.g.,* 149 CONG. REC. 5,731 (2003) (statement of Sen. Santorum) ("Why are we here? We are here because the Supreme Court defended the indefensible . . . . We have responded to the Supreme Court."); *see also* 148 CONG. REC. 14,273 (2002) (statement of Rep. Linder) (rejecting proposition that Congress has "no right to legislate a ban on this horrible practice because the Supreme Court says [it] cannot").

[32] Gonzales v. Carhart, 550 U.S. 124, 164–66 (2007); *see* Nat'l Abortion Fed'n v. Ashcroft, 330 F. Supp. 2d 436, 482 (S.D.N.Y. 2004) ("Congress did not . . . carefully consider the evidence before arriving at its findings."), *aff'd sub nom.* Nat'l Abortion Fed'n v. Gonzales, 437 F.3d 278 (2d Cir. 2006); *see also* Planned Parenthood Fed'n of Am. v. Ashcroft, 320 F. Supp. 2d 957, 1019 (N.D. Cal. 2004) ("[N]one of the six physicians who testified before Congress

Many of the Act's recitations are incorrect.[33] For example, Congress determined that no medical schools provide instruction on intact D&E.[34] But in fact, numerous leading medical schools teach the procedure.[35]

More important, Congress claimed there was a medical consensus that the banned procedure is never necessary.[36] But the evidence "very clearly demonstrate[d] the opposite."[37]

Similarly, Congress found that "[t]here is no credible medical evidence that partial-birth abortions are safe or are safer than other abortion procedures."[38] But the congressional record includes letters from numerous individual physicians stating that pregnant women's health would be jeopardized under the Act, as well as statements from nine professional associations, including ACOG, the American Public Health Association, and the California Medical Association, attesting that intact D&E carries meaningful safety advantages over

---

had ever performed an intact D&E. Several did not provide abortion services at all; and one was not even an obgyn . . . . [T]he oral testimony before Congress was not only unbalanced, but intentionally polemic."), *aff'd*, 435 F.3d 1163 (9th Cir. 2006); Carhart v. Ashcroft, 331 F. Supp. 2d 805, 1011 (D. Neb. 2004) ("Congress arbitrarily relied upon the opinions of doctors who claimed to have no (or very little) recent and relevant experience with surgical abortions, and disregarded the views of doctors who had significant and relevant experience with those procedures."), *aff'd*, 413 F.3d 791 (8th Cir. 2005).

[33] *Gonzales*, 550 U.S. at 164–66.

[34] §2(14)(B), 117 Stat. 1204, notes following 18 U.S.C. § 1531 (2000 ed., Supp. IV), p. 769, ¶(14)(B) (Congressional Findings).

[35] *See Planned Parenthood Fed'n of Am.*, 320 F. Supp. 2d at 1029; *Nat'l Abortion Fed'n*, 330 F. Supp. 2d at 479; *see also* Brief for American College of Gynecologists as Amicus Curiae at 18, *Gonzales*, 550 U.S. 124 [hereinafter Brief for ACOG] ("Among the schools that now teach the intact variant are Columbia, Cornell, Yale, New York University, Northwestern, University of Pittsburgh, University of Pennsylvania, University of Rochester, and University of Chicago.").

[36] Congressional Findings (1), in notes following 18 U.S.C. § 1531 (2000 ed., Supp. IV), p. 767.

[37] *Planned Parenthood Fed'n of Am.*, 320 F. Supp. 2d at 1025; *See also* Carhart v. Ashcroft, 331 F. Supp. 2d 805, 1008–09 (D. Neb. 2004) ("[T]here was no evident consensus in the record that Congress compiled. There was, however, a substantial body of medical opinion presented to Congress in opposition. If anything . . . the congressional record establishes that there was a 'consensus' in favor of the banned procedure."); *Nat'l Abortion Fed'n*, 330 F. Supp. 2d at 488 ("The congressional record itself undermines [Congress'] finding" that there is a medical consensus that intact D&E "is never medically necessary and should be prohibited." (internal quotation marks omitted)).

[38] Congressional Findings (14)(B), in notes following 18 U.S.C. § 1531 (2000 ed., Supp. IV), p. 769.

other methods.[39] No comparable medical groups supported the ban. In fact, "all of the government's own witnesses disagreed with many of the specific congressional findings."[40]

C

In contrast to Congress, the District Courts made findings after full trials at which all parties had the opportunity to present their best evidence. The courts had the benefit of "much more extensive medical and scientific evidence . . . concerning the safety and necessity of intact D&Es."[41]

During the District Court trials, "numerous" "extraordinarily accomplished" and "very experienced" medical experts explained that, in certain circumstances and for certain women, intact D&E is safer than alternative procedures and necessary to protect women's health.[42]

According to the expert testimony plaintiffs introduced, the safety advantages of intact D&E are marked for women with certain medical conditions, for example, uterine scarring, bleeding disorders, heart disease, or compromised immune systems.[43] Further, plaintiffs' experts testified that intact D&E is significantly safer for women with certain pregnancy-related conditions, such as placenta previa and accreta, and for women carrying fetuses with certain abnormalities, such as severe hydrocephalus.[44]

---

[39] *See Nat'l Abortion Fed'n*, 330 F. Supp. 2d at 490; *see also Planned Parenthood Fed'n of Am.*, 320 F. Supp. 2d at 1021 ("Congress in its findings . . . chose to disregard the statements by ACOG and other medical organizations.").

[40] *Planned Parenthood Fed'n of Am.*, 320 F. Supp. 2d at 1024.

[41] *Id.* at 1014; *cf. Nat'l Abortion Fed'n*, 330 F. Supp. 2d at 482 (District Court "heard more evidence during its trial than Congress heard over the span of eight years.").

[42] *Carhart*, 331 F. Supp. 2d at 1024–27; *see Planned Parenthood Fed'n of Am.*, 320 F. Supp. 2d at 1001 ("[A]ll of the doctors who actually perform intact D&Es concluded that in their opinion and clinical judgment, intact D&Es remain the safest option for certain individual women under certain individual health circumstances, and are significantly safer for these women than other abortion techniques, and are thus medically necessary."); *cf.* Gonzales v. Carhart, 550 U.S. 124, 161 (2007) ("Respondents presented evidence that intact D&E may be the safest method of abortion, for reasons similar to those adduced in Stenberg.").

[43] *See Carhart*, 331 F. Supp. 2d at 924–29, 1026–27; *Nat'l Abortion Fed'n*, 330 F. Supp. 2d at 472–73; *Planned Parenthood Fed'n of Am.*, 320 F. Supp. 2d at 992–94, 1001.

[44] *See Carhart*, 331 F. Supp. 2d at 924, 1026–27; *Nat'l Abortion Fed'n*, 330 F.

Intact D&E, plaintiffs' experts explained, provides safety benefits over D&E by dismemberment for several reasons: First, intact D&E minimizes the number of times a physician must insert instruments through the cervix and into the uterus, and thereby reduces the risk of trauma to, and perforation of, the cervix and uterus—the most serious complication associated with nonintact D&E.[45] Second, removing the fetus intact, instead of dismembering it in utero, decreases the likelihood that fetal tissue will be retained in the uterus, a condition that can cause infection, hemorrhage, and infertility.[46] Third, intact D&E diminishes the chances of exposing the patient's tissues to sharp bony fragments sometimes resulting from dismemberment of the fetus.[47] Fourth, intact D&E takes less operating time than D&E by dismemberment, and thus may reduce bleeding, the risk of infection, and complications relating to anesthesia.[48]

Based on thoroughgoing review of the trial evidence and the congressional record, each of the District Courts to consider the issue rejected Congress' findings as unreasonable and not supported by the evidence.[49] The trial courts concluded, in contrast to Congress' findings, that "significant medical authority supports the proposition that in some circumstances, [intact D&E] is the safest procedure."[50; 51 [FN5]]

Supp. 2d at 473–74; *Planned Parenthood Fed'n of Am.*, 320 F. Supp. 2d at 992–94, 1001; *see also* Stenberg v. Carhart, 530 U.S. 914, 929 (2000); Brief for ACOG, *supra* note 35, at 2, 13–16.

[45] *See Carhart*, 331 F. Supp. 2d at 923–28, 1025; *Nat'l Abortion Fed'n*, 330 F. Supp. 2d at 471; *Planned Parenthood Fed'n of Am.*, 320 F. Supp. 2d at 982, 1001.

[46] *See Carhart*, 331 F. Supp. 2d at 923–28, 1025–26; *Nat'l Abortion Fed'n*, 330 F. Supp. 2d at 472; *Planned Parenthood Fed'n of Am.*, 320 F. Supp. 2d at 1001.

[47] *See Carhart*, 331 F. Supp. 2d at 923–28, 1026; *Nat'l Abortion Fed'n*, 330 F. Supp. 2d at 471; *Planned Parenthood Fed'n of Am.*, 320 F. Supp. 2d at 1001.

[48] *See Carhart*, 331 F. Supp. 2d at 923–28, 1026; *Nat'l Abortion Fed'n*, 330 F. Supp. 2d at 472; *Planned Parenthood Fed'n of Am.*, 320 F. Supp. 2d at 1001; *see also Stenberg*, 530 U.S. at 928–29, 932; Brief for ACOG, *supra* note 35, at 2, 11–13.

[49] *See Carhart*, 331 F. Supp. 2d at 1008–27; *Nat'l Abortion Fed'n*, 330 F. Supp. 2d at 482, 488–91; *Planned Parenthood Fed'n of Am.*, 320 F. Supp. 2d at 1032.

[50] *Planned Parenthood Fed'n of Am.*, 320 F. Supp. 2d at 1033 (quoting *Stenberg*, 530 U.S. at 932); *accord Carhart*, 331 F. Supp. 2d at 1008–09, 1017–18; *Nat'l Abortion Fed'n*, 330 F. Supp. 2d at 480–82; *cf. Stenberg*, 530 U.S. at 932 ("[T]he record shows that significant medical authority supports the proposition that in some circumstances, [intact D&E] would be the safest procedure.").

[51 [FN5]] Even the District Court for the Southern District of New York, which was more skeptical of the health benefits of intact D&E, *see* Gonzales v.

The District Courts' findings merit this Court's respect.[52] Today's opinion supplies no reason to reject those findings. Nevertheless, despite the District Courts' appraisal of the weight of the evidence, and in undisguised conflict with *Stenberg*, the Court asserts that the Partial-Birth Abortion Ban Act can survive "when . . . medical uncertainty persists."[53] This assertion is bewildering. Not only does it defy the Court's longstanding precedent affirming the necessity of a health exception, with no carve-out for circumstances of medical uncertainty;[54] it gives short shrift to the records before us, carefully canvassed by the District Courts. Those records indicate that "the majority of highly-qualified experts on the subject believe intact D&E to be the safest, most appropriate procedure under certain circumstances."[55]

The Court acknowledges some of this evidence,[56] but insists that, because some witnesses disagreed with the ACOG and other experts' assessment of risk, the Act can stand.[57] In this insistence, the Court brushes under the rug the District Courts' well-supported findings that the physicians who testified that intact D&E is never necessary to preserve the health of a woman had slim authority for their opinions. They had no training for, or personal experience with, the intact D&E procedure, and many performed abortions only on rare occasions.[58] Even indulging the assumption that the Government witnesses were equally qualified to evaluate the relative risks of abortion procedures, their testimony could not erase the "significant medical

---

Carhart, 550 U.S. 124, 161–62, recognized: "[T]he Government's own experts disagreed with almost all of Congress's factual findings"; a "significant body of medical opinion" holds that intact D&E has safety advantages over nonintact D&E; "[p]rofessional medical associations have also expressed their view that [intact D&E] may be the safest procedure for some women"; and "[t]he evidence indicates that the same disagreement among experts found by the Supreme Court in Stenberg existed throughout the time that Congress was considering the legislation, despite Congress's findings to the contrary." *Nat'l Abortion Fed'n*, 330 F. Supp. 2d at 480–82.

[52] *See, e.g.*, FED. R. CIV. P. 52(a); Salve Regina College v. Russell, 499 U.S. 225, 233 (1991).

[53] *Gonzales*, 550 U.S. at 163.

[54] *Id.* at 171–73 (Ginsburg, J., dissenting).

[55] *Planned Parenthood Fed'n of Am.*, 320 F. Supp. 2d at 1034; *see Gonzales*, 550 U.S. at 176–79 (Ginsburg, J., dissenting).

[56] *Gonzales*, 550 U.S. at 161–62.

[57] *Id.* at 161–63, 166–67.

[58] *See Planned Parenthood Fed'n of Am.*, 320 F. Supp. 2d at 980; Carhart v. Ashcroft, 331 F. Supp. 2d 805, 1025 (D. Neb. 2004); *cf.* Nat'l Abortion Fed'n v. Ashcroft, 330 F. Supp. 2d 436, 462–64 (S.D.N.Y. 2004).

authority support[ing] the proposition that in some circumstances, [intact D&E] would be the safest procedure."[59; 60 [FN6]]

II

A

The Court offers flimsy and transparent justifications for upholding a nationwide ban on intact D&E sans any exception to safeguard a women's health. Today's ruling, the Court declares, advances "a premise central to [*Casey*'s] conclusion"—i.e., the Government's "legitimate and substantial interest in preserving and promoting fetal life."[61] But the Act scarcely furthers that interest: The law saves not a single fetus from destruction, for it targets only a method of performing abortion.[62] And surely the statute was not designed to protect the lives or health of pregnant women.[63] In short, the Court upholds a law that, while doing nothing to "preserv[e] . . . fetal life,"[64] bars a woman

---

[59] Stenberg v. Carhart, 530 U.S. 914, 932 (2000).

[60] [FN6] The majority contends that "[i]f the intact D&E procedure is truly necessary in some circumstances, it appears likely an injection that kills the fetus is an alternative under the Act that allows the doctor to perform the procedure." *Gonzales*, 550 U.S. at 164. But a "significant body of medical opinion believes that inducing fetal death by injection is almost always inappropriate to the preservation of the health of women undergoing abortion because it poses tangible risk and provides no benefit to the woman." *Carhart*, 331 F. Supp. 2d at 1028 (internal quotation marks omitted), *aff'd*, 413 F.3d 791 (8th Cir. 2005). In some circumstances, injections are "absolutely [medically] contraindicated." *Id.* at 1027; *see also id.* at 907–12; *Nat'l Abortion Fed'n*, 330 F. Supp. 2d at 474–75; *Planned Parenthood Fed'n of Am.*, 320 F. Supp. 2d at 995–97. The Court also identifies medical induction of labor as an alternative. *See Gonzales*, 550 U.S. at 140. That procedure, however, requires a hospital stay, ibid., rendering it inaccessible to patients who lack financial resources, and it too is considered less safe for many women, and impermissible for others. *See Carhart*, 331 F. Supp. 2d at 940–49, 1017; *Nat'l Abortion Fed'n*, 330 F. Supp. 2d at 468–70; *Planned Parenthood Fed'n of Am.*, 320 F. Supp. 2d at 961 n.5, 992–94, 1000–02.

[61] *Gonzales*, 550 U.S. at 145; *see also id.* at 146 ("[W]e must determine whether the Act furthers the legitimate interest of the Government in protecting the life of the fetus that may become a child.").

[62] *See Stenberg*, 530 U.S. at 930.

[63] *Id.* at 951 (Ginsburg, J., concurring); *cf.* Planned Parenthood of Se. Pa. v. Casey, 505 U.S. 833, 846 (1992) (recognizing along with the State's legitimate interest in the life of the fetus, its "legitimate interes[t] . . . in protecting the health of the woman" (emphasis added)).

[64] *Gonzales*, 550 U.S. at 145.

from choosing intact D&E although her doctor "reasonably believes [that procedure] will best protect [her]."[65]

As another reason for upholding the ban, the Court emphasizes that the Act does not proscribe the nonintact D&E procedure.[66] But why not, one might ask. Nonintact D&E could equally be characterized as "brutal,"[67] involving as it does "tear[ing] [a fetus] apart" and "ripp[ing] off" its limbs.[68] "[T]he notion that either of these two equally gruesome procedures . . . is more akin to infanticide than the other, or that the State furthers any legitimate interest by banning one but not the other, is simply irrational."[69]

Delivery of an intact, albeit nonviable, fetus warrants special condemnation, the Court maintains, because a fetus that is not dismembered resembles an infant.[70] But so, too, does a fetus delivered intact after it is terminated by injection a day or two before the surgical evacuation,[71] or a fetus delivered through medical induction or cesarean.[72] Yet, the availability of those procedures—along with D&E by dismemberment—the Court says, saves the ban on intact D&E from a declaration of unconstitutionality.[73] Never mind that the procedures deemed acceptable might put a woman's health at greater risk.[74]

Ultimately, the Court admits that "moral concerns" are at work, concerns that could yield prohibitions on any abortion.[75] Notably, the concerns expressed are untethered to any ground genuinely serving the Government's interest in preserving life. By allowing such concerns to carry the day and case, overriding fundamental rights, the Court dishonors our precedent.[76]

---

[65] *Stenberg*, 530 U.S. at 946 (Stevens, J., concurring).

[66] *Gonzales*, 550 U.S. at 164.

[67] *Id.* at 157.

[68] *Id.* at 135, 135–37.

[69] *Stenberg*, 530 U.S. at 946–47 (Stevens, J., concurring).

[70] *Gonzales*, 550 U.S. at 158.

[71] *Id.* at 136, 164–66.

[72] *Id.* at 140.

[73] *Id.* at 164–67.

[74] *Id.* at 180 & n.6 (Ginsburg, J., dissenting); *cf. id.* at 136, 161–63 (majority opinion).

[75] *See id.* at 158 (majority opinion) ("Congress could . . . conclude that the type of abortion proscribed by the Act requires specific regulation because it implicates additional ethical and moral concerns that justify a special prohibition.").

[76] *See, e.g.*, Planned Parenthood of Se. Pa. v. Casey, 505 U.S. 833, 850 (1992) ("Some of us as individuals find abortion offensive to our most basic principles of morality, but that cannot control our decision. Our obligation is to define the liberty of all, not to mandate our own moral code."); Lawrence v. Texas, 539 U.S. 558, 571 (2003) (Though "[f]or many persons [objections to homosexual

Revealing in this regard, the Court invokes an antiabortion shibboleth for which it concededly has no reliable evidence: Women who have abortions come to regret their choices, and consequently suffer from "[s]evere depression and loss of esteem."[77; 78 [Fn7]] Because of

---

conduct] are not trivial concerns but profound and deep convictions accepted as ethical and moral principles," the power of the State may not be used "to enforce these views on the whole society through operation of the criminal law." (citing *Casey*, 505 U.S. at 850)).

[77] *Gonzales*, 550 U.S. at 159.

[78 [FN7]] The Court is surely correct that, for most women, abortion is a painfully difficult decision. *See id.* at 158–59. But "neither the weight of the scientific evidence to date nor the observable reality of 33 years of legal abortion in the United States comports with the idea that having an abortion is any more dangerous to a woman's long-term mental health than delivering and parenting a child that she did not intend to have . . . ." Susan A. Cohen, *Abortion and Mental Health: Myths and Realities*, 9 GUTTMACHER POL'Y REV. 8 (2006). *See generally* Emily Bazelon, *Is There a Post-Abortion Syndrome?*, N.Y. TIMES MAG., Jan. 21, 2007, at 40. *See also, e.g.*, AM. PSYCHOLOGICAL ASS'N, APA BRIEFING PAPER ON THE IMPACT OF ABORTION (2005) (rejecting theory of a postabortion syndrome and stating that "[a]ccess to legal abortion to terminate an unwanted pregnancy is vital to safeguard both the physical and mental health of women"); Sarah Schmiege & Nancy Felipe Russo, *Depression and Unwanted First Pregnancy: Longitudinal Cohort Study*, 331 BRIT. MED. J. 1303 (2005) (finding no credible evidence that choosing to terminate an unwanted first pregnancy contributes to risk of subsequent depression); Anne C. Gilchrist, Philip C. Hannaford, Peter Frank & Clifford R. Kay, *Termination of Pregnancy and Psychiatric Morbidity*, 167 BRIT. J. PSYCHIATRY 243, 247–48 (1995) (finding, in a cohort of more than 13,000 women, that the rate of psychiatric disorder was no higher among women who terminated pregnancy than among those who carried pregnancy to term); Nada L. Stodland, *The Myth of the Abortion Trauma Syndrome*, 268 JAMA 2078, 2079 (1992) ("Scientific studies indicate that legal abortion results in fewer deleterious sequelae for women compared with other possible outcomes of unwanted pregnancy. There is no evidence of an abortion trauma syndrome."); AM. PSYCHOLOGICAL ASS'N, COUNCIL POLICY MANUAL: (N)(I)(3), PUBLIC INTEREST (1989) (declaring assertions about widespread severe negative psychological effects of abortion to be "without fact"). *But see* Jesse R. Cougle, David C. Reardon, & Priscilla K. Coleman, *Generalized Anxiety Following Unintended Pregnancies Resolved Through Childbirth and Abortion: A Cohort Study of the 1995 National Survey of Family Growth*, 19 J. ANXIETY DISORDERS 137, 142 (2005) (advancing theory of a postabortion syndrome but acknowledging that "no causal relationship between pregnancy outcome and anxiety could be determined" from study); David C. Reardon et al., *Psychiatric Admissions of Low-Income Women following Abortion and Childbirth*, 168 CANADIAN MED. ASS'N J. 1253, 1255–56 (2003) (concluding that psychiatric admission rates were higher for women who had an abortion compared with women who delivered); *cf.* Brenda Major, *Psychological Implications of Abortion—Highly Charged and Rife with Misleading Research*, 168 CANADIAN MED. ASS'N J.

women's fragile emotional state and because of the "bond of love the mother has for her child," the Court worries, doctors may withhold information about the nature of the intact D&E procedure.[79; 80 [FN8]] The solution the Court approves, then, is not to require doctors to inform women, accurately and adequately, of the different procedures and their attendant risks.[81] Instead, the Court deprives women of the right to make an autonomous choice, even at the expense of their safety.[82 [FN9]]

This way of thinking reflects ancient notions about women's place in the family and under the Constitution—ideas that have long since been discredited.[83]

1257, 1258 (2003) (critiquing Reardon study for failing to control for a host of differences between women in the delivery and abortion samples).

[79] *Gonzales*, 550 U.S. at 158–59.

[80 [FN8]] Notwithstanding the "bond of love" women often have with their children, *see id.*, not all pregnancies, this Court has recognized, are wanted, or even the product of consensual activity. *See Casey*, 505 U.S. at 891 ("[O]n an average day in the United States, nearly 11,000 women are severely assaulted by their male partners. Many of these incidents involve sexual assault."); *see also* Susan S. Glander, Mary Lou Moore, Robert Michielutte & Linn H. Parsons, *The Prevalence of Domestic Violence Among Women Seeking Abortion*, 91 OBSTETRICS & GYNECOLOGY 1002 (1998); Melisa M. Holmes, Heidi S. Resnick, Dean G. Kilpatrick & Connie L. Best, *Rape-Related Pregnancy: Estimates and Descriptive Characteristics from a National Sample of Women*, 175 AM. J. OBSTETRICS & GYNECOLOGY 320 (1996).

[81] *Cf. Casey*, 505 U.S. at 873 (plurality opinion) ("States are free to enact laws to provide a reasonable framework for a woman to make a decision that has such profound and lasting meaning.").

[82 [FN9]] Eliminating or reducing women's reproductive choices is manifestly not a means of protecting them. When safe abortion procedures cease to be an option, many women seek other means to end unwanted or coerced pregnancies. *See, e.g.*, WORLD HEALTH ORG., UNSAFE ABORTION: GLOBAL AND REGIONAL ESTIMATES OF THE INCIDENCE OF UNSAFE ABORTION AND ASSOCIATED MORTALITY IN 2000 3, 16 (4th ed. 2004) ("Restrictive legislation is associated with a high incidence of unsafe abortion" worldwide; unsafe abortion represents 13% of all "maternal" deaths); Stanley K. Henshaw, *Unintended Pregnancy and Abortion: A Public Health Perspective*, in A CLINICIAN'S GUIDE TO MEDICAL AND SURGICAL ABORTION 11, 19 (Maureen Paul, E. Steven Lichtenberg, Lynn Borgatta, David A. Grimes & Phillip G. Stubblefield eds., 1999) ("Before legalization, large numbers of women in the United States died from unsafe abortions."); HEATHER D. BOONSTRA, RACHEL BENSON GOLD, CORY L. RICHARDS & LAWRENCE B. FINER, ABORTION IN WOMEN'S LIVES 13 & fig. 2.2 (2006) ("as late as 1965, illegal abortion still accounted for an estimated . . . 17% of all officially reported pregnancy-related deaths"; "[d]eaths from abortion declined dramatically after legalization").

[83] *Compare, e.g.*, Muller v. Oregon, 208 U.S. 412, 422–23 (1908) ("protective" legislation imposing hours-of-work limitations on women only held permissible

Though today's majority may regard women's feelings on the matter as "self-evident,"[84] this Court has repeatedly confirmed that "[t]he destiny of the woman must be shaped . . . on her own conception of her spiritual imperatives and her place in society."[85]

B

In cases on a "woman's liberty to determine whether to [continue] her pregnancy," this Court has identified viability as a critical consideration.[86] "[T]here is no line [more workable] than viability," the Court explained in *Casey*, for viability is "the time at which there is a realistic possibility of maintaining and nourishing a life outside the womb, so that the independent existence of the second life can in reason and all fairness be the object of state protection that now overrides the rights of the woman. . . . In some broad sense it might be said that a woman who fails to act before viability has consented to the State's intervention on behalf of the developing child."[87]

Today, the Court blurs that line, maintaining that "[t]he Act [legitimately] appl[ies] both previability and postviability because . . . a fetus is a living organism while within the womb, whether or not it is viable outside the womb."[88] Instead of drawing the line at viability, the Court refers to Congress' purpose to differentiate "abortion and infanticide" based not on whether a fetus can survive outside the

---

in view of women's "physical structure and a proper discharge of her maternal funct[ion]"), *and* Bradwell v. State, 83 U.S. (16 Wall.) 130, 141 (1873) (Bradley, J., concurring) ("Man is, or should be, woman's protector and defender. The natural and proper timidity and delicacy which belongs to the female sex evidently unfits it for many of the occupations of civil life. . . . The paramount destiny and mission of woman are to fulfil[l] the noble and benign offices of wife and mother."), *with* United States v. Virginia, 518 U.S. 515, 533, 542 n.12 (1996) (State may not rely on "overbroad generalizations" about the "talents, capacities, or preferences" of women; "[s]uch judgments have . . . impeded . . . women's progress toward full citizenship stature throughout our Nation's history"), *and* Califano v. Goldfarb, 430 U.S. 199, 207 (1977) (gender-based Social Security classification rejected because it rested on "archaic and overbroad generalizations" "such as assumptions as to [women's] dependency" (internal quotation marks omitted)).

[84] *Gonzales*, 550 U.S. at 159.

[85] *Casey*, 505 U.S. at 852. *See also id.* at 877 (plurality opinion) ("[M]eans chosen by the State to further the interest in potential life must be calculated to inform the woman's free choice, not hinder it."); *Gonzales*, 550 U.S. at 171–72.

[86] *See Casey*, 505 U.S. at 869–70 (plurality opinion).

[87] *Id.* at 870.

[88] *Gonzales*, 550 U.S. at 147.

womb, but on where a fetus is anatomically located when a particular medical procedure is performed.[89]

One wonders how long a line that saves no fetus from destruction will hold in face of the Court's "moral concerns."[90] The Court's hostility to the right *Roe* and *Casey* secured is not concealed. Throughout, the opinion refers to obstetrician-gynecologists and surgeons who perform abortions not by the titles of their medical specialties, but by the pejorative label "abortion doctor."[91] A fetus is described as an "unborn child," and as a "baby;"[92] second-trimester, previability abortions are referred to as "late-term;" and the reasoned medical judgments of highly trained doctors are dismissed as "preferences" motivated by "mere convenience."[93] Instead of the heightened scrutiny we have previously applied, the Court determines that a "rational" ground is enough to uphold the Act.[94] And, most troubling, *Casey's* principles, confirming the continuing vitality of "the essential holding of *Roe*," are merely "assume[d]" for the moment,[95] rather than "retained" or "reaffirmed."[96]

III

A

The Court further confuses our jurisprudence when it declares that "facial attacks" are not permissible in "these circumstances," i.e., where medical uncertainty exists.[97] This holding is perplexing given that, in materially identical circumstances we held that a statute lacking a health exception was unconstitutional on its face.[98]

---

[89] *See id.* at 158 (quoting Congressional Findings (14)(G), in notes following 18 U.S.C. § 1531 (2000 ed., Supp. IV), p. 769).

[90] *See id.* at 182 (Ginsburg, J., dissenting); *cf. id.* at 186 (majority opinion) (noting that "[i]n this litigation" the Attorney General "does not dispute that the Act would impose an undue burden if it covered standard D&E").

[91] *Id.* at 129, 138, 144, 154, 155, 161, 163 (majority opinion).

[92] *Id.* at 134, 138–39.

[93] *Id.* at 134, 166.

[94] *Id.* at 158, 166–67.

[95] *Id.* at 146, 161.

[96] *Casey*, 505 U.S. at 846.

[97] *Gonzales*, 550 U.S. at 167; *see id.* ("In an as-applied challenge the nature of the medical risk can be better quantified and balanced than in a facial attack.").

[98] Stenberg v. Carhart, 530 U.S. 914, 930; *see id.* at 937 (in facial challenge, law held unconstitutional because "significant body of medical opinion believes [the] procedure may bring with it greater safety for some patients"

Without attempting to distinguish *Stenberg* and earlier decisions, the majority asserts that the Act survives review because respondents have not shown that the ban on intact D&E would be unconstitutional "in a large fraction of relevant cases."[99] But *Casey* makes clear that, in determining whether any restriction poses an undue burden on a "large fraction" of women, the relevant class is not "all women," nor "all pregnant women," nor even all women "seeking abortions."[100] Rather, a provision restricting access to abortion, "must be judged by reference to those [women] for whom it is an actual rather than an irrelevant restriction."[101] Thus the absence of a health exception burdens all women for whom it is relevant—women who, in the judgment of their doctors, require an intact D&E because other procedures would place their health at risk.[102; 103 [FN 10]]. It makes no sense to conclude that this facial challenge fails because respondents have not shown that a health exception is necessary for a large fraction of second-trimester abortions, including those for which a health exception is unnecessary: The very purpose of a health exception is to protect women in exceptional cases.

(emphasis added)); *see also* Sabri v. United States, 541 U.S. 600, 609–10 (2004) (identifying abortion as one setting in which we have recognized the validity of facial challenges); Richard H. Fallon, Jr., *Making Sense of Overbreadth*, 100 YALE L.J. 853, 859 n.29 (1991) ("[V]irtually all of the abortion cases reaching the Supreme Court since Roe v. Wade, 410 U. S. 113 (1973), have involved facial attacks on state statutes, and the Court, whether accepting or rejecting the challenges on the merits, has typically accepted this framing of the question presented."); *accord* Richard H. Fallon, Jr., *As-Applied and Facial Challenges and Third-Party Standing*, 113 HARV. L. REV. 1321, 1356 (2000); Michael C. Dorf, *Facial Challenges to State and Federal Statutes*, 46 STAN. L. REV. 235, 271–76 (1994).

[99] *Gonzales*, 550 U.S. at 167–68 (citing *Casey*, 505 U. S. at 895).

[100] 505 U. S. at 895

[101] *Id.*

[102] *Cf. Stenberg*, 530 U.S. at 934 (accepting the "relative rarity" of medically indicated intact D&Es as true but not "highly relevant"—for "the health exception question is whether protecting women's health requires an exception for those infrequent occasions"); Ayotte v. Planned Parenthood of N. New England, 546 U.S. 320, 328 (facial challenge entertained where "[i]n some very small percentage of cases . . . women . . . need immediate abortions to avert serious, and often irreversible damage to their health").

[103 [FN10]] There is, in short, no fraction because the numerator and denominator are the same: The health exception reaches only those cases where a woman's health is at risk. Perhaps for this reason, in mandating safeguards for women's health, we have never before invoked the "large fraction" test.

B

If there is anything at all redemptive to be said of today's opinion, it is that the Court is not willing to foreclose entirely a constitutional challenge to the Act. "The Act is open," the Court states, "to a proper as-applied challenge in a discrete case."[104] But the Court offers no clue on what a "proper" lawsuit might look like.[105] Nor does the Court explain why the injunctions ordered by the District Courts should not remain in place, trimmed only to exclude instances in which another procedure would safeguard a woman's health at least equally well. Surely the Court cannot mean that no suit may be brought until a woman's health is immediately jeopardized by the ban on intact D&E. A woman "suffer[ing] from medical complications,"[106] needs access to the medical procedure at once and cannot wait for the judicial process to unfold.[107]

The Court appears, then, to contemplate another lawsuit by the initiators of the instant actions. In such a second round, the Court suggests, the challengers could succeed upon demonstrating that "in discrete and well-defined instances a particular condition has or is likely to occur in which the procedure prohibited by the Act must be used."[108] One may anticipate that such a preenforcement challenge will be mounted swiftly, to ward off serious, sometimes irremediable harm, to women whose health would be endangered by the intact D&E prohibition.

The Court envisions that in an as-applied challenge, "the nature of the medical risk can be better quantified and balanced."[109] But it should not escape notice that the record already includes hundreds and hundreds of pages of testimony identifying "discrete and well-defined instances" in which recourse to an intact D&E would better protect the health of women with particular conditions.[110] Record evidence also documents that medical exigencies, unpredictable in advance, may indicate to a well-trained doctor that intact D&E is the

---

[104] *Gonzales*, 550 U.S. at 168; *see id.* at 167 ("The Government has acknowledged that preenforcement, as-applied challenges to the Act can be maintained.").

[105] *See id.* at 167–68.

[106] *Id.* at 168.

[107] *See Ayotte*, 546 U.S. at 328.

[108] *Gonzales*, 550 U.S. at 167.

[109] *Id.*

[110] *See id.* at 177–78 (Ginsburg, J., dissenting).

safest procedure.[111] In light of this evidence, our unanimous decision just one year ago in *Ayotte* counsels against reversal.[112]

The Court's allowance only of an "as-applied challenge in a discrete case,"[113]—jeopardizes women's health and places doctors in an untenable position. Even if courts were able to carve-out exceptions through piecemeal litigation for "discrete and well-defined instances,"[114] women whose circumstances have not been anticipated by prior litigation could well be left unprotected. In treating those women, physicians would risk criminal prosecution, conviction, and imprisonment if they exercise their best judgment as to the safest medical procedure for their patients. The Court is thus gravely mistaken to conclude that narrow as-applied challenges are "the proper manner to protect the health of the woman."[115]

IV

As the Court wrote in *Casey*, "overruling *Roe*'s central holding would not only reach an unjustifiable result under principles of stare decisis, but would seriously weaken the Court's capacity to exercise the judicial power and to function as the Supreme Court of a Nation dedicated to the rule of law."[116] "[T]he very concept of the rule of law underlying our own Constitution requires such continuity over time that a respect for precedent is, by definition, indispensable."[117]

Though today's opinion does not go so far as to discard *Roe* or *Casey*, the Court, differently composed than it was when we last considered a restrictive abortion regulation, is hardly faithful to our earlier invocations of "the rule of law" and the "principles of stare decisis." Congress imposed a ban despite our clear prior holdings that the State cannot proscribe an abortion procedure when its use is necessary to protect a woman's health.[118] Although Congress' findings

---

[111] *See id.*

[112] *See* 546 U.S. at 331 (remanding for reconsideration of the remedy for the absence of a health exception, suggesting that an injunction prohibiting unconstitutional applications might suffice).

[113] *Gonzales*, 550 U.S. at 168.

[114] *Id.* at 167.

[115] *Cf. id.*

[116] 505 U.S. at 865.

[117] *Id.* at 854. *See also id.* at 867 ("[T]o overrule under fire in the absence of the most compelling reason to reexamine a watershed decision would subvert the Court's legitimacy beyond any serious question.").

[118] *See Gonzales*, 505 U.S. at 174 n.4 (Ginsburg, J., dissenting).

could not withstand the crucible of trial, the Court defers to the legislative override of our Constitution-based rulings.[119] A decision so at odds with our jurisprudence should not have staying power.

In sum, the notion that the Partial-Birth Abortion Ban Act furthers any legitimate governmental interest is, quite simply, irrational. The Court's defense of the statute provides no saving explanation. In candor, the Act, and the Court's defense of it, cannot be understood as anything other than an effort to chip away at a right declared again and again by this Court—and with increasing comprehension of its centrality to women's lives.[120] When "a statute burdens constitutional rights and all that can be said on its behalf is that it is the vehicle that legislators have chosen for expressing their hostility to those rights, the burden is undue."[121]

*　　*　　*

For the reasons stated, I dissent from the Court's disposition and would affirm the judgments before us for review.

---

[119] *See id.* at 174–76.

[120] *See id.* at 171 n.2; *id.* at 174 n.4

[121] Stenberg v. Carhart, 530 U.S. 914, 952 (Ginsburg, J., concurring) (quoting Hope Clinic v. Ryan, 195 F.3d 857, 881 (7th Cir. 1999) (Posner, C.J., dissenting)).

MINORITY RIGHTS

GRATZ V. BOLLINGER

RICCI V. DESTEFANO

ADARAND CONSTRUCTORS, INC. V. PEÑA

VANCE V. BALL STATE UNIVERSITY

SHELBY COUNTY V. HOLDER

*MASTERPIECE CAKE SHOP V.
COLORADO CIVIL RIGHTS COMMISSION*

MINORITY RIGHTS

"We should not be held back from pursuing our full talents, from contributing what we could contribute the society, because we fit into a certain mold—because we belong to a group that historically has been the object of discrimination."

When Ruth Bader Ginsburg began her legal career, discrimination against minorities, both *de jure* and *de facto*, was prevalent throughout the country and formal legal protections for civil rights were virtually non-existent. Over the ensuing decades, that changed completely. But by 2019—Ginsburg's twenty-sixth year on the Supreme Court—she found herself dissenting frequently from decisions of the Court's conservative majority, which she believed threatened the gains of the previous sixty years.

Ginsburg matriculated at Harvard Law School in 1956.[1] At that time, *Brown v. Board of Education*—the landmark Supreme Court decision finding school segregation unconstitutional—was only two years old.[2] Virtually every American institution of power—and every lawmaking body and court—was dominated by old, white men.

Ginsburg's early life made her acutely aware of the routine discrimination faced by women and minorities. She was a descendant of Russian Jews—her father having emigrated to the U.S. at the age of 13. She remembered one family vacation where she saw a sign outside a bed-and-breakfast which read "No Dogs Or Jews Allowed."[3] Ginsburg's mother died the day before her high school graduation; after the funeral "the Bader house filled with mourners, but only the men were allowed to participate in the minyan, the quorum for the official prayers. The teenaged Ruth took note."[4] Later, in her first year of law school, Ginsburg—who finished first in her undergraduate class at Cornell University, an Ivy League institution[5]—was called to account to the Dean of Harvard Law School to justify "taking a place

---

[1] RUTH BADER GINSBURG, MY OWN WORDS, (2016).

[2] Brown v. Bd. of Educ., 347 U.S. 483 (1954).

[3] LINDA HIRSHMAN, SISTERS IN LAW: HOW SANDRA DAY O'CONNOR AND RUTH BADER GINSBURG WENT TO THE SUPREME COURT AND CHANGED THE WORLD 5–6 (2015); IRIN CARMON & SHANA KNIZHNIK, NOTORIOUS RBG: THE LIFE AND TIMES OF RUTH BADER GINSBURG 26 (2015).

[4] JEFFREY TOOBIN, THE OATH: THE OBAMA WHITE HOUSE AND THE SUPREME COURT 58 (2012).

[5] HIRSHMAN, *supra* note 3, at 14.

a man would otherwise have had."[6] Upon finishing law school—again first in her class—Ginsburg had trouble finding work because she was a woman.[7]

Beyond her personal experiences, Ginsburg's established judicial philosophy was shaped through the influence of her college mentor, renowned liberal professor and anti-McCarthyite activist Robert Cushman.[8] As one scholar has stated, "Using classical liberal political theory, Cushman helped Ginsburg to 'see the grievances of a disempowered group,' both personally—for 'women like herself'—and broadly, imbuing her with 'an overall commitment to equality for all disempowered people.'"[9] Indeed, Ginsburg has traced her desire to become a lawyer to her work with Cushman, as she was inspired by the tenacity and courage of lawyers defending individuals hauled before Congress to account for their alleged Communist leanings during the "Red Scare" of the McCarthy era.[10]

Ginsburg's early years as a lawyer and law professor were marked by sweeping changes in the status of legal protections for minorities and women. The first came in 1961, through a policy created during the Kennedy Administration which required that all federal "government contractors and sub-contractors" take "affirmative action" not to "discriminate" based on "race, creed, color, or national origin."[11] The expansion of formal legal protections continued with the Civil Rights Act of 1964, which is broadly considered the most sweeping civil rights legislation in American history. Though the Act contains numerous significant provisions, of major importance was Title VII, which made it unlawful for employers with more than fifteen employees "to discriminate against any individual with respect to his compensation, terms, conditions, or privileges of employment, because of such individual's race, color, religion, sex, or national origin."[12] This landmark law provided the first robust legal protection from discrimination in the workplace for racial minorities and women. The very

---

[6] *Id.* at 15.

[7] *Id.* at 20.

[8] *Id.* at 11.

[9] *Id.* Cushman's theories are discussed at length in Robert Cushman, *Civil Liberty After the War*, 38 AM. POL. SCI. REV. 12–13 (1944).

[10] HIRSHMAN, *supra* note 3, at 11. Ginsburg has stated elsewhere that after Cushman pointed out to her that lawyers had come to the rescue of those hauled before Congress, she "got the idea that being a lawyer was a pretty good thing because in addition to practicing a profession, you could do something good for your society." CARMON & KNIZHNIK, *supra* note 3, at 30.

[10] HIRSHMAN, *supra* note 3, at 11.

[11] Exec. Order No. 10,925, 26 Fed. Reg. 1977 (Mar. 6, 1961).

[12] Civil Rights Act of 1964, 42 U.S.C. §§ 2000e(b), 2000e-2(a)(1) (1964).

next year, Congress passed the Voting Rights Act of 1965, which was enacted to forbid any "standard, practice, or procedure . . . imposed or applied . . . to deny or abridge the right of any citizen of the United States to vote on account of race or color."[13]

In just half a decade, the scope of legal protection available to minorities and women had broadened exponentially, shielding them from discrimination in hiring and working and safeguarding their ability to vote. In each of these areas, protections would be expanded in various ways in the ensuing decades—but all would also come under attack.

Never does Justice Ginsburg advocate more forcefully than when she believes a litigant's civil rights have been threatened. In all six dissents featured in this section, Justice Ginsburg sides with her perceived David against Goliath. As she has demonstrated throughout her career, she seems especially engaged when the facts before her present individuals "harmed, terribly and irreparably, by large forces well beyond their control."[14] Her dissents frequently "direct her audience's attention to the lack of equality between the plaintiff and the large social institutions," and emphasize that those individuals "had only the law to make them whole when the blunt forces of these institutions bore down on them."[15]

Ginsburg's early, personal experiences with discrimination inform the conclusion that her judicial philosophy is firmly grounded in an objective reality. She doesn't view the Constitution as a hermetically-sealed parchment whose meaning was frozen in 1789.[16] Instead, she observes the tangible effects of discrimination on real people living in the real world, and asks if such discrimination can reasonably be remedied using the Constitution's broadly egalitarian language, as well as the principles which Ginsburg believes its language encompasses.[17]

---

[13] The quoted language appeared in the original codification of the Voting Rights Act of 1965 at 42 U.S.C. § 1973 and was subsequently transferred after a reconfiguration of the Voting Rights Act to 52 U.S.C. § 10301 (2014).

[14] HIRSHMAN, *supra* note 3, at 281.

[15] *Id.* at 281–82.

[16] For a lay-friendly (and somewhat tongue-in-cheek) review of this method of approach to Constitutional interpretation, see Jill Lepore, *The History Test: How Should the Courts Use History?*, NEW YORKER (Mar. 27, 2017), https://www.newyorker.com/magazine/2017/03/27/weaponizing-the-past.

[17] Ginsburg's philosophy hews closely to that articulated by John Hart Ely—perhaps the most influential liberal legal scholar of the twentieth century—who wrote, in his seminal work *Democracy and Distrust*, that when a law is "withholding something to which the Constitution gives us a presumptive constitutional entitlement, such as the right to vote[, t]hat right simply cannot be denied. . . . The Court's job in such cases is to look at the world as it exists and ask whether such a right is in fact being abridged, and if it is, to consider

The implications of Ginsburg's philosophy are perhaps most evident in her dissents on affirmative action. In the years following its creation, affirmative action policies began to be implemented by colleges and universities in their admissions selection criteria. A 1978 Supreme Court decision permitted the consideration of race in admissions policies generally, but also struck down the specific policy under review.[18] The continued viability of such race-conscious policies was thus on tenuous legal footing until they were specifically affirmed by the Supreme Court in a 2003 case, *Grutter v. Bollinger*.[19] However, in two other cases—*Gratz v. Bollinger*,[20] decided the same day as *Grutter*, and *Fisher v. Univ. of Texas at Austin*, decided in 2013[21]—the Court sought to limit the very right it had affirmed in *Grutter*, which

---

what reasons might be adduced in support of the deprivation, without regard to what actually occasioned it. To the extent that there is a stoppage, the system is malfunctioning, and the Court should unblock it without caring how it got that way." JOHN HART ELY, DEMOCRACY AND DISTRUST: A THEORY OF JUDICIAL REVIEW 136 (1980).

[18] The case was *Regents of the University of California v. Bakke*, 438 U.S. 265 (1978). As Justice Kennedy later explained in *Fisher v. University of Texas at Austin*, 570 U.S. 297 (2013), another affirmative action case, "Justice Powell['s opinion in *Bakke*] identified one compelling interest that could justify the consideration of race: the interest in the educational benefits that flow from a diverse student body." *Id.* at 308. Despite this holding, the *Bakke* court went on to invalidate the affirmative action policy in question as an impermissible numerical racial "set-aside" which failed to account for the individual characteristics of applicants to the Medical School of the University of California at Davis. *Bakke*, 438 U.S. at 315–19.

[19] In *Grutter v. Bollinger*, 539 U.S. 306 (2003), the Court held that the educational benefit of "student body diversity is a compelling state interest that can justify the use of race in university admissions." *Id.* at 325.

[20] In *Gratz v. Bollinger*, 539 U.S. 244 (2003), the Court found "that the University [of Michigan's undergraduate admissions affirmative action] policy, which automatically distributes 20 points [out of a total possible 150 points], or one-fifth of the [100] points needed to guarantee admission, to every single "underrepresented minority" applicant solely because of race, is not narrowly tailored to achieve the interest in educational diversity that [the University] claim[ed] justifies their program." *Id.* at 270.

[21] In *Fisher*, the Court held that the lower courts "confined the strict scrutiny inquiry in too narrow a way by deferring to the University's good faith in its use of racial classifications and affirming the grant of summary judgment on that basis" and sent the case back to the lower courts "so that the admissions process can be considered and judged under a correct analysis." Fisher v. Univ. of Tex. at Austin, 570 U.S. 297, 314 (2013). In other words, the Court found that the lower courts should not have taken UT-Austin at its word that its affirmative action policy was properly and legally implemented, thereby implying, without directly stating, that the policy in question was constitutionally impermissible.

led Ginsburg to author two of the dissents that feature here.

Ginsburg was galled that the majority in *Gratz* seemed to ignore that "[i]n the wake 'of a system of racial caste only recently ended'" in the United States, "large disparities [between races] endure."[22] She argued in her dissent that "[w]ithout recourse to [affirmative action] plans, institutions of higher learning may resort to camouflage," hiding the actions they take to remedy such disparities, and that a "fully disclosed College affirmative action program is preferable to achieving similar numbers through winks, nods, and disguises."[23]

That dissent, which takes the majority to task for failing to recognize the realities to which colleges and universities must adhere when attempting to achieve diversity in admissions, squares perfectly with Ginsburg's view of herself "as a kind of teacher to get [Justices on the Court] to think" about civil rights issues from a different perspective.[24] Ginsburg has confessed to being "inspired by" the "example" of Thurgood Marshall, in his pre-judicial work as a civil rights lawyer, who worked with the NAACP Legal Defense and Education Fund "to educate the U.S. Supreme Court, step by step, about the pernicious effects of race discrimination"; as Ginsburg has stated, she "copied [Marshall's] strategy of educating judicial audiences in measured movements, in ways digestible by, and palatable to, the decisionmakers."[25]

Ginsburg's dissents continue such work day in and day out. "She's sounding an alarm and wants people to take notice," the head of one

---

[22] *Gratz*, 539 U.S. at 299 (Ginsburg, J., dissenting) (quoting Adarand Constructors, Inc. v. Peña, 515 U.S. 200, 273 (1995) (Ginsburg, J., dissenting)).

[23] *Id.* at 304–05 (Ginsburg, J., dissenting). As another scholar of the Court has observed, Ginsburg "believe[s] that for the most part government and businesses could give advantages to racial minorities, either to redress prior discrimination or to foster the goal of diversity." TOOBIN, *supra* note 4, at 210. Indeed, she joined a 2017 dissent by Justice Breyer in which he wrote that there is a "legal and practical difference between the use of race-conscious criteria . . . to keep the races apart, and the use of race-conscious criteria . . . to bring the races together." Parents Involved in Cmty. Sch. v. Seattle Sch. Dist. No. 1, 51 U.S. 701, 829 (2007) (Breyer, J., dissenting). For further discussion of this case by Ginsburg herself, see RUTH BADER GINSBURG, *Remarks on the Value of Diversity: International Affirmative Action*, *in* MY OWN WORDS: RUTH BADER GINSBURG, *supra* note **Error! Bookmark not defined.**, at 273.

[24] Jessica Weisberg, *Supreme Court Justice Ruth Bader Ginsburg: I'm Not Going Anywhere*, ELLE (Sept. 23, 2014), https://www.elle.com/culture/career-politics/interviews/a14788/supreme-court-justice-ruth-bader-ginsburg/.

[25] RUTH BADER GINSBURG, Brown v. Board of Education *in International Context*, *in* MY OWN WORDS: RUTH BADER GINSBURG *supra* note **Error! Bookmark not defined.**, at 264.

advocacy group has observed.[26] Her judicial philosophy is ever cognizant of the reality identified by renowned legal scholar John Hart Ely, who observed that "[n]o matter how open the process, those with most of the votes are in a position to vote themselves advantages at the expense of others, or otherwise to refuse to take their interests into account."[27]

Sometimes, Ely's observation is true even of "those with most of the votes" on the Court itself. In her dissent in *Shelby County, Ala. v. Holder*, Ginsburg, who normally eschewed any criticism of her colleagues that could be construed as personal, excoriated the Court's majority for its "hubris" in selectively interpreting evidence in the record to vitiate the functional ability of the Voting Rights Act to protect the rights and interests of minority voters.[28] As Ginsburg details at great length in her dissent,[29] the Voting Rights Act had been reauthorized and extended numerous times since its passage in 1965, with Congress finding that even as registration and voting rates of minority citizens increased, more subtle attempts to "reduce the impact of minority votes, in contrast to direct attempts to block access to the ballot," continued to metastasize.[30] As a result, in 2006 Congress had found "countless 'examples of flagrant racial discrimination' since the last reauthorization" in 1982 that were so "'serious and widespread in covered jurisdictions that [the Act] is still needed.'"[31] Ginsburg charged that the Court essentially ignored the bulk of these findings, instead citing abstract principles regarding the "equal sovereignty"[32] the states ostensibly share with the federal government in order to justify rendering the functional protections of the Voting Rights Act impotent. In a particularly pointed jab at the majority—which Ginsburg believed selectively disregarded the more damning portions of the voluminous evidence of voter discrimination in the record in order to effectuate a desired result—Ginsburg likened the Court's holding

---

[26] Linda Greenhouse, *Oral Dissents Give Ginsburg a New Voice on Court*, N.Y. TIMES (May 31, 2007), https://www.nytimes.com/2007/05/31/washington/31scotus.html (quoting Debra L. Ness, president of the National Partnership for Women and Families, an advocacy group that focuses on the workplace).

[27] ELY, *supra* note 17, at 135.

[28] Shelby Cty. v. Holder, 570 U.S. 529, 587, 590 (2013) (Ginsburg, J., dissenting).

[29] *See id.* at 560–66, 570–80.

[30] *Id.* at 563.

[31] *Id.* at 565 (quoting Shelby Cty. v. Holder, 679 F.3d 848, 865–73 (D.C. Cir. 2012)).

[32] *See id.* at 542–45 (majority opinion).

to "throwing away your umbrella in a rainstorm because you are not getting wet."[33]

Ginsburg has also "sounded the alarm" with respect to gay rights. There were essentially no formal federal legal protections for gay rights prior to 2008; as recently as 2004, the populations of eleven different states passed statewide bans on gay marriage, all on the same day.[34] The election of Barack Obama as President led to the establishment of a patchwork of benefits for the LGBT community, including an extension of federal hate crimes laws to include attacks based on sexual orientation and gender identity; the extension of same-sex domestic partner benefits to federal employees; and the repeal of "Don't Ask, Don't Tell," which allowed gay, lesbian, and bisexual Americans to serve openly in the armed forces.[35] Then, in 2015, the Supreme Court ruled in *Obergefell v. Hodges* that the right to marry may not be denied to couples of the same sex, and that states must recognize lawful same-sex marriages performed in other states.[36] Justice Ginsburg was part of the Court's slim 5–4 majority in that case. The passage of *Obergefell* led to further formal legal protections for the LGBT community, including equal treatment under federal tax law for gay married couples and the recognition by the Social Security Administration of valid same-sex marriages for purposes of entitlement to Social Security benefits.[37]

Despite so many gains in so few years, stumbling blocks inevitably appeared. In *Masterpiece Cakeshop, Ltd., v. Colorado Civil Rights Commission*, a 5–4 majority of the Supreme Court ruled that a Colorado baker's rights under the Free Exercise Clause of the First Amendment and other federal laws trumped a gay couple's right not to face discrimination for their sexual orientation under a Colorado civil rights law.[38] Ginsburg's dissent suggested hypocrisy on behalf of the majority; while Ginsburg cited numerous propositions of law in the majority opinion "with which [she] agree[d]," she believed the majority was wrong to rule against the gay couple in question, as all of

---

[33] *Id.* at 590 (Ginsburg, J., dissenting).

[34] *Voters Pass All 11 Bans on Gay Marriage*, NBCNews.com, Nov. 3, 2004, http://www.nbcnews.com/id/6383353/ns/politics/t/voters-pass-all-bans-gay-marriage/.

[35] Office of the Press Sec'y, The White House, *Fact Sheet: Obama Administration's Record and the LGBT Community*, WHITE HOUSE (June 9, 2016) https://obamawhitehouse.archives.gov/the-press-office/2016/06/09/fact-sheet-obama-administrations-record-and-lgbt-community.

[36] *See* Obergefell v. Hodges, 135 S. Ct. 2584, 2604–05, 2607–08 (2015).

[37] Office of the Press Sec'y, *supra* note 35.

[38] *See* Masterpiece Cakeshop, Ltd. v. Colo. Civil Rights Comm'n, 138 S. Ct. 1719, 1729–321 (2018).

the "statements [quoted by the majority] point[ed] in the opposite direction."[39] She noted with pique that the majority had opted for the curtailment of gay rights using a Colorado law that, in Ginsburg's view, was plainly drafted and ratified by the duly-elected legislature of Colorado to effectuate the exact opposite purpose.[40]

*   *   *

In speaking on "the external impact of dissenting opinions," Ginsburg herself has frequently quoted the words of former Chief Justice Hughes set forth in the General Introduction to this text.[41] On civil rights, Ginsburg embodies the bulwark of Hughes's "intelligence of a future day." Ginsburg "always thought she was entitled to anything available to any other human of any gender,"[42] and she adheres to that same view when it comes to "including all marginalized groups into equal participation in national life."[43]

In short, Ginsburg reads the Constitution for the principles it espouses, she looks at society for what it is, and she sees the yawning gap between the two. With every dissent, she fights—if not to fill it, then to light the path for those who follow.

---

[39] *Id.* at 1748–51 (Ginsburg, J., dissenting).

[40] *See id.*

[41] GINSBURG, *supra* note **Error! Bookmark not defined.**, at 282–83.

[42] HIRSHMAN, *supra* note 3, at 17.

[43] *Id.* at 11–12.

GRATZ

"The stain of generations of racial oppression is still visible in our society, and the determination to hasten its removal remains vital."

The Case

Since the 1970s, one application of the practice known as "affirmative action" has been the use of race-conscious policies in the university admissions process. A 1978 Supreme Court decision, *Regents of the University of California v. Bakke*,[1] permitted the consideration of race in academic admission policies generally, insofar as considering race advanced the "compelling governmental interest" of promoting "the educational benefits that flow from a diverse student body."[2] To be constitutional, however, a university's use of race in its admissions program needed to employ measures that were "narrowly tailored."[3] To that end, the *Bakke* Court decided that colleges could only consider race as one of a range of factors in making their admission decisions and that race was never permitted to be a determinative factor—as it was in systems using racial quotas or which reserved seats for minority applicants.

Gratz v. Bollinger stemmed from a lawsuit by two applicants to the University of Michigan's College of Literature, Science, and the Arts (LSA). Both claimed they were denied admission because they were white.[4] Beginning in 1998, the University used an applicant-ranking system based on earned points; applicants could earn up to 150 points

---

[1] 438 U.S. 265 (1978).

[2] The quoted language comes from *Fisher v. University of Texas at Austin*, 570 U.S. 297, 308 (2013), which was summarizing an extended discussion in *Bakke*, 438 U.S. at 307–09, 311–15.

[3] Adarand Constructors, Inc. v. Peña, 515 U.S. 200, 224 (1995).

[4] Specifically, the students filed a class action alleging "violations and threatened violations of the rights of the plaintiffs and the class they represent to equal protection of the laws under the Fourteenth Amendment . . . and for racial discrimination in violation of 42 U.S.C. §§ 1981, 1983 and 2000d *et seq.*" *Gratz*, 539 U.S. at 252 (internal quotation marks omitted).

and were guaranteed admission if they scored at least 100. Points were issued based on a variety of factors, including high school grade point averages and standardized test scores. But "[o]f particular significance," the Court noted, was that "under a 'miscellaneous' category, an applicant was entitled to 20 points based upon his or her membership in an underrepresented racial or ethnic minority group."[5] Challenging this rubric, the white applicants alleged, in essence, that the minority applicants were effectively guaranteed admission by the structure of the point system simply because they were minorities, whereas white applicants were unfairly disadvantaged by not receiving automatic points based solely on the immutable characteristic of their race.

The United States District Court for the Eastern District of Michigan held that the University's points system passed muster under the framework established in *Bakke*, which had specifically outlawed racial quotas. The District Court found the points system "was not the functional equivalent of a quota because minority candidates were not insulated from review by virtue of those points."[6] That decision was appealed to the United States Court of Appeals for the Sixth Circuit. Before the appellate court reached a judgment, the Supreme Court agreed to hear a separate affirmative action case also involving the University of Michigan: *Grutter v. Bollinger*,[7] in which the Sixth Circuit had upheld the race-conscious admissions policy used by the University's law school. The Supreme Court agreed to take up *Gratz* directly, alongside *Grutter*, so it "could address the constitutionality of the consideration of race in university admissions in a wider range of circumstances."[8]

The Court issued its opinions in both *Grutter* and *Gratz* on the same day in 2003. *Grutter* reaffirmed the Court's commitment to the principal holding in *Bakke*: that the educational benefit of "student body diversity is a compelling state interest that can justify the use of race in university admissions."[9] The majority in *Grutter*—comprised of Justice O'Connor, who wrote the opinion, along with Justices Stevens, Souter, Ginsburg, and Breyer—also upheld the admissions policy of the University of Michigan Law School as sufficiently narrowly tailored in line with the principles announced in *Bakke*. Yet in *Gratz*, a different majority of the Court, comprised this time of Chief Justice Rehnquist and Justices O'Connor, Scalia, Kennedy, and Thomas, sought to limit the very right the Court reaffirmed in *Grutter*.

---

[5] *Id.* at 255.
[6] *Id.* at 258.
[7] 539 U.S. 306 (2003).
[8] *Gratz*, 539 U.S. at 260.
[9] *Grutter*, 539 U.S. at 325.

Justice Rehnquist's Majority Opinion

In an opinion by Chief Justice Rehnquist, the *Gratz* majority held that the University's LSA admissions policy, "which automatically distributes 20 points, or one-fifth of the points needed to guarantee admission, to every single 'underrepresented minority' applicant solely because of race, is not narrowly tailored to achieve the interest in educational diversity that [the University] claim[ed] justifies their program."[10] The majority observed that under the approach described in *Bakke*, "each characteristic of a particular applicant was to be considered in assessing the applicant's entire application," but that the LSA policy did "not provide such individualized consideration" because it "ha[d] the effect of making 'the factor of race . . . decisive' for virtually every minimally qualified underrepresented minority applicant."[11] In other words, as observed by Justice O'Connor in her concurring opinion, the LSA "procedures . . . do not provide for a meaningful individualized review of applicants."[12]

Instead of a points system, Justice Rehnquist suggested the use of a race-conscious admissions system like the Harvard College Admissions Program, which had been discussed in and attached to Justice Powell's opinion in *Bakke*. Unlike the LSA points system, Harvard's race-conscious admissions criteria were not determinative because they did not favor minority applicants simply because of their minority status, but instead considered how that status might influence their holistic contribution to campus diversity. For example, Harvard's criteria would view favorably a minority applicant who "grew up in an inner-city ghetto of semi-literate parents [and] whose academic achievement was lower but who had demonstrated energy and leadership," but still allowed for the possibility of that applicant losing out to a white applicant with "extraordinary artistic talent."[13] The majority believed Harvard's approach to be constitutionally viable because it explicitly noted that "'the critical criteria are often individual qualities or experience *not dependent upon race but sometimes associated with it.*'"[14]

In a brief concurrence, Justice Thomas helped to further limit the

---

[10] *Gratz*, 539 U.S. at 270.

[11] *Id.* at 271–72 (quoting Regents of Univ. of Cal. v. Bakke, 438 U.S. 265, 317 (1978)).

[12] *Id.* at 276 (O'Connor, J., concurring).

[13] *Id.* at 272 (majority opinion) (quoting *Bakke*, 438 U.S. at 324, in turn quoting a "statement" by the Harvard College Admissions Program).

[14] *Id.* at 272–73 (quoting *Bakke*, 438 U.S. at 324, in turn quoting a "statement" by the Harvard College Admissions Program) (emphasis supplied by Chief Justice Rehnquist).

relevance of the contrast between the Harvard and LSA policies: "[t]he LSA policy falls . . . because it does not sufficiently allow for the consideration of nonracial distinctions among underrepresented minority applicants."[15]

Justice Ginsburg's Dissent

Justice Ginsburg's dissent took issue with the fundamental premises underlying not only the majority opinion, but the Court's entire affirmative action jurisprudence dating back to *Bakke.* Ginsburg argued that this line of cases had, in effect, been blind to the objective realities faced by racial minorities in the United States, and, if it were not, the outcome of both *Gratz* and other cases would have been substantially different.

Ginsburg first observed that "[i]n the wake 'of a system of racial caste only recently ended'" in the United States, "large disparities [between races] endure."[16] She then catalogued numerous such "disparities" to support her position that the *Gratz* majority improperly continued *Bakke*'s determination "that the same standard of review controls judicial inspection of all official race classifications."[17] By ignoring the historical animus faced by various minorities in the United States, she explained, the majority allowed itself to analyze racial preferences in college admissions as if white students and minority students were on a level playing field. As Ginsburg ably demonstrated, they were not.

The crux of Ginsburg's argument was that policies and practices which may be constitutionally proscribed for one purpose may be constitutionally prescribed for another. In her words, "[a]ctions designed to burden groups long denied full citizenship stature are not sensibly ranked with measures taken to hasten the day when entrenched discrimination and its aftereffects have been extirpated."[18] In further parsing this distinction, Ginsburg quoted an esteemed appellate court judge (aptly named Judge Wisdom), writing near the height of the Civil Rights Movement, who observed as follows:

> "The Constitution is both color blind and color conscious. To avoid conflict with the equal protection clause, a classification that denies a benefit, causes harm, or imposes a burden must

---

[15] *Id.* at 281 (Thomas, J., concurring).

[16] *Id.* at 299 (Ginsburg, J., dissenting) (quoting Adarand Constructors, Inc. v. Peña, 515 U.S. 200, 273 (1995) (Ginsburg, J., dissenting)).

[17] *Id.* at 298.

[18] *Id.* at 301.

not be based on race. In that sense, the Constitution is color blind. But the Constitution is color conscious to prevent discrimination being perpetuated and to undo the effects of past discrimination."[19]

Applying this logic to the points system at issue in *Gratz*, Ginsburg saw "no constitutional infirmity" because "[e]very applicant admitted under" that system was "qualified to attend the College."[20]

Ginsburg concluded by taking the majority to task for failing to recognize how, she feared, colleges and universities would, in light of *Gratz*, attempt to achieve diversity in admissions. She argued that "[w]ithout recourse to [affirmative action] plans, institutions of higher learning may resort to camouflage," hiding the actions they take to remedy such disparities. [21] By Ginsburg's accounting, "honesty is the best policy"—meaning, in this context, that a "fully disclosed College affirmative action program is preferable to achieving similar numbers through winks, nods, and disguises."[22]

---

[19] *Id.* at 302 (quoting United States v. Jefferson Cty. Bd. of Ed., 372 F.2d 836, 876 (5th Cir. 1966)).

[20] *Id.* at 303.

[21] *Id.* at 304.

[22] *Id.* at 304–05.

GRATZ V. BOLLINGER

JUSTICE GINSBURG, with whom JUSTICE SOUTER joins,
DISSENTING.[1]

I

Educational institutions, the Court acknowledges, are not barred from any and all consideration of race when making admissions decisions.[2] But the Court once again maintains that the same standard of review controls judicial inspection of all official race classifications.[3] This insistence on "consistency,"[4] would be fitting were our Nation free of the vestiges of rank discrimination long reinforced by law.[5] But we are not far distant from an overtly discriminatory past, and the effects of centuries of law-sanctioned inequality remain painfully evident in our communities and schools.

In the wake "of a system of racial caste only recently ended,"[6] large disparities endure. Unemployment,[7] [FN 1] poverty,[8] [FN 2] and access to

---

[1] Justice Breyer joins Part I of this opinion.

[2] *Id.* at 268 (majority opinion); *see* Grutter v. Bollinger, 539 U.S. 306, 326–33 (2003).

[3] *Gratz*, 539 U.S. at 270 (quoting Adarand Constructors, Inc. v. Peña, 515 U.S. 200, 224 (1995); Richmond v. J. A. Croson Co., 488 U.S. 469, 494 (1989) (plurality opinion)).

[4] *Adarand*, 515 U.S. at 224.

[5] *See id.* at 274–76 & n.8 (Ginsburg, J., dissenting).

[6] *Id.* at 273.

[7] [FN 1] *See, e.g.*, U.S. CENSUS BUREAU, STATISTICAL ABSTRACT OF THE UNITED STATES: 2002 368 tbl. 562 (2002) [hereinafter Statistical Abstract] (unemployment rate among whites was 3.7% in 1999, 3.5% in 2000, and 4.2% in 2001; during those years, the unemployment rate among African-Americans was 8.0%, 7.6%, and 8.7%, respectively; among Hispanics, 6.4%, 5.7%, and 6.6%).

[8] [FN 2] *See, e.g.*, U.S. CENSUS BUREAU, POVERTY IN THE UNITED STATES: 2000 p. 291 tbl. A (2001) (In 2000, 7.5% of non-Hispanic whites, 22.1% of African-Americans, 10.8% of Asian-Americans, and 21.2% of Hispanics were living in poverty.); SARAH STAVETEIG & ALYSSA WIGTON, RACIAL AND ETHNIC DISPARITIES: KEY FINDINGS FROM THE NATIONAL SURVEY OF AMERICA'S FAMILIES 1 (Urban Institute Report B-5, 2000) ("Blacks, Hispanics, and Native Ameri-

health care[9] [FN 3] vary disproportionately by race. Neighborhoods and schools remain racially divided.[10] [FN 4] African-American and Hispanic children are all too often educated in poverty-stricken and underperforming institutions.[11] [FN 5] Adult African Americans and Hispanics generally earn less than whites with equivalent levels of education.[12] [FN 6] Equally credentialed job applicants receive different receptions depending on their race.[13] [FN 7] Irrational prejudice is still encoun-

---

cans . . . each have poverty rates almost twice as high as Asians and almost three times as high as whites.").

[9] [FN 3] *See, e.g.*, U.S. CENSUS BUREAU, HEALTH INSURANCE COVERAGE: 2000 391 tbl. A (2001) (In 2000, 9.7% of non-Hispanic whites were without health insurance, as compared to 18.5% of MricanAmericans, 18.0% of Asian-Americans, and 32.0% of Hispanics.); Timothy A. Waidmann & Shruti Rajan, *Race and Ethnic Disparities in Health Care Access and Utilization: An Examination of State Variation*, 57 MED. CARE RES. & REV. 55, 56 (2000) ("On average, Latinos and African Americans have both worse health and worse access to effective health care than do non-Hispanic whites . . . .").

[10] [FN 4] *See, e.g.*, JOHN ICELAND & DANIEL H. WEINBERG, U.S. CENSUS BUREAU, RACIAL AND ETHNIC RESIDENTIAL SEGREGATION IN THE UNITED STATES: 1980-2000 (2002) (documenting residential segregation); ERICA FRANKENBERG, CHUNGMEI LEE & GARY ORFIELD, A MULTIRACIAL SOCIETY WITH SEGREGATED SCHOOLS: ARE WE LOSING THE DREAM? 4 (2003) ("[W]hites are the most segregated group in the nation's public schools; they attend schools, on average, where eighty percent of the student body is white."); *id.* at 28 ("[A]lmost three-fourths of black and Latino students attend schools that are predominantly minority . . . . More than one in six black children attend a school that is 99-100% minority . . . . One in nine Latino students attend virtually all minority schools.").

[11] [FN 5] *See, e.g.*, James E. Ryan, *Schools, Race, and Money*, 109 YALE L.J. 249, 273–74 (1999) ("Urban public schools are attended primarily by African-American and Hispanic students"; students who attend such schools are disproportionately poor, score poorly on standardized tests, and are far more likely to drop out than students who attend nonurban schools.).

[12] [FN 6] *See, e.g.*, Statistical Abstract, *supra* note 7, at 140 tbl. 211.

[13] [FN 7] *See, e.g.*, Harry J. Holzer, *Career Advancement Prospects and Strategies for Low-Wage Minority Workers*, in LOW-WAGE WORKERS IN THE NEW ECONOMY 228 (Richard Kazis & Marc S. Miller eds., 2001) ("[I]n studies that have sent matched pairs of minority and white applicants with apparently equal credentials to apply for jobs, whites routinely get more interviews and job offers than   either black or Hispanic applicants."); Marianne Bertrand & Sendhil Mullainathan, *Are Emily and Brendan More Employable than Lakisha and Jamal? A Field Experiment on Labor Market Discrimination*, 4 AM. ECON. REV. 991 (2004), Ronald Mincy, *The Urban Institute Audit Studies: Their Research and Policy Context*, in CLEAR AND CONVINCING EVIDENCE: MEASUREMENT OF DISCRIMINATION IN AMERICA 165–86 (Michael Fix & Raymond J. Struyk eds., 1993).

tered in real estate markets[14] [FN 8] and consumer transactions.[15] [FN 9] "Bias both conscious and unconscious, reflecting traditional and unexamined habits of thought, keeps up barriers that must come down if equal opportunity and nondiscrimination are ever genuinely to become this country's law and practice."[16]

The Constitution instructs all who act for the government that they may not "deny to any person . . . the equal protection of the laws."[17] In implementing this equality instruction, as I see it, government decisionmakers may properly distinguish between policies of exclusion and inclusion.[18] Actions designed to burden groups long denied full citizenship stature are not sensibly ranked with measures taken to hasten the day when entrenched discrimination and its aftereffects have been extirpated.[19]

---

[14] [FN 8] *See, e.g.*, MARGERY TURNER ET AL., DISCRIMINATION IN METROPOLITAN HOUSING MARKETS: NATIONAL RESULTS FROM PHASE I HDS 2000 i, iii (2002), http://www.huduser.org/Publications/pdf/Phase1_Report.pdf (paired testing in which "two individuals-one minority and the other white-pose as otherwise identical home seekers, and visit real estate or rental agents to inquire about the availability of advertised housing units" revealed that "discrimination still persists in both rental and sales markets of large metropolitan areas nationwide"); MARGERY AUSTIN TURNER & FELICITY SKIDMORE, MORTGAGE LENDING DISCRIMINATION: A REVIEW OF EXISTING EVIDENCE 2 (1999) (Existing research evidence shows that minority homebuyers in the United States "face discrimination from mortgage lending institutions.").

[15] [FN 9] *See, e.g.*, Ian Ayres, *Further Evidence of Discrimination in New Car Negotiations and Estimates of Its Cause*, 94 MICH. L. REV. 109, 109–10 (1995) (study in which 38 testers negotiated the purchase of more than 400 automobiles confirmed earlier finding "that dealers systematically offer lower prices to white males than to other tester types").

[16] Adarand Constructors, Inc. v. Peña, 515 U.S. 200, 274 (Ginsburg, J., dissenting); *see generally* Linda Hamilton Krieger, *Civil Rights Perestroika: Intergroup Relations After Affirmative Action*, 86 CAL. L. REV. 1251, 1276–91 (1998).

[17] U.S. CONST. amend. XIV, § 1.

[18] See Wygant v. Jackson Bd. of Ed., 476 U.S. 267, 316 (1986) (Stevens, J., dissenting).

[19] See Stephen L. Carter, *When Victims Happen To Be Black*, 97 YALE L.J. 420, 433–34 (1988) ("[T]o say that two centuries of struggle for the most basic of civil rights have been mostly about freedom from racial categorization rather than freedom from racial oppressio[n] is to trivialize the lives and deaths of those who have suffered under racism. To pretend . . . that the issue presented in [Regents of Univ. of Cal. v. Bakke, 438 U.S. 265 (1978)] was the same as the issue in [Brown v. Bd. of Ed., 347 U.S. 483 (1954)] is to pretend that history never happened and that the present doesn't exist." (alteration in original)).

Our jurisprudence ranks race a "suspect" category, "not because [race] is inevitably an impermissible classification, but because it is one which usually, to our national shame, has been drawn for the purpose of maintaining racial inequality."[20] But where race is considered "for the purpose of achieving equality,"[21] no automatic proscription is in order.

For, as insightfully explained: "The Constitution is both color blind and color conscious. To avoid conflict with the equal protection clause, a classification that denies a benefit, causes harm, or imposes a burden must not be based on race. In that sense, the Constitution is color blind. But the Constitution is color conscious to prevent discrimination being perpetuated and to undo the effects of past discrimination."[22]

The mere assertion of a laudable governmental purpose, of course, should not immunize a race-conscious measure from careful judicial inspection.[23] Close review is needed "to ferret out classifications in reality malign, but masquerading as benign,"[24] and to "ensure that preferences are not so large as to trammel unduly upon the opportunities of others or interfere too harshly with legitimate expectations of persons in once preferred groups."[25]

II

Examining in this light the admissions policy employed by the University of Michigan's College of Literature, Science, and the Arts (College), and for the reasons well stated by Justice Souter, I see no

---

[20] Norwalk Core v. Norwalk Redevelopment Agency, 395 F.2d 920, 931–32 (2d Cir. 1968) (footnote omitted).

[21] *Id.* at 932.

[22] United States v. Jefferson Cty. Bd. of Ed., 372 F.2d 836, 876 (5th Cir. 1966); *see* Herbert Wechsler, *The Nationalization of Civil Liberties and Civil Rights*, 12 TEX. Q. 10, 23 (Supp. 968) (Brown may be seen as disallowing racial classifications that "impl[y] an invidious assessment" while allowing such classifications when "not invidious in implication" but advanced to "correct inequalities"). Contemporary human rights documents draw just this line; they distinguish between policies of oppression and measures designed to accelerate de facto equality. *See* Grutter v. Bollinger, 539 U.S. 306, 344 (2003) (Ginsburg, J., concurring) (citing International Convention on the Elimination of All Forms of Racial Discrimination, *opened for signature* Dec. 21, 1965, 94 U.S.T. 1120, 660 U.N.T.S. 195; Convention on the Elimination of All Forms of Discrimination Against Women, Sept. 3, 1981, 1249 U.N.T.S. 13).

[23] See *Jefferson Cty.*, 372 F.2d at 876 ("The criterion is the relevancy of color to a legitimate governmental purpose.").

[24] Adarand Constructors, Inc. v. Peña, 515 U.S. 200, 275 (1995) (Ginsburg, J., dissenting).

[25] *Id.* at 276.

constitutional infirmity.[26] Like other top ranking institutions, the College has many more applicants for admission than it can accommodate in an entering class.[27] Every applicant admitted under the current plan, petitioners do not here dispute, is qualified to attend the College.[28] The racial and ethnic groups to which the College accords special consideration (African-Americans, Hispanics, and Native-Americans) historically have been relegated to inferior status by law and social practice; their members continue to experience class based discrimination to this day.[29] There is no suggestion that the College adopted its current policy in order to limit or decrease enrollment by any particular racial or ethnic group, and no seats are reserved on the basis of race.[30] Nor has there been any demonstration that the College's program unduly constricts admissions opportunities for students who do not receive special consideration based on race.[31; 32 [FN 10]]

---

[26] *See* Gratz v. Bollinger, 539 U.S. 244, 293–98 (Souter, J., dissenting).

[27] Appendix to Petition for Writ of Certiorari 108a, *Gratz*, 539 U.S. 244 (No. 02-516).

[28] *Id.* at 111a.

[29] *See Gratz*, 539 U.S. at 298–301.

[30] *See* Brief for Respondent Bollinger et al. at 10, *Gratz*, 539 U.S. 244 (No.02-516); Transcript of Oral Argument at 41–42, *Gratz*, 539 U.S. 244 (No.02-516) (in the range between 75 and 100 points, the review committee may look at applications individually and ignore the points).

[31] *Cf.* Goodwin Liu, *The Causation Fallacy:* Bakke *and the Basic Arithmetic of Selective Admissions*, 100 MICH. L. REV. 1045, 1049 (2002) ("In any admissions process where applicants greatly outnumber admittees, and where white applicants greatly outnumber minority applicants, substantial preferences for minority applicants will not significantly diminish the odds of admission facing white applicants.").

[32 [FN 10]] The United States points to the "percentage plans" used in California, Florida, and Texas as one example of a "race-neutral alternativ[e]" that would permit the College to enroll meaningful numbers of minority students. Brief for United States as Amicus Curiae at 14, *Gratz*, 539 U.S. 244 (No. 02-516); *see* U.S. COMM'N ON CIVIL RIGHTS, BEYOND PERCENTAGE PLANS: THE CHALLENGE OF EQUAL OPPORTUNITY IN HIGHER EDUCATION 1 (2002), (percentage plans guarantee admission to state universities for a fixed percentage of the top students from high schools in the State). Calling such 10% or 20% plans "race-neutral" seems to me disingenuous, for they "unquestionably were adopted with the specific purpose of increasing representation of African-Americans and Hispanics in the public higher education system." Brief for Respondent Bollinger et al., *supra* note 30, at 44; *see* CATHERINE L. HORN & STELLA M. FLORES, PERCENT PLANS IN COLLEGE ADMISSIONS: A COMPARATIVE ANALYSIS OF THREE STATES' EXPERIENCES 14–19 (2003), https://civilrights project.ucla.edu/research/college-access/admissions/percent-plans-in-college-admissions-a-comparative-analysis-of-three-states2019-experiences/horn-percentpl ans-2003.pdf. Percentage plans depend for their effectiveness on continued

The stain of generations of racial oppression is still visible in our society,[33] and the determination to hasten its removal remains vital. One can reasonably anticipate, therefore, that colleges and universities will seek to maintain their minority enrollment and the networks and opportunities thereby opened to minority graduates whether or not they can do so in full candor through adoption of affirmative action plans of the kind here at issue. Without recourse to such plans, institutions of higher education may resort to camouflage. For example, schools may encourage applicants to write of their cultural traditions in the essays they submit, or to indicate whether English is their second language. Seeking to improve their chances for admission, applicants may highlight the minority group associations to which they belong, or the Hispanic surnames of their mothers or grandparents. In turn, teachers' recommendations may emphasize who a student is as much as what he or she has accomplished.[34] If honesty is the best policy, surely Michigan's accurately described, fully disclosed College affirmative action program is preferable to achieving similar numbers through winks, nods, and disguises.[35] [FN 11]

For the reasons stated, I would affirm the judgment of the District Court.

---

racial segregation at the secondary school level: They can ensure significant minority enrollment in universities only if the majority-minority high school population is large enough to guarantee that, in many schools, most of the students in the top 10% or 20% are minorities. Moreover, because such plans link college admission to a single criterion-high school class rank-they create perverse incentives. They encourage parents to keep their children in low-performing segregated schools, and discourage students from taking challenging classes that might lower their grade point averages. *See* Jeffrey Selingo, *What States Aren't Saying About the 'X-Percent Solution'*, CHRON. OF HIGHER EDUC., June 2, 2000, at A31. And even if percentage plans could boost the sheer numbers of minority enrollees at the undergraduate level, they do not touch enrollment in graduate and professional schools.

[33] *See* Krieger, *supra* note 16, at 1253.

[34] *See, e.g.*, Jacques Steinberg, Using Synonyms for Race, College Strives for Diversity, N.Y. TIMES, Dec. 8, 2002, § 1, at 1 col. 3 (describing admissions process at Rice University); *cf.* Brief for United States as Amicus Curiae, supra note 32, at 14–15 (suggesting institutions could consider, inter alia, "a history of overcoming disadvantage," "reputation and location of high school," and "individual outlook as reflected by essays").

[35] [FN 11] Contrary to the Court's contention, I do not suggest "changing the Constitution so that it conforms to the conduct of the universities." *Gratz*, 539 U.S. at 275 n.22. In my view, the Constitution, properly interpreted, permits government officials to respond openly to the continuing importance of race. *See id.* at 301–02 (Ginsburg, J., dissenting). Among constitutionally permissible options, those that candidly disclose their consideration of race seem to me preferable to those that conceal it.

Ricci

"Removing overtly race-based job classifications did not usher in genuinely equal opportunity. More subtle—and sometimes unconscious—forms of discrimination replaced once undisguised restrictions."

The Case

In 2003, 118 firefighters in New Haven, Connecticut, took examinations to qualify for promotion to the rank of lieutenant or captain. The examination results determined which firefighters would be eligible for promotions over the subsequent two years and in what order they would be considered for promotion. "Many firefighters studied for months, at considerable personal and financial cost."[1]

The examinations showed that white candidates outperformed minority candidates.[2] A "rancorous" public debate ensued during which some firefighters argued the test results should be discarded because they were discriminatory, while other firefighters asserted the exams were fair and neutral, regardless of the racial balance of the outcome, and the City should therefore rely on the test results when determining promotions.[3] City officials believed they had no

---

[1] Ricci v. DeStefano, 557 U.S. 557, 562 (2009).

[2] Specifically, the majority opinion described the breakdown of passage rates as follows: Seventy-seven candidates completed the lieutenant examination—43 whites, 19 blacks, and 15 Hispanics. Of those, 34 candidates passed—25 whites, 6 blacks, and 3 Hispanics. Eight lieutenant positions were vacant at the time of the examination. As the rule of three [by which "the relevant hiring authority must fill each vacancy by choosing one candidate from the top three scorers on the list" (*id.* at 564)] operated, this meant that the top 10 candidates were eligible for an immediate promotion to lieutenant. All 10 were white. Subsequent vacancies would have allowed at least 3 black candidates to be considered for promotion to lieutenant. Forty-one candidates completed the captain examination—25 whites, 8 blacks, and 8 Hispanics. Of those, 22 candidates passed—16 whites, 3 blacks, and 3 Hispanics. Seven captain positions were vacant at the time of the examination. Under the rule of three, 9 candidates were eligible for an immediate promotion to captain—7 whites and 2 Hispanics.
Id. at 566 (internal citations omitted).

[3] *See id.* at 567–68.

choice in the matter, fearing that if they adhered to the examination results, they would face a lawsuit by the minority firefighters. Both sides, however—the firefighters who were pleased with the results and those who wanted the results discarded—threatened to file discrimination lawsuits if their viewpoint did not prevail. Ultimately, the City sided with those who protested the examination results, and threw them out.

Seventeen white firefighters and one Hispanic firefighter, most of whom would likely have been promoted based on their good performance on the examinations, sued the City and some of its officials.[4] The suit alleged that by throwing out the examination results, the City had discriminated against the plaintiffs based on their race in violation of both Title VII of the Civil Rights Act of 1964 and the Equal Protection Clause of the Fourteenth Amendment.

A Brief Explanation of Relevant Title VII Law

Title VII prohibits employment discrimination on the basis of the protected traits of race, color, religion, sex, and national original.[5] As originally enacted, Title VII's "principal nondiscrimination provision held employers liable only for disparate treatment."[6] "Disparate treatment cases 'present the most easily understood type of discrimination,'"[7] and occur where an employer has intentionally "'treated [a] particular person less favorably than others because of' a protected trait."[8]

Title VII also "prohibits . . . in some cases, practices that are not intended to discriminate but in fact have a disproportionately adverse effect on minorities."[9] This second type of discrimination, known as "disparate impact," was first recognized by the Supreme Court in two cases from the 1970s[10] and was formally codified as part of Title VII when the Civil Rights Act of 1964 was amended by the Civil Rights

---

[4] The name of the case comes from the lead plaintiff, Frank Ricci, a firefighter who took the examination, and one of the defendants, then-Mayor of New Haven John DeStefano. *See id.* at 574–75.

[5] *See* Title VII of the Civil Rights Act of 1964, 42 U.S.C. §§ 2000e to 2000e-17.

[6] *Ricci*, 557 U.S. at 577.

[7] *Id.* (quoting Int'l Bhd. of Teamsters v. United States, 431 U.S. 324, 335 n.15 (1977)).

[8] *Id.* (quoting Watson v. Fort Worth Bank & Tr., 487 U.S. 977, 985–86 (1988)).

[9] *Id.*

[10] Griggs v. Duke Power Co., 401 U.S. 424 (1971); Albemarle Paper Co. v. Moody, 422 U.S. 405 (1975).

Act of 1991.[11] Under the disparate impact statute, an "employer may defend against liability by demonstrating that the [challenged] practice is 'job related for the position in question and consistent with business necessity.'"[12] But even if the employer meets that burden, "a plaintiff may still succeed by showing that the employer refuses to adopt an available alternative employment practice that has less disparate impact and serves the employer's legitimate needs."[13]

The firefighters who brought suit in *Ricci* were alleging disparate-treatment discrimination under Title VII. As we shall see below, however, discussion of the concept of disparate-impact discrimination is also necessary to understand both the arguments made in response to the firefighters' claim and the reasoning of both the majority and dissenting opinions.

The Case in the Lower Courts

After the initial lawsuit was filed and the discovery process was concluded, both the plaintiffs and the defendants filed motions for summary judgment. The firefighters alleged the City's failure to certify the examination results was "based on the race of the successful candidates," such that the City "discriminated against them in violation of Title VII's disparate-treatment provision."[14] That argument did not prevail, as the United States District Court for the District of Connecticut granted summary judgment for the City and its officials. The court's reasoning was twofold: 1) City officials did not have to certify the results of an examination which they believed would subject the City to a disparate-impact suit just because they could not "pinpoint [the examination's] deficiency explaining its disparate impact" upon different races; and (2) City officials' "'motivation to avoid making promotions based on a test with a racially disparate impact . . . does not, as a matter of law, constitute discriminatory intent' under Title VII."[15] The United States Court of Appeals for the Second Circuit affirmed the district court, though not without the vocal dissent of some of its members.[16]

---

[11] *See Ricci*, 557 U.S. at 577–78.

[12] *Id.* at 578 (quoting 42 U.S.C. § 2000e-2(k)(1)(A)(i)).

[13] *Id.* (citing 42 U.S.C. § 2000e-2(k)(1)(A)(ii), (C)).

[14] *Id.* at 578–79.

[15] *Id.* at 576 (quoting Ricci v. DeStefano, 554 F. Supp. 2d 142, 156, 160 (D. Conn. 2006)).

[16] *See id.*

Justice Kennedy's Majority Opinion

Writing for a 5–4 majority, Justice Kennedy's opinion began with an undisputed premise: "Whatever the City's ultimate aim—however well-intentioned or benevolent it might have seemed—the City made its employment decision because of race."[17] The only question, then, became "whether the City had a lawful justification for its race-based action"—in short, "whether the purpose to avoid disparate-impact liability excused what otherwise would be prohibited disparate-treatment discrimination."[18] In deciding this matter, Kennedy said that the majority's decision must "provide guidance to employers and courts for situations when these two prohibitions could be in conflict absent a rule to reconcile them," and that any such guidance "must be consistent with the important purpose of Title VII—that the workplace be an environment free of discrimination, where race is not a barrier to opportunity."[19]

After discussing numerous potential resolutions offered by the parties addressing the inherent tension between Title VII's conflicting prohibitions, and rejecting all of them as too extreme in one direction or the other, Kennedy found that a test adopted in another area of constitutional jurisprudence—that of the Equal Protection—occupied the middle ground and lent itself well to resolution of the tension in question. The Court had previously held "that certain government actions to remedy past racial discrimination—actions that are themselves based on race—are constitutional only where there is a 'strong basis in evidence' that the remedial actions were necessary."[20] Kennedy further expounded the rationale behind the development of this test before concluding that applying "the strong-basis-in-evidence standard to Title VII gives effect to both the disparate-treatment and disparate-impact provisions, allowing violations of one in the name of compliance with the other only in certain, narrow circumstances."[21]

That standard was ideal because it both "leaves ample room for employers' voluntary compliance efforts, which are essential to the statutory scheme and to Congress's efforts to eradicate workplace discrimination," and "appropriately constrains employers' discretion in making race-based decisions: It limits that discretion to cases in which there is a strong basis in evidence of disparate-impact liability, but it is not so restrictive that it allows employers to act only when

---

[17] *Id.* at 579–80.
[18] *Id.* at 580.
[19] *Id.*
[20] *Id.* at 582 (quoting Richmond v. J. A. Croson Co., 488 U.S. 469, 500 (1989) (internal quotation marks omitted)).
[21] *Id.* at 583.

there is a provable, actual violation."[22] Accordingly, the majority held that "before an employer can engage in intentional discrimination for the asserted purpose of avoiding or remedying an unintentional disparate impact, the employer must have a strong basis in evidence to believe it will be subject to disparate-impact liability if it fails to take the race-conscious, discriminatory action."[23]

These conclusions seemed to indicate the majority was preparing to rule in favor of the City on the grounds that its officials had a "strong basis in evidence" to believe they would be subject to disparate-impact liability if they certified the examination results. Indeed, City officials had argued just that: they believed that they effectively had no choice but to discard the examination results because the numerical disparities in passage rates meant that "the tests appear[ed] to violate Title VII's disparate-impact provisions."[24] But surprisingly, the majority did not agree.

Instead, the majority found that a "showing of a significant statistical disparity" in passage rates "and nothing more" was "far from a strong basis in evidence that the City would have been liable" for disparate-impact discrimination because it did not also show that the examinations "were not job related and consistent with business necessity, or if there existed an equally valid, less-discriminatory alternative that served the City's needs but that the City refused to adopt."[25] To the contrary, the majority found "no evidence—let alone the required strong basis in evidence—that the tests were flawed because they were not job-related or because other, equally valid and less discriminatory tests were available to the City,"[26] and cited substantial evidence from the record to support both findings.[27] Ultimately, the majority concluded, "Fear of litigation alone cannot justify an employer's reliance on race to the detriment of individuals who passed the examinations and qualified for promotions."[28]

---

[22] *Id.*

[23] *Id.* at 585.

[24] *Id.* at 579 (quoting Brief for Respondents at 12, *Ricci*, 557 U.S. 557 (Nos. 07-1427, 08-328)).

[25] *Id.* at 587.

[26] *Id.* at 592.

[27] *See generally id.* at 561–92.

[28] *Id.* at 592. Because the Court decided the case based on Title VII alone, it did not "reach the question whether respondents' actions may have violated the Equal Protection Clause." *Id.* at 563.

Justice Ginsburg's Dissent

Justice Ginsburg's dissent directly assaulted the majority's holding and the evidence supporting it, and did not mince words: "The Court today holds that New Haven has not demonstrated 'a strong basis in evidence' for its plea. In so holding, the Court pretends that the City rejected the test results solely because the higher scoring candidates were white. That pretension, essential to the Court's disposition, ignores substantial evidence of multiple flaws in the tests New Haven used. The Court similarly fails to acknowledge the better tests used in other cities, which have yielded less racially skewed outcomes."[29] She then dismantled, piece by piece, the majority's logic, and did so by citing to facts in the record which, in her view, the majority had intentionally overlooked.

Ginsburg believed that the majority's "recitation of the facts le[ft] out important parts of the story."[30] She began by tracing the history of racial discrimination in firefighting, "a profession in which the legacy of racial discrimination casts an especially long shadow," and said that it was "against this backdrop of entrenched inequality that the promotion process at issue in this litigation should be assessed."[31] She then expounded at length how the underlying structure of the City's examination was fundamentally flawed. She focused especially on testimony by a representative of the company that created the examination who stated "that the City never asked whether alternative methods might better measure the qualities of a successful fire officers, including leadership skills and command presence."[32]

Ginsburg observed that the majority acknowledged that the "stark disparities" in passage rates "sufficed to state a prima facie case under Title VII's disparate-impact provision."[33] She then cited the example of another Connecticut city which switched from examination methods similar to those at issue in this case to others which more accurately "addressed the sort of real-life scenarios fire officers encounter on the job," after which that city "had seen minorities fairly represented in its exam results."[34] She also identified substantial evidence from the record, including testimony by a senior expert in the field of firefighter testing, showing that the design of New Haven's test specifically led to a "relatively high adverse impact," whereas other forms of testing would have a "significantly and dramatically

---

[29] *Id.* at 608–09 (Ginsburg, J., dissenting).
[30] *Id.* at 609.
[31] *See id.* at 609, 611.
[32] *Id.* at 611–12.
[33] *Id.* at 612.
[34] *Id.* at 614 (internal quotation marks omitted).

less adverse impact,"[35] and even statements by the City's own lawyer asserting that the examination was not optimally designed "to identify solutions to real problems on the fire ground" and that the examination results practically invited a Title VII lawsuit because of their significantly adverse impact.[36]

For Ginsburg, these and other facts from the record led to the inevitable conclusion that the City had not discriminated on the basis of race because "'all the test results were discarded, no one was promoted, and firefighters of every race will have to participate in another selection process to be considered for promotion.'"[37] In Ginsburg's view, the City's conduct was appropriate. Ginsburg would therefore have held "that an employer who jettisons a selection device when its disproportionate racial impact becomes apparent does not violate Title VII's disparate-treatment bar automatically or at all" if the employer has "good cause to believe the device would not withstand examination for business necessity," as required by Title VII.[38]

Accordingly, Ginsburg excoriated the majority for its new "strong basis in evidence" standard, calling the standard "enigmatic" and "barely described," lambasting the "justifications" for it as "unimpressive," and predicting that in the future it would make "voluntary compliance a hazardous venture."[39] In other words, Ginsburg feared that at best, the new standard would make it much more difficult for employers to determine when they should take action to remedy possible discrimination, and at worst, it would create a chilling effect on anti-discriminatory action.

Instead, Ginsburg reiterated that the "business necessity" standard—the one contemplated by the Civil Rights Act of 1991—remained the appropriate standard. Ginsburg then set out to apply that standard to the facts of the case. She discussed at length substantial evidence from the record ignored by the majority—including evidence supporting the proposition that "[r]elying heavily on written tests to select fire officers is a questionable practice"—to reach the conclusion that "it is unsurprising that most municipal employers do not evaluate their fire-officer candidates as New Haven does."[40]

Due to the substance and volume of this evidence, Ginsburg concluded she would have reached quite a different holding from the majority: that "New Haven had ample cause to believe its selection

[35] *Id.* at 615 (internal quotation marks omitted).
[36] *Id.* at 617–18 (internal quotation marks omitted).
[37] *Id.* at 619 (quoting Ricci v. DeStefano, 554 F. Supp. 2d 142, 158 (D. Conn. 2006)).
[38] *Id.* at 625–26; *see also* 42 U.S.C. § 2000e-2(k)(1)(A)(i).
[39] *Ricci*, 557 U.S. at 627, 629–30 (Ginsburg, J., dissenting).
[40] *Id.* at 633–34.

process was flawed and not justified by business necessity," meaning the City's failure to certify the exam results did not violate Title VII on disparate-treatment grounds.[41] Using one of her characteristic bits of rhetorical flourish, Ginsburg insisted that the majority simply ignored those difficult facts which did not fit within its narrative:

> Like the chess player who tries to win by sweeping the opponent's pieces off the table, the Court simply shuts from its sight the formidable obstacles New Haven would have faced in defending against a disparate-impact suit."[42]

Ginsburg believed that the City had acted appropriately because it "had good cause to fear disparate-impact liability," and regardless lamented that the majority supplied "no tenable explanation why the evidence of the tests" multiple deficiencies does "not create at least a triable issue under a strong-basis-in-evidence standard."[43]

Ultimately, Ginsburg's view can be summarized succinctly in her own words, written specifically in response to the concurring opinion authored by Justice Alito: "[W]hen employers endeavor to avoid exposure to disparate-impact liability, they do not thereby encounter liability for disparate treatment."[44] In holding otherwise, the majority rested its judgment on a "false premise"—that the examination results showed "'a significant statistical disparity,' but 'nothing more.'"[45] By making this "choice," Ginsburg lamented that the majority broke the promise of the Court's earlier decisions and the Civil Rights Act of 1991 "that groups long denied equal opportunity would not be held back by tests 'fair in form, but discriminatory in operation.'"[46]

---

[41] *See id.* at 632.

[42] *Id.* at 636.

[43] *Id.* at 638.

[44] *Id.* at 643.

[45] *Id.* at 644 (quoting majority opinion at 587).

[46] *Id.* (quoting Griggs v. Duke Power Co., 401 U.S. 424, 431 (1971)).

Ricci v. DeStefano

Justice Ginsburg, with whom Justice Stevens, Justice Souter, and Justice Breyer join, Dissenting.

In assessing claims of race discrimination, "[c]ontext matters."[1] In 1972, Congress extended Title VII of the Civil Rights Act of 1964 to cover public employment. At that time, municipal fire departments across the country, including New Haven's, pervasively discriminated against minorities. The extension of Title VII to cover jobs in firefighting effected no overnight change. It took decades of persistent effort, advanced by Title VII litigation, to open firefighting posts to members of racial minorities.

The white firefighters who scored high on New Haven's promotional exams understandably attract this Court's sympathy. But they had no vested right to promotion. Nor have other persons received promotions in preference to them. New Haven maintains that it refused to certify the test results because it believed, for good cause, that it would be vulnerable to a Title VII disparate-impact suit if it relied on those results. The Court today holds that New Haven has not demonstrated "a strong basis in evidence" for its plea.[2] In so holding, the Court pretends that "[t]he City rejected the test results solely because the higher scoring candidates were white."[3] That pretension, essential to the Court's disposition, ignores substantial evidence of multiple flaws in the tests New Haven used. The Court similarly fails to acknowledge the better tests used in other cities, which have yielded less racially skewed outcomes.[4] [FN 1]

---

[1] Grutter v. Bollinger, 539 U.S. 306, 327 (2003).

[2] *Ricci*, 557 U.S. at 563.

[3] *Id.* at 580.

[4] [FN 1] Never mind the flawed tests New Haven used and the better selection methods used elsewhere, Justice Alito's concurring opinion urges. Overriding all else, racial politics, fired up by a strident African-American pastor, were at work in New Haven. *See id.* at 563–69. Even a detached and disinterested observer, however, would have every reason to ask: Why did such racially skewed results occur in New Haven, when better tests likely would have produced less disproportionate results?

By order of this Court, New Haven, a city in which African-Americans and Hispanics account for nearly 60 percent of the population, must today be served—as it was in the days of undisguised discrimination—by a fire department in which members of racial and ethnic minorities are rarely seen in command positions. In arriving at its order, the Court barely acknowledges the path marking decision in *Griggs v. Duke Power Co.*,[5] which explained the centrality of the disparate-impact concept to effective enforcement of Title VII. The Court's order and opinion, I anticipate, will not have staying power.

I

A

The Court's recitation of the facts leaves out important parts of the story. Firefighting is a profession in which the legacy of racial discrimination casts an especially long shadow. In extending Title VII to state and local government employers in 1972, Congress took note of a U. S. Commission on Civil Rights (USCCR) report finding racial discrimination in municipal employment even "more pervasive than in the private sector."[6] According to the report, overt racism was partly to blame, but so too was a failure on the part of municipal employers to apply merit-based employment principles. In making hiring and promotion decisions, public employers often "rel[ied] on criteria unrelated to job performance," including nepotism or political patronage.[7] Such flawed selection methods served to entrench preexisting racial hierarchies. The USCCR report singled out police and fire departments for having "[b]arriers to equal employment . . . greater . . . than in any other area of State or local government," with African-Americans "hold[ing] almost no positions in the officer ranks."[8]

The city of New Haven (City) was no exception. In the early 1970's, African-Americans and Hispanics composed 30 percent of New Haven's population, but only 3.6 percent of the City's 502 firefighters. The racial disparity in the officer ranks was even more pronounced: "[O]f the 107 officers in the Department only one was black, and he held the lowest rank above private."[9]

---

[5] 401 U.S. 424 (1971).

[6] H.R. REP. NO. 92-238, at 17 (1971).

[7] 118 CONG. REC. 1,817 (1972).

[8] *Id.; see also* NAT'L COMM'N ON FIRE PREVENTION & CONTROL, AMERICA BURNING 5 (1973) ("Racial minorities are under-represented in the fire departments in nearly every community in which they live.").

[9] Firebird Soc'y of New Haven, Inc. v. New Haven Bd. of Fire Comm'rs, 66

Following a lawsuit and settlement agreement,[10] the City initiated efforts to increase minority representation in the New Haven Fire Department (Department). Those litigation-induced efforts produced some positive change. New Haven's population includes a greater proportion of minorities today than it did in the 1970's: Nearly 40 percent of the City's residents are African-American and more than 20 percent are Hispanic. Among entry-level firefighters, minorities are still underrepresented, but not starkly so. As of 2003, African-Americans and Hispanics constituted 30 percent and 16 percent of the City's firefighters, respectively. In supervisory positions, however, significant disparities remain. Overall, the senior officer ranks (captain and higher) are nine percent African-American and nine percent Hispanic. Only one of the Department's 21 fire captains is African-American.[11] It is against this backdrop of entrenched inequality that the promotion process at issue in this litigation should be assessed.

B

By order of its charter, New Haven must use competitive examinations to fill vacancies in fire officer and other civil-service positions. Such examinations, the City's civil service rules specify, "shall be practical in nature, shall relate to matters which fairly measure the relative fitness and capacity of the applicants to discharge the duties of the position which they seek, and shall take into account character, training, experience, physical and mental fitness."[12] The City may choose among a variety of testing methods, including written and oral exams and "[p]erformance tests to demonstrate skill and ability in performing actual work."[13]

New Haven, the record indicates, did not closely consider what sort of "practical" examination would "fairly measure the relative fitness and capacity of the applicants to discharge the duties" of a fire officer. Instead, the City simply adhered to the testing regime outlined in its two-decades-old contract with the local firefighters' union: a written exam, which would account for 60 percent of an applicant's total score, and an oral exam, which would account for the remaining 40 percent.[14] In soliciting bids from exam development companies, New Haven made clear that it would entertain only "proposals that

---

F.R.D. 457, 460 (D. Conn. 1975).

[10] *See id.*

[11] *See* App. at A1588, Ricci v. DeStefano, 530 F.3d 87 (No. 06-4996-cv) (2d Cir. 2008) (per curiam) [hereinafter CA2 App.].

[12] *Id.* at A331.

[13] *Id.* at A332.

[14] *Id.* at A1045.

include a written component that will be weighted at 60%, and an oral component that will be weighted at 40%."[15] Chad Legel, a representative of the winning bidder, Industrial / Organizational Solutions, Inc. (IOS), testified during his deposition that the City never asked whether alternative methods might better measure the qualities of a successful fire officer, including leadership skills and command presence.[16]

Pursuant to New Haven's specifications, IOS developed and administered the oral and written exams. The results showed significant racial disparities. On the lieutenant exam, the pass rate for African-American candidates was about one-half the rate for Caucasian candidates; the pass rate for Hispanic candidates was even lower. On the captain exam, both African-American and Hispanic candidates passed at about half the rate of their Caucasian counterparts.[17] More striking still, although nearly half of the 77 lieutenant candidates were African-American or Hispanic, none would have been eligible for promotion to the eight positions then vacant. The highest scoring African-American candidate ranked 13th; the top Hispanic candidate was 26th. As for the seven then-vacant captain positions, two Hispanic candidates would have been eligible, but no African-Americans. The highest scoring African-American candidate ranked 15th.[18]

These stark disparities, the Court acknowledges, sufficed to state a prima facie case under Title VII's disparate-impact provision.[19] New Haven thus had cause for concern about the prospect of Title VII litigation and liability. City officials referred the matter to the New Haven Civil Service Board (CSB), the entity responsible for certifying the results of employment exams.

Between January and March 2004, the CSB held five public meetings to consider the proper course. At the first meeting, New Haven's Corporation Counsel, Thomas Ude, described the legal standard governing Title VII disparate-impact claims. Statistical imbalances alone, Ude correctly recognized, do not give rise to liability. Instead, presented with a disparity, an employer "has the opportunity and the burden of proving that the test is job-related and consistent with

---

[15] *Id.* at A342.

[16] *See id.* at A522 ("I was under contract and had responsibility only to create the oral interview and the written exam.").

[17] *See* App. at 225–26, Ricci v. DeStefano, 557 U.S. 557 (Nos. 07-1428, 08-328) (2009).

[18] *See id.* at 218–19.

[19] *See Ricci*, 557 U.S. at 586 ("The pass rates of minorities . . . f[e]ll well below the 80-percent standard set by the [Equal Employment Opportunity Commission (EEOC)] to implement the disparate-impact provision of Title VII.").

business necessity."[20] A Title VII plaintiff may attempt to rebut an employer's showing of job-relatedness and necessity by identifying alternative selection methods that would have been at least as valid but with "less of an adverse or disparate or discriminatory effect."[21] Accordingly, the CSB Commissioners understood, their principal task was to decide whether they were confident about the reliability of the exams: Had the exams fairly measured the qualities of a successful fire officer despite their disparate results? Might an alternative examination process have identified the most qualified candidates without creating such significant racial imbalances?

Seeking a range of input on these questions, the CSB heard from test takers, the test designer, subject-matter experts, City officials, union leaders, and community members. Several candidates for promotion, who did not yet know their exam results, spoke at the CSB's first two meetings. Some candidates favored certification. The exams, they emphasized, had closely tracked the assigned study materials. Having invested substantial time and money to prepare themselves for the test, they felt it would be unfair to scrap the results.[22]

Other firefighters had a different view. A number of the exam questions, they pointed out, were not germane to New Haven's practices and procedures.[23] At least two candidates opposed to certification noted unequal access to study materials. Some individuals, they asserted, had the necessary books even before the syllabus was issued. Others had to invest substantial sums to purchase the materials and "wait a month and a half for some of the books because they were on back-order."[24] These disparities, it was suggested, fell at least in part along racial lines. While many Caucasian applicants could obtain materials and assistance from relatives in the fire service, the overwhelming majority of minority applicants were "first-generation firefighters" without such support networks.[25]

A representative of the Northeast Region of the International Association of Black Professional Firefighters, Donald Day, also spoke at the second meeting. Statistical disparities, he told the CSB, had been present in the Department's previous promotional exams. On earlier tests, however, a few minority candidates had fared well enough to earn promotions.[26] Day contrasted New Haven's experience with that of nearby Bridgeport, where minority firefighters held one-third of

[20] CA2 App., *supra* note 11, at A724.

[21] *Id.*; *see also id.* at A738.

[22] *See, e.g., id.* at A772–A773, A785–A789.

[23] *See, e.g., id.* at A774–A784.

[24] *Id.* at A858.

[25] *See id.* at A857–A861, A886–A887.

[26] *Id.* at A828; *see also* App., *supra* note 17, at 218–219.

lieutenant and captain positions. Bridgeport, Day observed, had once used a testing process similar to New Haven's, with a written exam accounting for 70 percent of an applicant's score, an oral exam for 25 percent, and seniority for the remaining five percent.[27] Bridgeport recognized, however, that the oral component, more so than the written component, addressed the sort of "real-life scenarios" fire officers encounter on the job.[28] Accordingly, that city "changed the relative weights" to give primacy to the oral exam. Since that time, Day reported, Bridgeport had seen minorities "fairly represented" in its exam results.[29]

The CSB's third meeting featured IOS representative Legel, the leader of the team that had designed and administered the exams for New Haven. Several City officials also participated in the discussion. Legel described the exam development process in detail. The City, he recounted, had set the "parameters" for the exams, specifically, the requirement of written and oral components with a 60/40 weighting.[30] For security reasons, Department officials had not been permitted to check the content of the questions prior to their administration. Instead, IOS retained a senior fire officer from Georgia to review the exams "for content and fidelity to the source material."[31] Legel defended the exams as "facially neutral," and stated that he "would stand by the[ir] validity."[32] City officials did not dispute the neutrality of IOS's work. But, they cautioned, even if individual exam questions had no intrinsic bias, the selection process as a whole may nevertheless have been deficient. The officials urged the CSB to consult with experts about the "larger picture."[33]

At its fourth meeting, CSB solicited the views of three individuals with testing-related expertise. Dr. Christopher Hornick, an industrial/organizational psychology consultant with 25 years' experience with police and firefighter testing, described the exam results as having "relatively high adverse impact."[34] Most of the tests he had developed, Hornick stated, exhibited "significantly and dramatically less adverse impact."[35] Hornick downplayed the notion of "facial neutrality." It was more important, he advised the CSB, to consider "the broader issue of how your procedures and your rules and the types of

---

[27] CA2 App., *supra* note 11, at A830.
[28] *Id.* at A832.
[29] *Id.*
[30] *Id.* at A923, A974.
[31] *Id.* at A936.
[32] *Id.* at A962.
[33] *Id.* at A1012.
[34] *Id.* at A1028.
[35] *Id.* at A1029.

tests that you are using are contributing to the adverse impact."[36]

Specifically, Hornick questioned New Haven's union-prompted 60/40 written/oral examination structure, noting the availability of "different types of testing procedures that are much more valid in terms of identifying the best potential supervisors in [the] fire department."[37] He suggested, for example, "an assessment center process, which is essentially an opportunity for candidates . . . to demonstrate how they would address a particular problem as opposed to just verbally saying it or identifying the correct option on a written test."[38] Such selection processes, Hornick said, better "identif[y] the best possible people" and "demonstrate dramatically less adverse impacts."[39] Hornick added:

"I've spoken to at least 10,000, maybe 15,000 firefighters in group settings in my consulting practice and I have never one time ever had anyone in the fire service say to me, 'Well, the person who answers— gets the highest score on a written job knowledge, multiple-guess test makes the best company officer.' We know that it's not as valid as other procedures that exist."[40]

Hornick described the written test itself as "reasonably good,"[41] but he criticized the decision not to allow Department officials to check the content. According to Hornick, this "inevitably" led to "test[ing] for processes and procedures that don't necessarily match up into the department."[42] He preferred "experts from within the department who have signed confidentiality agreements . . . to make sure that the terminology and equipment that's being identified from standardized reading sources apply to the department."[43]

Asked whether he thought the City should certify the results, Hornick hedged: "There is adverse impact in the test. That will be identified in any proceeding that you have. You will have industrial psychology experts, if it goes to court, on both sides. And it will not be a pretty or comfortable position for anyone to be in."[44] Perhaps, he suggested, New Haven might certify the results but immediately

---

[36] *Id.* at A1038.

[37] *Id.* at A1032.

[38] *Id.* at A1039–A1040.

[39] *Id.*

[40] *Id.* at A1033; *see also id.* at A1042–A1043 ("I think a person's leadership skills, their command presence, their interpersonal skills, their management skills, their tactical skills could have been identified and evaluated in a much more appropriate way.").

[41] *Id.* at A1041.

[42] *Id.* at A1034–A1035.

[43] *Id.* at A1035.

[44] *Id.* at A1040–A1041.

begin exploring "alternative ways to deal with these issues" in the future.[45]

The two other witnesses made relatively brief appearances. Vincent Lewis, a specialist with the Department of Homeland Security and former fire officer in Michigan, believed the exams had generally tested relevant material, although he noted a relatively heavy emphasis on questions pertaining to being an "apparatus driver." He suggested that this may have disadvantaged test takers "who had not had the training or had not had an opportunity to drive the apparatus."[46] He also urged the CSB to consider whether candidates had, in fact, enjoyed equal access to the study materials.[47]

Janet Helms, a professor of counseling psychology at Boston College, observed that two-thirds of the incumbent fire officers who submitted job analyses to IOS during the exam design phase were Caucasian. Members of different racial groups, Helms told the CSB, sometimes do their jobs in different ways, "often because the experiences that are open to white male firefighters are not open to members of these other under-represented groups."[48] The heavy reliance on job analyses from white firefighters, she suggested, may thus have introduced an element of bias.[49]

The CSB's fifth and final meeting began with statements from City officials recommending against certification. Ude, New Haven's counsel, repeated the applicable disparate-impact standard:

"[A] finding of adverse impact is the beginning, not the end, of a review of testing procedures. Where a procedure demonstrates adverse impact, you look to how closely it is related to the job that you're looking to fill and you also look at whether there are other ways to test for those qualities, those traits, those positions that are equally valid with less adverse impact."[50]

New Haven, Ude and other officials asserted, would be vulnerable to Title VII liability under this standard. Even if the exams were "facially neutral," significant doubts had been raised about whether they properly assessed the key attributes of a successful fire officer.[51] More-

---

[45] *Id.* at A1041.

[46] *Id.* at A1051.

[47] *Id. Cf.* Ricci v. DeStefano, 557 U.S. 557, 613–14 (2009) (Ginsburg, J., dissenting).

[48] CA2 App., *supra* note 11, at A1063–A1064.

[49] *Id.* at A1063.

[50] *Id.* at A1100–A1101.

[51] *Id.* at A1103; *see also id.* at A1125 ("Upon close reading of the exams, the questions themselves would appear to test a candidate's ability to memorize textbooks but not necessarily to identify solutions to real problems on the fire ground.").

over, City officials reminded the CSB, Hornick and others had identified better, less discriminatory selection methods–such as assessment
centers or exams with a more heavily weighted oral component.[52]

After giving members of the public a final chance to weigh in, the
CSB voted on certification, dividing 2 to 2. By rule, the result was
noncertification. Voting no, Commissioner Webber stated, "I originally
was going to vote to certify. . . . But I've heard enough testimony here
to give me great doubts about the test itself and . . . some of the procedures. And I believe we can do better."[53] Commissioner Tirado likewise concluded that the "flawed" testing process counseled against
certification.[54] Chairman Segaloff and Commissioner Caplan voted to
certify. According to Segaloff, the testimony had not "compelled [him]
to say this exam was not job-related," and he was unconvinced that
alternative selection processes would be "less discriminatory."[55] Both
Segalhoff and Caplan, however, urged the City to undertake civil service reform.[56]

C

Following the CSB's vote, petitioners—17 white firefighters and
one Hispanic firefighter, all of whom had high marks on the exams—
filed suit in the United States District Court for the District of Connecticut. They named as defendants—respondents here—the City,
several City officials, a local political activist, and the two CSB members who voted against certifying the results. By opposing certification, petitioners alleged, respondents had discriminated against them
in violation of Title VII's disparate-treatment provision and the Fourteenth Amendment's Equal Protection Clause. The decision not to
certify, respondents answered, was a lawful effort to comply with Title VII's disparate-impact provision and thus could not have run afoul
of Title VII's prohibition of disparate treatment. Characterizing respondents' stated rationale as a mere pretext, petitioners insisted
that New Haven would have had a solid defense to any disparate-
impact suit.

In a decision summarily affirmed by the Court of Appeals, the District Court granted summary judgment for respondents.[57] Under Second Circuit precedent, the District Court explained, "the intent to

[52] *Id.* at A1108–A1109, A1129–A1130.
[53] *Id.* at A1157.
[54] *Id.* at A1158.
[55] *Id.* at A1159–A1160.
[56] *Id.* at A1150–A1154.
[57] Ricci v. DeStefano, 554 F. Supp. 2d 142 (D. Conn. 2006), *aff'd*, 530 F.3d 87
(2d Cir. 2008) (per curiam).

remedy the disparate impact" of a promotional exam "is not equivalent to an intent to discriminate against non-minority applicants."[58] Rejecting petitioners' pretext argument, the court observed that the exam results were sufficiently skewed "to make out a prima facie case of discrimination" under Title VII's disparate-impact provision.[59] Had New Haven gone forward with certification and been sued by aggrieved minority test takers, the City would have been forced to defend tests that were presumptively invalid. And, as the CSB testimony of Hornick and others indicated, overcoming that presumption would have been no easy task.[60] Given Title VII's preference for voluntary compliance, the court held, New Haven could lawfully discard the disputed exams even if the City had not definitively "pinpoint[ed]" the source of the disparity and "ha[d] not yet formulated a better selection method."[61]

Respondents were no doubt conscious of race during their decision-making process, the court acknowledged, but this did not mean they had engaged in racially disparate treatment. The conclusion they had reached and the action thereupon taken were race-neutral in this sense: "[A]ll the test results were discarded, no one was promoted, and firefighters of every race will have to participate in another selection process to be considered for promotion."[62] New Haven's action, which gave no individual a preference, "was 'simply not analogous to a quota system or a minority set-aside where candidates, on the basis of their race, are not treated uniformly.'"[63] For these and other reasons, the court also rejected petitioners' equal protection claim.

II

A

Title VII became effective in July 1965. Employers responded to the law by eliminating rules and practices that explicitly barred racial minorities from "white" jobs. But removing overtly race-based job classifications did not usher in genuinely equal opportunity. More subtle—and sometimes unconscious—forms of discrimination replaced once undisguised restrictions.

---

[58] *Id.* at 157 (quoting Hayden v. Cty. of Nassau, 180 F.3d 42, 51 (2d Cir. 1999)).

[59] *Id.* at 158.

[60] *Id.* at 153–56.

[61] *Id.* at 156.

[62] *Id.* at 158.

[63] *Id.* at 157 (quoting *Hayden*, 180 F.3d at 50).

In *Griggs v. Duke Power Co.*,[64] this Court responded to that reality and supplied important guidance on Title VII's mission and scope. Congress, the landmark decision recognized, aimed beyond "disparate treatment"; it targeted "disparate impact" as well. Title VII's original text, it was plain to the Court, "proscribe[d] not only overt discrimination but also practices that are fair in form, but discriminatory in operation."[65; 66 [FN 2]] Only by ignoring *Griggs* could one maintain that intentionally disparate treatment alone was Title VII's "original, foundational prohibition," and disparate impact a mere afterthought.[67]

Griggs addressed Duke Power Company's policy that applicants for positions, save in the company's labor department, be high school graduates and score satisfactorily on two professionally prepared aptitude tests. "[T]here was no showing of a discriminatory purpose in the adoption of the diploma and test requirements."[68] The policy, however, "operated to render ineligible a markedly disproportionate number of [African-Americans]."[69] At the time of the litigation, in North Carolina, where the Duke Power plant was located, 34 percent of white males, but only 12 percent of African-American males, had high school diplomas.[70] African-Americans also failed the aptitude tests at a significantly higher rate than whites.[71] Neither requirement had been "shown to bear a demonstrable relationship to successful performance of the jobs for which it was used."[72]

The Court unanimously held that the company's diploma and test

---

[64] 401 U.S. 424 (1971).

[65] *Id.* at 431.

[66] [FN 2] The Court's disparate-impact analysis rested on two provisions of Title VII: §703(a)(2), which made it unlawful for an employer "to limit, segregate, or classify his employees in any way which would deprive or tend to deprive any individual of employment opportunities or otherwise adversely affect his status as an employee, because of such individual's race, color, religion, sex, or national origin"; and §703(h), which permitted employers "to act upon the results of any professionally developed ability test provided that such test, its administration or action upon the results is not designed, intended or used to discriminate because of race, color, religion, sex or national origin." *Griggs*, 401 U.S. at 426 n.1 (1971) (quoting 78 Stat. 255 (1964) (codified as amended at 42 U.S.C. §2000e-2(a)(2), (h))); *see also id.* at 433–36 (explaining that §703(h) authorizes only tests that are "demonstrably a reasonable measure of job performance").

[67] *Cf.* Ricci v. DeStefano, 557 U.S. 557, 581 (2009).

[68] *Griggs*, 401 U.S. at 428.

[69] *Id.* at 429.

[70] *Id.* at 430 n.6.

[71] *Id.*

[72] *Id.* at 431.

requirements violated Title VII. "[T]o achieve equality of employment opportunities," the Court comprehended, Congress "directed the thrust of the Act to the consequences of employment practices, not simply the motivation."[73] That meant "unnecessary barriers to employment" must fall, even if "neutral on their face" and "neutral in terms of intent."[74] "The touchstone" for determining whether a test or qualification meets Title VII's measure, the Court said, is not "good intent or the absence of discriminatory intent"; it is "business necessity."[75] Matching procedure to substance, the *Griggs* Court observed, Congress "placed on the employer the burden of showing that any given requirement . . . ha[s] a manifest relationship to the employment in question."[76]

In *Albemarle Paper Co. v. Moody*,[77] the Court, again without dissent, elaborated on *Griggs*. When an employment test "select[s] applicants for hire or promotion in a racial pattern significantly different from the pool of applicants," the Court reiterated, the employer must demonstrate a "manifest relationship" between test and job.[78] Such a showing, the Court cautioned, does not necessarily mean the employer prevails: "[I]t remains open to the complaining party to show that other tests or selection devices, without a similarly undesirable racial effect, would also serve the employer's legitimate interest in 'efficient and trustworthy workmanship.'"[79]

Federal trial and appellate courts applied *Griggs* and *Albemarle* to disallow a host of hiring and promotion practices that "operate[d] as 'built in headwinds' for minority groups."[80] Practices discriminatory in effect, courts repeatedly emphasized, could be maintained only upon an employer's showing of "an overriding and compelling business purpose."[81; 82 [FN 3]] That a practice served "legitimate management

---

[73] *Id.* at 429, 432.
[74] *Id.* at 430, 431.
[75] *Id.* at 431, 432.
[76] *Id.* at 432.
[77] 422 U.S. 405 (1975).
[78] *Id.* at 425.
[79] *Id.*
[80] *Griggs*, 401 U.S. at 432.
[81] Chrisner v. Complete Auto Transit, Inc., 645 F.2d 1251, 1261 n.9 (6th Cir. 1981).
[82] [FN 3] *See also* Dothard v. Rawlinson, 433 U.S. 321, 332 n.14 (1977) ("a discriminatory employment practice must be shown to be necessary to safe and efficient job performance to survive a Title VII challenge"); Williams v. Colorado Springs, Colo., Sch. Dist. # 11, 641 F.2d 835, 840–41 (10th Cir. 1981) ("The term 'necessity' connotes that the exclusionary practice must be shown to be of great importance to job performance."); Kirby v. Colony Furniture Co., 613 F.2d 696, 705 n.6 (8th Cir. 1980) ("the proper standard for determining

functions" did not, it was generally understood, suffice to establish business necessity.[83] Among selection methods cast aside for lack of a "manifest relationship" to job performance were a number of written hiring and promotional examinations for firefighters.[84] [FN 4]

Moving in a different direction, in *Wards Cove Packing Co. v. Atonio*,[85] a bare majority of this Court significantly modified the *Griggs-Albemarle* delineation of Title VII's disparate-impact proscription. As to business necessity for a practice that disproportionately excludes members of minority groups, *Wards Cove* held, the employer bears only the burden of production, not the burden of persuasion.[86] And in place of the instruction that the challenged practice "must have a manifest relationship to the employment in question,"[87] *Wards Cove* said that the practice would be permissible as long as it "serve[d], in a significant way, the legitimate employment goals of the employer."[88]

In response to *Wards Cove* and "a number of [other] recent decisions by the United States Supreme Court that sharply cut back on the scope and effectiveness of [civil rights] laws," Congress enacted the Civil Rights Act of 1991.[89] Among the 1991 alterations, Congress

---

whether 'business necessity' justifies a practice which has a racially discriminatory result is not whether it is justified by routine business considerations but whether there is a compelling need for the employer to maintain that practice and whether the employer can prove there is no alternative to the challenged practice"); Pettway v. Am. Cast Iron Pipe Co., 494 F.2d 211, 244 n.87 (5th Cir. 1974) ("this doctrine of business necessity . . . connotes an irresistible demand" (internal quotation marks omitted)); United States v. Bethlehem Steel Corp., 446 F.2d 652, 662 (2d Cir. 1971) (an exclusionary practice "must not only directly foster safety and efficiency of a plant, but also be essential to those goals"); Robinson v. Lorillard Corp., 444 F.2d 791, 798 (4th Cir. 1971) ("The test is whether there exists an overriding legitimate business purpose such that the practice is necessary to the safe and efficient operation of the business.").

[83] *Williams*, 641 F.2d 835, 840–41 (10th Cir. 1981) (internal quotation marks omitted).

[84] [FN 4] *See, e.g.*, Nash v. Jacksonville, 837 F.2d 1534 (11th Cir. 1988), *vacated*, 490 U.S. 1103 (1989), *opinion reinstated*, 905 F.2d 355 (11th Cir. 1990); Vulcan Pioneers, Inc. v. N.J. Dept. of Civil Serv., 832 F.2d 811 (3d Cir. 1987); Guardians Assn. of N.Y. City Police Dept. v. Civil Serv. Comm'n, 630 F.2d 79 (2d Cir. 1980); Ensley Branch of NAACP v. Seibels, 616 F.2d 812 (5th Cir. 1980); Firefighters Inst. for Racial Equality v. St. Louis, 616 F.2d 350 (8th Cir. 1980); Boston Chapter, NAACP, Inc. v. Beecher, 504 F.2d 1017 (1st Cir. 1974).

[85] 490 U.S. 642 (1989).

[86] *Id.* at 659–60.

[87] Griggs v. Duke Power Co., 401 U.S. 424, 432 (1971).

[88] Wards Cove Packing Co., Inc. v. Atonio, 490 U. S. 642, 659 (1989).

[89] H.R. REP. NO. 102-40, pt. 2, at 2 (1991).

formally codified the disparate-impact component of Title VII. In so amending the statute, Congress made plain its intention to restore "the concepts of 'business necessity' and 'job related' enunciated by the Supreme Court in *Griggs v. Duke Power Co.* . . . and in other Supreme Court decisions prior to *Wards Cove Packing Co. v. Atonio.*"[90] Once a complaining party demonstrates that an employment practice causes a disparate impact, amended Title VII states, the burden is on the employer "to demonstrate that the challenged practice is job related for the position in question and consistent with business necessity."[91] If the employer carries that substantial burden, the complainant may respond by identifying "an alternative employment practice" which the employer "refuses to adopt."[92]

B

Neither Congress' enactments nor this Court's Title VII precedents (including the now-discredited decision in *Wards Cove*) offer even a hint of "conflict" between an employer's obligations under the statute's disparate-treatment and disparate-impact provisions.[93] Standing on an equal footing, these twin pillars of Title VII advance the same objectives: ending workplace discrimination and promoting genuinely equal opportunity.[94]

Yet the Court today sets at odds the statute's core directives. When an employer changes an employment practice in an effort to comply with Title VII's disparate-impact provision, the Court reasons, it acts "because of race"—something Title VII's disparate-treatment provision[95] generally forbids.[96] This characterization of an employer's compliance-directed action shows little attention to Congress' design or to the *Griggs* line of cases Congress recognized as path-marking.

"[O]ur task in interpreting separate provisions of a single Act is to give the Act the most harmonious, comprehensive meaning possible in light of the legislative policy and purpose."[97] A particular phrase need not "extend to the outer limits of its definitional possibilities" if an incongruity would result.[98] Here, Title VII's disparate-treatment

---

[90] Civil Rights Act of 1991, Pub. L. No. 102-166 § 3(2), 105 Stat. 1071 (1991).

[91] 42 U.S.C. §2000e-2(k)(1)(A)(i).

[92] 42 U.S.C. § 2000e-2(k)(1)(A)(ii), (C).

[93] *Cf.* Ricci v. DeStefano, 557 U.S. 557, 579–80 (2009).

[94] *See* McDonnell Douglas Corp. v. Green, 411 U.S. 792, 800 (1973).

[95] *See* 42 U.S.C. § 2000e-2(a)(1).

[96] *Ricci*, 557 U.S. at 579–80.

[97] Weinberger v. Hynson, Westcott & Dunning, Inc., 412 U.S. 609, 631–32 (1973) (internal quotation marks omitted).

[98] Dolan v. Postal Serv., 546 U.S. 481, 486 (2006).

and disparate-impact proscriptions must be read as complementary.

In codifying the *Griggs* and *Albemarle* instructions, Congress declared unambiguously that selection criteria operating to the disadvantage of minority group members can be retained only if justified by business necessity.[99] [FN 5] In keeping with Congress' design, employers who reject such criteria due to reasonable doubts about their reliability can hardly be held to have engaged in discrimination "because of" race. A reasonable endeavor to comply with the law and to ensure that qualified candidates of all races have a fair opportunity to compete is simply not what Congress meant to interdict. I would therefore hold that an employer who jettisons a selection device when its disproportionate racial impact becomes apparent does not violate Title VII's disparate-treatment bar automatically or at all, subject to this key condition: The employer must have good cause to believe the device would not withstand examination for business necessity.[100]

EEOC's interpretative guidelines are corroborative. "[B]y the enactment of title VII," the guidelines state, "Congress did not intend to expose those who comply with the Act to charges that they are violating the very statute they are seeking to implement."[101] Recognizing EEOC's "enforcement responsibility" under Title VII, we have previously accorded the Commission's position respectful consideration.[102] Yet the Court today does not so much as mention EEOC's counsel.

Our precedents defining the contours of Title VII's disparate-treatment prohibition further confirm the absence of any intra-statutory discord. In *Johnson v. Transportation Agency, Santa Clara Cty.*,[103] we upheld a municipal employer's voluntary affirmative-action plan against a disparate-treatment challenge. Pursuant to the plan, the employer selected a woman for a road-dispatcher position, a job category traditionally regarded as "male." A male applicant who had a slightly higher interview score brought suit under Title VII. This Court rejected his claim and approved the plan, which allowed consideration of gender as "one of numerous factors."[104] Such consid-

---

[99] [FN 5] What was the "business necessity" for the tests New Haven used? How could one justify, e.g., the 60/40 written/oral ratio, *see Ricci*, 557 U.S. at 611–12, 614–16 (Ginsburg, J., dissenting), under that standard? Neither the Court nor the concurring opinions attempt to defend the ratio.

[100] *Cf.* Faragher v. Boca Raton, 524 U.S. 775, 806 (1998) (observing that it accords with "clear statutory policy" for employers "to prevent violations" and "make reasonable efforts to discharge their duty" under Title VII).

[101] 29 C.F.R. § 1608.1(a) (2008).

[102] *See, e.g.,* Albemarle Paper Co. v. Moody, 422 U.S. 405, 431 (1975); Griggs v. Duke Power Co., 401 U.S. 424, 434 (1971).

[103] 480 U.S. 616 (1987).

[104] *Id.* at 638.

eration, we said, is "fully consistent with Title VII" because plans of that order can aid "in eliminating the vestiges of discrimination in the workplace."[105]

This litigation does not involve affirmative action. But if the voluntary affirmative action at issue in *Johnson* does not discriminate within the meaning of Title VII, neither does an employer's reasonable effort to comply with Title VII's disparate-impact provision by refraining from action of doubtful consistency with business necessity.

C

To "reconcile" the supposed "conflict" between disparate treatment and disparate impact, the Court offers an enigmatic standard.[106] Employers may attempt to comply with Title VII's disparate-impact provision, the Court declares, only where there is a "strong basis in evidence" documenting the necessity of their action.[107] The Court's standard, drawn from inapposite equal protection precedents, is not elaborated. One is left to wonder what cases would meet the standard and why the Court is so sure this case does not.

1

In construing Title VII, I note preliminarily, equal protection doctrine is of limited utility. The Equal Protection Clause, this Court has held, prohibits only intentional discrimination; it does not have a disparate-impact component.[108] Title VII, in contrast, aims to eliminate all forms of employment discrimination, unintentional as well as deliberate. Until today,[109] this Court has never questioned the constitutionality of the disparate-impact component of Title VII, and for good reason. By instructing employers to avoid needlessly exclusionary selection processes, Title VII's disparate-impact provision calls for a "race-neutral means to increase minority . . . participation"— something this Court's equal protection precedents also encourage.[110] "The very radicalism of holding disparate impact doctrine unconstitutional as a matter of equal protection," moreover, "suggests that only

---

[105] *Id.* at 642.

[106] Ricci v. DeStefano, 557 U.S. 557, 578–80.

[107] *Id.* at 582.

[108] *See* Pers. Adm'r of Mass. v. Feeney, 442 U.S. 256, 272 (1979); Washington v. Davis, 426 U.S. 229, 239 (1976).

[109] *Cf. Ricci*, 557 U.S. at 584; *id.* at 594 (Scalia, J., concurring).

[110] *See* Adarand Constructors, Inc. v. Peña, 515 U.S. 200, 238 (1995) (quoting Richmond v. J. A. Croson Co., 488 U.S. 469, 507 (1989)).

a very uncompromising court would issue such a decision."[111]

The cases from which the Court draws its strong-basis-in-evidence standard are particularly inapt; they concern the constitutionality of absolute racial preferences.[112] An employer's effort to avoid Title VII liability by repudiating a suspect selection method scarcely resembles those cases. Race was not merely a relevant consideration in *Wygant* and *Croson*; it was the decisive factor. Observance of Title VII's disparate-impact provision, in contrast, calls for no racial preference, absolute or otherwise. The very purpose of the provision is to ensure that individuals are hired and promoted based on qualifications manifestly necessary to successful performance of the job in question, qualifications that do not screen out members of any race.[113] [FN 6]

2

The Court's decision in this litigation underplays a dominant Title VII theme. This Court has repeatedly emphasized that the statute "should not be read to thwart" efforts at voluntary compliance.[114] Such compliance, we have explained, is "the preferred means of achieving [Title VII's] objectives."[115] The strong-basis-in-evidence standard, however, as barely described in general, and cavalierly applied in this case, makes voluntary compliance a hazardous venture.

---

[111] Richard A. Primus, *Equal Protection and Disparate Impact: Round Three*, 117 HARV. L. REV. 493, 585 (2003).

[112] *See* Wygant v. Jackson Bd. of Educ., 476 U.S. 267, 277 (1986) (plurality opinion) (invalidating a school district's plan to lay off nonminority teachers while retaining minority teachers with less seniority); *Croson*, 488 U.S. at 499–500 (rejecting a set-aside program for minority contractors that operated as "an unyielding racial quota").

[113] [FN 6] Even in Title VII cases involving race-conscious (or gender-conscious) affirmative-action plans, the Court has never proposed a strong-basis-in-evidence standard. In *Johnson v. Transportation Agency, Santa Clara Cty.*, 480 U.S. 616 (1987), the Court simply examined the municipal employer's action for reasonableness: "Given the obvious imbalance in the Skilled Craft category, and given the Agency's commitment to eliminating such imbalances, it was plainly not unreasonable for the Agency . . . to consider as one factor the sex of [applicants] in making its decision." *Id.* at 637. *See also* Local No. 93, Int'l Ass'n of Firefighters v. Cleveland, 478 U.S. 501, 516 (1986) ("Title VII permits employers and unions voluntarily to make use of reasonable race-conscious affirmative action.").

[114] *Johnson*, 480 U.S. at 630.

[115] *Local No. 93*, 478 U.S. at 515; *see also* Kolstad v. Am. Dental Ass'n, 527 U.S. 526, 545 (1999) ("Dissuading employers from [taking voluntary action] to prevent discrimination in the workplace is directly contrary to the purposes underlying Title VII."); 29 C.F.R. § 1608.1(c).

As a result of today's decision, an employer who discards a dubious selection process can anticipate costly disparate-treatment litigation in which its chances for success—even for surviving a summary-judgment motion—are highly problematic. Concern about exposure to disparate-impact liability, however well grounded, is insufficient to insulate an employer from attack. Instead, the employer must make a "strong" showing that (1) its selection method was "not job related and consistent with business necessity," or (2) that it refused to adopt "an equally valid, less-discriminatory alternative."[116] It is hard to see how these requirements differ from demanding that an employer establish "a provable, actual violation" against itself.[117] There is indeed a sharp conflict here, but it is not the false one the Court describes between Title VII's core provisions. It is, instead, the discordance of the Court's opinion with the voluntary compliance ideal.[118; 119 [FN 7]]

3

The Court's additional justifications for announcing a strong-basis-in-evidence standard are unimpressive. First, discarding the results of tests, the Court suggests, calls for a heightened standard because it "upset[s] an employee's legitimate expectation."[120] This rationale puts the cart before the horse. The legitimacy of an employee's expectation depends on the legitimacy of the selection method. If an employer reasonably concludes that an exam fails to identify the most qualified individuals and needlessly shuts out a segment of the applicant pool, Title VII surely does not compel the employer to hire or promote based on the test, however unreliable it may be. Indeed, the statute's

---

[116] Ricci v. DeStefano, 557 U.S. 557, 587 (2009).

[117] *Cf. id.* at 583.

[118] *Cf.* Wygant v. Jackson Bd. of Educ., 476 U.S. 267, 290 (O'Connor, J., concurring in part and concurring in judgment) ("The imposition of a requirement that public employers make findings that they have engaged in illegal discrimination before they [act] would severely undermine public employers' incentive to meet voluntarily their civil rights obligations.").

[119] [FN 7] Notably, prior decisions applying a strong-basis-in-evidence standard have not imposed a burden as heavy as the one the Court imposes today. In *Croson,* the Court found no strong basis in evidence because the City had offered "nothing approaching a prima facie case." Richmond v. J. A. Croson Co., 488 U.S. 469, 500 (1989). The Court did not suggest that anything beyond a prima facie case would have been required. In the context of race-based electoral districting, the Court has indicated that a "strong basis" exists when the "threshold conditions" for liability are present. Bush v. Vera, 517 U.S. 952, 978 (1996) (plurality opinion).

[120] *Ricci,* 557 U.S. at 585.

prime objective is to prevent exclusionary practices from "operat[ing] to 'freeze' the status quo."[121]

Second, the Court suggests, anything less than a strong-basis-in-evidence standard risks creating "a de facto quota system, in which . . . an employer could discard test results . . . with the intent of obtaining the employer's preferred racial balance."[122] Under a reasonableness standard, however, an employer could not cast aside a selection method based on a statistical disparity alone.[123] [FN 8] The employer must have good cause to believe that the method screens out qualified applicants and would be difficult to justify as grounded in business necessity. Should an employer repeatedly reject test results, it would be fair, I agree, to infer that the employer is simply seeking a racially balanced outcome and is not genuinely endeavoring to comply with Title VII.

D

The Court stacks the deck further by denying respondents any chance to satisfy the newly announced strong-basis-in-evidence standard. When this Court formulates a new legal rule, the ordinary course is to remand and allow the lower courts to apply the rule in the first instance.[124] I see no good reason why the Court fails to follow that course in this case. Indeed, the sole basis for the Court's peremptory ruling is the demonstrably false pretension that respondents showed "nothing more" than "a significant statistical disparity."[125; 126 [FN 9]]

---

[121] Griggs v. Duke Power Co., 401 U.S. 424, 430 (1971).

[122] *Ricci*, 557 U.S. at 581–82.

[123] [FN 8] Infecting the Court's entire analysis is its insistence that the City rejected the test results "in sole reliance upon race-based statistics." *Id.* at 584; *see also id.* at 579–80, 585–87. But as the part of the story the Court leaves out, *see id.* at 608–18, so plainly shows—the long history of rank discrimination against African-Americans in the firefighting profession, the multiple flaws in New Haven's test for promotions—"sole reliance" on statistics certainly is not descriptive of the CSB's decision.

[124] *See, e.g.*, Johnson v. California, 543 U.S. 499, 515 (2005); Pullman-Standard v. Swint, 456 U.S. 273, 291 (1982).

[125] *Ricci*, 557 U.S. at 587; *see id.* at 630 n.8 (Ginsburg, J., dissenting).

[126] [FN 9] The Court's refusal to remand for further proceedings also deprives respondents of an opportunity to invoke 42 U.S.C. § 2000e-12(b) as a shield to liability. Section 2000e-12(b) provides:

> "In any action or proceeding based on any alleged unlawful employment practice, no person shall be subject to any liability or punishment for or on account of (1) the commission by such person of an unlawful employment practice if he pleads and proves that the act or

III

A

Applying what I view as the proper standard to the record thus far made, I would hold that New Haven had ample cause to believe its selection process was flawed and not justified by business necessity. Judged by that standard, petitioners have not shown that New Haven's failure to certify the exam results violated Title VII's disparate-treatment provision.[127] [FN 10]

The City, all agree, "was faced with a prima facie case of disparate-impact liability."[128] The pass rate for minority candidates was half the rate for nonminority candidates, and virtually no minority candidates would have been eligible for promotion had the exam results been certified. Alerted to this stark disparity, the CSB heard expert and lay testimony, presented at public hearings, in an endeavor to ascertain whether the exams were fair and consistent with business necessity. Its investigation revealed grave cause for concern about the exam process itself and the City's failure to consider alternative selection devices.

Chief among the City's problems was the very nature of the tests for promotion. In choosing to use written and oral exams with a 60/40 weighting, the City simply adhered to the union's preference and apparently gave no consideration to whether the weighting was likely to

---

omission complained of was in good faith, in conformity with, and in reliance on any written interpretation or opinion of the [EEOC] . . . . Such a defense, if established, shall be a bar to the action or proceeding, notwithstanding that (A) after such act or omission, such interpretation or opinion is modified or rescinded or is determined by judicial authority to be invalid or of no legal effect . . . ."

Specifically, given the chance, respondents might have called attention to the EEOC guidelines set out in 29 C.F.R. §§ 1608.3 and 1608.4 (2008). The guidelines recognize that employers may "take affirmative action based on an analysis which reveals facts constituting actual or potential adverse impact." 29 C.F.R. § 1608.3(a). If "affirmative action" is in order, so is the lesser step of discarding a dubious selection device.

127 [FN 10] The lower courts focused on respondents' "intent" rather than on whether respondents in fact had good cause to act. *See* Ricci v. DeStefano, 554 F. Supp. 2d 142, 157 (D. Conn. 2006). Ordinarily, a remand for fresh consideration would be in order. But the Court has seen fit to preclude further proceedings. I therefore explain why, if final adjudication by this Court is indeed appropriate, New Haven should be the prevailing party.

128 *Ricci*, 557 U.S. at 586.

identify the most qualified fire-officer candidates.129 [FN 11] There is strong reason to think it was not.

Relying heavily on written tests to select fire officers is a questionable practice, to say the least. Successful fire officers, the City's description of the position makes clear, must have the "[a]bility to lead personnel effectively, maintain discipline, promote harmony, exercise sound judgment, and cooperate with other officials."130 These qualities are not well measured by written tests. Testifying before the CSB, Christopher Hornick, an exam-design expert with more than two decades of relevant experience, was emphatic on this point: Leadership skills, command presence, and the like "could have been identified and evaluated in a much more appropriate way."131

Hornick's commonsense observation is mirrored in case law and in Title VII's administrative guidelines. Courts have long criticized written firefighter promotion exams for being "more probative of the test-taker's ability to recall what a particular text stated on a given topic than of his firefighting or supervisory knowledge and abilities."132 A fire officer's job, courts have observed, "involves complex behaviors, good interpersonal skills, the ability to make decisions under tremendous pressure, and a host of other abilities—none of which is easily measured by a written, multiple choice test."133; 134 [FN 12] Interpreting

---

129 [FN 11] This alone would have posed a substantial problem for New Haven in a disparate-impact suit, particularly in light of the disparate results the City's scheme had produced in the past. *See id.* at 612–15 (Ginsburg, J., dissenting). Under the Uniform Guidelines on Employee Selection Procedures (Uniform Guidelines), employers must conduct "an investigation of suitable alternative selection procedures." 29 C.F.R. § 1607.3(B); *see also* Officers for Justice v. Civil Serv. Comm'n, 979 F.2d 721, 728 (9th Cir. 1992) ("before utilizing a procedure that has an adverse impact on minorities, the City has an obligation pursuant to the Uniform Guidelines to explore alternative procedures and to implement them if they have less adverse impact and are substantially equally valid"). It is no answer to "presume" that the two-decades-old 60/40 formula was adopted for a "rational reason" because it "was the result of a union-negotiated collective bargaining agreement." *Cf. Ricci*, 557 U.S. at 589. That the parties may have been "rational" says nothing about whether their agreed-upon selection process was consistent with business necessity. It is not at all unusual for agreements negotiated between employers and unions to run afoul of Title VII. *See, e.g.*, Peters v. Mo.-Pac. R.R. Co., 483 F.2d 490, 497 (5th Cir. 1973) (an employment practice "is not shielded [from the requirements of Title VII] by the facts that it is the product of collective bargaining and meets the standards of fair representation").

130 CA2 App., *supra* note 11, at A432.

131 *Id.* at A1042–A1043.

132 Vulcan Pioneers, Inc. v. N.J. Dep't of Civil Serv., 625 F. Supp. 527, 539 (D.N.J. 1985).

133 Firefighters Inst. for Racial Equal. v. City of St. Louis, 616 F.2d 350, 359

the Uniform Guidelines, EEOC and other federal agencies responsible for enforcing equal opportunity employment laws have similarly recognized that, as measures of "interpersonal relations" or "ability to function under danger (e.g., firefighters)," "[p]encil-and-paper tests . . . generally are not close enough approximations of work behaviors to show content validity."[135; 136 [FN 13]]

Given these unfavorable appraisals, it is unsurprising that most municipal employers do not evaluate their fire-officer candidates as New Haven does. Although comprehensive statistics are scarce, a 1996 study found that nearly two-thirds of surveyed municipalities used assessment centers ("simulations of the real world of work") as part of their promotion processes.[137] That figure represented a marked increase over the previous decade, so the percentage today may well be even higher. Among municipalities still relying in part on written exams, the median weight assigned to them was 30 percent—half the weight given to New Haven's written exam.[138]

Testimony before the CSB indicated that these alternative methods were both more reliable and notably less discriminatory in operation.

(8th Cir. 1980).

[134 [FN 12]] *See also* Nash v. Consol. City of Jacksonville, 837 F.2d 1534, 1538 (11th Cir.) ("the examination did not test the one aspect of job performance that differentiated the job of firefighter engineer from fire lieutenant (combat): supervisory skills"); Firefighters Inst. for Racial Equal. v. City of St. Louis, 549 F.2d 506, 512 (8th Cir. 1977) ("there is no good pen and paper test for evaluating supervisory skills"); Boston Chapter, NAACP, Inc. v. Beecher, 504 F.2d 1017, 1023 (1974) ("[T]here is a difference between memorizing . . . fire fighting terminology and being a good fire fighter. If the Boston Red Sox recruited players on the basis of their knowledge of baseball history and vocabulary, the team might acquire [players] who could not bat, pitch or catch.").

[135] Adoption of Questions and Answers to Clarify and Provide a Common Interpretation of the Uniform Guidelines on Employee Selection Process, 44 Fed. Reg. 12,007 (March 2, 1979); *see also* 29 C.F.R. § 1607.15(C)(4).

[136 [FN 13]] *Cf.* Gillespie v. Wisconsin, 771 F.2d 1035, 1043 (7th Cir. 1985) (courts must evaluate "the degree to which the nature of the examination procedure approximates the job conditions"). In addition to "content validity," the Uniform Guidelines discuss "construct validity" and "criterion validity" as means by which an employer might establish the reliability of a selection method. *See* 29 C.F.R. § 1607.14(B)–(D). Content validity, however, is the only type of validity addressed by the parties and "the only feasible type of validation in these circumstances." Brief for Industrial-Organizational Psychologists as Amicus Curiae at 7 n.2, Ricci v. DeStefano, 557 U.S. 557 (Nos. 07-1428, 08-328) (2009) [hereinafter I-O Psychologists Brief].

[137] Phillip E. Lowry, *A Survey of the Assessment Center Process in the Public Sector*, 25 PUB. PERSONNEL MGMT. 307, 315 (1996).

[138] *Id.* at 309.

According to Donald Day of the International Association of Black Professional Firefighters, nearby Bridgeport saw less skewed results after switching to a selection process that placed primary weight on an oral exam.[139] And Hornick described assessment centers as "demonstrat[ing] dramatically less adverse impacts" than written exams.[140; 141 [FN 14]] Considering the prevalence of these proven alternatives, New Haven was poorly positioned to argue that promotions based on its outmoded and exclusionary selection process qualified as a business necessity.[142; 143 [FN 15]]

Ignoring the conceptual and other defects in New Haven's selection process, the Court describes the exams as "painstaking[ly]" developed to test "relevant" material and on that basis finds no substantial risk of disparate-impact liability.[144] Perhaps such reasoning would have

---

[139] CA2 App., *supra* note 11, at A830–A832; *Ricci*, 557 U.S. at 613–14 (Ginsburg, J., dissenting).

[140] CA2 App., *supra* note 11, at A1040.

[141] [FN 14] *See also* GEORGE C. THORNTON III & DEBORAH E. RUPP, ASSESSMENT CENTERS IN HUMAN RESOURCE MANAGEMENT 15 (2006) ("Assessment centers predict future success, do not cause adverse impact, and are seen as fair by participants."); WAYNE F. CASCIO & HERMAN AGUINIS, APPLIED PSYCHOLOGY IN HUMAN RESOURCE MANAGEMENT 372 (6th ed. 2005) ("research has demonstrated that adverse impact is less of a problem in an [assessment center] as compared to an aptitude test"); *cf.* Firefighters Inst. for Racial Equal. v. City of St. Louis, 549 F.2d 506, 513 (8th Cir. 1977) (recommending assessment centers as an alternative to written exams).

[142] *Cf.* Robinson v. Lorillard Corp., 444 F.2d 791, 798 n.7 (4th Cir. 1971) ("It should go without saying that a practice is hardly 'necessary' if an alternative practice better effectuates its intended purpose or is equally effective but less discriminatory.").

[143] [FN 15] Finding the evidence concerning these alternatives insufficiently developed to "create a genuine issue of fact," *Ricci*, 557 U.S. at 591, the Court effectively confirms that an employer cannot prevail under its strong-basis-in-evidence standard unless the employer decisively proves a disparate-impact violation against itself. The Court's specific arguments are unavailing. First, the Court suggests, changing the oral/written weighting may have violated Title VII's prohibition on altering test scores. *Id.* at 590. No one is arguing, however, that the results of the exams given should have been altered. Rather, the argument is that the City could have availed itself of a better option when it initially decided what selection process to use. Second, with respect to assessment centers, the Court identifies "statements to the CSB indicat[ing] that the Department could not have used [them] for the 2003 examinations." *Id.* at 591. The Court comes up with only a single statement on this subject— an offhand remark made by petitioner Ricci, who hardly qualifies as an expert in testing methods. *See id.* at 574. Given the large number of municipalities that regularly use assessment centers, it is impossible to fathom why the City, with proper planning, could not have done so as well.

[144] *See id.* at 588.

sufficed under *Wards Cove*, which permitted exclusionary practices as long as they advanced an employer's "legitimate" goals.[145] But Congress repudiated *Wards Cove* and reinstated the "business necessity" rule attended by a "manifest relationship" requirement.[146] Like the chess player who tries to win by sweeping the opponent's pieces off the table, the Court simply shuts from its sight the formidable obstacles New Haven would have faced in defending against a disparate-impact suit.[147]

That IOS representative Chad Legel and his team may have been diligent in designing the exams says little about the exams' suitability for selecting fire officers. IOS worked within the City's constraints. Legel never discussed with the City the propriety of the 60/40 weighting and "was not asked to consider the possibility of an assessment center."[148] The IOS exams, Legel admitted, had not even attempted to assess "command presence": "[Y]ou would probably be better off with an assessment center if you cared to measure that."[149]

In addition to the highly questionable character of the exams and the neglect of available alternatives, the City had other reasons to worry about its vulnerability to disparate-impact liability. Under the City's ground rules, IOS was not allowed to show the exams to anyone in the New Haven Fire Department prior to their administration. This "precluded [IOS] from being able to engage in [its] normal subject matter expert review process"—something Legel described as "very critical."[150] As a result, some of the exam questions were confusing or irrelevant, and the exams may have over-tested some subject-matter areas while missing others.[151] Testimony before the CSB also raised questions concerning unequal access to study materials[152] and the potential bias introduced by relying principally on job analyses

---

[145] Wards Cove Packing Co. v. Atonio, 490 U.S. 642, 659 (1989).
[146] *See* Griggs v. Duke Power Co., 401 U.S. 424, 431–32 (1971); *see also Ricci*, 557 U.S. at 623.
[147] See Lanning v. Se. Pa. Transp. Auth., 181 F.3d 478, 489 (3d Cir. 1999) ("Judicial application of a standard focusing solely on whether the qualities measured by an . . . exam bear some relationship to the job in question would impermissibly write out the business necessity prong of the Act's chosen standard.").
[148] CA2 App., *supra* note 11, at A522; *see also id.* at A467.
[149] *Id.* at A521; *cf.* Boston Chapter, NAACP, Inc., v. Beecher, 504 F.2d 1017, 1021–22 (1st Cir. 1974) ("A test fashioned from materials pertaining to the job . . . superficially may seem job-related. But what is at issue is whether it demonstrably selects people who will perform better the required on-the-job behaviors.").
[150] CA2 App., *supra* note 11, at A477, A506.
[151] *See, e.g., id.* at A1034–A1035, A1051.
[152] *See id.* at A857–A861.

from nonminority fire officers to develop the exams.[153; 154 [FN 16]]

The Court criticizes New Haven for failing to obtain a "technical report" from IOS, which, the Court maintains, would have provided "detailed information to establish the validity of the exams."[155] The record does not substantiate this assertion. As Legel testified during his deposition, the technical report merely summarized "the steps that [IOS] took methodologically speaking," and would not have established the exams' reliability.[156]

In sum, the record solidly establishes that the City had good cause to fear disparate-impact liability. Moreover, the Court supplies no tenable explanation why the evidence of the tests' multiple deficiencies does not create at least a triable issue under a strong-basis-in-evidence standard.

B

Concurring in the Court's opinion, Justice Alito asserts that summary judgment for respondents would be improper even if the City had good cause for its noncertification decision. A reasonable jury, he maintains, could have found that respondents were not actually motivated by concern about disparate-impact litigation, but instead sought only "to placate a politically important [African-American] constituency."[157] As earlier noted, I would not oppose a remand for

---

[153] *See id.* at A1063–A1064; *see also* Ricci v. DeStefano, 557 U.S. 557, 613–14, 616–17 (2009).

[154] [FN 16] The I-O Psychologists Brief identifies still other, more technical flaws in the exams that may well have precluded the City from prevailing in a disparate-impact suit. Notably, the exams were never shown to be suitably precise to allow strict rank ordering of candidates. A difference of one or two points on a multiple-choice exam should not be decisive of an applicant's promotion chances if that difference bears little relationship to the applicant's qualifications for the job. Relatedly, it appears that the line between a passing and failing score did not accurately differentiate between qualified and unqualified candidates. A number of fire-officer promotional exams have been invalidated on these bases. *See, e.g.,* Guardians Ass'n of N.Y.C. Police Dep't, Inc. v. Civil Serv. Comm'n of N.Y.C., 630 F.2d 79, 105 (2d Cir. 1980) ("When a cutoff score unrelated to job performance produces disparate racial results, Title VII is violated."); Vulcan Pioneers, Inc. v. N.J. Dep't of Civil Serv., 625 F. Supp. 527, 538 (D.N.J. 1985) ("[T]he tests here at issue are not appropriate for ranking candidates.").

[155] *Ricci,* 557 U.S. at 589.

[156] CA2 App., *supra* note 11, at A461; *see also id.* at A462 (the report "doesn't say anything that other documents that already existed wouldn't say").

[157] *Ricci,* 557 U.S. at 597.

further proceedings fair to both sides.[158] It is the Court that has chosen to short-circuit this litigation based on its pretension that the City has shown, and can show, nothing more than a statistical disparity.[159] Justice Alito compounds the Court's error.

Offering a truncated synopsis of the many hours of deliberations undertaken by the CSB, Justice Alito finds evidence suggesting that respondents' stated desire to comply with Title VII was insincere, a mere "pretext" for discrimination against white firefighters.[160] In support of his assertion, Justice Alito recounts at length the alleged machinations of Rev. Boise Kimber (a local political activist), Mayor John DeStefano, and certain members of the mayor's staff.[161]

Most of the allegations Justice Alito repeats are drawn from petitioners' statement of facts they deem undisputed, a statement displaying an adversarial zeal not uncommonly found in such presentations.[162] [FN 17] What cannot credibly be denied, however, is that the decision against certification of the exams was made neither by Kimber nor by the mayor and his staff. The relevant decision was made by the CSB, an unelected, politically insulated body. It is striking that Justice Alito's concurrence says hardly a word about the CSB itself, perhaps because there is scant evidence that its motivation was

---

[158] *See id.* at 632 n.10 (Ginsburg, J., dissenting).

[159] *See id.* at 630–31, 630 n.8.

[160] *Id.* at 596–97 (Alito, J., concurring).

[161] *See id.* at 598–604.

[162] [FN 17] Some of petitioners' so-called facts find little support in the record, and many others can scarcely be deemed material. Petitioners allege, for example, that City officials prevented New Haven's fire chief and assistant chief from sharing their views about the exams with the CSB. Petition for Writ of Certiorari app. at 228a, *Ricci*, 557 U.S. 557 (No. 07-1428). None of the materials petitioners cite, however, "suggests" that this proposition is accurate. *Cf. Ricci*, 557 U.S. at 600 (Alito, J., concurring). In her deposition testimony, City official Karen Dubois-Walton specifically denied that she or her colleagues directed the chief and assistant chief not to appear. Petition for Writ of Certiorari, *supra*, app. at 850a. Moreover, contrary to the insinuations of petitioners and Justice Alito, the statements made by City officials before the CSB did not emphasize allegations of cheating by test takers. *Cf. Ricci*, 557 U.S. at 602 (Alito, J., concurring). In her deposition, Dubois-Walton acknowledged sharing the cheating allegations not with the CSB, but with a different City commission. Petition for Writ of Certiorari, *supra*, app. at 837a. Justice Alito also reports that the City's attorney advised the mayor's team that the way to convince the CSB not to certify was "to focus on something other than 'a big discussion re: adverse impact' law." *Ricci*, 557 U.S. at 603–04 (Alito, J., concurring) (quoting Petition for Writ of Certiorari, *supra*, app. at 458a). This is a misleading abbreviation of the attorney's advice. Focusing on the exams' defects and on disparate-impact law is precisely what he recommended. *See* Petition for Writ of Certiorari, *supra*, app. at 458a–459a.

anything other than to comply with Title VII's disparate-impact provision. Notably, petitioners did not even seek to take depositions of the two commissioners who voted against certification. Both submitted uncontested affidavits declaring unequivocally that their votes were "based solely on [their] good faith belief that certification" would have discriminated against minority candidates in violation of federal law.[163]

Justice Alito discounts these sworn statements, suggesting that the CSB's deliberations were tainted by the preferences of Kimber and City officials, whether or not the CSB itself was aware of the taint. Kimber and City officials, Justice Alito speculates, decided early on to oppose certification and then "engineered" a skewed presentation to the CSB to achieve their preferred outcome.[164]

As an initial matter, Justice Alito exaggerates the influence of these actors. The CSB, the record reveals, designed and conducted an inclusive decision-making process, in which it heard from numerous individuals on both sides of the certification question.[165] Kimber and others no doubt used strong words to urge the CSB not to certify the exam results, but the CSB received "pressure" from supporters of certification as well as opponents.[166] Petitioners, for example, engaged counsel to speak on their behalf before the CSB. Their counsel did not mince words: "[I]f you discard these results," she warned, "you will get sued. You will force the taxpayers of the city of New Haven into protracted litigation."[167]

The local firefighters union—an organization required by law to represent all the City's firefighters—was similarly outspoken in favor of certification. Discarding the test results, the union's president told the CSB, would be "totally ridiculous."[168] He insisted, inaccurately, that the City was not at risk of disparate-impact liability because the exams were administered pursuant to "a collective bargaining agreement."[169] Never mentioned by Justice Alito in his attempt to show testing expert Christopher Hornick's alliance with the City,[170] the CSB solicited Hornick's testimony at the union's suggestion, not the

---

[163] CA2 App., *supra* note 11, at A1605, A1611.

[164] *Ricci*, 557 U.S. at 606 (Alito, J., concurring).

[165] *See, e.g.*, CA2 App., *supra* note 11, at A1090.

[166] *Cf. Ricci*, 557 U.S. at 600–01 (Alito, J., concurring).

[167] CA2 App., *supra* note 11, at A816; *see also id.* at A788.

[168] *Id.* at A806.

[169] *Id.* at A1137; *cf. Ricci*, 557 U.S. at 632 n.11 (Ginsburg, J., dissenting).

[170] *Ricci*, 557 U.S. at 603–04 (Alito, J., concurring).

City's.[171] Hornick's cogent testimony raised substantial doubts about the exams' reliability.[172; 173 [FN 18]]

There is scant cause to suspect that maneuvering or overheated rhetoric, from either side, prevented the CSB from evenhandedly assessing the reliability of the exams and rendering an independent, good-faith decision on certification. Justice Alito acknowledges that the CSB had little patience for Kimber's antics.[174; 175 [FN 19]] As to petitioners, Chairman Segaloff—who voted to certify the exam results—dismissed the threats made by their counsel as unhelpful and needlessly "inflammatory."[176] Regarding the views expressed by City officials, the CSB made clear that they were entitled to no special weight.[177; 178 [FN 20]]

In any event, Justice Alito's analysis contains a more fundamental flaw: It equates political considerations with unlawful discrimination. As Justice Alito sees it, if the mayor and his staff were motivated by their desire "to placate a . . . racial constituency,"[179] then they engaged in unlawful discrimination against petitioners. But Justice Alito fails to ask a vital question: "[P]lacate" how? That political officials would

---

[171] CA2 App., *supra* note 11, at A1128.

[172] *See Ricci*, 557 U.S. at 615–16 (Ginsburg, J., dissenting).

[173] [FN 18] City officials, Justice Alito reports, sent Hornick newspaper accounts and other material about the exams prior to his testimony. *Ricci*, 557 U.S. at 603 (Alito, J., concurring). Some of these materials, Justice Alito intimates, may have given Hornick an inaccurate portrait of the exams. But Hornick's testimony before the CSB, viewed in full, indicates that Hornick had an accurate understanding of the exam process. Much of Hornick's analysis focused on the 60/40 weighting of the written and oral exams, something that neither the Court nor the concurrences even attempt to defend. It is, moreover, entirely misleading to say that the City later hired union-proposed Hornick as a "rewar[d]" for his testimony. *Cf. id.* at 604.

[174] *Id.* at 600–02.

[175] [FN 19] To be clear, the Board of Fire Commissioners on which Kimber served is an entity separate from the CSB. Kimber was not a member of the CSB. Kimber, Justice Alito states, requested a private meeting with the CSB. *Id.* at 599. There is not a shred of evidence that a private meeting with Kimber or anyone else took place.

[176] CA2 App., *supra* note 11, at A821.

[177] *Id.* at A1080.

[178] [FN 20] Justice Alito points to evidence that the mayor had decided not to make promotions based on the exams even if the CSB voted to certify the results, going so far as to prepare a press release to that effect. *Ricci*, 557 U.S. at 604 (Alito, J., concurring). If anything, this evidence reinforces the conclusion that the CSB—which made the noncertification decision—remained independent and above the political fray. The mayor and his staff needed a contingency plan precisely because they did not control the CSB.

[179] *Id.* at 597.

have politics in mind is hardly extraordinary, and there are many ways in which a politician can attempt to win over a constituency—including a racial constituency—without engaging in unlawful discrimination. As courts have recognized, "[p]oliticians routinely respond to bad press . . . , but it is not a violation of Title VII to take advantage of a situation to gain political favor."[180]

The real issue, then, is not whether the mayor and his staff were politically motivated; it is whether their attempt to score political points was legitimate (i.e., nondiscriminatory). Were they seeking to exclude white firefighters from promotion (unlikely, as a fair test would undoubtedly result in the addition of white firefighters to the officer ranks), or did they realize, at least belatedly, that their tests could be toppled in a disparate-impact suit? In the latter case, there is no disparate-treatment violation. Justice Alito, I recognize, would disagree. In his view, an employer's action to avoid Title VII disparate-impact liability qualifies as a presumptively improper race-based employment decision.[181] I reject that construction of Title VII.[182] As I see it, when employers endeavor to avoid exposure to disparate-impact liability, they do not thereby encounter liability for disparate treatment.

Applying this understanding of Title VII, supported by *Griggs* and the long line of decisions following *Griggs*,[183] the District Court found no genuine dispute of material fact. That court noted, particularly, the guidance furnished by Second Circuit precedent.[184] Petitioners' allegations that City officials took account of politics, the District Court determined, simply "d[id] not suffice" to create an inference of unlawful discrimination.[185] The noncertification decision, even if undertaken "in a political context," reflected a legitimate "intent not to implement a promotional process based on testing results that had an adverse impact."[186] Indeed, the District Court perceived "a total absence of any evidence of discriminatory animus towards [petitioners]."[187] Perhaps the District Court could have been more expansive in its discussion of these issues, but its conclusions appear entirely

---

[180] Henry v. Jones, 507 F.3d 558, 567 (7th Cir. 2007).

[181] *See Ricci*, 557 U.S. at 596–97 (Alito, J., concurring).

[182] *See id.* at 624–26 (Ginsburg, J., dissenting).

[183] *See id.* at 623–24 & nn. 3–4.

[184] *See id.* at 619.

[185] Ricci v. DeStefano, 554 F. Supp. 2d 142, 160 n.12 (D. Conn. 2006).

[186] *Id.* at 158, 160.

[187] *Id.* at 158; *see also id.* at 162 ("Nothing in the record in this case suggests that the City defendants or CSB acted 'because of' discriminatory animus toward [petitioners] or other non-minority applicants for promotion.").

consistent with the record before it.[188] [FN 21]

It is indeed regrettable that the City's noncertification decision would have required all candidates to go through another selection process. But it would have been more regrettable to rely on flawed exams to shut out candidates who may well have the command presence and other qualities needed to excel as fire officers. Yet that is the choice the Court makes today. It is a choice that breaks the promise of *Griggs* that groups long denied equal opportunity would not be held back by tests "fair in form, but discriminatory in operation."[189]

*   *   *

This case presents an unfortunate situation, one New Haven might well have avoided had it utilized a better selection process in the first place. But what this case does not present is race-based discrimination in violation of Title VII. I dissent from the Court's judgment, which rests on the false premise that respondents showed "a significant statistical disparity," but "nothing more."[190]

---

[188] [FN 21] The District Court, Justice Alito writes, "all but conceded that a jury could find that the City's asserted justification was pretextual" by "admitt[ing] that 'a jury could rationally infer that city officials worked behind the scenes to sabotage the promotional examinations because they knew that, were the exams certified, the Mayor would incur the wrath of [Rev. Boise] Kimber and other influential leaders of New Haven's African-American community.'" *Ricci*, 557 U.S. at 598, 607–08 (Alito, J., concurring) (quoting *Ricci*, 554 F. Supp. 2d at 162). The District Court drew the quoted passage from petitioners' lower court brief, and used it in reference to a First Amendment claim not before this Court. In any event, it is not apparent why these alleged political maneuvers suggest an intent to discriminate against petitioners. That City officials may have wanted to please political supporters is entirely consistent with their stated desire to avoid a disparate-impact violation. *Cf.* Ashcroft v. Iqbal, 556 U.S. 662, 682 (2009) (allegations that senior Government officials condoned the arrest and detention of thousands of Arab Muslim men following the September 11 attacks failed to establish even a "plausible inference" of unlawful discrimination sufficient to survive a motion to dismiss).

[189] Griggs v. Duke Power Co., 401 U.S. 424, 431 (1971).

[190] *See Ricci*, 557 U.S. at 587.

ADARAND

"Bias both conscious and unconscious, reflecting traditional and unexamined habits of thought, keeps up barriers that must come down if equal opportunity and nondiscrimination are ever genuinely to become this country's law and practice."

The Case

In *Adarand Contractors, Inc. v. Peña*,[1] the Court faced a challenge to federal incentives designed to promote the hiring of subcontractors owned by traditionally under-represented minorities. Pursuant to the Small Business Act ("SBA"), small businesses "owned and controlled by socially and economically disadvantaged individuals" received a hiring preference when bidding for government contracts, along with other preferential treatment aimed at boosting their participation in government projects. Under the terms of the SBA, ownership by at least 51% of individuals qualifying as "socially and economically disadvantaged" entitled a company to a rebuttable presumption of disadvantage, regardless of whether the business was *in fact* socially or economically underprivileged.

In *Adarand*, the U.S. Department of Transportation awarded the prime contract for a Colorado highway construction project to Mountain Gravel & Construction Company. Mountain Gravel then solicited bids from subcontractors for the installation of guardrails. The bids of two subcontractors were at issue: Adarand, which submitted the lowest bid, and Gonzales Construction Company, a minority owned business. Because Gonzales qualified as disadvantaged, their higher bid was more financially attractive to Mountain Gravel due to additional payments it would receive through the SBA's program.

The contract was awarded to Gonzales, and Adarand brought suit, claiming entitlement to the contract due to its lower bid. Adarand argued that the federal government's financial incentives for hiring minority subcontractors were unconstitutional because they relied on the race of the competitors, which the Fourteenth Amendment prohibited. The United States District Court for the District of Colorado

---

[1] 515 U.S. 200 (1995).

disagreed and ruled against Adarand. On appeal, the Tenth Circuit affirmed the District Court and, in so doing, applied "intermediate scrutiny" to the race-based classifications of the SBA.

Constitutional Tiers of Scrutiny

Generally, when the federal government acts and is subsequently sued on a claim that the action was discriminatory, the courts review the constitutionality of the action under one of three general tests or "tiers of scrutiny." In *Adarand*, the Supreme Court focused heavily on whether the Tenth Circuit chose the correct tier.

The highest level of scrutiny is "strict scrutiny." Under strict scrutiny, the government must prove that a law or policy both serves a compelling state interest and is narrowly tailored to achieve that interest. The most common instances in which strict scrutiny is applied are governmental bans on political or content-related speech; laws that discriminate based on race, national origin, religion, or alienage; and when a so-called "fundamental right," such as the right to marriage or the right to vote, is challenged. In general, the Supreme Court will rarely uphold laws that discriminate on these bases.

The second tier of scrutiny is intermediate scrutiny, which the Tenth Circuit applied in *Adarand*. For a law or government action to survive intermediate scrutiny, the government must prove that the law or action serves an important governmental objective and is substantially related to achieving that objective. Intermediate scrutiny is most commonly used in analyzing laws that discriminate on the basis of gender or sex and in cases involving certain regulations or limits on speech. The courts have explained the need for this heightened scrutiny by pointing to historical discrimination against such groups, or because of the importance of the right being protected.

The lowest level of scrutiny is called "rational basis review." This test simply asks whether the challenged law or policy is rationally related to a legitimate government interest. If a rational basis is found—even if it was not the basis the government actually provided—the challenged law or policy is upheld. This test is generally applied to any law or regulation challenged on the basis that it is arbitrary and to laws which discriminate on the basis of age or disability.

Justice O'Connor's Majority Opinion

Prior to *Adarand*, there had been some inconsistency in the Supreme Court's approach to governmental racial classifications: courts in different cases applied differing levels of scrutiny to race-based governmental action.[2] In her majority opinion, Justice O'Connor unequivocally adopted strict scrutiny as the proper test, holding "that all racial classifications, imposed by whatever federal, state, or local governmental actor, must be analyzed by a reviewing court under strict scrutiny. In other words, such classifications are constitutional only if they are narrowly tailored measures that further compelling governmental interests."[3]

With respect to the specific facts before it, the Court held that the Tenth Circuit used the wrong test in considering Adarand's challenge and sent the case back for reconsideration.[4] But the decision had much broader consequences for future laws designed to redress historical racial discrimination. The majority in *Adarand* did observe that "[t]he unhappy persistence of both the practice and the lingering effects of racial discrimination against minority groups in this country is an unfortunate reality, and government is not disqualified from acting in response to it."[5] But the practical implication of the Court's ruling meant the government would find it difficult to utilize racial classifications for the purpose of correcting past injustices due to the exacting strict scrutiny standard such policies would have to survive.

Justice Ginsburg's Dissent

Justice Ginsburg cleverly designed her dissent to minimize the primary implication of the majority's decision: that laws designed to redress historical discrimination would be unlikely to survive a constitutional strict scrutiny analysis. Her dissent attempted to soften the blow of the majority's opinion and was an effort to salvage government strategies, which, up until this point, were doing significant work in correcting the lingering effects of past wrongs. Accordingly, Justice Ginsburg wrote "to underscore not the differences the several opinions[6] in this case display, but the considerable field of agreement—the common understandings and concerns—revealed in opinions that together speak for a majority of the Court."[7]

---

[2] The majority opinion discusses this history at length; *see* 515 U.S. at 212–27.

[3] *Id.* at 227.

[4] *Id.* at 237–38.

[5] *Id.* at 237.

[6] In addition to the majority opinion and Justice Ginsburg's dissent, Justice Scalia had filed a concurring opinion and Justice Stevens and Justice Souter had both filed dissenting opinions.

[7] *Id.* at 271 (Ginsburg, J., dissenting).

Ginsburg first traced the Court's own regretful history of ill-preparedness "to say that there is in this land no superior race, no race inferior to any other" before listing numerous examples of continued "persisten[t] racial inequality" and noting the "majority's acknowledgment of Congress' authority to act affirmatively, not only to end discrimination, but also to counteract discrimination's lingering effects."[8] Through artful analysis, Justice Ginsburg effectively undermined the majority's controlling premise: that equality can be reached through leveling the playing field while ignoring the starting positions of the players.

In her conclusion, she argued "strict scrutiny," as interpreted by the majority, actually *helped* affirmative action policies, and selectively quoted the majority to establish its opinion "usefully reiterates that 'the purpose of strict scrutiny is precisely to distinguish legitimate from illegitimate uses of race in governmental decisionmaking,' to 'differentiate between permissible and impermissible governmental use of race,' and 'to distinguish between a "No Trespassing" sign and a welcome mat.'"[9] In other words, Justice Ginsburg not only invited future litigants to use the Court's own reasoning—which implicitly offered a means to undermine laws designed to help minorities—to argue that well-designed affirmative action policies could withstand strict scrutiny analysis, but also laid out a road map demonstrating how to do so. Indeed, it appeared that Ginsburg openly welcomed such efforts: earlier in her dissent she wrote, "given this history and its practical consequences, Congress surely can conclude that a carefully designed affirmative action program may help to realize, finally, the 'equal protection of the laws' the Fourteenth Amendment has promised since 1868."[10]

---

[8] *Id.* at 273–74.

[9] *Id.* at 275–76 (quoting majority opinion at 228–29) (some internal quotation marks omitted).

[10] *Id.* at 274.

ADARAND CONSTRUCTORS, INC. V. PEÑA

JUSTICE GINSBURG, with whom JUSTICE BREYER joins,
DISSENTING.

For the reasons stated by Justice Souter, and in view of the attention the political branches are currently giving the matter of affirmative action, I see no compelling cause for the intervention the Court has made in this case. I further agree with Justice Stevens that, in this area, large deference is owed by the Judiciary to "Congress' institutional competence and constitutional authority to overcome historic racial subjugation."[1; 2] [FN 1] I write separately to underscore not the differences the several opinions in this case display, but the considerable field of agreement—the common understandings and concerns—revealed in opinions that together speak for a majority of the Court.

I

The statutes and regulations at issue, as the Court indicates, were adopted by the political branches in response to an "unfortunate reality": "[t]he unhappy persistence of both the practice and the lingering effects of racial discrimination against minority groups in this country."[3] The United States suffers from those lingering effects because, for most of our Nation's history, the idea that "we are just one race,"[4] was not embraced. For generations, our lawmakers and judges were

---

[1] *Id.* at 253 (Stevens, J., dissenting); *see id.* at 254–55.

[2] [FN 1] On congressional authority to enforce the equal protection principle, *see, e.g.,* Heart of Atlanta Motel, Inc. v. United States, 379 U.S. 241, 286 (1964) (Douglas, J., concurring) (recognizing Congress' authority, under § 5 of the Fourteenth Amendment, to "pu[t] an end to all obstructionist strategies and allo[w] every person-whatever his race, creed, or color-to patronize all places of public accommodation without discrimination whether he travels interstate or intrastate."); *id.* at 291, 293 (Goldberg, J., concurring) ("primary purpose of the Civil Rights Act of 1964 . . . is the vindication of human dignity"; "Congress clearly had authority under both § 5 of the Fourteenth Amendment and the Commerce Clause" to enact the law); GERALD GUNTHER, CONSTITUTIONAL LAW 147–51 (12th ed. 1991).

[3] *Adarand Constructors,* 515 U.S. at 237 (majority opinion).

[4] *Id.* at 239 (Scalia, J., concurring in part and concurring in judgment).

unprepared to say that there is in this land no superior race, no race inferior to any other. In *Plessy v. Ferguson*,[5] not only did this Court endorse the oppressive practice of race segregation, but even Justice Harlan, the advocate of a "color-blind" Constitution, stated:

> "The white race deems itself to be the dominant race in this country. And so it is, in prestige, in achievements, in education, in wealth and in power. So, I doubt not, it will continue to be for all time, if it remains true to its great heritage and holds fast to the principles of constitutional liberty."[6]

Not until *Loving v. Virginia*,[7] which held unconstitutional Virginia's ban on interracial marriages, could one say with security that the Constitution and this Court would abide no measure "designed to maintain White Supremacy."[8; 9 [FN 2]]

The divisions in this difficult case should not obscure the Court's recognition of the persistence of racial inequality and a majority's acknowledgment of Congress' authority to act affirmatively, not only to end discrimination, but also to counteract discrimination's lingering effects.[10] Those effects, reflective of a system of racial caste only recently ended, are evident in our workplaces, markets, and neighborhoods. Job applicants with identical resumes, qualifications, and interview styles still experience different receptions, depending on their race.[11 [FN 3]] White and African American consumers still en-

---

[5] 163 U.S. 537 (1896).

[6] *Id.* at 559 (Harlan, J., dissenting).

[7] 388 U.S. 1 (1967).

[8] *Id.* at 11.

[9] [FN 2] The Court, in 1955 and 1956, refused to rule on the constitutionality of antimiscegenation laws; it twice declined to accept appeals from the decree on which the Virginia Supreme Court of Appeals relied in *Loving*. *See* Naim v. Naim, 197 Va. 80, 87 S.E.2d 749 (1955), *vacated and remanded*, 350 U.S. 891 (1955), *reinstated and aff'd*, 197 Va. 734, 90 S.E.2d 849, *appeal dismissed*, 350 U.S. 985 (1956). *Naim* expressed the state court's view of the legislative purpose served by the Virginia law: "to preserve the racial integrity of [Virginia's] citizens"; to prevent "the corruption of blood," "a mongrel breed of citizens," and "the obliteration of racial pride." 197 Va. at 90, 87 S.E.2d at 756.

[10] *Adarand Constructors*, 515 U.S. at 237 (majority opinion); *see also id.* at 269–70 (Souter, J., dissenting).

[11] [FN 3] *See, e.g.*, H. CROSS, G. KENNEDY, J. MELL & W. ZIMMERMANN, EMPLOYER HIRING PRACTICES: DIFFERENTIAL TREATMENT OF HISPANIC AND ANGLO JOB SEEKERS 42 (Urban Institute Report 90-4, 1990) (e.g., Anglo applicants sent out by investigators received 52% more job offers than matched Hispanics); MARGERY TURNER, MICHAEL FIX & RAYMOND STRUYK, OPPORTUNITIES DENIED, OPPORTUNITIES DIMINISHED: RACIAL DISCRIMINATION IN HIRING xi (Urban In-

counter different deals.[12] [FN 4] People of color looking for housing still face discriminatory treatment by landlords, real estate agents, and mortgage lenders.[13] [FN 5]

Minority entrepreneurs sometimes fail to gain contracts though they are the low bidders, and they are sometimes refused work even after winning contracts.[14] [FN 6] Bias both conscious and unconscious, reflecting traditional and unexamined habits of thought,[15] [FN 7] keeps up barriers that must come down if equal opportunity and nondiscrimination are ever genuinely to become this country's law and practice.

Given this history and its practical consequences, Congress surely can conclude that a carefully designed affirmative action program may help to realize, finally, the "equal protection of the laws" the Fourteenth Amendment has promised since 1868.[16] [FN 8]

---

stitute Report 91-9, 1991) ("In one out of five audits, the white applicant was able to advance farther through the hiring process than his black counterpart. In one out of eight audits, the white was offered a job although his equally qualified black partner was not. In contrast, black auditors advanced farther than their white counterparts only 7 percent of the time, and received job offers while their white partners did not in 5 percent of the audits.").

[12] [FN 4] *See, e.g.*, Ian Ayres, *Fair Driving: Gender and Race Discrimination in Retail Car Negotiations*, 104 HARV. L. REV. 817, 821–22, 819, 828 (1991) ("blacks and women simply cannot buy the same car for the same price as can white men using identical bargaining strategies"; the final offers given white female testers reflected 40 percent higher markups than those given white male testers; final offer markups for black male testers were twice as high, and for black female testers three times as high as for white male testers).

[13] [FN 5] *See, e.g.*, A COMMON DESTINY: BLACKS AND AMERICAN SOCIETY 50 (G. Jaynes & R. Williams eds., 1989) ("[I]n many metropolitan areas one quarter to one-half of all [housing] inquiries by blacks are met by clearly discriminatory responses."); MARGERY TURNER, RAYMOND STRUYK & JOHN YINGER, U.S. DEPT. OF HOUSING AND URBAN DEVELOPMENT, HOUSING DISCRIMINATION STUDY: SYNTHESIS i–vii (1991) (1989 audit study of housing searches in 25 metropolitan areas; over half of African-American and Hispanic testers seeking to rent or buy experienced some form of unfavorable treatment compared to paired white testers); Peter J. Leahy, *Are Racial Factors Important for the Allocation of Mortgage Money?*, 44 AM. J. ECON. & SOC. 185, 193 (1985) (controlling for socioeconomic factors, and concluding that "even when neighborhoods appear to be similar on every major mortgage-lending criterion except race, mortgage-lending outcomes are still unequal").

[14] [FN 6] *See, e.g.*, Associated Gen. Contractors v. Coal. for Econ. Equity, 950 F.2d 1401, 1415 (9th Cir. 1991) (detailing examples in San Francisco).

[15] [FN 7] *Cf.* Wygant v. Jackson Bd. of Ed., 476 U.S. 267, 318 (1986) (Stevens, J., dissenting); Califano v. Goldfarb, 430 U.S. 199, 222–23 (1977) (Stevens, J., concurring in judgment).

[16] [FN 8] On the differences between laws designed to benefit a historically dis-

II

The lead opinion uses one term, "strict scrutiny," to describe the standard of judicial review for all governmental classifications by race.[17] But that opinion's elaboration strongly suggests that the strict standard announced is indeed "fatal" for classifications burdening groups that have suffered discrimination in our society. That seems to me, and, I believe, to the Court, the enduring lesson one should draw from *Korematsu v. United States*;[18] for in that case, scrutiny the Court described as "most rigid,"[19] nonetheless yielded a pass for an odious, gravely injurious racial classification.[20] A *Korematsu*-type classification, as I read the opinions in this case, will never again survive scrutiny: Such a classification, history and precedent instruct, properly ranks as prohibited.

For a classification made to hasten the day when "we are just one race,"[21] however, the lead opinion has dispelled the notion that "strict scrutiny" is " 'fatal in fact.'"[22] Properly, a majority of the Court calls for review that is searching, in order to ferret out classifications in reality malign, but masquerading as benign.[23] The Court's once lax review of sex-based classifications demonstrates the need for such suspicion.[24] Today's decision thus usefully reiterates that the purpose

---

favored group and laws designed to burden such a group, *see, e.g.*, Stephen L. Carter, *When Victims Happen To Be Black*, 97 Yale L.J. 420, 433–34 (1988) ("[W]hatever the source of racism, to count it the same as racialism, to say that two centuries of struggle for the most basic of civil rights have been mostly about freedom from racial categorization rather than freedom from racial oppression, is to trivialize the lives and deaths of those who have suffered under racism. To pretend . . . that the issue presented in *Bakke* was the same as the issue in *Brown* is to pretend that history never happened and that the present doesn't exist.").

[17] *Adarand Constructors*, 515 U.S. at 235–37.

[18] 323 U.S. 214 (1944).

[19] *Id.* at 216.

[20] *Adarand Constructors*, 515 U.S. at 214–15.

[21] *Id.* at 239 (Scalia, J., concurring in part and concurring in judgment)

[22] *Id.* at 237 (majority opinion) (quoting Fullilove v. Klutznick, 448 U.S. 448, 519 (1980) (Marshall, J., concurring in judgment)).

[23] See *id.* at 228–29.

[24] *See, e.g.*, Hoyt v. Florida, 368 U.S. 57, 60 (1961) (upholding women's "privilege" of automatic exemption from jury service); Goesaert v. Cleary, 335 U.S. 464 (1948) (upholding Michigan law barring women from employment as bartenders); *see also* John D. Johnston, Jr. & Charles L. Knapp, *Sex Discrimination by Law: A Study in Judicial Perspective*, 46 N.Y.U. L. Rev. 675 (1971).

of strict scrutiny "is precisely to distinguish legitimate from illegitimate uses of race in governmental decisionmaking,"[25] "to 'differentiate between' permissible and impermissible governmental use of race,"[26] to distinguish" 'between a "No Trespassing" sign and a welcome mat.'"[27]

Close review also is in order for this further reason. As Justice Souter points out,[28] and as this very case shows, some members of the historically favored race can be hurt by catchup mechanisms designed to cope with the lingering effects of entrenched racial subjugation. Court review can ensure that preferences are not so large as to trammel unduly upon the opportunities of others or interfere too harshly with legitimate expectations of persons in once-preferred groups.[29]

*   *   *

While I would not disturb the programs challenged in this case, and would leave their improvement to the political branches, I see today's decision as one that allows our precedent to evolve, still to be informed by and responsive to changing conditions.

---

[25] *Adarand Constructors*, 515 U.S. at 228 (majority opinion).

[26] *Id.*

[27] *Id.* at 229.

[28] *Id.* at 270 (Souter, J., dissenting).

[29] *See, e.g.*, Bridgeport Guardians, Inc. v. Bridgeport Civil Serv. Comm'n, 482 F.2d 1333, 1341 (2d Cir. 1973).

VANCE

"Congress has, in the recent past, intervened to correct this Court's wayward interpretations of Title VII. The ball is once again in Congress' court to correct the error into which this Court has fallen, and to restore the robust protections against workplace harassment the Court weakens today."

Brief Overview of Relevant Employment Discrimination Law

In *Vance v. Ball State University*, the Court investigated the nuanced meaning of the term "supervisor" as used in employment discrimination law. Both the facts of the case and the Court's opinion are easier to understand after reading a brief summary of the relevant applicable law.

Title VII of the Civil Rights Act of 1964 outlaws discrimination based upon "race, color, religion, sex, or national origin."[1] One type of prohibited discrimination recognized by the Supreme Court is the presence of a "hostile work environment," which the Court has held exists when "the work environment [is] so pervaded by discrimination that the terms and conditions of employment were altered."[2] Liability for such harassment depends in part upon who the harassing employee is and ultimately turns on whether that employee counts as a "supervisor"—a question which, until *Vance*, had not been definitively answered.[3]

At the outset of the majority opinion, Justice Alito explained why this question matters and how it framed the legal issue taken up by the Court:

> Under Title VII, an employer's liability for [workplace] harassment may depend on the status of the harasser. If the harassing employee is the victim's co-worker, the employer is liable only if it was negligent in controlling working conditions. In cases in which the harasser is a "supervisor," however, different rules apply. If the supervisor's harassment

---

[1] 42 U.S.C. § 2000e-2(a)(1).

[2] Vance v. Ball State Univ., 570 U.S. 421, 427 (2013).

[3] *See id.* at 423.

culminates in a tangible employment action, the employer is strictly liable. But if no tangible employment action is taken, the employer may escape liability by establishing, as an affirmative defense, that (1) the employer exercised reasonable care to prevent and correct any harassing behavior and (2) that the plaintiff unreasonably failed to take advantage of the preventive or corrective opportunities that the employer provided. Under this framework, therefore, it matters whether a harasser is a "supervisor" or simply a co-worker.[4]

Brief Factual and Procedural History

Maetta Vance, an African-American woman, was employed by Ball State University ("BSU") in various capacities in the University's Dining Services department—eventually rising to the position of "full-time catering assistant."[5] In her complaint, which was filed in the United States District Court for the Southern District of Indiana, Vance alleged that she had experienced racial harassment and discrimination, much of which was allegedly directed at her by Saundra Davis, a white female employed by BSU as a "catering specialist."[6] Vance alleged she reported Davis's behavior to the University, and that it attempted to address the problem, but that the harassment nonetheless continued. In her lawsuit, Vance claimed Davis was her supervisor, making BSU vicariously liable for the presence of a racially hostile work environment under the framework described by Justice Alito at his opinion's outset (as quoted above).

The district court granted summary judgment for BSU, finding the University could not be held vicariously liable for Vance's harassment "because Davis could not 'hire, fire, demote, promote, transfer, or discipline' Vance and, as a result, was not Vance's supervisor."[7] The district court also found that "BSU could not be liable in negligence because it responded reasonably to the incidents of which it was aware."[8] The Seventh Circuit affirmed the district court, explaining that under its precedent, supervisor status requires "the power to hire, fire, demote, promote, transfer, or discipline an employee,"[9] and

---

[4] *Id.* at 424 (internal citations omitted).

[5] *See id.*

[6] *Id.*

[7] *Id.* at 425–26 (quoting Vance v. Ball State Univ., No. 1:06-cv-1452-SEB-JMS, 2008 WL 4247836, at *12 (S.D. Ind. Sept. 10, 2008) (internal citation omitted)).

[8] *Id.*

[9] Vance v. Ball State Univ., 646 F.3d 461, 470 (7th Cir. 2011) (quoting Hall v.

Davis did not have any of these powers over Vance. Accordingly, the circuit court held, BSU could not be held liable unless Vance could prove it had been negligent, and the court found no evidence to support such a finding.[10]

Justice Alito's Majority Opinion

Writing for a 5–4 majority, Justice Alito affirmed the judgment of the Seventh Circuit, holding "that an employee is a 'supervisor' for purposes of vicarious liability under Title VII if he or she is empowered by the employer to take tangible employment actions against the victim,"[11] which the majority defined as the ability "to effect a significant change in employment status, such as hiring, firing, failing to promote, reassignment with significantly different responsibilities, or a decision causing a significant change in benefits."[12] In so holding, the majority explicitly "reject[ed] the nebulous definition of a 'supervisor' advocated" by the Equal Employment Opportunity Commission ("EEOC") "and substantially adopted by several courts of appeals," construing Vance's reliance "on colloquial uses of the term 'supervisor'" as "misplaced," and labelling "her contention that [the Court's] cases require the EEOC's abstract definition" as "simply wrong."[13]

Though the majority opinion is long, its discussion essentially boils down to a protracted attempt to distinguish between the legal meaning of the word "supervisor" as the majority construed it[14] and the word's more colloquial meaning adopted by the EEOC and some courts of appeal, "which tie[d] supervisor status to the ability to exercise significant direction over another's daily work" without the concomitant ability to take "tangible employment actions" against the

---

Bodine Elec. Co., 276 F.3d 345, 355 (7th Cir. 2002)).

[10] *See id.* at 470–73.

[11] *Id.* at 424.

[12] *Id.* at 431 (quoting Burlington Indus., Inc. v. Ellerth, 524 U.S. 742, 761 (1998)). It should be noted, as the majority does later in its opinion, that "supervisor" "is not a term used by Congress in Title VII," but one adopted by the Court in two of its prior cases "as a label for the class of employees whose misconduct may give rise to vicarious employer liability" in certain Title VII actions. *See id.* at 436.

[13] *Id.* at 431–32.

[14] *See id.* at 439–46 (stating that "the answer to th[e] question" of who is a supervisor for Title VII purposes "is implicit in the characteristics of the framework that" the Court had adopted in two 1998 Title VII cases addressing the issue in related contexts: *Burlington Industries, Inc. v. Ellerth*, 524 U.S. 742 (1998), and *Faragher v. City of Boca Raton*, 524 U.S. 775 (1998)).

ostensible subordinate.[15] The majority's stated purpose in this endeavor was to create a "framework" for determining supervisory status that was "easily workable" and applicable "without undue difficulty" by trial courts, as opposed to the approach of the EEOC, advocated by Vance, which the majority criticized as both "a study in ambiguity" and "vague"[16] and which made "the determination of supervisor status depend on a highly case-specific evaluation of numerous factors."[17] Notably, the majority asserted its framework did nothing to hinder the ability of Title VII plaintiffs to succeed on their claims: if the harasser were a supervisor, the existing legal framework would still apply, and if not, "a plaintiff could still prevail by showing that his or her employer was negligent in failing to prevent harassment from taking place."[18] Ultimately, the majority was "confident that, in every case, the approach" it adopted would "be more easily administrable than the approach advocated by the dissent."[19]

Justice Ginsburg's Dissent

In her dissent, Justice Ginsburg characteristically criticized the majority for its disregard of the nuanced realities of human existence and for "ignor[ing]" the actual "conditions under which members of the work force labor."[20] In Ginsburg's view, context was everything, and the EEOC properly determined that "the appropriate question" to ask when determining supervisory status was two-pronged: "Has the employer given the alleged harasser authority to take tangible employment actions *or* to control the conditions under which subordinates do their daily work? If the answer to either inquiry [is] yes, vicarious liability [is] in order, for the superior-subordinate working arrangement facilitating the harassment [is] of the employer's making."[21]

To support her position, Justice Ginsburg spent much of her dissent discussing numerous real-world examples, all drawn from various federal lawsuits, where a man "vested with authority to control the conditions of a subordinate's daily work life used his position to aid his harassment. But in none of them would the Court's severely confined definition of supervisor yield vicarious liability for the employer" despite the fact that, "[a]s anyone with work experience would

---

[15] *Id.* at 424, 431.

[16] *Id.* at 442, 443.

[17] *Id.* at 432.

[18] *Id.* at 448–49.

[19] *Id.* at 450.

[20] *Id.* at 451 (Ginsburg, J., dissenting).

[21] *Id.*

immediately grasp," the men in question "wielded employer-conferred supervisory authority over their victims. Each man's discriminatory harassment derived force from, and was facilitated by, the control reins he held."[22] Ginsburg believed these cases demonstrated that the EEOC's definition of "supervisor" was appropriate because it not only "has the ring of truth and, therefore, powerfully persuasive force," but also recognized that "context is often key" in determining the nature of a supervisory relationship.[23] Implicit in Ginsburg's assessment was that the majority's attempt to create an "easily workable" "framework"[24] was simply not possible when the "realities of the workplace" were honestly considered—realities to which Ginsburg said the majority was "blind."[25] For this reason, Ginsburg had little faith in the majority's reassurance that harassment victims could still prevail by proving negligence on behalf of employers because the realities of many working environments mean that an "employee may have a reputation as a harasser among those in his vicinity, but" it is possible that "no complaint makes its way up to management."[26]

Ultimately, Ginsburg believed that the majority had supplanted "the robust protection against workplace discrimination Congress intended Title VII to secure"[27] with fundamentally inferior priorities such as a rigid focus on "the virtues of simplicity and administrability."[28] Again, she emphasized the impossibility of knowing the true nature of an employment relationship without context: "no crisp definition of supervisor could supply the unwavering line the Court desires" because "[o]ne cannot know whether an employer has vested supervisory authority in an employee, and whether harassment is aided by that authority, without looking to the particular working relationship between the harasser and the victim."[29] She lamented that the majority, "insistent on constructing artificial categories where context should be key," had proceeded "on an immoderate and unrestrained course to corral Title VII,"[30] engineering a shift in the analytical framework of Title VII that would result "in a decidedly employer-friendly direction."[31] The only solution Ginsburg saw to this

---

[22] *Id.* at 455–61.

[23] *Id.* at 463.

[24] *See id.* at 432 (majority opinion).

[25] *Id.* at 455 (Ginsburg, J., dissenting).

[26] *Id.* at 466.

[27] *Id.* 463–64 (quoting Ledbetter v. Goodyear Tire & Rubber Co., Inc., 550 U.S. 618, 660 (2007) (Ginsburg, J., dissenting)).

[28] *Id.* at 463.

[29] *Id.* at 465.

[30] *Id.* at 470.

[31] *Id.* at 466.

problem was legislative; accordingly, she closed her dissent, as she had in other cases, with an appeal to Congress: "The ball is once again in Congress' court to correct the error into which this Court has fallen, and to restore the robust protections against workplace harassment the Court weakens today."[32]

---

[32] *Id.* at 470–71.

VANCE V. BALL STATE UNIVERSITY

JUSTICE GINSBURG, with whom JUSTICE BREYER, JUSTICE SOTOMAYOR, and JUSTICE KAGAN join, DISSENTING.

In *Faragher v. Boca Raton*[1] and *Burlington Industries, Inc. v. Ellerth*,[2] this Court held that an employer can be vicariously liable under Title VII of the Civil Rights Act of 1964 for harassment by an employee given supervisory authority over subordinates. In line with those decisions, in 1999, the Equal Employment Opportunity Commission (EEOC) provided enforcement guidance "regarding employer liability for harassment by supervisors based on sex, race, color, religion, national origin, age, disability, or protected activity."[3] Addressing who qualifies as a supervisor, the EEOC answered: (1) an individual authorized "to undertake or recommend tangible employment decisions affecting the employee," including "hiring, firing, promoting, demoting, and reassigning the employee"; or (2) an individual authorized "to direct the employee's daily work activities."[4]

The Court today strikes from the supervisory category employees who control the day-to-day schedules and assignments of others, confining the category to those formally empowered to take tangible employment actions. The limitation the Court decrees diminishes the force of *Faragher* and *Ellerth*, ignores the conditions under which members of the work force labor, and disserves the objective of Title VII to prevent discrimination from infecting the Nation's workplaces. I would follow the EEOC's Guidance and hold that the authority to direct an employee's daily activities establishes supervisory status under Title VII.

---

[1] 524 U.S. 775 (1998).
[2] 524 U.S. 742 (1998).
[3] U.S. Equal Emp. Opportunity Comm'n, Guidance on Vicarious Employer Liability For Unlawful Harassment by Supervisors, 8 FEP Manual (BNA) 405:7651 (2003) [hereinafter EEOC Guidance].
[4] *Id.* at 405:7654.

I

A

Title VII makes it "an unlawful employment practice for an employer" to "discriminate against any individual with respect to" the "terms, conditions, or privileges of employment, because of such individual's race, color, religion, sex, or national origin."[5] The creation of a hostile work environment through harassment, this Court has long recognized, is a form of proscribed discrimination.[6]

What qualifies as harassment? Title VII imposes no "general civility code."[7] It does not reach "the ordinary tribulations of the workplace," for example, "sporadic use of abusive language" or generally boorish conduct.[8] To be actionable, charged behavior need not drive the victim from her job, but it must be of such severity or pervasiveness as to pollute the working environment, thereby "alter[ing] the conditions of the victim's employment."[9]

In *Faragher* and *Ellerth*, this Court established a framework for determining when an employer may be held liable for its employees' creation of a hostile work environment. Recognizing that Title VII's definition of "employer" includes an employer's "agent[s],"[10] the Court looked to agency law for guidance in formulating liability standards.[11] In particular, the Court drew upon §219(2)(d) of the Restatement (Second) of Agency (1957), which makes an employer liable for the conduct of an employee, even when that employee acts beyond the scope of her employment, if the employee is "aided in accomplishing" a tort "by the existence of the agency relation."[12]

Stemming from that guide, *Faragher* and *Ellerth* distinguished between harassment perpetrated by supervisors, which is often enabled by the supervisor's agency relationship with the employer, and harassment perpetrated by co-workers, which is not similarly facilitated.[13]

---

[5] 42 U.S.C. § 2000e-2(a).

[6] Oncale v. Sundowner Offshore Servs., Inc., 523 U.S. 75, 78 (1998); Meritor Sav. Bank, FSB v. Vinson, 477 U.S. 57, 65–66 (1986).

[7] *Oncale*, 523 U.S. at 81.

[8] BARBARA LINDEMANN & DAVID KADUE, SEXUAL HARASSMENT IN EMPLOYMENT LAW 175 (1992); *see also* 1 BARBARA LINDEMANN & PAUL GROSSMAN, EMPLOYMENT DISCRIMINATION LAW 1335–43 (4th ed. 2007).

[9] Harris v. Forklift Sys., Inc., 510 U.S. 17, 21–22 (1993).

[10] 42 U.S.C. § 2000e(b).

[11] Faragher v. City of Boca Raton, 524 U.S. 775, 791, 801 (1998); Burlington Indus., Inc. v. Ellerth, 524 U.S. 742, 755–760 (1998).

[12] *See Faragher*, 524 U.S. at 801; *Ellerth*, 524 U.S. at 758.

[13] *Faragher*, 524 U.S. at 801–03; *Ellerth*, 524 U.S. at 763–65.

If the harassing employee is a supervisor, the Court held, the employer is vicariously liable whenever the harassment culminates in a tangible employment action.[14] The term "tangible employment action," *Ellerth* observed, "constitutes a significant change in employment status, such as hiring, firing, failing to promote, reassignment with significantly different responsibilities, or a decision causing a significant change in benefits."[15] Such an action, the Court explained, provides "assurance the injury could not have been inflicted absent the agency relation."[16]

An employer may also be held vicariously liable for a supervisor's harassment that does not culminate in a tangible employment action, the Court next determined. In such a case, however, the employer may avoid liability by showing that (1) it exercised reasonable care to prevent and promptly correct harassing behavior, and (2) the complainant unreasonably failed to take advantage of preventative or corrective measures made available to her.[17] The employer bears the burden of establishing this affirmative defense by a preponderance of the evidence.[18]

In contrast, if the harassing employee is a co-worker, a negligence standard applies. To satisfy that standard, the complainant must show that the employer knew or should have known of the offensive conduct but failed to take appropriate corrective action.[19]

B

The distinction *Faragher* and *Ellerth* drew between supervisors and co-workers corresponds to the realities of the workplace. Exposed to a fellow employee's harassment, one can walk away or tell the offender to "buzz off." A supervisor's slings and arrows, however, are not so easily avoided. An employee who confronts her harassing supervisor risks, for example, receiving an undesirable or unsafe work assignment or an unwanted transfer. She may be saddled with an excessive workload or with placement on a shift spanning hours disruptive of her family life. And she may be demoted or fired. Facing such dangers, she may be reluctant to blow the whistle on her superior, whose "power and authority invests his or her harassing conduct

---

[14] *Faragher*, 524 U.S. at 807–08; *Ellerth*, 524 U.S. at 764–65.

[15] *Ellerth*, 524 U.S. at 761.

[16] *Id.* at 761–62.

[17] *Faragher*, 524 U.S. at 807; *Ellerth*, 524 U.S. at 765.

[18] *Faragher*, 524 U.S. at 807; *Ellerth*, 524 U.S. at 765.

[19] *See Faragher*, 524 U.S. at 799; *Ellerth*, 524 U.S. at 758–59; *see also* 29 C.F.R. § 1604.11(d) (2012); EEOC Guidance, *supra* note 3, at 405:7652.

with a particular threatening character."[20] In short, as *Faragher* and *Ellerth* recognized, harassment by supervisors is more likely to cause palpable harm and to persist unabated than similar conduct by fellow employees.

II

While *Faragher* and *Ellerth* differentiated harassment by supervisors from harassment by co-workers, neither decision gave a definitive answer to the question: Who qualifies as a supervisor? Two views have emerged. One view, in line with the EEOC's Guidance, counts as a supervisor anyone with authority to take tangible employment actions or to direct an employee's daily work activities.[21] The other view ranks as supervisors only those authorized to take tangible employment actions.[22]

Notably, respondent Ball State University agreed with petitioner Vance and the United States, as *amicus curiae*, that the tangible-employment-action-only test "does not necessarily capture all employees who may qualify as supervisors."[23] "[V]icarious liability," Ball State acknowledged, "also may be triggered when the harassing employee has the authority to control the victim's daily work activities in a way that materially enables the harassment."[24]

The different view taken by the Court today is out of accord with the agency principles that, *Faragher* and *Ellerth* affirmed, govern Title VII.[25] It is blind to the realities of the workplace, and it discounts the guidance of the EEOC, the agency Congress established to interpret, and superintend the enforcement of, Title VII. Under that guidance, the appropriate question is: Has the employer given the alleged harasser authority to take tangible employment actions or to control the conditions under which subordinates do their daily work? If the answer to either inquiry is yes, vicarious liability is in order, for the

---

[20] *Ellerth*, 524 U.S. at 763; *see also Faragher*, 524 U.S. at 803; Brief for Respondent at 23, Vance v. Ball State Univ., 570 U.S. 421 (2013) (No. 11-556) ("The potential threat to one's livelihood or working conditions will make the victim think twice before resisting harassment or fighting back.").

[21] *E.g.*, Mack v. Otis Elevator Co., 326 F.3d 116, 127 (2d Cir. 2003); Whitten v. Fred's, Inc., 601 F.3d 231, 246 (4th Cir. 2010); EEOC Guidance, *supra* note 3, at 405:7654.

[22] *E.g.*, Noviello v. City of Boston, 398 F.3d 76, 96 (1st Cir. 2005); Parkins v. Civil Constructors of Ill., Inc., 163 F.3d 1027, 1034 (7th Cir. 1998); Joens v. John Morrell & Co., 354 F.3d 938, 940–41 (8th Cir. 2004).

[23] Brief for Respondent, *supra* note 20, at 1.

[24] *Id.* at 1–2.

[25] *See Vance*, 570 U.S. at 452–54 (Ginsburg, J., dissenting).

superior-subordinate working arrangement facilitating the harassment is of the employer's making.

A

Until today, our decisions have assumed that employees who direct subordinates' daily work are supervisors. In *Faragher*, the city of Boca Raton, Florida, employed Bill Terry and David Silverman to oversee the city's corps of ocean lifeguards.[26] Terry and Silverman "repeatedly subject[ed] Faragher and other female lifeguards to uninvited and offensive touching," and they regularly "ma[de] lewd remarks, and [spoke] of women in offensive terms."[27] Terry told a job applicant that "female lifeguards had sex with their male counterparts," and then "asked whether she would do the same."[28] Silverman threatened to assign Faragher to toilet-cleaning duties for a year if she refused to date him.[29] In words and conduct, Silverman and Terry made the beach a hostile place for women to work.

As Chief of Boca Raton's Marine Safety Division, Terry had authority to "hire new lifeguards (subject to the approval of higher management), to supervise all aspects of the lifeguards' work assignments, to engage in counseling, to deliver oral reprimands, and to make a record of any such discipline."[30] Silverman's duties as a Marine Safety lieutenant included "making the lifeguards' daily assignments, and . . . supervising their work and fitness training."[31] Both men "were granted virtually unchecked authority over their subordinates, directly controlling and supervising all aspects of Faragher's day-to-day activities."[32]

We may assume that Terry would fall within the definition of supervisor the Court adopts today.[33; 34 [FN 1]] But nothing in the *Faragher*

---

[26] Faragher v. City of Boca Raton, 524 U.S. 775, 780 (1998).

[27] *Id.* (internal quotation marks omitted).

[28] *Id.* at 782.

[29] *Id.* at 780.

[30] *Id.* at 781.

[31] *Id.*

[32] *Id.* at 808 (internal quotation marks and brackets omitted).

[33] *See* Vance v. Ball State Univ., 570 U.S. 421, 431 (2013).

[34] [FN 1] It is not altogether evident that Terry would qualify under the Court's test. His authority to hire was subject to approval by higher management, *Faragher*, 524 U.S. at 781 (1998), and there is scant indication that he possessed other powers on the Court's list. The Court observes that Terry was able to "recommen[d]," and "initiat[e]" tangible employment actions. *Vance*, 570 U.S. at 437 n.8 (internal quotation marks omitted). Nothing in the *Faragher* record, however, shows that Terry had authority to take such actions himself. Faragher's complaint alleged that Terry said he would never promote

record shows that Silverman would. Silverman had oversight and as-signment responsibilities—he could punish lifeguards who would not date him with full-time toilet-cleaning duty—but there was no evi-dence that he had authority to take tangible employment actions.[35] Holding that Boca Raton was vicariously liable for Silverman's har-assment,[36] the Court characterized him as Faragher's supervisor,[37] and there was no dissent on that point.[38]

Subsequent decisions reinforced *Faragher's* use of the term "su-pervisor" to encompass employees with authority to direct the daily work of their victims. In *Pennsylvania State Police v. Suders*,[39] for example, the Court considered whether a constructive discharge occa-sioned by supervisor harassment ranks as a tangible employment ac-tion. The harassing employees lacked authority to discharge or demote the complainant, but they were "responsible for the day-to-day supervision" of the workplace and for overseeing employee shifts.[40] Describing the harassing employees as the complainant's "supervisors," the Court proceeded to evaluate the complainant's con-structive discharge claim under the *Ellerth* and *Faragher* frame-work.[41]

It is true, as the Court says,[42] that *Faragher* and later cases did not squarely resolve whether an employee without power to take tan-gible employment actions may nonetheless qualify as a supervisor. But in laboring to establish that Silverman's supervisor status, un-disputed in *Faragher*, is not dispositive here, the Court misses the forest for the trees. *Faragher* illustrates an all-too-plain reality: A su-pervisor with authority to control subordinates' daily work is no less aided in his harassment than is a supervisor with authority to fire, demote, or transfer. That Silverman could threaten Faragher with toilet-cleaning duties while Terry could orally reprimand her was in-consequential in *Faragher*, and properly so. What mattered was that both men took advantage of the power vested in them as agents of

---

a female lifeguard to the rank of lieutenant, *Faragher*, 524 U.S. at 780, but that statement hardly suffices to establish that he had ultimate promotional authority. Had Boca Raton anticipated the position the Court today an-nounces, the city might have urged classification of Terry as Faragher's supe-rior, but not her "supervisor."

[35] *See Faragher*, 524 U.S. at 780–81.

[36] *Id.* at 808–09.

[37] *See id.* at 780.

[38] *See id.* at 810 (Thomas, J., dissenting).

[39] 542 U.S. 129, 140 (2004).

[40] Suders v. Easton, 325 F.3d 432, 450 n.11 (3d Cir. 2003).

[41] *Suders*, 542 U.S. at 134, 140–41.

[42] Vance v. Ball State Univ., 570 U.S. 421, 437–38, 438 n.11 (2013).

Boca Raton to facilitate their abuse.[43] And when, assisted by an agency relationship, in-charge superiors like Silverman perpetuate a discriminatory work environment, our decisions have appropriately held the employer vicariously liable, subject to the above-described affirmative defense.[44]

B

Workplace realities fortify my conclusion that harassment by an employee with power to direct subordinates' day-to-day work activities should trigger vicarious employer liability. The following illustrations, none of them hypothetical, involve in-charge employees of the kind the Court today excludes from supervisory status.[45] [FN 2]

Yasharay Mack: Yasharay Mack, an African-American woman, worked for the Otis Elevator Company as an elevator mechanic's helper at the Metropolitan Life Building in New York City. James Connolly, the "mechanic in charge" and the senior employee at the site, targeted Mack for abuse. He commented frequently on her "fantastic ass," "luscious lips," and "beautiful eyes," and, using deplorable racial epithets, opined that minorities and women did not "belong in the business." Once, he pulled her on his lap, touched her buttocks, and tried to kiss her while others looked on. Connolly lacked authority to take tangible employment actions against mechanic's helpers, but he did assign their work, control their schedules, and direct the particulars of their workdays. When he became angry with Mack, for example, he denied her overtime hours. And when she complained about the mistreatment, he scoffed, "I get away with everything."[46]

Donna Rhodes: Donna Rhodes, a seasonal highway maintainer for the Illinois Department of Transportation, was responsible for plowing snow during winter months. Michael Poladian was a "Lead Lead Worker" and Matt Mara, a "Technician" at the maintenance yard where Rhodes worked. Both men assembled plow crews and managed the work assignments of employees in Rhodes's position, but neither had authority to hire, fire, promote, demote, transfer, or discipline

---

[43] *See Faragher*, 524 U.S. at 801 (Silverman and Terry "implicitly threaten[ed] to mis-use their supervisory powers to deter any resistance or complaint.").

[44] *See Vance*, 570 U.S. at 453 (Ginsburg, J., dissenting).

[45] [FN 2] The illustrative cases reached the appellate level after grants of summary judgment in favor of the employer. Like the Courts of Appeals in each case, I recount the facts in the light most favorable to the employee, the nonmoving party.

[46] *See* Mack v. Otis Elevator Co., 326 F.3d 116, 120–21, 125–26 (2d Cir. 2003) (internal quotation marks omitted).

employees. In her third season working at the yard, Rhodes was verbally assaulted with sex-based invectives and a pornographic image was taped to her locker. Poladian forced her to wash her truck in subzero temperatures, assigned her undesirable yard work instead of road crew work, and prohibited another employee from fixing the malfunctioning heating system in her truck. Conceding that Rhodes had been subjected to a sex-based hostile work environment, the Department of Transportation argued successfully in the District Court and Court of Appeals that Poladian and Mara were not Rhodes's supervisors because they lacked authority to take tangible employment actions against her.[47]

Clara Whitten: Clara Whitten worked at a discount retail store in Belton, South Carolina. On Whitten's first day of work, the manager, Matt Green, told her to "give [him] what [he] want[ed]" in order to obtain approval for long weekends off from work. Later, fearing what might transpire, Whitten ignored Green's order to join him in an isolated storeroom. Angered, Green instructed Whitten to stay late and clean the store. He demanded that she work over the weekend despite her scheduled day off. Dismissing her as "dumb and stupid," Green threatened to make her life a "living hell." Green lacked authority to fire, promote, demote, or otherwise make decisions affecting Whitten's pocketbook. But he directed her activities, gave her tasks to accomplish, burdened her with undesirable work assignments, and controlled her schedule. He was usually the highest ranking employee in the store, and both Whitten and Green considered him the supervisor.[48]

Monika Starke: CRST Van Expedited, Inc., an interstate transit company, ran a training program for newly hired truckdrivers requiring a 28-day on-the-road trip. Monika Starke participated in the program. Trainees like Starke were paired in a truck cabin with a single "lead driver" who lacked authority to hire, fire, promote, or demote, but who exercised control over the work environment for the duration of the trip. Lead drivers were responsible for providing instruction on CRST's driving method, assigning specific tasks, and scheduling rest stops. At the end of the trip, lead drivers evaluated trainees' performance with a nonbinding pass or fail recommendation that could lead to full driver status. Over the course of Starke's training trip, her first lead driver, Bob Smith, filled the cabin with vulgar sexual remarks, commenting on her breast size and comparing the gear stick to genitalia. A second lead driver, David Goodman, later forced her into

---

[47] *See* Rhodes v. Ill Dep't of Transp., 359 F.3d 498, 501–03, 506–07 (7th Cir. 2004).

[48] *See* Whitten v. Fred's, Inc., 601 F.3d 231, 236, 244–47 (4th Cir. 2010) (internal quotation marks omitted).

unwanted sex with him, an outrage to which she submitted, believing it necessary to gain a passing grade.[49]

In each of these cases, a person vested with authority to control the conditions of a subordinate's daily work life used his position to aid his harassment. But in none of them would the Court's severely confined definition of supervisor yield vicarious liability for the employer. The senior elevator mechanic in charge, the Court today tells us, was Mack's co-worker, not her supervisor. So was the store manager who punished Whitten with long hours for refusing to give him what he wanted. So were the lead drivers who controlled all aspects of Starke's working environment, and the yard worker who kept other employees from helping Rhodes to control the heat in her truck.

As anyone with work experience would immediately grasp, James Connolly, Michael Poladian, Matt Mara, Matt Green, Bob Smith, and David Goodman wielded employer-conferred supervisory authority over their victims. Each man's discriminatory harassment derived force from, and was facilitated by, the control reins he held.[50] Under any fair reading of Title VII, in each of the illustrative cases, the superior employee should have been classified a supervisor whose conduct would trigger vicarious liability.[51] [FN 3]

---

[49] *See* Equal Emp't Opportunity Comm'n v. CRST Van Expedited, Inc., 679 F.3d 657, 665–66, 684–85 (8th Cir. 2012).

[50] *Cf.* Burlington N. & Santa Fe Ry. Co. v. White, 548 U.S. 53, 70–71 (2006) ("Common sense suggests that one good way to discourage an employee . . . from bringing discrimination charges would be to insist that she spend more time performing the more arduous duties and less time performing those that are easier or more agreeable.").

[51] [FN 3] The Court misses the point of the illustrations. *See* Vance v. Ball State Univ., 570 U.S. 421, 447–49, 448 nn.15–16 (2013). Even under a vicarious liability rule, the Court points out, employers might escape liability for reasons other than the harasser's status as supervisor. For example, Rhodes might have avoided summary judgment in favor of her employer; even so, it would have been open to the employer to raise and prove to a jury the *Faragher/Ellerth* affirmative defense, *see id.* at 453 (Ginsburg, J., dissenting). No doubt other barriers also might impede an employee from prevailing, for example, Whitten's and Starke's intervening bankruptcies, *see* Whitten v. Fred's Inc., No. 8:08-0218-HMH-BHH, 2010 WL 2757005 (D.S.C. July 12, 2010); *CRST Van Expedited*, 679 F.3d at 678 & n.14, or Mack's withdrawal of her complaint for reasons not apparent from the record, *see* Vance, 570 U.S. at 448 n.16. That, however, is no reason to restrict the definition of supervisor in a way that leaves out those genuinely in charge.

C

Within a year after the Court's decisions in *Faragher* and *Ellerth*, the EEOC defined "supervisor" to include any employee with "authority to undertake or recommend tangible employment decisions," or with "authority to direct [another] employee's daily work activities."[52] That definition should garner "respect proportional to its 'power to persuade.'"[53; 54 [FN 4]]

The EEOC's definition of supervisor reflects the agency's "informed judgment" and "body of experience" in enforcing Title VII.[55] For 14 years, in enforcement actions and litigation, the EEOC has firmly adhered to its definition.[56]

In developing its definition of supervisor, the EEOC paid close attention to the *Faragher* and *Ellerth* framework. An employer is vicariously liable only when the authority it has delegated enables actionable harassment, the EEOC recognized.[57] For that reason, a supervisor's authority must be "of a sufficient magnitude so as to assist the harasser . . . in carrying out the harassment."[58] Determining whether an employee wields sufficient authority is not a mechanical inquiry, the EEOC explained; instead, specific facts about the employee's job function are critical.[59] Thus, an employee with authority to increase another's workload or assign undesirable tasks may rank

---

[52] EEOC Guidance, *supra* note 3, at 405:7654.

[53] United States v. Mead Corp., 533 U.S. 218, 235 (2001) (quoting Skidmore v. Swift & Co., 323 U.S. 134, 140 (1944)); *see also* Crawford v. Metro. Gov't of Nashville & Davidson Cty., 555 U.S. 271, 276 (2009) (EEOC guidelines merited Skidmore deference); Fed. Express Corp. v. Holowecki, 552 U.S. 389, 399–403 (2008) (same); Meritor Sav. Bank, FSB v. Vinson, 477 U.S. 57, 65 (1986) (same).

[54] [FN 4] Respondent's *amici* maintain that the EEOC Guidance is ineligible for deference under *Skidmore v. Swift & Co.*, 323 U.S. 134 (1944), because it interprets *Faragher* and *Burlington Industries, Inc. v. Ellerth*, 524 U.S. 742 (1998), not the text of Title VII. *See* Brief for Society for Human Resource Management et al. at 11–16, *Vance*, 570 U.S. 421 (No. 11-556). They are mistaken. The EEOC Guidance rests on the employer liability framework set forth in *Faragher* and *Ellerth*, but both the framework and EEOC Guidance construe the term "agent" in 42 U.S.C. § 2000e(b).

[55] *Meritor*, 447 U.S. at 65 (internal quotation marks omitted).

[56] *See* Brief for United States as Amicus Curiae at 28, *Vance*, 570 U.S. 421 (No. 11-556) (citing numerous briefs in the Courts of Appeals setting forth the EEOC's understanding).

[57] EEOC Guidance, *supra* note 3, at 405:7654.

[58] *Id.*

[59] *Id.* at 405:7653–7654.

as a supervisor, for those powers can enable harassment.[60] On the other hand, an employee "who directs only a limited number of tasks or assignments" ordinarily would not qualify as a supervisor, for her harassing conduct is not likely to be aided materially by the agency relationship.[61]

In my view, the EEOC's definition, which the Court puts down as "a study in ambiguity,"[62] has the ring of truth and, therefore, powerfully persuasive force. As a precondition to vicarious employer liability, the EEOC explained, the harassing supervisor must wield authority of sufficient magnitude to enable the harassment. In other words, the aided-in-accomplishment standard requires "something more than the employment relation itself."[63] Furthermore, as the EEOC perceived, in assessing an employee's qualification as a supervisor, context is often key.[64] I would accord the agency's judgment due respect.

III

Exhibiting remarkable resistance to the thrust of our prior decisions, workplace realities, and the EEOC's Guidance, the Court embraces a position that relieves scores of employers of responsibility for the behavior of the supervisors they employ. Trumpeting the virtues of simplicity and administrability, the Court restricts supervisor status to those with power to take tangible employment actions. In so restricting the definition of supervisor, the Court once again shuts from sight the "robust protection against workplace discrimination Congress intended Title VII to secure."[65]

A

The Court purports to rely on the *Ellerth* and *Faragher* framework to limit supervisor status to those capable of taking tangible employment actions.[66] That framework, we are told, presupposes "a sharp line between co-workers and supervisors."[67] The definition of supervisor decreed today, the Court insists, is "clear," "readily applied," and

---

[60] *Id.* at 405:7654.

[61] *Id.* at 405:7655.

[62] Vance v. Ball State Univ., 570 U.S. 421, 442 (2013).

[63] Burlington Indus., Inc. v. Ellerth, 524 U.S. 742, 760 (1998).

[64] *See Vance*, 570 U.S. at 465–66 (Ginsburg, J., dissenting).

[65] Ledbetter v. Goodyear Tire & Rubber Co., 550 U.S. 618, 660 (2007) (Ginsburg, J., dissenting).

[66] *Vance*, 570 U.S. at 432, 439–40.

[67] *Id.* at 439.

"easily workable,"[68] when compared to the EEOC's vague standard.[69]

There is reason to doubt just how "clear" and "workable" the Court's definition is. A supervisor, the Court holds, is someone empowered to "take tangible employment actions against the victim, i.e., to effect a 'significant change in employment status, such as hiring, firing, failing to promote, reassignment with significantly different responsibilities, or a decision causing a significant change in benefits.'"[70] Whether reassignment authority makes someone a supervisor might depend on whether the reassignment carries economic consequences.[71] The power to discipline other employees, when the discipline has economic consequences, might count, too.[72] So might the power to initiate or make recommendations about tangible employment actions.[73] And when an employer "concentrates all decision-making authority in a few individuals" who rely on information from "other workers who actually interact with the affected employee," the other workers may rank as supervisors (or maybe not; the Court does not commit one way or the other).[74]

Someone in search of a bright line might well ask, what counts as "significantly different responsibilities"? Can any economic consequence make a reassignment or disciplinary action "significant," or is there a minimum threshold? How concentrated must the decision-making authority be to deem those not formally endowed with that authority nevertheless "supervisors"? The Court leaves these questions unanswered, and its liberal use of "mights" and "mays"[75] dims the light it casts.[76] [FN 5]

---

[68] *Id.* at 432, 441.

[69] *Id.* at 443.

[70] *Id.* at 431 (quoting Burlington Indus., Inc. v. Ellerth, 524 U.S. 742, 761 (1998)).

[71] *Id.* at 438 n.9.

[72] *Id.*

[73] *Id.* at 437 n.8.

[74] *Id.* at 446–47.

[75] *Id.* at 437 n.8, 438 n.9, 447.

[76] [FN 5] Even the Seventh Circuit, whose definition of supervisor the Court adopts in large measure, has candidly acknowledged that, under its definition, supervisor status is not a clear and certain thing. *See* Doe v. Oberweis Dairy, 456 F.3d 704, 717 (2006) ("The difficulty of classification in this case arises from the fact that Nayman, the shift supervisor, was in between the paradigmatic classes [of supervisor and co-worker]. He had supervisory responsibility in the sense of authority to direct the work of the [ice-cream] scoopers, and he was even authorized to issue disciplinary write-ups, but he had no authority to fire them. He was either an elevated coworker or a diminished supervisor.").

That the Court has adopted a standard, rather than a clear rule, is not surprising, for no crisp definition of supervisor could supply the unwavering line the Court desires. Supervisors, like the workplaces they manage, come in all shapes and sizes. Whether a pitching coach supervises his pitchers (can he demote them?), or an artistic director supervises her opera star (can she impose significantly different responsibilities?), or a law firm associate supervises the firm's paralegals (can she fire them?) are matters not susceptible to mechanical rules and on-off switches. One cannot know whether an employer has vested supervisory authority in an employee, and whether harassment is aided by that authority, without looking to the particular working relationship between the harasser and the victim. That is why *Faragher* and *Ellerth* crafted an employer liability standard embracive of all whose authority significantly aids in the creation and perpetuation of harassment.

The Court's focus on finding a definition of supervisor capable of instant application is at odds with the Court's ordinary emphasis on the importance of particular circumstances in Title VII cases.[77; 78 [FN 6]] The question of supervisory status, no less than the question whether retaliation or harassment has occurred, "depends on a constellation of surrounding circumstances, expectations, and relationships."[79] The EEOC's Guidance so perceives.

B

As a consequence of the Court's truncated conception of supervisory authority, the *Faragher* and *Ellerth* framework has shifted in a decidedly employer-friendly direction. This realignment will leave many harassment victims without an effective remedy and undermine Title VII's capacity to prevent workplace harassment.

---

[77] *See, e.g.*, Burlington N. v. Santa Fe Ry. Co. v. White, 548 U.S. 53, 69 (2006) ("[T]he significance of any given act of retaliation will often depend upon the particular circumstances."); Harris v. Forklift Sys., Inc., 510 U.S. 17, 23 (1993) ("[W]hether an environment is 'hostile' or 'abusive' can be determined only by looking at all the circumstances.").

[78 [FN 6]] The Court worries that the EEOC's definition of supervisor will confound jurors who must first determine whether the harasser is a supervisor and second apply the correct employer liability standard. *Vance*, 570 U.S. at 443–45, 444 n.13, 445 n.14. But the Court can point to no evidence that jury instructions on supervisor status in jurisdictions following the EEOC Guidance have in fact proved unworkable or confusing to jurors. Moreover, under the Court's definition of supervisor, jurors in many cases will be obliged to determine, as a threshold question, whether the alleged harasser possessed supervisory authority. *See id.* at 437.

[79] Oncale v. Sundowner Offshore Servs., Inc., 523 U.S. 75, 81–82 (1998).

The negligence standard allowed by the Court[80] scarcely affords the protection the *Faragher* and *Ellerth* framework gave victims harassed by those in control of their lives at work. Recall that an employer is negligent with regard to harassment only if it knew or should have known of the conduct but failed to take appropriate corrective action.[81] It is not uncommon for employers to lack actual or constructive notice of a harassing employee's conduct.[82] An employee may have a reputation as a harasser among those in his vicinity, but if no complaint makes its way up to management, the employer will escape liability under a negligence standard.[83]

Faragher is illustrative. After enduring unrelenting harassment, Faragher reported Terry's and Silverman's conduct informally to Robert Gordon, another immediate supervisor.[84] But the lifeguards were "completely isolated from the City's higher management," and it did not occur to Faragher to pursue the matter with higher ranking city officials distant from the beach.[85] Applying a negligence standard, the Eleventh Circuit held that, despite the pervasiveness of the harassment, and despite Gordon's awareness of it, Boca Raton lacked constructive notice and therefore escaped liability.[86] Under the vicarious liability standard, however, Boca Raton could not make out the affirmative defense, for it had failed to disseminate a policy against sexual harassment.[87]

On top of the substantive differences in the negligence and vicarious liability standards, harassment victims, under today's decision, are saddled with the burden of proving the employer's negligence whenever the harasser lacks the power to take tangible employment actions. *Faragher* and *Ellerth*, by contrast, placed the burden squarely on the employer to make out the affirmative defense.[88] This allocation of the burden was both sensible and deliberate: An employer has superior access to evidence bearing on whether it acted reasonably to prevent or correct harassing behavior, and superior resources to marshal that evidence.[89]

---

[80] *See Vance*, 570 U.S. at 445–46.
[81] *See* 29 C.F.R. § 1604.11(d); EEOC Guidance, *supra* note 3, at 405:7652 to 405:7653.
[82] *See* LINDEMANN & GROSSMAN, *supra* note 8, at 1378–79.
[83] *Id.* at 1378.
[84] Faragher v. City of Boca Raton, 524 U.S. 775, 782–83 (1998).
[85] *Id.* at 783, 808 (internal quotation marks omitted).
[86] *Id.* at 784–85.
[87] *Id.* at 808–09.
[88] *See* Pa. State Police v. Suders, 542 U.S. 129, 146 (2004) (citing Burlington Indus., Inc. v. Ellerth, 524 U.S. 742, 765 (1998); *Faragher*, 524 U.S. at 807).
[89] *See Suders*, 542 U.S. at 146 n.7 ("The employer is in the best position to

Faced with a steeper substantive and procedural hill to climb, victims like Yasharay Mack, Donna Rhodes, Clara Whitten, and Monika Starke likely will find it impossible to obtain redress. We can expect that, as a consequence of restricting the supervisor category to those formally empowered to take tangible employment actions, victims of workplace harassment with meritorious Title VII claims will find suit a hazardous endeavor.[90] [FN 7]

Inevitably, the Court's definition of supervisor will hinder efforts to stamp out discrimination in the workplace. Because supervisors are comparatively few, and employees are many, "the employer has a greater opportunity to guard against misconduct by supervisors than by common workers," and a greater incentive to "screen [supervisors], train them, and monitor their performance."[91] Vicarious liability for employers serves this end. When employers know they will be answerable for the injuries a harassing jobsite boss inflicts, their incentive to provide preventative instruction is heightened. If vicarious liability is confined to supervisors formally empowered to take tangible employment actions, however, employers will have a diminished incentive to train those who control their subordinates' work activities and schedules, i.e., the supervisors who "actually interact" with employees.[92]

IV

I turn now to the case before us. Maetta Vance worked as substitute server and part-time catering assistant for Ball State University's Banquet and Catering Division. During the period in question, she alleged, Saundra Davis, a catering specialist, and other Ball State employees subjected her to a racially hostile work environment. Applying controlling Circuit precedent, the District Court and Seventh Circuit concluded that Davis was not Vance's supervisor, and reviewed Ball State's liability for her conduct under a negligence standard.[93] Because

---

know what remedial procedures it offers to employees and how those procedures operate.").

[90] [FN 7] Nor is the Court's confinement of supervisor status needed to deter insubstantial claims. Under the EEOC Guidance, a plaintiff must meet the threshold requirement of actionable harassment and then show that her supervisor's authority was of "sufficient magnitude" to assist in the harassment. *See* EEOC Guidance, *supra* note 3, at 405:7652, 405:7654.

[91] *Faragher*, 524 U.S. at 803.

[92] Vance v. Ball State Univ., 570 U.S. 421, 447 (2013).

[93] Vance v. Ball State Univ., 646 F.3d 461, 470–471 (7th Cir. 2011); Petition for Writ of Certiorari app. at 53a–55a, 59a–60a, *Vance*, 570 U.S. 421 (No. 11-556).

I would hold that the Seventh Circuit erred in restricting supervisor status to employees formally empowered to take tangible employment actions, I would remand for application of the proper standard to Vance's claim. On this record, however, there is cause to anticipate that Davis would not qualify as Vance's supervisor.[94] [FN 8]

Supervisor status is based on "job function rather than job title," and depends on "specific facts" about the working relationship.[95] Vance has adduced scant evidence that Davis controlled the conditions of her daily work. Vance stated in an affidavit that the general manager of the Catering Division, Bill Kimes, was charged with "overall supervision in the kitchen," including "reassign[ing] people to perform different tasks," and "control[ling] the schedule."[96] The chef, Shannon Fultz, assigned tasks by preparing "prep lists" of daily duties.[97] There is no allegation that Davis had a hand in creating these prep lists, nor is there any indication that, in fact, Davis otherwise controlled the particulars of Vance's workday. Vance herself testified that she did not know whether Davis was her supervisor.[98]

True, Davis' job description listed among her responsibilities "[l]ead[ing] and direct[ing] kitchen part-time, substitute, and student employee helpers via demonstration, coaching, and overseeing their work."[99] And another employee testified to believing that Davis was "a supervisor."[100] But because the supervisor-status inquiry should focus on substance, not labels or paper descriptions, it is doubtful that this slim evidence would enable Vance to survive a motion for summary judgment. Nevertheless, I would leave it to the Seventh Circuit to decide, under the proper standard for supervisory status, what impact, if any, Davis' job description and the co-worker's statement should have on the determination of Davis' status.[101] [FN 9]

---

[94] [FN 8] In addition to concluding that Davis was not Vance's supervisor, the District Court held that the conduct Vance alleged was "neither sufficiently severe nor pervasive to be considered objectively hostile for the purposes of Title VII." Petition for Writ of Certioari, *supra* note 93, app. at 66a. The Seventh Circuit declined to address this issue. *See Vance,* 646 F.3d at 471. If the case were remanded, the Court of Appeals could resolve the hostile environment issue first, and then, if necessary, Davis' status as supervisor or co-worker.

[95] EEOC Guidance, *supra* note 3, at 405:7654; *see Vance,* 570 U.S. at 462–63 (Ginsburg, J., dissenting).

[96] App. at 431, *Vance,* 570 U.S. 421 (No. 11-556).

[97] *Id.* at 277–279, 427.

[98] *Id.* at 198.

[99] *Id.* at 13.

[100] *Id.* at 386.

[101] [FN 9] The Court agrees that Davis "would probably not qualify" as Vance's supervisor under the EEOC's definition. *Vance,* 570 U.S. at 459. Then why,

V

Regrettably, the Court has seized upon Vance's thin case to narrow the definition of supervisor, and thereby manifestly limit Title VII's protections against workplace harassment. Not even Ball State, the defendant-employer in this case, has advanced the restrictive definition the Court adopts.[102] Yet the Court, insistent on constructing artificial categories where context should be key, proceeds on an immoderate and unrestrained course to corral Title VII.

Congress has, in the recent past, intervened to correct this Court's wayward interpretations of Title VII.[103] The ball is once again in Congress' court to correct the error into which this Court has fallen, and to restore the robust protections against workplace harassment the Court weakens today.

*   *   *

For the reasons stated, I would reverse the judgment of the Seventh Circuit and remand the case for application of the proper standard for determining who qualifies as a supervisor.

---

one might ask, does the Court nevertheless reach out to announce its restrictive standard in this case, one in which all parties, including the defendant-employer, accept the fitness for Title VII of the EEOC's Guidance? *See Id.* at 455 (Ginsburg, J., dissenting).

[102] *See id.* at 455 (Ginsburg, J., dissenting).

[103] *See* Lilly Ledbetter Fair Pay Act of 2009, Pub. L. No. 111-2, 123 Stat. 5, superseding Ledbetter v. Goodyear Tire & Rubber Co., 550 U.S. 618 (2007); *see also* Civil Rights Act of 1991, Pub. L. No. 102-166, 105 Stat. 1071, superseding in part, Lorance v. AT&T Techs., Inc., 490 U.S. 900 (1989); Martin v. Wilks, 490 U.S. 755 (1989); Wards Cove Packing Co. v. Atonio, 490 U.S. 642 (1989); and Price Waterhouse v. Hopkins, 490 U.S. 228 (1989).

SHELBY COUNTY

"Hubris is a fit word for today's demolition of the Voting Rights Act."

Brief Procedural History

The Voting Rights Act of 1965 ("VRA" or "the Act") was enacted to end discriminatory practices in the South hindering African-Americans from exercising the right to vote guaranteed the Fifteenth Amendment. Such practices included literacy tests, poll taxes, strict registration and licensing requirements, the need for vouchers from registered voters, and similar restrictions, all aimed at preventing blacks from voting.

Shelby County, Alabama v. Holder concerns the constitutionality of Sections 4 and 5 of the Act. These sections required states with a history of discrimination to obtain federal approval before enacting any election law to ensure the law "had neither 'the purpose [nor] the effect of denying or abridging the right to vote on account of race or color.'"[1] This was known as the "preclearance" requirement of the VRA. A state subject to preclearance could only change its voting laws if the proposed changes were approved by the Attorney General of the United States or a panel of three federal judges from the United States District Court for the District of Columbia.

Section 4(b) applied the preclearance requirement only to those jurisdictions that, prior to 1964, either imposed a test or device as a prerequisite to voting or which had voter turnout of less than 50% in the 1964 Presidential election. These were called "covered jurisdictions." In 1965, the covered jurisdictions included Alabama, Georgia, Louisiana, Mississippi, South Carolina, and Virginia, as well as select counties in North Carolina and one county in Arizona.

Sections 4(b) and 5 of the VRA were intended to be temporary, expiring after five years. However, those sections were both reauthorized and expanded by Congress numerous times between 1970 and 2006, when the Act was reauthorized for 25 years and its scope expanded once more.[2] One covered jurisdiction was Shelby County,

---

[1] Shelby Cty. v. Holder, 570 U.S. 529, 537 (2013) (quoting Section 5 of the Voting Rights Act).

[2] The majority opinion describes these various reauthorizations in detail. *See id.* at 538–40.

Alabama—one of the named parties in the case—which challenged the constitutionality of the 2006 reauthorization. The District Court ruled against the county and upheld the Act, finding "that the evidence before Congress in 2006 was sufficient to justify reauthorizing § 5 and continuing the § 4(b) coverage formula."[3] The United States Court of Appeals for the District of Columbia Circuit affirmed the lower court, though not without noting "that the evidence for singling out the covered jurisdictions was 'less robust' and that the issue presented 'a close question.'"[4]

Chief Justice Roberts' Majority Opinion

Writing for a 5–4 majority, the Chief Justice began by calling the VRA's measures "unprecedented"[5] and continuously emphasizing the "extraordinary" nature of the Act. Indeed, the opening sentence of the majority opinion states that the Act "employed extraordinary measures to address an extraordinary problem." He would use the word "extraordinary" eight more times in the nine-page opinion.[6] This emphasis is key to understanding the majority's subsequent rationale: while previous majorities of the Court had upheld the VRA by reasoning that "'exceptional conditions can justify legislative measures not otherwise appropriate,'"[7] the *Shelby County* majority determined that because the Act contains "extraordinary measures," its "'burdens . . . must be justified by current needs'"[8]—especially when, as the majority observed, the Act "sharply departs from" the "basic principles" of federalism, including the "'fundamental principle of *equal* sovereignty' among the States," by exposing them to disparate treatment.[9]

The majority concluded that while in 1966 "these departures from the basic features of our system of government" were "justified" by the realities of Jim Crow, "[n]early 50 years later, things have changed dramatically,"[10] such that current needs no longer justified imposition of the Act's stringent preclearance requirements. Citing evidence in

---

[3] *Id.* at 541.

[4] *Id.* (quoting Shelby Cty. v. Holder, 679 F.3d 848, 879 (D.C. Cir. 2012)).

[5] *Id.* at 534.

[6] *See id.* at 534, 536, 545, 546, 549, 552, 555, 557.

[7] *Id.* at 535 (quoting South Carolina v. Katzenbach, 383 U.S. 301, 309 (1966)).

[8] *Id.* at 536 (quoting Nw. Austin Mun. Util. Dist. No. One v. Holder, 557 U.S. 193, 203 (2009)).

[9] *Id.* at 544 (quoting *Nw. Austin*, 557 U.S. at 203 (emphasis added by Chief Justice Roberts)).

[10] *Id.* at 545, 547.

the Congressional Record, the Chief Justice agreed with Shelby County that in "the covered jurisdictions, '[v]oter turnout and registration rates now approach parity. Blatantly discriminatory evasions of federal decrees are rare. And minority candidates hold office at unprecedented levels.'"[11] Especially persuasive for the majority was the fact that "Census Bureau data from the most recent election indicate that African–American voter turnout exceeded white voter turnout in five of the six States originally covered by § 5, with a gap in the sixth State of less than one half of one percent."[12] Yet despite "these improvements," the majority noted—while conceding that those improvements transpired "no doubt . . . in large part *because of* the Voting Rights Act"[13]—the Act's "extraordinary and unprecedented features were reauthorized—as if nothing had changed"—and in fact, had "grown even stronger."[14]

Accordingly, the majority found that the Act's "'current burdens'" were no longer justified by "'current needs.'"[15] The majority believed that Congress continued to treat covered jurisdictions as if they still behaved as they did in 1965, ignoring the positive "developments" of the ensuing 40 years of history and instead "ke[pt] the focus on decades-old data relevant to decades-old problems, rather than current data reflecting current needs."[16] The majority concluded that "no one can fairly say" the current situation "shows anything approaching the 'pervasive,' 'flagrant,' 'widespread,' and 'rampant' discrimination that faced Congress in 1965."[17] The majority thus declared Section 4(b) of the VRA unconstitutional, asserting that the "formula in that section can no longer be used as a basis for subjecting jurisdictions to preclearance."[18]

While the Chief Justice stressed that the majority "issue[d] no holding on § 5 itself" and that "Congress may draft another formula based on current conditions,"[19] the effect of the ruling was to vitiate the entire Voting Rights Act. Without a coverage formula in place mandating which jurisdictions were subject to preclearance, the result was that no jurisdictions were subject to preclearance. The protections enshrined in the Act were therefore functionally extirpated

---

[11] *Id.* at 547 (quoting *Nw. Austin*, 557 U.S. at 202).
[12] *Id.* at 548.
[13] *Id.*
[14] *Id.* at 549.
[15] *Id.* at 550–51 (quoting *Nw. Austin*, 557 U.S. at 203).
[16] *Id.* at 553.
[17] *Id.* at 554 (quoting South Carolina v. Katzenbach, 383 U.S. 301, 308, 315, 331 (1966); *Nw. Austin*, 557 U.S. at 201).
[18] *Id.* at 557.
[19] *Id.*

as a result of the majority's holding; as Justice Ginsburg noted in her dissent, "without [§ 4(b)'s] formula, § 5 is immobilized."[20]

Justice Thomas' Concurring Opinion

Justice Thomas wrote separately to explain that he would also find § 5 of the VRA unconstitutional. Repeating much of the same language in the majority opinion quoted above, Justice Thomas concluded that the majority "compellingly demonstrate[d] that Congress had failed to justify 'current burdens' with a record demonstrating 'current needs,'" "leaving the inevitable conclusion unstated" that § 5 was unconstitutional on the same grounds as § 4(b).[21]

Justice Ginsburg's Dissent

Justice Ginsburg believed that Congress was well within its constitutional authority to enforce the Fifteenth Amendment "by appropriate legislation" such as the VRA, and had justifiably concluded that the preclearance requirement should remain in force because "continuance would facilitate completion of the impressive gains thus far made" and "guard against backsliding."[22] She termed Jim Crow laws the "first generation barriers experienced by minority voters" justifying passage of the Act, and observed that while the Act had successfully eliminated those barriers, "second-generation barriers" remained in the form of more subtle efforts to "reduce the impact of minority votes, in contrast to direct attempts to block access to the ballot."[23] For Ginsburg, the Act was plainly justified as an endeavor to stymy such barriers.

Ginsburg next traced the history of Congressional authority to enforce the Fifteenth Amendment, finding that authority "broad," before presenting an extensive survey of more recent attempts by covered jurisdictions to restrict minority voting rights which "fill[ed] the pages of the legislative record" and provided more than "sufficient" evidence to support the 2006 reauthorization and expansion of the Act.[24] Notably, Ginsburg pointed to numerous specific examples of such second-generation barriers in Alabama itself, including an attempt by one municipality located in Shelby County to eliminate a majority-black

---

[20] *Id.* at 559 n.1 (Ginsburg, J., dissenting).
[21] *Id.* at 559 (Thomas, J., concurring) (quoting majority opinion at 542).
[22] *Id.* at 559–60 (Ginsburg, J., dissenting) (quoting U.S. CONST. amend. XV, § 2).
[23] *Id.* at 563.
[24] *See id.* at 566–80.

voting district.[25] She also quoted recordings from an FBI sting operation in which Alabama state legislators were caught on tape using racial slurs and brainstorming ways to reduce African-American turnout in local elections.[26] While Justice Ginsburg stopped short of directly stating that Shelby County's successful attempt to challenge the preclearance requirement was self-serving, the implication was obvious.

Ultimately, Justice Ginsburg asserted that the majority made "no genuine attempt to engage with the massive legislative record that Congress assembled,"[27] and instead selectively cherry-picked certain evidence that supported the outcome it wished to reach. Ginsburg called the majority's "demolition of the VRA" an act of "[h]ubris" and, in a particularly pointed jab, likened the majority's decision to "throw[ ] out preclearance when it has worked and [was] continuing to work to stop discriminatory changes" as akin to "throwing away your umbrella in a rainstorm because you are not getting wet."[28] Ginsburg would have held that "Congress had more than a reasonable basis to conclude that the existing coverage formula was not out of sync with conditions on the ground in covered areas" because "second-generation barriers to minority voting rights ha[d] emerged in the covered jurisdictions as attempted *substitutes* for the first-generation barriers that originally triggered preclearance for those jurisdictions."[29] By ignoring this "powerful evidence" and—to borrow the majority's most-repeated word—the "extraordinary" record supporting the 2006 reauthorization, Ginsburg lamented that the majority had "err[ed] egregiously by overriding Congress' decision."[30]

---

[25] *See id.* at 581–85.

[26] *See id.* at 584.

[27] *Id.* at 580.

[28] *Id.* at 587, 590.

[29] *Id.* at 592.

[30] *Id.* at 592–93.

SHELBY COUNTY V. HOLDER

JUSTICE GINSBURG, with whom JUSTICE BREYER, JUSTICE SOTOMAYOR, and JUSTICE KAGAN join, DISSENTING.

In the Court's view, the very success of §5 of the Voting Rights Act demands its dormancy. Congress was of another mind. Recognizing that large progress has been made, Congress determined, based on a voluminous record, that the scourge of discrimination was not yet extirpated. The question this case presents is who decides whether, as currently operative, §5 remains justifiable,[1] [FN 1] this Court, or a Congress charged with the obligation to enforce the post-Civil War Amendments "by appropriate legislation." With overwhelming support in both Houses, Congress concluded that, for two prime reasons, §5 should continue in force, unabated. First, continuance would facilitate completion of the impressive gains thus far made; and second, continuance would guard against backsliding. Those assessments were well within Congress' province to make and should elicit this Court's unstinting approbation.

I

"[V]oting discrimination still exists; no one doubts that."[2] But the Court today terminates the remedy that proved to be best suited to block that discrimination. The Voting Rights Act of 1965 (VRA) has worked to combat voting discrimination where other remedies had been tried and failed. Particularly effective is the VRA's requirement of federal preclearance for all changes to voting laws in the regions of the country with the most aggravated records of rank discrimination against minority voting rights.

A century after the Fourteenth and Fifteenth Amendments guaranteed citizens the right to vote free of discrimination on the basis of

---

1 [FN 1] The Court purports to declare unconstitutional only the coverage formula set out in §4(b). *See id.* at 556–57 (majority opinion). But without that formula, §5 is immobilized.

2 *Id.* at 536.

race, the "blight of racial discrimination in voting" continued to "infec[t] the electoral process in parts of our country."[3] Early attempts to cope with this vile infection resembled battling the Hydra. Whenever one form of voting discrimination was identified and prohibited, others sprang up in its place. This Court repeatedly encountered the remarkable "variety and persistence" of laws disenfranchising minority citizens.[4] To take just one example, the Court, in 1927, held unconstitutional a Texas law barring black voters from participating in primary elections;[5] in 1944, the Court struck down a "reenacted" and slightly altered version of the same law;[6] and in 1953, the Court once again confronted an attempt by Texas to "circumven[t]" the Fifteenth Amendment by adopting yet another variant of the all-white primary.[7]

During this era, the Court recognized that discrimination against minority voters was a quintessentially political problem requiring a political solution. As Justice Holmes explained: If "the great mass of the white population intends to keep the blacks from voting," "relief from [that] great political wrong, if done, as alleged, by the people of a State and the State itself, must be given by them or by the legislative and political department of the government of the United States."[8]

Congress learned from experience that laws targeting particular electoral practices or enabling case-by-case litigation were inadequate to the task. In the Civil Rights Acts of 1957, 1960, and 1964, Congress authorized and then expanded the power of "the Attorney General to seek injunctions against public and private interference with the right to vote on racial grounds."[9] But circumstances reduced the ameliorative potential of these legislative Acts:

"Voting suits are unusually onerous to prepare, sometimes requiring as many as 6,000 man-hours spent combing through registration records in preparation for trial. Litigation has been exceedingly slow, in part because of the ample opportunities for delay afforded voting officials and others involved in the proceedings. Even when favorable decisions have finally been obtained, some of the States affected have merely switched to discriminatory devices not covered by the federal decrees or have enacted difficult new tests designed to prolong the existing disparity between white and Negro registration. Alternatively, certain local officials have defied and evaded court orders or have

---

[3] South Carolina v. Katzenbach, 383 U.S. 301, 308 (1966).
[4] *Id.* at 311.
[5] Nixon v. Herndon, 273 U.S. 536, 541 (1927).
[6] Smith v. Allwright, 321 U.S. 649, 658 (1944).
[7] Terry v. Adams, 345 U.S. 461, 469 (1953).
[8] Giles v. Harris, 189 U.S. 475, 488 (1903).
[9] *Katzenbach*, 383 U.S. at 313.

simply closed their registration offices to freeze the voting rolls."[10] Patently, a new approach was needed.

Answering that need, the Voting Rights Act became one of the most consequential, efficacious, and amply justified exercises of federal legislative power in our Nation's history. Requiring federal preclearance of changes in voting laws in the covered jurisdictions—those States and localities where opposition to the Constitution's commands were most virulent—the VRA provided a fit solution for minority voters as well as for States. Under the preclearance regime established by §5 of the VRA, covered jurisdictions must submit proposed changes in voting laws or procedures to the Department of Justice (DOJ), which has 60 days to respond to the changes.[11] A change will be approved unless DOJ finds it has "the purpose [or] . . . the effect of denying or abridging the right to vote on account of race or color."[12] In the alternative, the covered jurisdiction may seek approval by a three-judge District Court in the District of Columbia.

After a century's failure to fulfill the promise of the Fourteenth and Fifteenth Amendments, passage of the VRA finally led to signal improvement on this front. "The Justice Department estimated that in the five years after [the VRA's] passage, almost as many blacks registered [to vote] in Alabama, Mississippi, Georgia, Louisiana, North Carolina, and South Carolina as in the entire century before 1965."[13] And in assessing the overall effects of the VRA in 2006, Congress found that "[s]ignificant progress has been made in eliminating first generation barriers experienced by minority voters, including increased numbers of registered minority voters, minority voter turnout, and minority representation in Congress, State legislatures, and local elected offices. This progress is the direct result of the Voting Rights Act of 1965."[14] On that matter of cause and effects there can be no genuine doubt.

Although the VRA wrought dramatic changes in the realization of minority voting rights, the Act, to date, surely has not eliminated all vestiges of discrimination against the exercise of the franchise by minority citizens. Jurisdictions covered by the preclearance requirement

---

[10] *Id.* at 314 (footnote omitted).

[11] Voting Rights Act of 1965, § 5, 79 Stat. 439 (codified at 42 U.S.C. § 1973c(a)).

[12] *Id.*

[13] Chandler Davidson, *The Voting Rights Act: A Brief History,* in CONTROVERSIES IN MINORITY VOTING 7, 21 (Bernard Grofman & Chandler Davidson eds., 1992).

[14] Fannie Lou Hamer, Rosa Parks, and Coretta Scott King Voting Rights Act Reauthorization and Amendments Act of 2006 (hereinafter 2006 Reauthorization), § 2(b)(1), 120 Stat. 577.

continued to submit, in large numbers, proposed changes to voting laws that the Attorney General declined to approve, auguring that barriers to minority voting would quickly resurface were the pre-clearance remedy eliminated.[15] Congress also found that as "registration and voting of minority citizens increas[ed], other measures may be resorted to which would dilute increasing minority voting strength."[16] Efforts to reduce the impact of minority votes, in contrast to direct attempts to block access to the ballot, are aptly described as "second-generation barriers" to minority voting.

Second-generation barriers come in various forms. One of the blockages is racial gerrymandering, the redrawing of legislative districts in an "effort to segregate the races for purposes of voting."[17] Another is adoption of a system of at-large voting in lieu of district-by-district voting in a city with a sizable black minority. By switching to at-large voting, the overall majority could control the election of each city council member, effectively eliminating the potency of the minority's votes.[18] A similar effect could be achieved if the city engaged in discriminatory annexation by incorporating majority-white areas into city limits, thereby decreasing the effect of VRA-occasioned increases in black voting. Whatever the device employed, this Court has long recognized that vote dilution, when adopted with a discriminatory purpose, cuts down the right to vote as certainly as denial of access to the ballot.[19]

In response to evidence of these substituted barriers, Congress reauthorized the VRA for five years in 1970, for seven years in 1975, and for 25 years in 1982.[20] Each time, this Court upheld the reauthorization as a valid exercise of congressional power.[21] As the 1982

---

[15] City of Rome v. United States, 446 U.S. 156, 181 (1980).

[16] *Id.* (quoting H.R. REP. NO. 94-196, at 10 (1975)); *see also* Shaw v. Reno, 509 U.S. 630, 640 (1993) ("[I]t soon became apparent that guaranteeing equal access to the polls would not suffice to root out other racially discriminatory voting practices" such as voting dilution).

[17] *Shaw*, 509 U.S. at 642.

[18] Bernard Grofman & Chandler Davidson, *The Effect of Municipal Election Structure on Black Representation in Eight Southern States*, in QUIET REVOLUTION IN THE SOUTH 301, 319 (Chandler Davidson & Bernard Grofman eds., 1994).

[19] *Shaw*, 509 U.S. at 640–41; Allen v. State Bd. of Elections, 393 U.S. 544, 569 (1969); Reynolds v. Sims, 377 U.S. 533, 555 (1964); *see also* H.R. REP. NO. 109-478, at 6 (2006) (although "[d]iscrimination today is more subtle than the visible methods used in 1965," "the effect and results are the same, namely a diminishing of the minority community's ability to fully participate in the electoral process and to elect their preferred candidates").

[20] Shelby Cty. v. Holder, 570 U.S. 529, 538–39 (2013).

[21] *Id.* at 539.

reauthorization approached its 2007 expiration date, Congress again considered whether the VRA's preclearance mechanism remained an appropriate response to the problem of voting discrimination in covered jurisdictions.

Congress did not take this task lightly. Quite the opposite. The 109th Congress that took responsibility for the renewal started early and conscientiously. In October 2005, the House began extensive hearings, which continued into November and resumed in March 2006.[22] In April 2006, the Senate followed suit, with hearings of its own.[23] In May 2006, the bills that became the VRA's reauthorization were introduced in both Houses.[24] The House held further hearings of considerable length, as did the Senate, which continued to hold hearings into June and July.[25] In mid-July, the House considered and rejected four amendments, then passed the reauthorization by a vote of 390 yeas to 33 nays.[26] The bill was read and debated in the Senate, where it passed by a vote of 98 to 0.[27] President Bush signed it a week later, on July 27, 2006, recognizing the need for "further work . . . in the fight against injustice," and calling the reauthorization "an example of our continued commitment to a united America where every person is valued and treated with dignity and respect."[28]

In the long course of the legislative process, Congress "amassed a sizable record."[29] The House and Senate Judiciary Committees held 21 hearings, heard from scores of witnesses, received a number of investigative reports and other written documentation of continuing discrimination in covered jurisdictions. In all, the legislative record Congress compiled filled more than 15,000 pages.[30] The compilation presents countless "examples of flagrant racial discrimination" since the last reauthorization; Congress also brought to light systematic evidence that "intentional racial discrimination in voting remains so

---

[22] S. REP. NO. 109-295, at 2 (2006).

[23] *Id.*

[24] *Id.*

[25] H.R. REP. NO. 109-478, at 5 (2006); S. REP. NO. 109-295, at 3–4.

[26] 152 CONG. REC. H5207 (daily ed. July 13, 2006); Nathaniel Persily, The Promise and Pitfalls of the New Voting Rights Act, 117 YALE L.J. 174, 182–83 (2007).

[27] 152 CONG. REC. S8012 (daily ed. July 20, 2006).

[28] 152 CONG. REC. S8781 (daily ed. Aug. 3, 2006).

[29] Nw. Austin Mun. Util. Dist. No. One v. Holder, 557 U.S. 193, 205 (2009); *see also* Shelby Cty. v. Holder, 679 F.3d 848, 865–73 (D.C. Cir. 2012) (describing the "extensive record" supporting Congress' determination that "serious and widespread intentional discrimination persisted in covered jurisdictions").

[30] H.R. REP. NO. 109-478, at 5, 11–12; S. REP. NO. 109-295, at 2–4, 15.

serious and widespread in covered jurisdictions that section 5 pre-clearance is still needed."[31]

After considering the full legislative record, Congress made the following findings: The VRA has directly caused significant progress in eliminating first-generation barriers to ballot access, leading to a marked increase in minority voter registration and turnout and the number of minority elected officials.[32] But despite this progress, "second generation barriers constructed to prevent minority voters from fully participating in the electoral process" continued to exist, as well as racially polarized voting in the covered jurisdictions, which increased the political vulnerability of racial and language minorities in those jurisdictions.[33] Extensive "[e]vidence of continued discrimination," Congress concluded, "clearly show[ed] the continued need for Federal oversight" in covered jurisdictions.[34] The overall record demonstrated to the federal lawmakers that, "without the continuation of the Voting Rights Act of 1965 protections, racial and language minority citizens will be deprived of the opportunity to exercise their right to vote, or will have their votes diluted, undermining the significant gains made by minorities in the last 40 years."[35]

Based on these findings, Congress reauthorized preclearance for another 25 years, while also undertaking to reconsider the extension after 15 years to ensure that the provision was still necessary and effective.[36] The question before the Court is whether Congress had the authority under the Constitution to act as it did.

II

In answering this question, the Court does not write on a clean slate. It is well established that Congress' judgment regarding exercise of its power to enforce the Fourteenth and Fifteenth Amendments warrants substantial deference. The VRA addresses the combination of race discrimination and the right to vote, which is "preservative of all rights."[37] When confronting the most constitutionally invidious form of discrimination, and the most fundamental right in our democratic system, Congress' power to act is at its height.

The basis for this deference is firmly rooted in both constitutional text and precedent. The Fifteenth Amendment, which targets precisely

---

[31] *Shelby Cty.*, 679 F.3d at 866.
[32] 2006 Reauthorization § 2(b)(1), 120 Stat. 577, 557.
[33] 2006 Reauthorization § 2(b)(2)–(3), 120 Stat. at 577.
[34] 2006 Reauthorization § 2(b)(4)–(5), 120 Stat. at 577–78.
[35] 2006 Reauthorization § 2(b)(9), 120 Stat. at 578.
[36] 42 U.S.C. § 1973b(a)(7), (8) (2006 ed., Supp. V).
[37] Yick Wo v. Hopkins, 118 U.S. 356, 370 (1886).

and only racial discrimination in voting rights, states that, in this domain, "Congress shall have power to enforce this article by appropriate legislation."[38] [FN 2] In choosing this language, the Amendment's framers invoked Chief Justice Marshall's formulation of the scope of Congress' powers under the Necessary and Proper Clause:

> Let the end be legitimate, let it be within the scope of the constitution, and *all means which are appropriate, which are plainly adapted to that end,* which are not prohibited, but consist with the letter and spirit of the constitution, are constitutional.[39]

It cannot tenably be maintained that the VRA, an Act of Congress adopted to shield the right to vote from racial discrimination, is inconsistent with the letter or spirit of the Fifteenth Amendment, or any provision of the Constitution read in light of the Civil War Amendments. Nowhere in today's opinion, or in *Northwest Austin*,[40] [FN 3] is there clear recognition of the transformative effect the Fifteenth Amendment aimed to achieve. Notably, "the Founders' first successful amendment told Congress that it could 'make no law' over a certain domain"; in contrast, the Civil War Amendments used "language [that] authorized transformative new federal statutes to uproot all vestiges of unfreedom and inequality" and provided "sweeping enforcement powers . . . to enact 'appropriate' legislation targeting state abuses."[41]

---

[38] [FN 2] The Constitution uses the words "right to vote" in five separate places: the Fourteenth, Fifteenth, Nineteenth, Twenty-Fourth, and Twenty-Sixth Amendments. Each of these Amendments contains the same broad empowerment of Congress to enact "appropriate legislation" to enforce the protected right. The implication is unmistakable: Under our constitutional structure, Congress holds the lead rein in making the right to vote equally real for all U.S. citizens. These Amendments are in line with the special role assigned to Congress in protecting the integrity of the democratic process in federal elections. U.S. CONST. art. I, § 4 ("[T]he Congress may at any time by Law make or alter" regulations concerning the "Times, Places and Manner of holding Elections for Senators and Representatives."); Arizona v. Inter Tribal Council of Ariz., Inc., 570 U.S. 1 (2013); Shelby Cty. v. Holder, 570 U.S. 529, 539 (2013).

[39] McCulloch v. Maryland, 17 U.S. (4 Wheat.) 316, 421 (1819) (emphasis added).

[40] [FN 3] Acknowledging the existence of "serious constitutional questions," *see* *Shelby Cty.*, 570 U.S. at 555 (internal quotation marks omitted), does not suggest how those questions should be answered.

[41] AKHIL AMAR, AMERICA'S CONSTITUTION: A BIOGRAPHY 361, 363, 399 (2005); *see also* Michael W. McConnell, *Institutions and Interpretation: A Critique of*

The stated purpose of the Civil War Amendments was to arm Congress with the power and authority to protect all persons within the Nation from violations of their rights by the States. In exercising that power, then, Congress may use "all means which are appropriate, which are plainly adapted" to the constitutional ends declared by these Amendments.[42] So when Congress acts to enforce the right to vote free from racial discrimination, we ask not whether Congress has chosen the means most wise, but whether Congress has rationally selected means appropriate to a legitimate end. "It is not for us to review the congressional resolution of [the need for its chosen remedy]. It is enough that we be able to perceive a basis upon which the Congress might resolve the conflict as it did."[43]

Until today, in considering the constitutionality of the VRA, the Court has accorded Congress the full measure of respect its judgments in this domain should garner. *South Carolina v. Katzenbach* supplies the standard of review: "As against the reserved powers of the States, Congress may use any rational means to effectuate the constitutional prohibition of racial discrimination in voting."[44] Faced with subsequent reauthorizations of the VRA, the Court has reaffirmed this standard.[45] Today's Court does not purport to alter settled precedent establishing that the dispositive question is whether Congress has employed "rational means."

For three reasons, legislation reauthorizing an existing statute is especially likely to satisfy the minimal requirements of the rational-basis test. First, when reauthorization is at issue, Congress has already assembled a legislative record justifying the initial legislation. Congress is entitled to consider that preexisting record as well as the record before it at the time of the vote on reauthorization. This is especially true where, as here, the Court has repeatedly affirmed the statute's constitutionality and Congress has adhered to the very model the Court has upheld.[46]

City of Boerne v. Flores, 111 HARV. L. REV. 153, 182 (1997) (quoting Civil War-era framer that "the remedy for the violation of the fourteenth and fifteenth amendments was expressly not left to the courts. The remedy was legislative.").

[42] *McCulloch*, 17 U.S. at 421.

[43] Katzenbach v. Morgan, 384 U.S. 641, 653 (1966).

[44] 383 U.S. 301, 324 (1966).

[45] *E.g.*, City of Rome v. United States, 446 U.S. 156, 178 (1980).

[46] *See id.* at 174 ("The appellants are asking us to do nothing less than overrule our decision in *South Carolina v. Katzenbach* . . . , in which we upheld the constitutionality of the Act."); Lopez v. Monterey Cty., 525 U.S. 266, 283 (1999) (similar).

Second, the very fact that reauthorization is necessary arises because Congress has built a temporal limitation into the Act. It has pledged to review, after a span of years (first 15, then 25) and in light of contemporary evidence, the continued need for the VRA.[47]

Third, a reviewing court should expect the record supporting reauthorization to be less stark than the record originally made. Demand for a record of violations equivalent to the one earlier made would expose Congress to a catch-22. If the statute was working, there would be less evidence of discrimination, so opponents might argue that Congress should not be allowed to renew the statute. In contrast, if the statute was not working, there would be plenty of evidence of discrimination, but scant reason to renew a failed regulatory regime.[48]

This is not to suggest that congressional power in this area is limitless. It is this Court's responsibility to ensure that Congress has used appropriate means. The question meet for judicial review is whether the chosen means are "adapted to carry out the objects the amendments have in view."[49] The Court's role, then, is not to substitute its judgment for that of Congress, but to determine whether the legislative record sufficed to show that "Congress could rationally have determined that [its chosen] provisions were appropriate methods."[50]

In summary, the Constitution vests broad power in Congress to protect the right to vote, and in particular to combat racial discrimination in voting. This Court has repeatedly reaffirmed Congress' prerogative to use any rational means in exercise of its power in this area. And both precedent and logic dictate that the rational-means test should be easier to satisfy, and the burden on the statute's challenger should be higher, when what is at issue is the reauthorization of a remedy that the Court has previously affirmed, and that Congress found, from contemporary evidence, to be working to advance the legislature's legitimate objective.

III

The 2006 reauthorization of the Voting Rights Act fully satisfies the standard stated in *McCulloch*:[51] Congress may choose any means "appropriate" and "plainly adapted to" a legitimate constitutional end. As we shall see, it is implausible to suggest otherwise.

---

[47] *Cf.* Grutter v. Bollinger, 539 U.S. 306, 343 (2003) (anticipating, but not guaranteeing, that, in 25 years, "the use of racial preferences [in higher education] will no longer be necessary").

[48] *See* Persily, *supra* note 26, at 193–94.

[49] *Ex parte* Virginia, 100 U.S. 339, 346 (1880).

[50] *City of Rome*, 446 U.S. at 176–77.

[51] *McCulloch*, 17 U.S. at 421.

A

I begin with the evidence on which Congress based its decision to continue the preclearance remedy. The surest way to evaluate whether that remedy remains in order is to see if preclearance is still effectively preventing discriminatory changes to voting laws.[52] On that score, the record before Congress was huge. In fact, Congress found there were more DOJ objections between 1982 and 2004 (626) than there were between 1965 and the 1982 reauthorization (490).[53]

All told, between 1982 and 2006, DOJ objections blocked over 700 voting changes based on a determination that the changes were discriminatory.[54] Congress found that the majority of DOJ objections included findings of discriminatory intent,[55] and that the changes blocked by preclearance were "calculated decisions to keep minority voters from fully participating in the political process."[56] On top of that, over the same time period the DOJ and private plaintiffs succeeded in more than 100 actions to enforce the §5 preclearance requirements.[57]

In addition to blocking proposed voting changes through preclearance, DOJ may request more information from a jurisdiction proposing a change. In turn, the jurisdiction may modify or withdraw the proposed change. The number of such modifications or withdrawals provides an indication of how many discriminatory proposals are deterred without need for formal objection. Congress received evidence that more than 800 proposed changes were altered or withdrawn since the last reauthorization in 1982.[58; 59 [FN 4]] Congress also received

---

[52] See City of Rome, 446 U.S. at 181 (identifying "information on the number and types of submissions made by covered jurisdictions and the number and nature of objections interposed by the Attorney General" as a primary basis for upholding the 1975 reauthorization).

[53] 1 Voting Rights Act: Evidence of Continued Need: Hearing Before the Subcomm. on the Constitution of the H. Comm. on the Judiciary, 109th Cong., 2d Sess. 172 (2006) [hereinafter Evidence of Continued Need].

[54] H.R. REP. NO. 109-478, at 21.

[55] See Shelby Cty. v. Holder, 679 F.3d 848, 867 (D.C. Cir. 2012).

[56] H.R. REP. NO. 109-478, at 21.

[57] 1 Evidence of Continued Need, supra note 53, at 186, 250.

[58] H.R. REP. NO. 109-478, at 40–41.

[59] [FN 4] This number includes only changes actually proposed. Congress also received evidence that many covered jurisdictions engaged in an "informal consultation process" with DOJ before formally submitting a proposal, so that the deterrent effect of preclearance was far broader than the formal submissions alone suggest. The Continuing Need for Section 5 Pre-Clearance: Hearing Before the S. Comm. on the Judiciary, 109th Cong., 2d Sess. 53–54 (2006). All agree that an unsupported assertion about "deterrence" would not be

empirical studies finding that DOJ's requests for more information had a significant effect on the degree to which covered jurisdictions "compl[ied] with their obligatio[n]" to protect minority voting rights.[60]

Congress also received evidence that litigation under §2 of the VRA was an inadequate substitute for preclearance in the covered jurisdictions. Litigation occurs only after the fact, when the illegal voting scheme has already been put in place and individuals have been elected pursuant to it, thereby gaining the advantages of incumbency.[61] An illegal scheme might be in place for several election cycles before a §2 plaintiff can gather sufficient evidence to challenge it.[62] And litigation places a heavy financial burden on minority voters.[63] Congress also received evidence that preclearance lessened the litigation burden on covered jurisdictions themselves, because the preclearance process is far less costly than defending against a §2 claim, and clearance by DOJ substantially reduces the likelihood that a §2 claim will be mounted.[64]

The number of discriminatory changes blocked or deterred by the preclearance requirement suggests that the state of voting rights in the covered jurisdictions would have been significantly different absent this remedy. Surveying the type of changes stopped by the preclearance procedure conveys a sense of the extent to which §5 continues to protect minority voting rights. Set out below are characteristic examples of changes blocked in the years leading up to the 2006 reauthorization:

In 1995, Mississippi sought to reenact a dual voter registration system, "which was initially enacted in 1892 to disenfranchise Black voters," and for that reason, was struck down by a federal court in 1987.[65]

---

sufficient to justify keeping a remedy in place in perpetuity. *See* Shelby Cty. v. Holder, 570 U.S. 529, 550 (2013). But it was certainly reasonable for Congress to consider the testimony of witnesses who had worked with officials in covered jurisdictions and observed a real-world deterrent effect.

[60] *2 Evidence of Continued Need, supra* note 53, at 2555.

[61] *1 Evidence of Continued Need, supra* note 53, at 97.

[62] *1 Voting Rights Act: Section 5 of the Act—History, Scope, and Purpose: Hearing Before the Subcomm. on the Constitution of the H. Comm. on the Judiciary*, 109th Cong., 1st Sess. 92 (2005) [hereinafter Section 5 Hearing].

[63] *See id.* at 84.

[64] *Reauthorizing the Voting Rights Act's Temporary Provisions: Policy Perspectives and Views From the Field: Hearing Before the Subcomm. on the Constitution, Civil Rights and Prop. Rights of the S. Comm. on the Judiciary*, 109th Cong., 2d Sess. 13, 120–21 (2006); *see also* Brief for States of New York, California, Mississippi, and North Carolina as Amici Curiae at 8–9, *Shelby Cty.*, 570 U.S. 529 (No. 12-96) (Section 5 "reduc[es] the likelihood that a jurisdiction will face costly and protracted Section 2 litigation").

[65] H.R. REP. NO. 109-478, at 39 (2006).

Following the 2000 census, the City of Albany, Georgia, proposed a redistricting plan that DOJ found to be "designed with the purpose to limit and retrogress the increased black voting strength . . . in the city as a whole."[66]

In 2001, the mayor and all-white five-member Board of Aldermen of Kilmichael, Mississippi, abruptly canceled the town's election after "an unprecedented number" of African-American candidates announced they were running for office. DOJ required an election, and the town elected its first black mayor and three black aldermen.[67]

In 2006, this Court found that Texas' attempt to redraw a congressional district to reduce the strength of Latino voters bore "the mark of intentional discrimination that could give rise to an equal protection violation," and ordered the district redrawn in compliance with the VRA.[68] In response, Texas sought to undermine this Court's order by curtailing early voting in the district, but was blocked by an action to enforce the §5 preclearance requirement.[69]

In 2003, after African-Americans won a majority of the seats on the school board for the first time in history, Charleston County, South Carolina, proposed an at-large voting mechanism for the board. The proposal, made without consulting any of the African-American members of the school board, was found to be an "'exact replica'" of an earlier voting scheme that, a federal court had determined, violated the VRA.[70] DOJ invoked §5 to block the proposal.

In 1993, the City of Millen, Georgia, proposed to delay the election in a majority-black district by two years, leaving that district without representation on the city council while the neighboring majority-white district would have three representatives.[71] DOJ blocked the proposal. The county then sought to move a polling place from a predominantly black neighborhood in the city to an inaccessible location in a predominantly white neighborhood outside city limits.[72]

In 2004, Waller County, Texas, threatened to prosecute two black students after they announced their intention to run for office. The county then attempted to reduce the availability of early voting in that election at polling places near a historically black university.[73]

---

[66] *Id.* at 37 (internal quotation marks omitted).

[67] *Id.* at 36–37.

[68] League of United Latin Am. Citizens v. Perry, 548 U.S. 399, 440 (2006).

[69] See League of United Latin Am. Citizens v. Texas, No. 06-cv-1046 (W.D. Tex. Dec. 5, 2006), (order Doc. 8).

[70] Shelby Cty. v. Holder, 811 F. Supp. 2d 424, 483 (D.D.C. 2011); *see also* S. REP. NO. 109-295, at 309 (2006).

[71] *1 Section 5 Hearing, supra* note 62, at 744.

[72] *Id.* at 816.

[73] Shelby Cty. v. Holder, 679 F.3d 848, 865–66 (2012).

In 1990, Dallas County, Alabama, whose county seat is the City of Selma, sought to purge its voter rolls of many black voters. DOJ rejected the purge as discriminatory, noting that it would have disqualified many citizens from voting "simply because they failed to pick up or return a voter update form, when there was no valid requirement that they do so."[74]

These examples, and scores more like them, fill the pages of the legislative record. The evidence was indeed sufficient to support Congress' conclusion that "racial discrimination in voting in covered jurisdictions [remained] serious and pervasive."[75; 76 [FN 5]]

Congress further received evidence indicating that formal requests of the kind set out above represented only the tip of the iceberg. There was what one commentator described as an "avalanche of case studies of voting rights violations in the covered jurisdictions," ranging from "outright intimidation and violence against minority voters" to "more subtle forms of voting rights deprivations."[77] This evidence gave Congress ever more reason to conclude that the time had not yet come for relaxed vigilance against the scourge of race discrimination in voting.

True, conditions in the South have impressively improved since passage of the Voting Rights Act. Congress noted this improvement and found that the VRA was the driving force behind it.[78] But Congress also found that voting discrimination had evolved into subtler second-generation barriers, and that eliminating preclearance would risk loss of the gains that had been made.[79] Concerns of this order, the Court previously found, gave Congress adequate cause to reauthorize the VRA.[80] Facing such evidence then, the Court expressly

---

[74] *1 Section 5 Hearing, supra* note 62, at 356.

[75] *Shelby Cty.*, 679 F.3d at 865.

[76] [FN 5] For an illustration postdating the 2006 reauthorization, see *South Carolina v. United States*, 898 F. Supp. 2d 30 (D.D.C. 2012), which involved a South Carolina voter-identification law enacted in 2011. Concerned that the law would burden minority voters, DOJ brought a §5 enforcement action to block the law's implementation. In the course of the litigation, South Carolina officials agreed to binding interpretations that made it "far easier than some might have expected or feared" for South Carolina citizens to vote. *Id.* at 37. A three-judge panel precleared the law after adopting both interpretations as an express "condition of preclearance." *Id.* at 37–38. Two of the judges commented that the case demonstrated "the continuing utility of Section 5 of the Voting Rights Act in deterring problematic, and hence encouraging nondiscriminatory, changes in state and local voting laws." *Id.* at 54 (Bates, J., concurring).

[77] Persily, *supra* note 26, at 202 (footnote omitted).

[78] 2006 Reauthorization § 2(b)(1), 120 Stat. 577, 557.

[79] 2006 Reauthorization § 2(b)(2), (9), 120 Stat. at 577–78.

[80] City of Rome v. United States, 446 U.S. 156, 180–82 (1980) (congressional

rejected the argument that disparities in voter turnout and number of elected officials were the only metrics capable of justifying reauthorization of the VRA.[81]

B

I turn next to the evidence on which Congress based its decision to reauthorize the coverage formula in §4(b). Because Congress did not alter the coverage formula, the same jurisdictions previously subject to preclearance continue to be covered by this remedy. The evidence just described, of preclearance's continuing efficacy in blocking constitutional violations in the covered jurisdictions, itself grounded Congress' conclusion that the remedy should be retained for those jurisdictions.

There is no question, moreover, that the covered jurisdictions have a unique history of problems with racial discrimination in voting.[82] Consideration of this long history, still in living memory, was altogether appropriate. The Court criticizes Congress for failing to recognize that "history did not end in 1965."[83] But the Court ignores that "what's past is prologue."[84] And "[t]hose who cannot remember the past are condemned to repeat it."[85] Congress was especially mindful of the need to reinforce the gains already made and to prevent backsliding.[86]

Of particular importance, even after 40 years and thousands of discriminatory changes blocked by preclearance, conditions in the covered jurisdictions demonstrated that the formula was still justified by "current needs."[87]

Congress learned of these conditions through a report, known as the Katz study, that looked at §2 suits between 1982 and 2004.[88] Because the private right of action authorized by §2 of the VRA applies

---

reauthorization of the preclearance requirement was justified based on "the number and nature of objections interposed by the Attorney General" since the prior reauthorization; extension was "necessary to pre-serve the limited and fragile achievements of the Act and to promote further amelioration of voting discrimination") (internal quotation marks omitted).

[81] *Id.*

[82] Shelby Cty. v. Holder, 570 U.S. 529, 545–46 (2013).

[83] *Id.* at 552.

[84] WILLIAM SHAKESPEARE, THE TEMPEST act 2, sc. 1.

[85] 1 GEORGE SANTAYANA, THE LIFE OF REASON 284 (1905).

[86] 2006 Reauthorization §2 (b)(9), 120 Stat. 557, 578.

[87] Nw. Austin Mun. Util. Dist. No. One v. Holder, 557 U.S. 193, 203 (2009).

[88] *To Examine the Impact and Effectiveness of the Voting Rights Act: Hearing Before the Subcomm. on the Constitution of the H. Comm. on the Judiciary,* 109th Cong., 1st Sess. 964–1124 (2005) [hereinafter Impact and Effectiveness].

nationwide, a comparison of §2 lawsuits in covered and noncovered jurisdictions provides an appropriate yardstick for measuring differences between covered and noncovered jurisdictions. If differences in the risk of voting discrimination between covered and noncovered jurisdictions had disappeared, one would expect that the rate of successful §2 lawsuits would be roughly the same in both areas.[89] [FN 6] The study's findings, however, indicated that racial discrimination in voting remains "concentrated in the jurisdictions singled out for preclearance."[90]

Although covered jurisdictions account for less than 25 percent of the country's population, the Katz study revealed that they accounted for 56 percent of successful §2 litigation since 1982.[91] Controlling for population, there were nearly four times as many successful §2 cases in covered jurisdictions as there were in noncovered jurisdictions.[92] The Katz study further found that §2 lawsuits are more likely to succeed when they are filed in covered jurisdictions than in noncovered jurisdictions.[93] From these findings—ignored by the Court—Congress reasonably concluded that the coverage formula continues to identify the jurisdictions of greatest concern.

The evidence before Congress, furthermore, indicated that voting in the covered jurisdictions was more racially polarized than elsewhere in the country.[94] While racially polarized voting alone does not signal a constitutional violation, it is a factor that increases the vulnerability of racial minorities to discriminatory changes in voting law. The reason is twofold. First, racial polarization means that racial minorities are at risk of being systematically outvoted and having their interests underrepresented in legislatures. Second, "when political preferences fall along racial lines, the natural inclinations of incumbents and ruling parties to entrench themselves have predictable racial effects. Under circumstances of severe racial polarization, efforts to gain political advantage translate into race-specific disadvantages."[95]

---

[89] [FN 6] Because preclearance occurs only in covered jurisdictions and can be expected to stop the most obviously objectionable measures, one would expect a lower rate of successful §2 lawsuits in those jurisdictions if the risk of voting discrimination there were the same as elsewhere in the country.

[90] *Nw. Austin*, 557 U.S. at 203.

[91] *Impact and Effectiveness, supra* note 88, at 974.

[92] Shelby Cty. v. Holder, 679 F.3d 848, 874 (D.C. Cir. 2012).

[93] *Impact and Effectiveness, supra* note 88, at 974.

[94] H.R. REP. NO. 109-478, at 34–35 (2006).

[95] Stephen Ansolabehere, Nathaniel Persily & Charles Stewart, *Regional Differences in Racial Polarization in the 2012 Presidential Election: Implications for the Constitutionality of Section 5 of the Voting Rights Act*, 126 HARV. L. REV. F. 205, 209 (2013).

In other words, a governing political coalition has an incentive to prevent changes in the existing balance of voting power. When voting is racially polarized, efforts by the ruling party to pursue that incentive "will inevitably discriminate against a racial group."[96] Just as buildings in California have a greater need to be earthquake-proofed, places where there is greater racial polarization in voting have a greater need for prophylactic measures to prevent purposeful race discrimination. This point was understood by Congress and is well recognized in the academic literature.[97]

The case for retaining a coverage formula that met needs on the ground was therefore solid. Congress might have been charged with rigidity had it afforded covered jurisdictions no way out or ignored jurisdictions that needed superintendence. Congress, however, responded to this concern. Critical components of the congressional design are the statutory provisions allowing jurisdictions to "bail out" of preclearance, and for court-ordered "bail ins."[98] The VRA permits a jurisdiction to bail out by showing that it has complied with the Act for ten years, and has engaged in efforts to eliminate intimidation and harassment of voters.[99] It also authorizes a court to subject a noncovered jurisdiction to federal preclearance upon finding that violations of the Fourteenth and Fifteenth Amendments have occurred there.[100]

Congress was satisfied that the VRA's bailout mechanism provided an effective means of adjusting the VRA's coverage over time.[101] Nearly 200 jurisdictions have successfully bailed out of the preclearance requirement, and DOJ has consented to every bailout application filed by an eligible jurisdiction since the current bailout

---

[96] *Id.*

[97] *See* 2006 Reauthorization § 2(b)(3), 120 Stat. at 577 ("The continued evidence of racially polarized voting in each of the jurisdictions covered by the [preclearance requirement] demonstrates that racial and language minorities remain politically vulnerable"); H.R. REP. NO. 109-478, at 35; Chandler Davidson, *The Recent Evolution of Voting Rights Law Affecting Racial and Language Minorities, in* QUIET REVOLUTION IN THE SOUTH 21, 22 (Chandler Davidson & Bernard Grofman eds., 1994).

[98] *See* Nw. Austin Mun. Util. Dist. No. One v. Holder, 557 U.S. 193, 199 (2009).

[99] 42 U.S.C. § 1973b(a) (2006 ed. and Supp. V).

[100] 42 U.S.C. § 1973a(c) (2006 ed.).

[101] H.R. REP. NO. 109-478, at 25 (2006) (the success of bailout "illustrates that: (1) covered status is neither permanent nor over-broad; and (2) covered status has been and continues to be within the control of the jurisdiction such that those jurisdictions that have a genuinely clean record and want to terminate coverage have the ability to do so").

procedure became effective in 1984.[102] The bail-in mechanism has also worked. Several jurisdictions have been subject to federal preclearance by court orders, including the States of New Mexico and Arkansas.[103]

This experience exposes the inaccuracy of the Court's portrayal of the Act as static, unchanged since 1965. Congress designed the VRA to be a dynamic statute, capable of adjusting to changing conditions. True, many covered jurisdictions have not been able to bail out due to recent acts of noncompliance with the VRA, but that truth reinforces the congressional judgment that these jurisdictions were rightfully subject to preclearance, and ought to remain under that regime.

IV

Congress approached the 2006 reauthorization of the VRA with great care and seriousness. The same cannot be said of the Court's opinion today. The Court makes no genuine attempt to engage with the massive legislative record that Congress assembled. Instead, it relies on increases in voter registration and turnout as if that were the whole story.[104] Without even identifying a standard of review, the Court dismissively brushes off arguments based on "data from the record," and declines to enter the "debat[e about] what [the] record shows."[105] One would expect more from an opinion striking at the heart of the Nation's signal piece of civil-rights legislation.

I note the most disturbing lapses. First, by what right, given its usual restraint, does the Court even address Shelby County's facial challenge to the VRA? Second, the Court veers away from controlling precedent regarding the "equal sovereignty" doctrine without even acknowledging that it is doing so. Third, hardly showing the respect ordinarily paid when Congress acts to implement the Civil War Amendments, and as just stressed, the Court does not even deign to grapple with the legislative record.

A

Shelby County launched a purely facial challenge to the VRA's 2006 reauthorization. "A facial challenge to a legislative Act," the Court has other times said, "is, of course, the most difficult challenge to mount successfully, since the challenger must establish that no set

---

[102] Brief for Federal Respondent at 54, Shelby Cty. v. Holder, 570 U.S. 529 (2013) (No. 12-96).

[103] *Id.*, app. at 1a–3a.

[104] *See Shelby Cty.*, 570 U.S. at 551–52 (Ginsburg,. J, dissenting).

[105] *Id.* at 553 (majority opinion).

of circumstances exists under which the Act would be valid."[106]

"[U]nder our constitutional system[,] courts are not roving commissions assigned to pass judgment on the validity of the Nation's laws."[107] Instead, the "judicial Power" is limited to deciding particular "Cases" and "Controversies."[108] "Embedded in the traditional rules governing constitutional adjudication is the principle that a person to whom a statute may constitutionally be applied will not be heard to challenge that statute on the ground that it may conceivably be applied unconstitutionally to others, in other situations not before the Court."[109] Yet the Court's opinion in this case contains not a word explaining why Congress lacks the power to subject to preclearance the particular plaintiff that initiated this lawsuit—Shelby County, Alabama. The reason for the Court's silence is apparent, for as applied to Shelby County, the VRA's preclearance requirement is hardly contestable.

Alabama is home to Selma, site of the "Bloody Sunday" beatings of civil-rights demonstrators that served as the catalyst for the VRA's enactment. Following those events, Martin Luther King, Jr., led a march from Selma to Montgomery, Alabama's capital, where he called for passage of the VRA. If the Act passed, he foresaw, progress could be made even in Alabama, but there had to be a steadfast national commitment to see the task through to completion. In King's words, "the arc of the moral universe is long, but it bends toward justice."[110]

History has proved King right. Although circumstances in Alabama have changed, serious concerns remain. Between 1982 and 2005, Alabama had one of the highest rates of successful §2 suits, second only to its VRA-covered neighbor Mississippi.[111] In other words, even while subject to the restraining effect of §5, Alabama was found to have "deni[ed] or abridge[d]" voting rights "on account of race or color" more frequently than nearly all other States in the Union.[112] This fact prompted the dissenting judge below to concede that "a more narrowly tailored coverage formula" capturing Alabama and a handful of other jurisdictions with an established track record of racial discrimination in voting "might be defensible."[113] That is an understatement.

---

[106] United States v. Salerno, 481 U.S. 739, 745 (1987).

[107] Broadrick v. Oklahoma, 413 U.S. 601, 610–11 (1973).

[108] U.S. CONST. art. III, § 2.

[109] *Broadrick*, 413 U.S. at 610.

[110] GARY MAY, BENDING TOWARD JUSTICE: THE VOTING RIGHTS ACT AND THE TRANSFORMATION OF AMERICAN DEMOCRACY 144 (2013).

[111] Shelby Cty. v. Holder, 679 F.3d 848, 897 (D.C. Cir. 2012) (Williams, J., dissenting).

[112] 42 U S.C. § 1973(a).

[113] *Shelby Cty.*, 679 F.3d at 897 (Williams, J., dissenting).

Alabama's sorry history of §2 violations alone provides sufficient justification for Congress' determination in 2006 that the State should remain subject to §5's preclearance requirement.[114] [FN 7]

A few examples suffice to demonstrate that, at least in Alabama, the "current burdens" imposed by §5's preclearance requirement are "justified by current needs."[115] In the interim between the VRA's 1982 and 2006 reauthorizations, this Court twice confronted purposeful racial discrimination in Alabama. In *Pleasant Grove v. United States*,[116] the Court held that Pleasant Grove—a city in Jefferson County, Shelby County's neighbor—engaged in purposeful discrimination by annexing all-white areas while rejecting the annexation request of an adjacent black neighborhood. The city had "shown unambiguous opposition to racial integration, both before and after the passage of the federal civil rights laws," and its strategic annexations appeared to be an attempt "to provide for the growth of a monolithic white voting block" for "the impermissible purpose of minimizing future black voting strength."[117]

Two years before *Pleasant Grove*, the Court in *Hunter v. Underwood*[118] struck down a provision of the Alabama Constitution that prohibited individuals convicted of misdemeanor offenses "involving moral turpitude" from voting.[119] The provision violated the Fourteenth Amendment's Equal Protection Clause, the Court unanimously concluded, because "its original enactment was motivated by a desire to discriminate against blacks on account of race[,] and the [provision] continues to this day to have that effect."[120]

Pleasant Grove and *Hunter* were not anomalies. In 1986, a Federal District Judge concluded that the at-large election systems in several Alabama counties violated §2.[121] Summarizing its findings, the court

---

[114] [FN 7] This lawsuit was filed by Shelby County, a political subdivision of Alabama, rather than by the State itself. Nevertheless, it is appropriate to judge Shelby County's constitutional challenge in light of instances of discrimination statewide because Shelby County is subject to §5's preclearance requirement by virtue of Alabama's designation as a covered jurisdiction under §4(b) of the VRA. *See* Shelby Cty. v. Holder, 570 U.S. 529, 540 (2013). In any event, Shelby County's recent record of employing an at-large electoral system tainted by intentional racial discrimination is by itself sufficient to justify subjecting the county to §5's preclearance mandate. *See id.*, at 583 (Ginsburg, J., dissenting).

[115] Nw. Austin Mun. Util. Dist. No. One v. Holder, 557 U.S. 193, 203 (2009).

[116] 479 U.S. 462 (1987).

[117] *Id.* at 465, 471–72.

[118] 471 U.S. 222 (1985).

[119] *Id.* at 223 (internal quotation marks omitted).

[120] *Id.* at 233.

[121] Dillard v. Crenshaw Cty., 640 F. Supp. 1347, 1354–63 (M.D. Ala. 1986).

stated that "[f]rom the late 1800's through the present, [Alabama] has consistently erected barriers to keep black persons from full and equal participation in the social, economic, and political life of the state."[122]

The *Dillard* litigation ultimately expanded to include 183 cities, counties, and school boards employing discriminatory at-large election systems.[123] One of those defendants was Shelby County, which eventually signed a consent decree to resolve the claims against it.[124]

Although the *Dillard* litigation resulted in overhauls of numerous electoral systems tainted by racial discrimination, concerns about backsliding persist. In 2008, for example, the city of Calera, located in Shelby County, requested preclearance of a redistricting plan that "would have eliminated the city's sole majority-black district, which had been created pursuant to the consent decree in *Dillard*."[125] Although DOJ objected to the plan, Calera forged ahead with elections based on the un-precleared voting changes, resulting in the defeat of the incumbent African-American councilman who represented the former majority-black district. The city's defiance required DOJ to bring a §5 enforcement action that ultimately yielded appropriate redress, including restoration of the majority-black district.[126]

A recent FBI investigation provides a further window into the persistence of racial discrimination in state politics.[127] Recording devices worn by state legislators cooperating with the FBI's investigation captured conversations between members of the state legislature and their political allies. The recorded conversations are shocking. Members of the state Senate derisively refer to African-Americans as "Aborigines" and talk openly of their aim to quash a particular gambling-related referendum because the referendum, if placed on the ballot, might increase African-American voter turnout.[128] These conversations occurred not in the 1870's, or even in the 1960's, they took place in 2010.[129] The District Judge presiding over the criminal trial at

---

[122] *Id.* at 1360.

[123] Dillard v. Baldwin Cty. Bd. of Ed., 686 F. Supp. 1459, 1461 (M.D. Ala. 1988).

[124] See Dillard v. Crenshaw Cty., 748 F. Supp. 819 (M.D. Ala. 1990).

[125] Shelby Cty. v. Holder, 811 F. Supp. 2d 424, 443 (D.D.C. 2011).

[126] *Id.*; Brief for Respondent-Intervenors Earl Cunningham et al. at 20, Shelby Cty. v. Holder, 570 U.S. 529 (2013) (No. 12-96).

[127] *See* United States v. McGregor, 824 F. Supp. 2d 1339, 1344–48 (M.D. Ala. 2011).

[128] *Id.* at 1345–46 (internal quotation marks omitted); *see also id.* at 1345 (legislators and their allies expressed concern that if the referendum were placed on the ballot, "'[e]very black, every illiterate' would be 'bused [to the polls] on HUD financed buses'").

[129] *Id.* at 1344–45.

which the recorded conversations were introduced commented that the "recordings represent compelling evidence that political exclusion through racism remains a real and enduring problem" in Alabama.[130] Racist sentiments, the judge observed, "remain regrettably entrenched in the high echelons of state government."[131]

These recent episodes forcefully demonstrate that §5's preclearance requirement is constitutional as applied to Alabama and its political subdivisions.[132] [FN 8] And under our case law, that conclusion should suffice to resolve this case.[133]

This Court has consistently rejected constitutional challenges to legislation enacted pursuant to Congress' enforcement powers under the Civil War Amendments upon finding that the legislation was constitutional as applied to the particular set of circumstances before the Court.[134] A similar approach is warranted here.[135] [FN 9]

---

[130] *Id.* at 1347.

[131] *Id.*

[132] [FN 8] Congress continued preclearance over Alabama, including Shelby County, after considering evidence of current barriers there to minority voting clout. Shelby County, thus, is no "redhead" caught up in an arbitrary scheme. *See* Shelby Cty. v. Holder, 570 U.S. 529, 554 (2013).

[133] *See* United States v. Raines, 362 U.S. 17, 24–25 (1960) ("[I]f the complaint here called for an application of the statute clearly constitutional under the Fifteenth Amendment, that should have been an end to the question of constitutionality."); *see also* Nev. Dep't of Human Res. v. Hibbs, 538 U.S. 721, 743 (2003) (Scalia, J., dissenting) (where, as here, a state or local government raises a facial challenge to a federal statute on the ground that it exceeds Congress' enforcement powers under the Civil War Amendments, the challenge fails if the opposing party is able to show that the statute "could constitutionally be applied to some jurisdictions").

[134] See United States v. Georgia, 546 U.S. 151, 159 (2006) (Title II of the Americans with Disabilities Act of 1990 (ADA) validly abrogates state sovereign immunity "insofar as [it] creates a private cause of action . . . for conduct that actually violates the Fourteenth Amendment"); Tennessee v. Lane, 541 U.S. 509, 530–34 (2004) (Title II of the ADA is constitutional "as it applies to the class of cases implicating the fundamental right of access to the courts"); *Raines*, 362 U.S. at 24–26 (federal statute proscribing deprivations of the right to vote based on race was constitutional as applied to the state officials before the Court, even if it could not constitutionally be applied to other parties).

[135] [FN 9] The Court does not contest that Alabama's history of racial discrimination provides a sufficient basis for Congress to require Alabama and its political subdivisions to preclear electoral changes. Nevertheless, the Court asserts that Shelby County may prevail on its facial challenge to §4's coverage formula because it is subject to §5's preclearance requirement by virtue of that formula. *See Shelby Cty.*, 570 U.S. at 554–55 ("The county was selected [for preclearance] based on th[e] [coverage] formula."). This misses the reality

The VRA's exceptionally broad severability provision makes it particularly inappropriate for the Court to allow Shelby County to mount a facial challenge to §§4(b) and 5 of the VRA, even though application of those provisions to the county falls well within the bounds of Congress' legislative authority. The severability provision states:

> If any provision of [this Act] or the application thereof to any person or circumstances is held invalid, the remainder of [the Act] and the application of the provision to other persons not similarly situated or to other circumstances shall not be affected thereby.[136]

In other words, even if the VRA could not constitutionally be applied to certain States—e.g., Arizona and Alaska[137]—§1973p calls for those unconstitutional applications to be severed, leaving the Act in place for jurisdictions as to which its application does not transgress constitutional limits.

Nevertheless, the Court suggests that limiting the jurisdictional scope of the VRA in an appropriate case would be "to try our hand at updating the statute."[138] Just last Term, however, the Court rejected this very argument when addressing a materially identical severability provision, explaining that such a provision is "Congress' explicit textual instruction to leave unaffected the remainder of [the Act]" if any particular "application is unconstitutional."[139] Leaping to resolve Shelby County's facial challenge without considering whether application of the VRA to Shelby County is constitutional, or even addressing the VRA's severability provision, the Court's opinion can hardly be described as an exemplar of restrained and moderate decision-making. Quite the opposite. Hubris is a fit word for today's demolition of the VRA.

---

that Congress decided to subject Alabama to preclearance based on evidence of continuing constitutional violations in that State. *See id.* at 585 n.8 (Ginsburg, J., dissenting).

[136] 42 U.S.C. § 1973p.

[137] *See Shelby Cty.*, 570 U.S. at 542.

[138] *Id.* at 554.

[139] Nat'l Fed'n of Indep. Bus. v. Sebelius, 567 U.S. 519, 586 (2012) (plurality opinion) (internal quotation marks omitted); *id.* at 645–46 (Ginsburg, J., concurring in part, concurring in judgment in part, and dissenting in part) (agreeing with the plurality's severability analysis); *see also Raines*, 362 U.S. at 23 (a statute capable of some constitutional applications may nonetheless be susceptible to a facial challenge only in "that rarest of cases where this Court can justifiably think itself able confidently to discern that Congress would not have desired its legislation to stand at all unless it could validly stand in its every application").

B

The Court stops any application of §5 by holding that §4(b)'s coverage formula is unconstitutional. It pins this result, in large measure, to "the fundamental principle of equal sovereignty."[140] In *Katzenbach*, however, the Court held, in no uncertain terms, that the principle "*applies only to the terms upon which States are admitted to the Union,* and not to the remedies for local evils which have subsequently appeared."[141]

Katzenbach, the Court acknowledges, "rejected the notion that the [equal sovereignty] principle operate[s] as a bar on differential treatment outside [the] context [of the admission of new States]."[142] But the Court clouds that once clear understanding by citing dictum from *Northwest Austin* to convey that the principle of equal sovereignty "remains highly pertinent in assessing subsequent disparate treatment of States."[143] If the Court is suggesting that dictum in *Northwest Austin* silently overruled *Katzenbach*'s limitation of the equal sovereignty doctrine to "the admission of new States," the suggestion is untenable. *Northwest Austin* cited *Katzenbach*'s holding in the course of declining to decide whether the VRA was constitutional or even what standard of review applied to the question.[144] In today's decision, the Court ratchets up what was pure dictum in *Northwest Austin*, attributing breadth to the equal sovereignty principle in flat contradiction of *Katzenbach*. The Court does so with nary an explanation of why it finds *Katzenbach* wrong, let alone any discussion of whether *stare decisis* nonetheless counsels adherence to *Katzenbach*'s ruling on the limited "significance" of the equal sovereignty principle.

Today's unprecedented extension of the equal sovereignty principle outside its proper domain—the admission of new States—is capable of much mischief. Federal statutes that treat States disparately are

---

[140] *Shelby Cty.*, 570 U.S. at 544, 556.

[141] South Carolina v. Katzenbach, 383 U.S. 301, 328–29 (1966) (emphasis added).

[142] *Shelby Cty.*, 570 U.S. at 544 (citing *Katzenbach*, 383 U.S. at 328–29) (emphasis omitted).

[143] *Id.* (citing Nw. Austin Mun. Util. Dist. No. One v. Holder, 557 U.S. 193, 203 (2009)); *see also id.* at 556 (relying on *Northwest Austin*'s "emphasis on [the] significance" of the equal-sovereignty principle).

[144] *Nw. Austin*, 557 U.S. at 203–04.

hardly novelties.[145] Do such provisions remain safe given the Court's expansion of equal sovereignty's sway?

Of gravest concern, Congress relied on our path marking *Katzenbach* decision in each reauthorization of the VRA. It had every reason to believe that the Act's limited geographical scope would weigh in favor of, not against, the Act's constitutionality.[146] Congress could hardly have foreseen that the VRA's limited geographic reach would render the Act constitutionally suspect.[147]

In the Court's conception, it appears, defenders of the VRA could not prevail upon showing what the record overwhelmingly bears out, *i.e.*, that there is a need for continuing the preclearance regime in covered States. In addition, the defenders would have to disprove the existence of a comparable need elsewhere.[148] I am aware of no precedent for imposing such a double burden on defenders of legislation.

C

The Court has time and again declined to upset legislation of this genre unless there was no or almost no evidence of unconstitutional

---

[145] *See, e.g.*, 28 U.S.C. § 3704 (no State may operate or permit a sports-related gambling scheme, unless that State conducted such a scheme "at any time during the period beginning January 1, 1976, and ending August 31, 1990"); 26 U.S.C. § 142(l) (EPA required to locate green building project in a State meeting specified population criteria); 42 U.S.C. § 3796bb (at least 50 percent of rural drug enforcement assistance funding must be allocated to States with "a population density of fifty-two or fewer persons per square mile or a State in which the largest county has fewer than one hundred and fifty thousand people, based on the decennial census of 1990 through fiscal year 1997"); 42 U.S.C. §§ 13925, 13971 (similar population criteria for funding to combat rural domestic violence); 42 U.S.C. § 10136 (specifying rules applicable to Nevada's Yucca Mountain nuclear waste site, and providing that "[n]o State, other than the State of Nevada, may receive financial assistance under this subsection after December 22, 1987").

[146] *See, e.g.*, United States v. Morrison, 529 U.S. 598, 626–27 (2000) (confining preclearance regime to States with a record of discrimination bolstered the VRA's constitutionality).

[147] *See* Persily, *supra* note 26, at 195 ("[S]upporters of the Act sought to develop an evidentiary record for the principal purpose of explaining why the covered jurisdictions should remain covered, rather than justifying the coverage of certain jurisdictions but not others.").

[148] *See* Transcript of Oral Argument at 61–62, Shelby Cty. v. Holder, 570 U.S. 529 (2013) (No. 12-96) (suggesting that proof of egregious episodes of racial discrimination in covered jurisdictions would not suffice to carry the day for the VRA, unless such episodes are shown to be absent elsewhere).

action by States.[149] No such claim can be made about the congressional record for the 2006 VRA reauthorization. Given a record replete with examples of denial or abridgment of a paramount federal right, the Court should have left the matter where it belongs: in Congress' bailiwick.

Instead, the Court strikes §4(b)'s coverage provision because, in its view, the provision is not based on "current conditions."[150] It discounts, however, that one such condition was the preclearance remedy in place in the covered jurisdictions, a remedy Congress designed both to catch discrimination before it causes harm, and to guard against return to old ways.[151] Volumes of evidence supported Congress' determination that the prospect of retrogression was real. Throwing out preclearance when it has worked and is continuing to work to stop discriminatory changes is like throwing away your umbrella in a rainstorm because you are not getting wet.

But, the Court insists, the coverage formula is no good; it is based on "decades-old data and eradicated practices."[152] Even if the legislative record shows, as engaging with it would reveal, that the formula accurately identifies the jurisdictions with the worst conditions of voting discrimination, that is of no moment, as the Court sees it. Congress, the Court decrees, must "star[t] from scratch."[153] I do not see why that should be so.

Congress' chore was different in 1965 than it was in 2006. In 1965, there were a "small number of States . . . which in most instances were familiar to Congress by name," on which Congress fixed its attention.[154] In drafting the coverage formula, "Congress began work with reliable evidence of actual voting discrimination in a great majority of the States" it sought to target.[155] "The formula [Congress] eventually evolved to describe these areas" also captured a few States that had not been the subject of congressional factfinding.[156] Nevertheless, the Court upheld the formula in its entirety, finding it fair "to infer a significant danger of the evil" in all places the formula covered.[157]

---

[149] *See, e.g.*, City of Boerne v. Flores, 521 U.S. 507, 530 (1997) (legislative record "mention[ed] no episodes [of the kind the legislation aimed to check] occurring in the past 40 years").

[150] *Shelby Cty.*, 570 U.S. at 550.

[151] 2006 Reauthorization § 2(b)(3), (9), 120 Stat. 557, 577–78.

[152] *Shelby Cty.*, at 551.

[153] *Id.* at 556.

[154] South Carolina v. Katzenbach, 383 U.S. 301, 328 (1966).

[155] *Id.* at 329.

[156] *Id.*

[157] *Id.*

The situation Congress faced in 2006, when it took up reauthorization of the coverage formula, was not the same. By then, the formula had been in effect for many years, and all of the jurisdictions covered by it were "familiar to Congress by name."[158] The question before Congress: Was there still a sufficient basis to support continued application of the preclearance remedy in each of those already-identified places? There was at that point no chance that the formula might inadvertently sweep in new areas that were not the subject of congressional findings. And Congress could determine from the record whether the jurisdictions captured by the coverage formula still belonged under the preclearance regime. If they did, there was no need to alter the formula. That is why the Court, in addressing prior reauthorizations of the VRA, did not question the continuing "relevance" of the formula.

Consider once again the components of the record before Congress in 2006. The coverage provision identified a known list of places with an undisputed history of serious problems with racial discrimination in voting. Recent evidence relating to Alabama and its counties was there for all to see. Multiple Supreme Court decisions had upheld the coverage provision, most recently in 1999. There was extensive evidence that, due to the preclearance mechanism, conditions in the covered jurisdictions had notably improved. And there was evidence that preclearance was still having a substantial real-world effect, having stopped hundreds of discriminatory voting changes in the covered jurisdictions since the last reauthorization. In addition, there was evidence that racial polarization in voting was higher in covered jurisdictions than elsewhere, increasing the vulnerability of minority citizens in those jurisdictions. And countless witnesses, reports, and case studies documented continuing problems with voting discrimination in those jurisdictions. In light of this record, Congress had more than a reasonable basis to conclude that the existing coverage formula was not out of sync with conditions on the ground in covered areas. And certainly Shelby County was no candidate for release through the mechanism Congress provided.[159]

The Court holds §4(b) invalid on the ground that it is "irrational to base coverage on the use of voting tests 40 years ago, when such tests have been illegal since that time."[160] But the Court disregards what Congress set about to do in enacting the VRA. That extraordinary legislation scarcely stopped at the particular tests and devices that happened to exist in 1965. The grand aim of the Act is to secure to all

---

[158] *Id.* at 328.

[159] *See* Shelby Cty. v. Holder, 570 U.S. 529, 579–80, 583–85 (Ginsburg, J., dissenting).

[160] *Id.* at 556 (majority opinion).

in our polity equal citizenship stature, a voice in our democracy undiluted by race. As the record for the 2006 reauthorization makes abundantly clear, second-generation barriers to minority voting rights have emerged in the covered jurisdictions as attempted substitutes for the first-generation barriers that originally triggered preclearance in those jurisdictions.[161]

The sad irony of today's decision lies in its utter failure to grasp why the VRA has proven effective. The Court appears to believe that the VRA's success in eliminating the specific devices extant in 1965 means that preclearance is no longer needed.[162] With that belief, and the argument derived from it, history repeats itself. The same assumption—that the problem could be solved when particular methods of voting discrimination are identified and eliminated—was indulged and proved wrong repeatedly prior to the VRA's enactment. Unlike prior statutes, which singled out particular tests or devices, the VRA is grounded in Congress' recognition of the "variety and persistence" of measures designed to impair minority voting rights.[163] In truth, the evolution of voting discrimination into more subtle second-generation barriers is powerful evidence that a remedy as effective as preclearance remains vital to protect minority voting rights and prevent backsliding.

Beyond question, the VRA is no ordinary legislation. It is extraordinary because Congress embarked on a mission long delayed and of extraordinary importance: to realize the purpose and promise of the Fifteenth Amendment. For a half century, a concerted effort has been made to end racial discrimination in voting. Thanks to the Voting Rights Act, progress once the subject of a dream has been achieved and continues to be made.

The record supporting the 2006 reauthorization of the VRA is also extraordinary. It was described by the Chairman of the House Judiciary Committee as "one of the most extensive considerations of any piece of legislation that the United States Congress has dealt with in the 27½ years" he had served in the House.[164] After exhaustive evidence-gathering and deliberative process, Congress reauthorized the VRA, including the coverage provision, with overwhelming bipartisan support. It was the judgment of Congress that "40 years has not been a sufficient amount of time to eliminate the vestiges of discrimination following nearly 100 years of disregard for the dictates of the

---

[161] *See id.* at 563–64, 565–66, 573–75 (Ginsburg, J., dissenting).

[162] *Id.* at 554–55, 555–56.

[163] South Carolina v. Katzenbach, 383 U.S. 301, 311 (1966); *Shelby Cty.*, 383 U.S. at 560 (Ginsburg, J., dissenting).

[164] 152 CONG. REC. H5143 (daily ed. July 13, 2006) (statement of Rep. Sensenbrenner).

15th amendment and to ensure that the right of all citizens to vote is protected as guaranteed by the Constitution."[165] That determination of the body empowered to enforce the Civil War Amendments "by appropriate legislation" merits this Court's utmost respect. In my judgment, the Court errs egregiously by overriding Congress' decision.

*   *   *

For the reasons stated, I would affirm the judgment of the Court of Appeals.

---

[165] 2006 Reauthorization § 2(b)(7), 120 Stat. 577, 577.

MASTERPIECE CAKESHOP

"To repeat, the court affirms that Colorado law can protect gay persons, just as it can protect other classes of individuals, in acquiring whatever products and services they choose on the same terms and conditions as are offered to other members of the public."

The Case

In 2015, the United States Supreme Court held in *Obergefell v. Hodges* that "the right to marry is a fundamental right inherent in the liberty of the person, and, under the Fourteenth Amendment's Due Process and Equal Protection Clauses, couples of the same-sex may not be deprived of that right and that liberty."[1] Prior to *Obergefell*, state laws pertaining to LGBT rights ranged from robust protections, including the right to marry, to no protections whatsoever, including outright bans on same-sex marriage. Colorado fell somewhere in the middle: the Colorado Anti-Discrimination Act protected homosexuals from discrimination in places of public accommodation (a category which included private businesses engaged in sales to the public), but state law did not recognize same-sex marriages as valid.

In 2012, a same-sex couple visited Masterpiece Cakeshop, a Colorado bakery, and requested a cake for their wedding reception.[2] The owner, Jack Phillips, refused to create the cake because of his opposition to same-sex marriage due to his Christian faith; the couple subsequently filed a charge with the Colorado Civil Rights Commission alleging discrimination on the basis of sexual orientation.[3]

The Commission determined that Masterpiece Cakeshop had violated the Act, and found, after further investigation, that Phillips had declined to sell custom wedding cakes to approximately six other couples for identical reasons.[4] The Commission rejected Phillips' First

---

[1] Obergefell v. Hodges, 135 S. Ct. 2584, 2604 (2015).
[2] The couple had made arrangements to become legally married in Massachusetts, one of the states which recognized same-sex marriages at that time. *See* Masterpiece Cakeshop, Ltd. v. Colo. Civil Rights Comm'n, 138 S. Ct. 1719, 1724 (2018).
[3] *See id.* at 1724–25.
[4] *See id.* at 1725–26.

Amendment defense that a legal requirement to produce such cakes would violate his freedom of speech and right to free exercise of religion and ordered Phillips to "cease and desist from discriminating against . . . same-sex couples by refusing to sell them wedding cakes or any product [he] would sell to heterosexual couples."[5] On appeal, Colorado state courts affirmed the Commission's ruling and enforcement order, which led to an appeal to the United States Supreme Court.

Justice Kennedy's Majority Opinion

Justice Kennedy wrote the 5-4 majority opinion in *Obergefell*; it is therefore remarkable that he also authored the majority opinion in *Masterpiece Cakeshop*, in which a 7-2 majority of the Court reversed the Colorado courts, holding that the Colorado Civil Rights Commission failed in its "obligation of religious neutrality" and violated Phillips' right to free exercise of religion under the First Amendment.[6]

Kennedy framed the decision faced by the Court as balancing two separate principles: on one hand, that "society has come to the recognition that gay persons and gay couples cannot be treated as social outcasts or as inferior in dignity and worth"; on the other, that "religious and philosophical objections to gay marriage are protected views and in some instances protected forms of expression."[7] Kennedy then explained that while the Constitution's guarantee of the right to free exercise of religion is "protected"—a principle that the majority had discussed in Kennedy's *Obergefell* opinion—free exercise must nevertheless yield, in certain instances, where it might "deny protected persons equal access to goods and services under a neutral and generally applicable public accommodations law."[8]

Kennedy then observed, however, that Phillips was arguing a narrower point. Making the wedding cake required Phillips to "use his artistic skills to make an expressive statement;" the Commission's mandate compelling him to do so in support of a message conflicting with his religious beliefs would therefore be an unconstitutional infringement of his free speech rights.[9] At this point in the analysis, Kennedy appeared to be laying the foundation for a landmark ruling which would parse the competing interests at stake and definitively

---

[5] *Id.* at 1726 (internal quotation marks and citation omitted).
[6] *Id.* at 1723.
[7] *Id.* at 1727.
[8] *Id.*
[9] *See id.* at 1728.

limit the heretofore hazily interwoven boundaries of two of the Constitution's most fundamental protections.

But then, he punted. Kennedy had observed earlier in the opinion that "the delicate question of when the free exercise of religion must yield to an otherwise valid exercise of state power needed to be determined in an adjudication in which religious hostility on the part of the State itself would not be a factor in the balance the State sought to reach."[10] Kennedy believed that the "neutral and respectful consideration" to which Phillips' claims had been entitled had been "compromised" by the Colorado Civil Rights Commission, whose members had evinced "elements of a clear and impermissible hostility" toward Phillips' religious beliefs in their "treatment of his case."[11] At one hearing, Kennedy observed, Commission members implied "that religious beliefs and persons are less than fully welcome in Colorado's business community," while at another, a Commission member "even went so far as to compare Phillips' invocation of his sincerely held religious beliefs to defenses of slavery and the Holocaust."[12] Kennedy found this "sentiment" to be "inappropriate for a Commission charged with the solemn responsibility of fair and neutral enforcement of Colorado's antidiscrimination law—a law that protects discrimination on the basis of religion as well as sexual orientation," and was troubled that no other commissioners objected to the aforementioned comments on the record.[13] Accordingly, Kennedy stated, the majority could not "avoid the conclusion that these statements cast doubt on the fairness and impartiality of the Commission's adjudication of Phillips' case"—a conclusion compounded by the additional "indication of hostility" that was the "difference in treatment between" Phillips' case and the Commission's previous rulings in the favor of bakers who had refused to create cakes "with images that conveyed disapproval of same-sex marriage, along with religious text."[14]

The majority thus concluded that "the Commission's treatment of Phillips' case violated the State's duty under the First Amendment not to base laws or regulations on hostility to a religion or religious viewpoint."[15] The Commission had an obligation "to proceed in a manner neutral toward and tolerant of Phillips' religious beliefs," and

---

[10] *Id.* at 1724.
[11] *Id.* at 1729.
[12] *Id.*
[13] *Id.*
[14] *Id.* at 1730.
[15] *Id.* at 1731.

it failed to uphold this obligation.[16] For these reasons, the majority found that the Commission's order "must be set aside."[17]

The majority never addressed the substance of Phillips' free speech argument. It also declined to make a broader ruling on whether Phillips' free exercise rights would have been impinged upon had the Commission been neutral in its consideration of its case. By limiting its holding to a decision that the Colorado Civil Rights Commission had violated Phillips' free exercise rights, the Court delayed until another day an authoritative ruling on the broader issues underlying the case—and even suggested the possibility that a future, similar case could result in a different outcome, especially if religious objections were considered neutrally and "with tolerance" for all sides.[18]

Justice Ginsburg's Dissent

Justice Ginsburg began with the observation that there was "much" in the majority's opinion with which she agreed, and quoted as examples four specific passages evincing broad anti-discrimination principles.[19] But Ginsburg believed that the majority was wrong to rule in favor of Phillips, as the four "statements [which she had quoted] point[ed] in the opposite direction."[20]

Specifically, Ginsburg took issue with the majority's reliance on cases where the Commission ruled in favor of bakers who refused to place offensive messages on cakes (in all three cases, for a customer named William Jack) as implicit evidence of the Commission's discriminatory intent in Phillips' case. She expounded the majority's error as follows: "The bakers would have refused to make a cake with Jack's requested [offensive] message for any customer, regardless of his or her religion. And the bakers visited by Jack would have sold him any baked goods they would have sold anyone else."[21] By contrast, Phillips' refusal to sell to the same-sex couple in question was made "for no reason other than their sexual orientation"; had the couple been a heterosexual couple, they would have received the requested service.[22] "Colorado, the Court does not gainsay, prohibits precisely the discrimination [the same-sex couple] encountered. Jack, on the other hand, suffered no service refusal on the basis of his religion or

---

[16] *Id.*
[17] *Id.* at 1732.
[18] *See id.*
[19] *See id.* at 1748 (Ginsburg, J., dissenting).
[20] *Id.*
[21] *Id.* at 1750.
[22] *See id.*

any other protected characteristic. He was treated as any other customer would have been treated—no better, no worse," because no customer requesting the cake Jack requested would been served.[23] The majority therefore erred, in Ginsburg's view, because it found bias in part based on the *outcome* of the Commission's decisions—bakers who refused to make cakes with anti-gay messages were not punished, whereas Phillips was—without considering the *context* of those decisions, which Ginsburg demonstrated were neutral to religion.

Justice Ginsburg also took issue with the majority's reliance on comments by a minority of the Commission's members as evidence that the entire process resulting in a ruling against Phillips was tainted by anti-religious bias. She pointed out that the Colorado "proceedings involved several layers of independent decisionmaking, of which the Commission was but one," and that at every level Masterpiece Cakeshop had lost.[24] Ginsburg observed that the majority could identify no apparent hostility or anti-religious bias at any other level of the proceedings, such that "the comments of one or two Commissioners" should not "overcome" Phillips' blatant refusal to sell a wedding cake to a same-sex couple.[25] Reinforcing this point, she asked, rhetorically, "What prejudice infected the determinations of the adjudicators in the case before and after the Commission? The Court does not say."[26] For these reasons, Ginsburg concluded that "sensible application" of the Colorado Anti-Discrimination Act "to a refusal to sell any wedding cake to a gay couple should occasion affirmance of the [state court's] judgment" in favor of that couple, and stated that she "would so rule."[27]

---

[23] *Id.*
[24] *Id.* at 1751.
[25] *Id.*
[26] *Id.*
[27] *Id.* at 1752.

MASTERPIECE CAKE SHOP V. COLORADO CIVIL RIGHTS COMMISSION

JUSTICE GINSBURG, with whom JUSTICE SOTOMAYOR joins, DISSENTING.

There is much in the Court's opinion with which I agree. "[I]t is a general rule that [religious and philosophical] objections do not allow business owners and other actors in the economy and in society to deny protected persons equal access to goods and services under a neutral and generally applicable public accommodations law."[1] "Colorado law can protect gay persons, just as it can protect other classes of individuals, in acquiring whatever products and services they choose on the same terms and conditions as are offered to other members of the public."[2] "[P]urveyors of goods and services who object to gay marriages for moral and religious reasons [may not] put up signs saying 'no goods or services will be sold if they will be used for gay marriages.'"[3] Gay persons may be spared from "indignities when they seek goods and services in an open market."[4; 5 [FN 1]] I strongly disagree,

---

[1] *Id.* at 1727 (majority opinion).

[2] *Id.* at 1727–28.

[3] *Id.* at 1728–29.

[4] *Id.* at 1732.

[5] [FN 1] As Justice Thomas observes, the Court does not hold that wedding cakes are speech or expression entitled to First Amendment protection. *See id.* at 1740, (Thomas, J., concurring in part and concurring in judgment). Nor could it, consistent with our First Amendment precedents. Justice Thomas acknowledges that for conduct to constitute protected expression, the conduct must be reasonably understood by an observer to be communicative. *Id.* at 1724–25 (majority opinion) (citing Clark v. Cmty. for Creative Non-Violence, 468 U.S. 288, 294 (1984)). The record in this case is replete with Jack Phillips' own views on the messages he believes his cakes convey. *See id.* at 1742–43 (Thomas, J., concurring in part and concurring in judgment) (describing how Phillips "considers" and "sees" his work). But Phillips submitted no evidence showing that an objective observer understands a wedding cake to convey a message, much less that the observer understands the message to be the baker's, rather than the marrying couple's. Indeed, some in the wedding industry could not explain what message, or whose, a wedding cake conveys. *See* Simon Charsley, *Interpretation and Custom: The Case of the Wedding*

however, with the Court's conclusion that Craig and Mullins should lose this case. All of the above-quoted statements point in the opposite direction.

The Court concludes that "Phillips' religious objection was not considered with the neutrality that the Free Exercise Clause requires."[6] This conclusion rests on evidence said to show the Colorado Civil Rights Commission's hostility to religion. Hostility is discernible, the Court maintains, from the asserted "disparate consideration of Phillips' case compared to the cases of" three other bakers who refused to make cakes requested by William Jack, an amicus here.[7] The Court also finds hostility in statements made at two public hearings on Phillips' appeal to the Commission.[8] The different outcomes the Court features do not evidence hostility to religion of the kind we have previously held to signal a free-exercise violation, nor do the comments by one or two members of one of the four decision-making entities considering this case justify reversing the judgment below.

I

On March 13, 2014—approximately three months after the ALJ ruled in favor of the same-sex couple, Craig and Mullins, and two months before the Commission heard Phillips' appeal from that decision—William Jack visited three Colorado bakeries. His visits followed a similar pattern. He requested two cakes "made to resemble an open Bible. He also requested that each cake be decorated with Biblical verses. [He] requested that one of the cakes include an image of two groomsmen, holding hands, with a red 'X' over the image. On one cake, he requested [on] one side[,] . . . 'God hates sin. Psalm 45:7'

Cake, 22 MAN 93, 100–01 (1987) (no explanation of wedding cakes' symbolism was forthcoming "even amongst those who might be expected to be the experts"); *id.* at 104–05 (the cake cutting tradition might signify "the bride and groom . . . as appropriating the cake" from the bride's parents). And Phillips points to no case in which this Court has suggested the provision of a baked good might be expressive conduct. *Cf. Masterpiece Cakeshop*, 138 S. Ct. at 1743 n.2 (Thomas, J., concurring in part and concurring in judgment); Hurley v. Irish-Am. Gay, Lesbian, & Bisexual Grp. of Bos., Inc., 515 U.S. 557, 568–79 (1995) (citing previous cases recognizing parades to be expressive); Barnes v. Glen Theatre, Inc., 501 U.S. 560, 565 (1991) (noting precedents suggesting nude dancing is expressive conduct); Spence v. Washington, 418 U.S. 405, 410 (1974) (observing the Court's decades-long recognition of the symbolism of flags).
[6] *Masterpiece Cakeshop*, 138 S. Ct. at 1731.
[7] *Id.* at 1732.
[8] *Id.* at 1728–30.

and on the opposite side of the cake 'Homosexuality is a detestable sin. Leviticus 18:2.' On the second cake, [the one] with the image of the two groomsmen covered by a red 'X' [Jack] requested [these words]: 'God loves sinners' and on the other side 'While we were yet sinners Christ died for us. Romans 5:8.'"[9]

In contrast to Jack, Craig and Mullins simply requested a wedding cake: They mentioned no message or anything else distinguishing the cake they wanted to buy from any other wedding cake Phillips would have sold.

One bakery told Jack it would make cakes in the shape of Bibles, but would not decorate them with the requested messages; the owner told Jack her bakery "does not discriminate" and "accept[s] all humans."[10] The second bakery owner told Jack he "had done open Bibles and books many times and that they look amazing," but declined to make the specific cakes Jack described because the baker regarded the messages as "hateful."[11] The third bakery, according to Jack, said it would bake the cakes, but would not include the requested message.[12; 13 [FN 2]]

Jack filed charges against each bakery with the Colorado Civil Rights Division (Division). The Division found no probable cause to support Jack's claims of unequal treatment and denial of goods or services based on his Christian religious beliefs.[14] In this regard, the Division observed that the bakeries regularly produced cakes and other baked goods with Christian symbols and had denied other customer requests for designs demeaning people whose dignity the Colorado Antidiscrimination Act (CADA) protects.[15] The Commission summarily affirmed the Division's no-probable-cause finding.[16]

The Court concludes that "the Commission's consideration of Phillips' religious objection did not accord with its treatment of [the other bakers'] objections."[17] But the cases the Court aligns are hardly comparable. The bakers would have refused to make a cake with Jack's

---

[9] Petition for Writ of Certiorari app. at 319a, *Masterpiece Cakeshop*, 138 S. Ct. 1719 (No. 16-111); *see id.* at 300a, 310a.

[10] *Id.* at 301a (internal quotation marks omitted).

[11] *Id.* at 310a (internal quotation marks omitted).

[12] *Id.* at 319a.

[13] [FN 2] The record provides no ideological explanation for the bakeries' refusals. *Cf. Masterpiece Cakeshop*, 138 S. Ct. at 1734–35, 1738, 1739–40 (Gorsuch, J., concurring) (describing Jack's requests as offensive to the bakers' "secular" convictions).

[14] Petition for Writ of Certiorari, *supra* note 9, app. at 297a, 307a, 316a.

[15] *See id.* at 305a, 314a, 324a.

[16] *See id.* at 326a–331a.

[17] *Masterpiece Cakeshop*, 138 S. Ct. at 1730; *see also id.* at 1736–37 (Gorsuch, J., concurring).

requested message for any customer, regardless of his or her religion. And the bakers visited by Jack would have sold him any baked goods they would have sold anyone else. The bakeries' refusal to make Jack cakes of a kind they would not make for any customer scarcely resembles Phillips' refusal to serve Craig and Mullins: Phillips would not sell to Craig and Mullins, for no reason other than their sexual orientation, a cake of the kind he regularly sold to others. When a couple contacts a bakery for a wedding cake, the product they are seeking is a cake celebrating their wedding—not a cake celebrating heterosexual weddings or same-sex weddings—and that is the service Craig and Mullins were denied.[18] Colorado, the Court does not gainsay, prohibits precisely the discrimination Craig and Mullins encountered.[19] Jack, on the other hand, suffered no service refusal on the basis of his religion or any other protected characteristic. He was treated as any other customer would have been treated—no better, no worse.[20] [FN 3]

The fact that Phillips might sell other cakes and cookies to gay and lesbian customers[21] [FN 4] was irrelevant to the issue Craig and Mullins' case presented. What matters is that Phillips would not provide a good or service to a same-sex couple that he would provide to a heterosexual couple. In contrast, the other bakeries' sale of other goods to Christian customers was relevant: It shows that there were no goods

---

[18] *Cf. id.* at 1735–36, 1738–39 (Gorsuch, J., concurring).

[19] *See id.* at 1748 (Ginsburg, J., dissenting).

[20] [FN 3] Justice Gorsuch argues that the situations "share all legally salient features." *Id.* at 1735 (Gorsuch, J., concurring). But what critically differentiates them is the role the customer's "statutorily protected trait," *id.*, played in the denial of service. Change Craig and Mullins' sexual orientation (or sex), and Phillips would have provided the cake. Change Jack's religion, and the bakers would have been no more willing to comply with his request. The bakers' objections to Jack's cakes had nothing to do with "religious opposition to same-sex weddings." *Id.* at 1736. Instead, the bakers simply refused to make cakes bearing statements demeaning to people protected by CADA. With respect to Jack's second cake, in particular, where he requested an image of two groomsmen covered by a red "X" and the lines "God loves sinners" and "While we were yet sinners Christ died for us," the bakers gave not the slightest indication that religious words, rather than the demeaning image, prompted the objection. *See id.* at 1749 (Ginsburg, J., dissenting). Phillips did, therefore, discriminate because of sexual orientation; the other bakers did not discriminate because of religious belief; and the Commission properly found discrimination in one case but not the other. *Cf. id.* at 1735–37 (Gorsuch, J., concurring).

[21] [FN 4] *But see id.* at 1726 (majority opinion) (acknowledging that Phillips refused to sell to a lesbian couple cupcakes for a celebration of their union).

the bakeries would sell to a non-Christian customer that they would refuse to sell to a Christian customer.[22]

Nor was the Colorado Court of Appeals' "difference in treatment of these two instances . . . based on the government's own assessment of offensiveness."[23] Phillips declined to make a cake he found offensive where the offensiveness of the product was determined solely by the identity of the customer requesting it. The three other bakeries declined to make cakes where their objection to the product was due to the demeaning message the requested product would literally display. As the Court recognizes, a refusal "to design a special cake with words or images . . . might be different from a refusal to sell any cake at all."[24; 25 [FN 5]] The Colorado Court of Appeals did not distinguish Phillips and the other three bakeries based simply on its or the Division's finding that messages in the cakes Jack requested were offensive while any message in a cake for Craig and Mullins was not. The Colorado court distinguished the cases on the ground that Craig and Mullins were denied service based on an aspect of their identity that the State chose to grant vigorous protection from discrimination.[26] I do not read the Court to suggest that the Colorado Legislature's decision to include certain protected characteristics in CADA is an impermissible

---

[22] *Cf. id.* at 1730.

[23] *Id.* at 1731.

[24] *Id.* at 1723.

[25] [FN 5] The Court undermines this observation when later asserting that the treatment of Phillips, as compared with the treatment of the other three bakeries, "could reasonably be interpreted as being inconsistent as to the question of whether speech is involved." *Id.* at 1730. But recall that, while Jack requested cakes with particular text inscribed, Craig and Mullins were refused the sale of any wedding cake at all. They were turned away before any specific cake design could be discussed. (It appears that Phillips rarely, if ever, produces wedding cakes with words on them—or at least does not advertise such cakes. *See Wedding*, MASTERPIECE CAKESHOP, http://www. masterpiece-cakes.com/wedding-cakes (last visited June 1, 2018) (gallery with 31 wedding cake images, none of which exhibits words).) The Division and the Court of Appeals could rationally and lawfully distinguish between a case involving disparaging text and images and a case involving a wedding cake of unspecified design. The distinction is not between a cake with text and one without, *see Masterpiece Cakeshop*, 138 S. Ct. at 1737–38 (Gorsuch, J., concurring); it is between a cake with a particular design and one whose form was never even discussed.

[26] *See* Petition for Writ of Certiorari, *supra* note 9, app. 20a n.8 ("The Division found that the bakeries did not refuse [Jack's] request because of his creed, but rather because of the offensive nature of the requested message. . . . [T]here was no evidence that the bakeries based their decisions on [Jack's] religion . . . [whereas Phillips] discriminat[ed] on the basis of sexual orientation.").

government prescription of what is and is not offensive.[27] To repeat, the Court affirms that "Colorado law can protect gay persons, just as it can protect other classes of individuals, in acquiring whatever products and services they choose on the same terms and conditions as are offered to other members of the public."[28]

II

Statements made at the Commission's public hearings on Phillips' case provide no firmer support for the Court's holding today. Whatever one may think of the statements in historical context, I see no reason why the comments of one or two Commissioners should be taken to overcome Phillips' refusal to sell a wedding cake to Craig and Mullins. The proceedings involved several layers of independent decision-making, of which the Commission was but one.[29] First, the Division had to find probable cause that Phillips violated CADA. Second, the ALJ entertained the parties' cross-motions for summary judgment. Third, the Commission heard Phillips' appeal. Fourth, after the Commission's ruling, the Colorado Court of Appeals considered the case *de novo*. What prejudice infected the determinations of the adjudicators in the case before and after the Commission? The Court does not say. Phillips' case is thus far removed from the only precedent upon which the Court relies, *Church of Lukumi Babalu Aye, Inc. v. Hialeah*,[30] where the government action that violated a principle of religious neutrality implicated a sole decision-making body, the city council.[31]

*   *   *

For the reasons stated, sensible application of CADA to a refusal to sell any wedding cake to a gay couple should occasion affirmance of the Colorado Court of Appeals' judgment. I would so rule.

---

[27] *Cf. Masterpiece Cakeshop*, 138 S. Ct. at 1727–28.

[28] *Id.* at 1728.

[29] *See* Petition for Writ of Certiorari, *supra* note 9, app. 5a–6a.

[30] 508 U.S. 520 (1993).

[31] *See id.* at 526–28.

ABOUT THE AUTHOR

Sarah Wainwright is an attorney who researches and writes on the history and philosophy of American Law. Her interest in the profession stemmed from being raised—along with her sister—by her single mother, who, after taking up law as a second career, often had Sarah with her at her small solo practice. At a young age, Sarah was exposed to the legal profession at its most fundamental level—seeing the struggles of people whose lives were entangled in the family and criminal court systems. After finishing high school, Sarah studied art with the expectation of following a passion for painting, but after several years in the field, she missed the personal interactions and sense of purpose she remembered from her mother's office. Sarah decided to enroll in law school, and, after graduating and passing the bar, she returned to her hometown to practice alongside her mother and writes when time allows.